Ian Allan
abc

M

Aircraft
Markings

1986

LONDON

IAN ALLAN LTD

Contents

Photographs by Andrew March (APM), Daniel March (DJM), and Peter R. March (PRM)

This seventh edition published 1986

ISBN 0 7110 1589 9

Published by Ian Allan Ltd
and printed by Ian Allan Printing Ltd at their works
at Coombelands in Runnymede, England

Cover: BAe Harrier GR3 XZ996(C) of No 233 OCU, RAF Wittering at IAT Fairford in July 1985. *PRM*

Introduction

This seventh edition of *abc Military Aircraft Markings*, a companion to *abc Civil Aircraft Markings*, again sets out to list all current aircraft carrying service serial numbers that are based or might be seen in the British Isles. This includes all Royal Air Force, Royal Navy, Army Air Corps, Ministry of Defence (Procurement Executive) and manufacturers' test aircraft including those located overseas (but only if they are likely to return to the UK), USAF and USN machines based in the UK, and the current Irish Army Air Corps fleet. There is also coverage of USAF, US Army and USN aircraft normally based in North-West Europe and types that regularly visit from the USA, together with a selection of aircraft from other overseas air arms which might be seen visiting the UK from time to time. Veteran and vintage aircraft which carry overseas military markings but are based in the UK have been listed in a separate section. Wherever possible the operating units and bases of RAF, RN and Army Air Corps aircraft are detailed together with locations of civilian owned aircraft in military markings.

The term aircraft used here covers powered, manned aeroplanes, helicopters and gliders. It does not include un-manned target drones. The serials listed are in the main those presently displayed on the aircraft, whether it is a primary or a secondary identity such as an RAF Support Command 'M' or Royal Navy 'A' maintenance number. Aircraft used as targets on MoD ranges are generally omitted as access to view these machines is restricted. The serials of some incomplete aircraft have been included, such as the cockpit sections of machines displayed by the RAF Exhibition Flight at Abingdon, aircraft used by airfield fire sections and for service battle damage repair training (BDRT), together with significant parts of aircraft held by preservation groups and societies. A list of aircraft that appeared in the last edition, but which have now been removed is provided, along with the fates of the aircraft where they are known.

UK serials are listed in alphabetical and numerical order with the manufacturer and type detailed and the owner/operator and location shown for each. If the aircraft has an alternative, previous or current identifying serial or civil registration this is shown in brackets after the type. A cross reference to the many RAF 'M' and RN 'A' numbers is included. Where a serial is omitted in a sequence this indicates that no aircraft is carrying that number at present, having been written off, scrapped, sold abroad or allocated an alternative marking.

The unit code identification for all RAF, RN and AAC aircraft, as recorded up to 31 December, is shown in square brackets after the type. These unit markings are normally carried boldly on the sides of the fuselage or on the aircraft's fin. In the case of RAF and AAC machines currently in service they are usually single or pairs of letters or numbers, while the RN continues to use a well established system of three-figure codes between 000 and 999 together with a fin letter code denoting the aircraft's operational base. RN squadrons, units and bases are allocated blocks of numbers from which individual aircraft codes are issued. Codes change when aircraft move between units and therefore the markings shown in this edition might not be that currently painted on a particular aircraft, having been overtaken by events. To help identification of RN bases and landing platforms on ships a list of tail letter codes with their appropriate name, ship pennant number and type of vessel is included. The individual helicopter code numbers for each ship has been added as a new feature in this edition.

Current USAF and USN aircraft based in the UK are listed by type. The serial number actually displayed on the aircraft's tail is shown in full with appropriate fiscal year information also provided. Details of the operating wing and, where possible, the squadron allocation is added. For European and mainland USA aircraft a similar pattern is followed. The serial numbers of overseas service aircraft are as usually presented on the individual machine or as they are normally identified. Where possible the aircraft's base and operating unit has been shown. Likewise the listed historic aircraft show the number carried on the fuselage as principal means of identification.

Information shown is believed to be correct at 31 January 1986.

Acknowledgements

The compiler wishes to thank the many people who have taken trouble to send comments, criticism and other useful information following the publication of the previous edition of *abc Military Aircraft Markings*. In particular the following correspondents: J. R. Cross, J. Lake, P. C. Marygold, S. Newton, L. P. Robinson, K. Sloper, M. Thompson and G. Turner.

This compilation has relied heavily on the publications of the following aviation groups and societies: *Air North, Air Scotland* (The West of Scotland Aviation Group), *British Aviation Review* (British Aviation Research Group), *Flightpath* (The Cheshire Aviation Society), *Flypast* (Merseyside Aviation Society), *Hawkeye* (Gatwick Aviation Society), *Humberside Air Review* (Humberside Aviation Society), *Irish Air Letter, Osprey* (Solent Aviation Society), *Prestwick Airport Letter* (Prestwick Airport Aviation Group), *Scottish Air News* (Central Scotland Aviation Group), *Skyward* (Westcountry Aviation Society), *South East Aviation Review* (West London Aviation Group), *South West Aviation News* (South West Aviation Society), *Stansted Aviation Newsletter* (The Stansted Aviation Society), together with these publications: *Euromil — Foreign Military Air Arms to Europe* (Seefive Publications); *NATO to the UK 1985* (West London Aviation Group); *United States Military Aircraft to Europe* (Seefive Publications) and *Wrecks and Relics* (Midland Counties Publications).

The new edition of *abc Military Aircraft Markings* would not have been possible without considerable research and checking by Stephen Byles, Howard Curtis, Wal Gandy, Andrew and Daniel March and Brian Strickland.

PRM

Abbreviations

AAC	Army Air Corps
A&AEE	Aeroplane & Armament Experimental Establishment
AAS	Aeromedical Airlift Squadron
ABS	Air Base Squadron
ABW	Air Base Wing
ACCGS	Air Cadets Central Gliding School
ACCS	Airborne Command and Control Squadron
ACR	Armoured Cavalry Regiment
AEF	Air Experience Flight
AES	Air Engineering School
AETW	Air Engineering Training Wing
AEW	Airborne Early Warning
AFRES	Air Force Reserve
AIU	Accident Investigation Unit
AMS	Air Movements School
ANG	Air National Guard
APS	Aircraft Preservation Society
ARG	Air Refuelling Group
ARRS	Aerospace Rescue and Recovery Squadron
ARS	Air Refuelling Squadron
ARW	Air Refuelling Wing
ARW/LCF	Advanced Rotary Wing Lynx Conversion Flight
ARWS	Advanced Rotary Wing Squadron
ASF	Aircraft Servicing Flight
AS&RU	Aircraft Salvage and Repair Unit
ATC	Air Training Corps
ATCC	Air Traffic Control Centre
ATS	Aircrewman Training Squadron
AvCo	Aviation Company
AW	Armstrong Whitworth Aircraft/ Aircraft Workshops
AW&CW	Airborne Warning & Control Wing
BAC	British Aircraft Corporation
BAe	British Aerospace Company
BAOR	British Army of the Rhine
BAPC	British Aircraft Preservation Council
BATUS	British Army Training Unit Support
BDRF	Battle Damage Repair Flight
BDRT	Battle Damage Repair Training
BFWF	Basic Fixed Wing Flight
BGA	British Gliding Association
BHC	British Hovercraft Corporation
BP	Boulton & Paul
B-V	Boeing-Vertol
BW	Bomber Wing
CATCS	Central Air Traffic Control School
CBAS	Commando Brigade Air Squadron

CCF Combined Cadet Force
CDE Chemical Defence Establishment
CFS Central Flying School
CinC Commander in Chief
CSDE Central Servicing Development Establishment
CTE Central Training Establishment
CTTS Civilian Technical Training School
CV Chance-Vought
D-BD Dassault-Breguet Dornier
DH De Havilland
DHC De Havilland Canada
D&TS Development and Trials Squadron
ECS Electronic Countermeasures Squadron
EE English Electric
EMA East Midlands Airport
EoN Elliot's of Newbury
ETPS Empire Test Pilots School
EWAU Electronics Warfare Avionics Unit
FAA Fleet Air Arm
FBW Fly by wire
FCS Facility Checking Squadron
FE Further Education
FF&SS Fire Fighting & Safety School
FIS Fighter Interceptor Squadron
Flt Flight
FMA Fabrica Militar de Aviones
FONAC Flag Officer Naval Air Command
FRADU Fleet Requirements and Direction Unit
FRSB Fleet Reserve Storage Base
FSS Flying Selection School
FTS Flying Training School
FW Foster Wickner
GAL General Aircraft Ltd
GD General Dynamics
HMS Her Majesty's Ship
HP Handley-Page
HQ Headquarters
HS Hawker Siddeley
IAM Institute of Aviation Medicine
IWM Imperial War Museum
JATE Joint Air Transport Establishment
JMU Jaguar Maintenance Unit
JTU Joint Trials Unit
LCF Lynx Conversion Flight
LTF Lightning Training Flight
MAG Military Airlift Group
MAAG Military Air Advisory Group
MAS Military Airlift Squadron
MAW Military Airlift Wing
McD McDonnell Douglas
MGSP Mobile Glider Servicing Party
MoD(PE) Ministry of Defence (Procurement Executive)
Mod Modified
MR Maritime Reconnaissance
MU Maintenance Unit
NA North American
NAF Naval Air Facility
NASU Naval Air Support Unit
NHTU Naval Hovercraft Trials Unit
OCU Operational Conversion Unit
OEU Operation Evaluation Unit
OPITB Offshore Petroleum Industry Training Board
PAX Passenger procedural trainer
PRU Photographic Reconnaissance Unit
RAE Royal Aircraft Establishment
RAF Royal Aircraft Factory/ Royal Air Force
RAFC Royal Air Force College
RAFGSA Royal Air Force Gliding and Soaring Association
RAOC Royal Army Ordnance Corps
RCAF Royal Canadian Air Force
REME Royal Electrical & Mechanical Engineers
RM Royal Marines
RMC of S Royal Military College of Science
RN Royal Navy
RNAS Royal Naval Air Station
RNAY Royal Naval Aircraft Yard
RNEC Royal Naval Engineering College
RNEFTS Royal Naval Elementary Flying Training School
R-R Rolls-Royce
RS Reid & Sigrist
RS&RE Royal Signals and Radar Establishment
RW Reconnaissance Wing
SA Scottish Aviation
SAC Strategic Air Command
SAH School of Air Handling
SAL Scottish Aviation Limited
SAR Search and Rescue
Saro Saunders-Roe
SAREW Search & Rescue Engineering Wing
SARTF Search and Rescue Training Flight
SCF Scout Conversion Flight
SEPECAT Société Européene de Production de l'Avion ECAT
SHSU Sea Harrier Servicing Unit
SKTF Sea King Training Flight
SNCAN Société Nationale Aeronautique du Nord
SOS Special Operations Squadron
SoTT School of Technical Training
Sqn Squadron
SRW Strategic Reconnaissance Wing
TAS Tactical Airlift Squadron
TAW Tactical Airlift Wing
TCW Tactical Control Wing
Tech Coll Technical College
TFS Tactical Fighter Squadron
TFTAS Tactical Fighter Training Aggressor Squadron
TFW Tactical Fighter Wing
TMTS Trade Management Training School
TOEU Tornado Operational Evaluation Unit
TRS Tactical Reconnaissance Squadron
TRW Tactical Reconnaissance Wing
TTTE Tri-national Tornado Training Establishment
TWCU Tornado Weapons Conversion Unit
TWU Tactical Weapons Unit
UAS University Air Squadron
UK United Kingdom
UKAEA United Kingdom Atomic Energy Authority
US United States
USAF United States Air Force
USAREUR US Army Europe
USN United States Navy
VGS Volunteer Gliding School
VS Vickers-Supermarine
WO Written off
WRG Weather Reconnaissance Group
WRS Weather Reconnaissance Squadron
WS Westland
WW2 World War II

British Military Aircraft Serials

The Committee of Imperial Defence through its Air Committee introduced a standardised system of numbering aircraft in November 1912. The Air Department of the Admiralty was allocated the first batch 1-200 and used these to cover aircraft already in use and those on order. The Army was issued with the next block from 201-800, which included the number 304 which was given to the Cody Biplane now preserved in the Science Museum. By the outbreak of World War 1 the Royal Navy was on its second batch of serials 801-1600 and this system continued with alternating allocations between the Army and Navy until 1916 when number 10000, a Royal Flying Corps BE2C, was reached.

It was decided not to continue with five digit numbers but instead to start again from 1, prefixing RFC aircraft with the letter A and RNAS aircraft with the prefix N. The RFC allocations commenced with A1 an FE2D and before the end of the year had reached A9999 an Armstrong Whitworth FK8. The next group commenced with B1 and continued in logical sequence through the C, D, E and F prefixes. G was used on a limited basis to identity captured German aircraft, while H was the last block of wartime ordered aircraft. To avoid confusion I was not used, so the new postwar machines were allocated serials in the J range. A further minor change was made in the serial numbering system in August 1929 when it was decided to maintain four numerals after the prefix letter, thus omitting numbers 1 to 999. The new K series therefore commenced at K1000, which was allocated to an AW Atlas.

The Naval N prefix was not used in such a logical way. Blocks of numbers were allocated for specific types of aircraft such as seaplanes or flying boats. By the late 1920s the sequence had largely been used up and a new series using the prefix S was commenced. In 1930 separate naval allocations were stopped and subsequent serials were issued in the 'military' range which had by this time reached the K series. A further change in the pattern of allocations came in the L range. Commencing with L7272 numbers were issued in blocks with smaller blocks of serials between not used. These were known as blackout blocks. As M had already been used as a suffix for Maintenance Command instructional airframes it was not used as a prefix. Although N had previously been used for naval aircraft it was used again for serials allocated from 1937.

With the build-up to World War 2 the rate of allocations quickly accelerated and the prefix R was being used when war was declared. The letters O and Q were not allotted, and nor was S which had been used up to S1865 for naval aircraft before integration into the RAF series. By 1940 the serial Z9999 had been reached, as part of a blackout block, with the letters U and Y not used to avoid confusion. The option to recommence serial allocation at A1000 was not taken up; instead it was decided to use an alphabetical two-letter prefix with three numerals running from 100 to 999. Thus AA100 was allocated to a Blenheim IV.

This two-letter, three-numeral serial system which started in 1940 continues today with the current issue being in the ZF range. The letters C, I, O, Q, U and Y were, with one or two exceptions, not used. For various reasons the following letter combinations were not issued: DA, DB, DH, EA, GA to GZ, HA, JE, JH, JJ, NZ and SA to SK. The first postwar serials issued were in the VP range while the end of the WZs had been reached by the Korean War. At the current rate of issue the Z range should last out the remainder of this century.

Note: Whilst every effort has been made to ensure the accuracy of this publication no part of the contents has been obtained from official sources. The compiler will be pleased to continue to receive comments, corrections and further information for inclusion in subsequent editions of *Military Aircraft Markings*. A monthly up-date of additions, amendments and cancellations is published in *Aircraft Illustrated*.

British Military Aircraft Markings

Serial	Type (alternative identity)	Owner, Operator or Location	Notes
164	Bleriot Type XI (BAPC 106)	RAF Museum, Hendon	
168	Sopwith Tabloid Replica (G-BFDE)	Bomber Command Museum, Hendon	
304	Cody Biplane (BAPC 62)	Science Museum, South Kensington	
433	Bleriot Type XXVII (BAPC 107)	RAF Museum, Hendon	
2345	Vickers FB5 Gunbus Replica (G-ATVP)	RAF Museum, Hendon	
2699	RAF BE2C	Imperial War Museum, Duxford	
3066	Caudron GIII (G-AETA)	RAF Museum, Hendon	
5964	DH2 Replica (BAPC 112)	Leisure Sport/Middle Wallop	
6232	RAF BE2C Replica (BAPC 41)	RAF St Athan Historic Aircraft Collection	
8151	Sopwith Baby Replica (BAPC 137)	Leisure Sport, Thorpe Park	
8359	Short 184	FAA Museum, RNAS Yeovilton	
A1325	RAF BE2e	Mosquito Aircraft Museum, London Colney	
A1742	Scout D Replica (BAPC 38)	RAF St Athan Historic Aircraft Collection	
A4850	RAF SE5A Replica (BAPC176)	South Yorkshire Aviation Society, Worksop	
A8226	Sopwith 1½ Strutter Replica (G-BIDW)	RAF Museum, Hendon	
B1807	Sopwith Pup (G-EAVX)	Privately owned, Keynsham, Avon	
B4863	RAF SE5A Replica (BAPC 113) [G]	Leisure Sport, Thorpe Park	
B4863	Eberhardt SE5E (G-BLXT) [G]	Privately owned, Booker	
B6401	Sopwith Camel F1 Replica (G-AWYY/C1701)	FAA Museum, RNAS Yeovilton	
B7270	Sopwith Camel F1 Replica (G-BFCZ)	Privately owned, St Just	
C1381	Avro 504K Replica (BAPC177) [G]	RAF Museum Store, Henlow	
C1904	RAF SE5A Replica (G-PFAP) [OZ]	Privately owned, Bicester	
C4912	Bristol M1c Replica (BAPC 135)	Leisure Sport, Thorpe Park	
D3419	Sopwith Camel F1 Replica (BAPC 59)	RAF St Athan Historic Aircraft Collection	
D5329	Sopwith Dolphin	RAF Museum Store, Henlow	
D7560	Avro 504K	Science Museum, South Kensington	
D8096	Bristol Fighter (G-AEPH) [D]	Shuttleworth Collection, Old Warden	
E449	Avro 504K (G-EBJE)	RAF Museum, Hendon	
E2581	Bristol F2b Fighter	Imperial War Museum, Duxford	
E6452	SNCAN Stampe SV4C (G-AXNW)	Privately owned, Barton	
F344	Avro 504K Replica	RAF Museum Store, Henlow	
F373	Avro 504K Replica	RAF Museum Store, Henlow	
F760	SE5A Microlight Replica [A]	Privately owned, Redhill	
F904	RAF SE5A (G-EBIA)	Shuttleworth Collection, Old Warden	
F938	RAF SE5A (G-EBIC)	RAF Museum, Hendon	
F939	RAF SE5A (G-EBIB) [6]	Science Museum, South Kensington	
F943	RAF SE5A Replica (G-BIHF) [S]	Privately owned, Booker (*Lady Di*)	
F943	RAF SE5A Replica (G-BKDT)	Privately owned, Sherburn	
F1010	DH9A [19]	Bomber Command Museum, Hendon	
F3556	RAF RE8	Imperial War Museum, Duxford	
F5447	RAF SE5A Replica (G-BKER) [N]	Privately owned, Glasgow	
F5459	RAF SE5A Replica (BAPC 142) [Y]	Cornwall Aero Park, Helston	
F-5459	RAF SE5A Replica (G-INNY)	Privately owned, Old Sarum	
F6314	Sopwith Camel [B]	RAF Museum, Hendon	
F8010	RAF SE5A Replica (G-BDWJ) [19]	Privately owned, Booker	
F8614	Vickers Vimy Replica (G-AWAU)	Bomber Command Museum, Hendon	
H1968	Avro 504K Replica (BAPC 42)	RAF St Athan Historic Aircraft Collection	
H2311	Avro 504K (G-ABAA)	RAF Museum Store, Henlow	
H5199	Avro 504K (G-ACNB, G-ADEV, E3404)	Shuttleworth Collection, Old Warden	

Notes	Serial	Type (alternative identity)	Owner, Operator or Location
	J7326	DH Humming Bird (G-EBQP)	Russavia Collection, Duxford
	J8067	Pterodactyl 1a	Science Museum, South Kensington
	J9941	Hawker Hart (G-ABMR) [57]	RAF Museum, Cardington
	K1786	Hawker Tomtit (G-AFTA)	Shuttleworth Collection, Old Warden
	K1930	Hawker Fury Replica (G-BKBB)	Privately owned, St Just
	K2050	Hawker Fury Replica (G-ASCM)	Privately owned, Stapleford
	K2059	Isaacs Fury (G-PFAR)	Privately owned, Dunkeswell
	K2567	DH Tiger Moth (G-MOTH)	Russavia Collection, Duxford
	K2568	DH Tiger Moth (G-APMM)	Privately owned, Bedford
	K2571	DH Tiger Moth	Privately owned, Lutterworth
	K2572	DH Tiger Moth (G-AOZH)	Privately owned, Shoreham
	K3215	Avro Tutor (G-AHSA)	Shuttleworth Collection, Old Warden
	K3584	DH Queen Bee (BAPC186)	Privately owned, Manchester
	K4232	Avro Rota (SE-AZB)	RAF Museum, Hendon
	K4235	Avro Rota (G-AHMJ)	Shuttleworth Collection, Old Warden
	K4972	Hawker Hart Trainer IIA (1746M)	RAF Museum, Hendon
	K5054	Supermarine Spitfire Replica	Privately owned, Swindon
	K5414	Hawker Hind (G-AENP/ BAPC 78) [XV]	Shuttleworth Collection, Old Warden
	K6038	Westland Wallace II	RAF Museum Store, Cardington
	K7271	Hawker Fury II Replica (BAPC 148)	RAF Cosford Aerospace Museum
	K8042	Gloster Gladiator (8372M)	Battle of Britain Museum, Hendon
	K9942	VS Spitfire IA (8383M) [SD-V]	RAF Museum, Hendon
	L1592	Hawker Hurricane I [KW-Z]	Science Museum, South Kensington
	L1592	Hawker Hurricane I Replica (BAPC 63) [KW-Z]	Torbay Aircraft Museum, Paignton
	L2301	VS Walrus (G-AIZG)	FAA Museum, RNAS Yeovilton
	L2940	Blackburn Skua	FAA Museum, RNAS Yeovilton
	L5343	Fairey Battle I	RAF St Athan Historic Aircraft Collection
	L6906	Miles Magister (BAPC 44)	Privately owned, Wroughton
	L8032	Gloster Gladiator (G-AMRK)	Shuttleworth Collection, Old Warden
	L8756	Bristol Bolingbroke (RCAF 10001) [XD-E]	Battle of Britain Museum, Hendon
	N220	Supermarine S5 replica (G-BDFF)	Privately owned, Bodmin
	N248	Supermarine S6A	Southampton Hall of Aviation
	N1671	Boulton Paul Defiant I (8370M) [EW-D]	Battle of Britain Museum, Hendon
	N1854	Fairey Fulmar II (G-AIBE)	FAA Museum, RNAS Yeovilton
	N2078	Sopwith Baby	FAA Museum, RNAS Yeovilton
	N2276	Gloster Sea Gladiator (N5903) [H]	FAA Museum, RNAS Yeovilton
	N2980	Vickers Wellington BIA [R]	Brooklands Museum, Weybridge
	N3788	Miles Magister (G-AKPF)	Privately owned, Bassingbourn
	N4172	Fairey Albacore [5A]	FAA Museum at St Just
	N4877	Avro Anson I (G-AMDA) [VX-F]	Skyfame Collection, Duxford
	N5180	Sopwith Pup (G-EBKY)	Shuttleworth Collection, Old Warden
	N5182	Sopwith Pup (G-APUP/B5292)	RAF Museum, Hendon
	N5195	Sopwith Pup (G-ABOX)	Museum of Army Flying, Middle Wallop
	N5445	DH Tiger Moth (G-AIXH/DE722)	Privately owned, Little Gransden
	N5492	Sopwith Triplane Replica (BAPC 111)	Leisure Sport, Thorpe Park
	N5628	Gloster Gladiator II	RAF Museum, Hendon
	N5912	Sopwith Triplane (8385M)	RAF Museum, Hendon
	N6004	Short Stirling 1	Cotswold Aircraft Restoration Group, RAF Innsworth
	N6452	Sopwith Pup Replica (G-BIAU)	FAA Museum, RNAS Yeovilton
	N6466	DH Tiger Moth (G-ANKZ)	Privately owned, Barton
	N6532	DH Tiger Moth (G-ANTS)	Strathallan Aircraft Collection
	N6720	DH Tiger Moth (7014M) [RUO-B]	No 1940 Sqn ATC, Levenshulme
	N6812	Sopwith Camel	Imperial War Museum, Lambeth
	N6847	DH Tiger Moth (G-APAL)	Privately owned, Little Gransden
	N6848	DH Tiger Moth (G-BALX)	Privately owned, Sedlescombe
	N6985	DH Tiger Moth (G-AHMN)	Museum of Army Flying, Middle Wallop
	N8224	DH Tiger Moth (G-AHUR)	Privately owned, Blackbushe
	N9191	DH Tiger Moth (G-ALND)	Privately owned, Shipdham
	N9238	DH Tiger Moth (G-ANEL)	Privately owned, Catterick
	N9389	DH Tiger Moth (G-ANJA)	Privately owned, Shipmeadow, Suffolk

Serial	Type (alternative identity)	Owner, Operator or Location	Notes
N9510	DH Tiger Moth (G-AOEL)	Royal Scottish Museum of Flight, East Fortune	
N9899	Supermarine Southampton	RAF Museum Store, Cardington	
P2183	Fairey Battle I [36]	RAF St Athan Historic Aircraft Collection	
P2617	Hawker Hurricane I (8373M) [AF-F]	Battle of Britain Museum, Hendon	
P3175	Hawker Hurricane I	Battle of Britain Museum, Hendon	
P6382	Miles Magister (G-AJRS)	Shuttleworth Collection, Old Warden	
P7350	VS Spitfire IIA (G-AWIJ) [EB-Z]	RAF Battle of Britain Flight, Coningsby	
P7540	VS Spitfire IIA [DU-W]	Dumfries & Galloway Aviation Museum, Tinwald Downs	
P9390	VS Spitfire I Replica (BAPC 71) [KL-B]	Norfolk & Suffolk Aviation Museum, Flixton	
P9444	VS Spitfire IA [RN-D]	Science Museum, South Kensington	
R1914	Miles Magister (G-AHUJ)	Strathallan Aircraft Collection	
R3950	Fairey Battle I (RCAF 1899)	Strathallan Aircraft Collection	
R4907	DH Tiger Moth (G-ANCS)	Privately owned, Norwich	
R4959	DH Tiger Moth (G-ARAZ) [59]	Privately owned, Goodwood	
R5086	DH Tiger Moth (G-APIH)	Privately owned, Little Gransden	
R5250	DH Tiger Moth (G-AODT)	Privately owned, Swanton Morley	
R5868	Avro Lancaster I (7325M) [PO-S]	Bomber Command Museum, Hendon	
R6915	VS Spitfire I	Imperial War Museum, Lambeth	
R9125	Westland Lysander III (8377M) [LX-L]	Battle of Britain Museum, Hendon	
S1287	Fairey Flycatcher Replica (G-BEYB) [5]	Privately owned, Middle Wallop/ Yeovilton	
S1595	Supermarine S6B	Science Museum, South Kensington	
S1595	Supermarine S6B Replica (BAPC 156)	Leisure Sport, Thorpe Park	
S3398	Spad XIII Replica (G-BFYO)	Privately owned, St Just	
S4523	Spad VII (N2727V)	Imperial War Museum, Duxford	
T5424	DH Tiger Moth (G-AJOA)	Privately owned, Chiseldon	
T5493	DH Tiger Moth (G-ANEF)	Privately owned, Cranwell	
T5854	DH Tiger Moth (G-ANKK)	Privately owned, Halfpenny Green	
T6296	DH Tiger Moth (8387M)	RAF Museum, Hendon	
T6313	DH Tiger Moth (G-AHVU)	Privately owned, Denham	
T6553	DH Tiger Moth (G-APIG) [N]	Privately owned, Avignon	
T6645	DH Tiger Moth (G-AIIZ)	Privately owned, Redhill	
T6818	DH Tiger Moth (G-ANKT)	Shuttleworth Collection, Old Warden	
T7281	DH Tiger Moth (G-ARTL)	Privately owned, Whitby	
T7404	DH Tiger Moth (G-ANMV)	Privately owned, Compton Abbas	
T7909	DH Tiger Moth (G-ANON)	Privately owned, Sherburn-in-Elmet	
T7997	DH Tiger Moth (G-AOBH)	Privately owned, Benington	
T8191	DH Tiger Moth	RN Historic Flight, RNAS Yeovilton	
T9707	Miles Magister (G-AKKR/8378M)	Greater Manchester Museum of Science and Industry	
T9738	Miles Magister (G-AKAT)	Newark Air Museum, Winthorpe	
V3388	Airspeed Oxford (G-AHTW)	Skyfame Collection, Duxford	
V7767	Hawker Hurricane Replica (BAPC 72)	Air Museum, North Weald	
V9281	Westland Lysander III (G-BCWL) [RU-M]	Privately owned, Hamble	
V9300	Westland Lysander	British Aerial Museum, Duxford	
V9441	Westland Lysander IIIA (RCAF2355/G-AZWT) [AR-A]	Strathallan Aircraft Collection	
W1048	HP Halifax II (8465M) [TL-S]	Bomber Command Museum, Hendon	
W4041	Gloster E28/39 [G]	Science Museum, South Kensington	
W4050	DH Mosquito 1	Mosquito Aircraft Museum, London Colney	
W5856	Fairey Swordfish II (G-BMGC)	Strathallan Aircraft Collection	
W5984	Fairey Swordfish II (HS618/ A2001) [5H]	FAA Museum, RNAS Yeovilton	
X4590	VS Spitfire I (8384M) [PR-F]	Battle of Britain Museum, Hendon	
X4936	VS Spitfire VB (AB910) [BP-O]	RAF Battle of Britain Memorial Flight, Coningsby	
Z2033	Fairey Firefly I (G-ASTL)	Skyfame Collection, Duxford	
Z7015	Hawker Sea Hurricane IB (G-BKTH)	Shuttleworth Collection, Duxford	
Z7197	Percival Proctor III (G-AKZN/ 8380M)	RAF St Athan Historic Aircraft Collection	
Z7258	DH Dragon Rapide (G-AHGD)	Privately owned, Booker	

Notes	Serial	Type (alternative identity)	Owner, Operator or Location
	AL246	Grumman Martlet I	FAA Museum, RNAS Yeovilton
	AP507	Cierva C30a (G-ACWP) [KX-P]	Science Museum, South Kensington
	AR213	VS Spitfire IA (G-AIST) [QG-A]	Privately owned, Booker
	AR501	VS Spitfire VC (G-AWII) [NN-D]	Shuttleworth Collection, Duxford
	BB807	Tiger Moth (G-ADWO)	Wessex Aviation Society, Wimborne
	BB814	DH Tiger Moth (G-AFWI)	RN Gliding Club, Lee-on-Solent
	BL614	VS Spitfire VB (AB871/4354M) [ZD-F]	Greater Manchester Museum of Science and Industry
	BM597	VS Spitfire VB (5713M) [PR-O]	RAF Church Fenton, on gate
	DE208	DH Tiger Moth (G-AGYU)	Privately owned, Nayland
	DE373	DH Tiger Moth T.2 (A680/A2127)	FAA Museum store, RNAS Yeovilton
	DE623	DH Tiger Moth (G-ANFI)	Privately owned, St Athan
	DE673	DH Tiger Moth (G-ADNZ/6948M)	Privately owned, Hampton
	DE992	DH Tiger Moth (G-AXXV)	Privately owned, Wellesbourne Mountford
	DF128	DH Tiger Moth (G-AOJJ) [RCO-U]	Privately owned, Booker
	DF130	DH Tiger Moth (G-BACK)	Privately owned, Laindon
	DF155	DH Tiger Moth (G-ANFV)	Privately owned, Lossiemouth
	DF198	DH Tiger Moth (G-BBRB)	Privately owned, Biggin Hill
	DG202	Gloster F9/40 Meteor (5758M)	RAF Cosford Aerospace Museum
	DG590	Miles Hawk Major (G-ADMW/8379M)	RAF Museum Store, Henlow
	DP872	Fairey Barracuda II	FAA Museum, St Just on rebuild
	DR613	FW Wicko GM1 (G-AFJB)	Privately owned, Berkswell
	DR628	Beech D.17s (N18V) [PB-1]	Privately owned, Duxford
	DV372	Avro Lancaster I	Imperial War Museum, Lambeth
	EE531	Gloster Meteor F4 (7090M)	Midland Air Museum, Coventry
	EE549	Gloster Meteor F4 (6372M/7008M)	RAF St Athan Historic Aircraft Collection
	EJ693	Hawker Tempest V [SA-J]	RAF Museum Store, Henlow
	EM727	DH Tiger Moth (G-AOXN)	Leicester Aircraft Preservation Group
	EM903	DH Tiger Moth (G-APBI)	Privately owned, Audley End
	EN398	VS Spitfire IX Replica (BAPC184) [JE-J]	Imperial War Museum, Duxford
	EP120	VS Spitfire VB (5377M/8070M) [QV-H]	RAF Wattisham
	EX280	NA Harvard IIB (G-TEAC) [G]	Privately owned, Bourn
	EX976	NA Harvard III	FAA Museum, RNAS Yeovilton
	EZ259	NA Harvard III (G-BMJW)	Privately owned, Bracknell
	EZ407	NA Harvard III	RN Historic Flight, Lee-on-Solent
	FE905	NA Harvard IIB (LN-BNM/12392)	RAF Museum Store, Cardington
	FE992	NA Harvard IIB (G-BDAM)	Privately owned, Lee-on-Solent
	FH153	NA Harvard IIB (G-BBHK) [GW-A]	Privately owned, Cardiff
	FR870	Curtiss Kittyhawk III (NL1009N) [GA-S]	Privately owned, Duxford
	FS728	NA Harvard IIB (G-BAFM)	Privately owned, Hamble
	FT239	NA Harvard IV (G-BIWX)	Privately owned, White Waltham
	FT375	NA Harvard IIB	MoD(PE) A&AEE Boscombe Down
	FT391	NA Harvard IIB (G-AZBN)	Privately owned, Staverton
	FX301	NA Harvard IIB (G-JUDI) [FD-NQ]	Privately owned, Ipswich
	FX442	NA Harvard IIB	Privately owned, Bournemouth
	HB275	Be.C-45 Expeditor II (N5063N)	Privately owned, White Waltham
	HB751	Fairchild Argus III (G-BCBL)	Privately owned, Little Gransden
	HD368	NA B-25J Mitchell (N9089Z/G-BKXW) [VO-A]	Aces High, Duxford
	HJ711	DH Mosquito NFII [VI-C]	Privately owned, York
	HM354	Percival Proctor III (G-ANPP)	Privately owned, Duxford
	HR723	HP Halifax II	Privately owned, Elvington
	HS503	Fairey Swordfish IV (BAPC 108)	RAF Museum store, Henlow
	HS649	VS Spitfire XVIII	Privately owned, Chichester
	HX922	DH Mosquito TT35 (G-AWJV) [EG-F] (really TA634)	Mosquito Aircraft Museum, London Colney
	JV482	Grumman Wildcat V	Ulster Aviation Society, Newtownards
	JV928	PBY-5A Catalina (G-BLSC)	Plane Sailing, Barkston Heath
	KB889	Avro Lancaster 10	Warbirds of GB, Bitteswell

Serial	Type (alternative identity)	Owner, Operator or Location	Notes
KB976	Avro Lancaster B10 (G-BCOH) [LQ-K]	Strathallan Aircraft Collection	
KD431	CV Corsair IV [E2-M]	FAA Museum, RNAS Yeovilton	
KE209	Grumman Hellcat II	FAA Museum, RNAS Yeovilton	
KE418	Hawker Tempest (rear fuselage)	RNEC, Manadon	
KF183	NA Harvard IIB	MoD(PE) A&AEE Boscombe Down	
KF388	NA Harvard IIB (nose only)	Wessex Aviation Society, Wimborne	
KF435	NA Harvard IIB	Privately owned, Camberley	
KF532	NA Harvard IIB (cockpit section)	Newark Air Museum, Winthrope	
KG374	Douglas Dakota C-4 (KN645/8355M)	RAF Cosford Aerospace Museum	
KG874	Douglas Dakota C-4 (TS423/ G-DAKS) [YS-L]	Aces High, North Weald	
KK995	Sikorsky Hoverfly I (KL110) [E]	RAF Museum, Hendon	
KN751	Consolidated Liberator VI	RAF Cosford Aerospace Museum	
KP208	Douglas Dakota C-4 [YS]	Airborne Forces Museum, Aldershot	
KX829	Hawker Hurricane IV [JV-I]	Birmingham Museum of Science & Industry	
LA198	VS Spitfire F21 (7118M) [JX-C]	RAF Locking, main gate	
LA226	VS Spitfire F21 (7119M)	RAF Memorial Chapel, Biggin Hill	
LA255	VS Spitfire F21 (6490M) [LX-V]	RAF Wittering	
LA564	VS Seafire F46	Privately owned, Newport Pagnell	
LB312	Taylorcraft Plus D (G-AHXE)	Privately owned, Shoreham	
LB375	Taylorcraft Plus D (G-AHGW)	Privately owned, Coventry	
LF363	Hawker Hurricane IIC [VY-X]	RAF Battle of Britain Flight, Coningsby	
LF738	Hawker Hurricane IIC (5405M)	RAF, RAeS Medway Branch, Rochester	
LF751	Hawker Hurricane IIC (5466M)	RAF, RAeS Medway Branch, Rochester	
LF858	DH Queen Bee (G-BLUZ)	Privately owned, Meppershall	
LH208	Airspeed Horsa I	Museum of Army Flying, Middle Wallop	
LS326	Fairey Swordfish II (G-AJVH) [5A]	RN Historic Flight, RNAS Yeovilton	
LZ551	DH Sea Vampire I	FAA Museum, RNAS Yeovilton	
LZ766	Percival Proctor III (G-ALCK)	Skyfame Collection, Duxford	
MF628	Vickers Wellington T10	Bomber Command Museum, Hendon	
MH434	VS Spitfire IX (G-ASJV) [ZD-B]	Privately owned, Duxford	
MJ627	VS Spitfire TIX (G-ASOZ/ G-BMSB)	Privately owned, Kenilworth	
MJ730	VS Spitfire IX (G-BLAS)	Privately owned, St Leonards on Sea	
MK356	VS Spitfire IX (5690M) [21-V]	RAF St Athan Historic Aircraft Collection	
ML407	VS Spitfire T9 (G-LFIX) [OU-V]	Privately owned, Middle Wallop	
ML417	VS Spitfire LFIXe (G-BJSG) (2I-T]	Privately owned, Duxford	
ML427	VS Spitfire IX [I-ST]	Birmingham Museum of Science & Industry	
ML796	Short Sunderland V	Imperial War Museum, Duxford	
ML824	Short Sunderland V [NS-Z]	Battle of Britain Museum, Hendon	
MN235	Hawker Typhoon IB	RAF Museum, Hendon	
MP345	Airspeed Oxford (G-AITB/ MP425)	RAF Museum Store, Cardington	
MT360	Auster 5 (G-AKWT)	Loughborough & Leicester Aircraft Museum	
MT438	Auster III (G-AREI)	Privately owned, Chessington	
MT847	VS Spitfire XIV (6960M)	RAF Cosford Aerospace Museum	
MV154	VS Spitfire HF VIII (G-BKMI/ A58-671)	Privately owned, Huntingdon	
MV262	VS Spitfire XIV [42-G]	Warbirds of GB, Bitteswell	
MV293	VS Spitfire XIV (G-SPIT/G-BGHB)	Privately owned, Ruskington, Lincs	
MV370	VS Spitfire XIV (G-FXIV) [AV-L]	Privately owned, Lower Upham	
MW100	Avro York C1 (G-AGNV/TS798)	RAF Cosford Aerospace Museum	
NF370	Fairey Swordfish III	Imperial War Museum, Lambeth	
NF389	Fairey Swordfish III [5B]	FAA Museum, Lee-on-Solent	
NF875	DH Dragon Rapide 6 (G-AGTM) [603/CH]	Russavia Collection, Duxford	
NH238	VS Spitfire IX (N238V/ G-MKIX) [D-A]	Warbirds of GB, Bitteswell	
NH799	VS Spitfire XIV	Warbirds of GB, Bitteswell	
NJ673	Auster 5D (G-AOCR)	Privately owned, Saltby	
NJ695	Auster 4 (G-AJXV)	Privately owned, Tollerton	
NJ703	Auster 5 (G-AKPI)	Privately owned, Doncaster	
NL985	DH Tiger Moth (7015M)	Vintage Aircraft Team, Cranfield	
NP181	Percival Proctor IV (G-AOAR)	Lashenden Air Warfare Museum, in store	

Notes	Serial	Type (alternative identity)	Owner, Operator or Location
	NP184	Percival Proctor IV (G-ANYP) [K]	Torbay Aircraft Museum, Paignton
	NP294	Percival Proctor IV [TS-M]	Lincolnshire Aviation Museum, East Kirkby
	NP303	Percival Proctor IV (G-ANZJ)	Privately owned, Caterham, Surrey
	NR747	DH Dragon Rapide (G-AJHO)	Privately owned, near Bassingbourn
	NV778	Hawker Tempest V (8386M)	RAF Museum, Hendon
	NX611	Avro Lancaster VII (G-ASXX/ 8375M) [YF-C]	Privately owned, East Kirkby
	PA474	Avro Lancaster I [SR-D]	RAF Battle of Britain Flight, Coningsby
	PG617	DH Tiger Moth (G-AYVY)	Privately owned, Ronaldsway
	PG651	DH Tiger Moth (G-AYUX)	Privately owned, Booker
	PG671	DH Tiger Moth (N82AM) [26]	Privately owned
	PK624	VS Spitfire F22 (8072M) [RAU-T]	RAF Abingdon, at main gate
	PK664	VS Spitfire F22 (7759M) (V6-B)	RAF Binbrook, at main gate
	PK683	VS Spitfire F24 (7150M)	Southampton Hall of Aviation
	PK724	VS Spitfire F24 (7288M)	RAF Museum, Hendon
	PL983	VS Spitfire XI (G-PRXI)	Privately owned, Duxford/Marseilles
	PM631	VS Spitfire XIX [DL-E]	RAF Battle of Britain Flight, Coningsby
	PM651	VS Spitfire XIX (7758M)	RAF Benson, at main gate
	PS853	VS Spitfire XIX	RAF Battle of Britain Flight, Coningsby
	PS915	VS Spitfire XIX (7711M)	RAF Battle of Britain Flight, BAe Preston
	PT462	VS Spitfire T9 (G-CTIX)	Privately owned, Micheldever, Hants
	PV202	VS Spitfire TIX (G-TRIX)	Privately owned, Micheldever, Hants
	PZ865	Hawker Hurricane II (G-AMAU)	RAF Battle of Britain Flight, Coningsby
	RA848	Slingsby Cadet TX1	Privately owned, Leeds
	RA854	Slingsby Cadet TX1	Privately owned, Wigan
	RA897	Slingsby Cadet TX1	Newark Air Museum store, Hucknall
	RD253	Bristol Beaufighter TFX (7931M)	RAF Museum, Hendon
	RF398	Avro Lincoln B2 (8376M)	RAF Cosford Aerospace Museum
	RG333	Miles Messenger IIA (G-AIEK)	Privately owned, Felton, Bristol
	RG333	Miles Messenger IIA (G-AKEZ)	Torbay Aircraft Museum, Paignton
	RH377	Miles Messenger 4A (G-ALAH)	The Aeroplane Collection, RAF Henlow
	RH378	Miles Messenger IIA (G-AJOE)	Cotswold Aircraft Restoration Group, RAF Innsworth
	RH746	Bristol Brigand TF1	North East Aircraft Museum, Usworth
	RL962	DH Dragon Rapide (G-AHED)	RAF Museum Store, Cardington
	RM221	Percival Proctor IV (G-ANXR)	Privately owned, Biggin Hill
	RM689	VS Spitfire XIV (G-ALGT) [AP-D]	Rolls-Royce, Filton
	RM694	VS Spitfire XIV (6640M)	Warbirds of GB, Bitteswell
	RR299	DH Mosquito T3 (G-ASKH) [HT-E]	British Aerospace, Hatfield
	RT520	Auster 4 (G-ALYB)	South Yorkshire A.P.S., Firbeck
	RW382	VS Spitfire XVIe (7245M/ 8075M)	RAF Uxbridge, London
	RW386	VS Spitfire XVIe (6944M/ G-BXVI) [RAK-A]	Warbirds of GB, Bitteswell
	RW388	VS Spitfire XVIe (6947M) [U4-U]	Stoke-on-Trent Museum
	RW393	VS Spitfire XVIe (7293M) [XT-A]	RAF Turnhouse, at main gate
	SL542	VS Spitfire XVIe (8390M) [4M-N]	RAF Coltishall, at main gate
	SL574	VS Spitfire XVIe (8391M) [AZ-B]	RAF Bentley Priory
	SL674	VS Spitfire XVIe (8392M)	RAF Memorial Chapel, Biggin Hill
	SM832	VS Spitfire XIV (G-WWII)	Warbirds of GB, Bitteswell
	SM969	VS Spitfire XVIII (G-BRAF)	Warbirds of GB, Bitteswell
	SX137	VS Seafire XVII	FAA Museum, RNAS Yeovilton
	SX300	VS Seafire XVII (A646)	Privately owned, Warwick
	SX336	VS Seafire XVII (A2055)	Privately owned, Twyford, Bucks
	TA122	DH Mosquito FBVI [UP-G]	Mosquito Aircraft Museum, London Colney
	TA634	DH Mosquito B35 (G-AWJV)	Mosquito Aircraft Museum, London Colney
	TA639	DH Mosquito TT35 (7806M)	RAF Cosford Aerospace Museum

Serial	*Type (alternative identity)*	*Owner, Operator or Location*	*Notes*
TA719	DH Mosquito TT35 (G-ASKC) [6T]	Skyfame Collection, Duxford	
TB252	VS Spitfire XVIe (7257M) [GW-H]	RAF Leuchars, at main gate	
TB382	VS Spitfire XVIe (7244M)	RAF Exhibition Flight, Abingdon	
TB752	VS Spitfire XVIe (7256M/ 8086M) [KH-Z]	RAF Manston, Memorial Hall	
TB863	VS Spitfire XVIe (G-CDAN)	Privately owned, Booker	
TB885	VS Spitfire LFXVIE	Shoreham Aircraft Preservation Society	
TD248	VS Spitfire XVIe (7246M) [DW-A]	RAF Sealand, at main gate	
TE184	VS Spitfire XVIe (6850M) [LA-A]	Ulster Folk & Transport Museum, County Down	
TE311	VS Spitfire XVIe (7241M)	RAF Exhibition Flight, Abingdon	
TE356	VS Spitfire XVIe (6709M/ 7001M)	RAF Leeming	
TE392	VS Spitfire XVIe (7000M)	Warbirds of GB, Bitteswell	
TE462	VS Spitfire XVIe (7243M)	Royal Scottish Museum of Flight, East Fortune	
TE476	VS Spitfire XVIe (7451M/ 8071M)	RAF Northolt at main gate	
TE517	VS Spitfire LFIX (2046/G-BIXP/ G-CCIX)	Privately owned, Micheldever, Hants	
TE566	VS Spitfire IX (G-BLCK)	Privately owned, St Leonards on Sea	
TF956	Hawker Sea Fury FB11 [123/T]	RN Historic Flight, RNAS Yeovilton	
TG263	Saro SRA1 (G-12-1)	Skyfame Collection, Duxford	
TG511	HP Hastings T5 (8554M)	RAF Cosford Aerospace Museum	
TG517	HP Hastings T5 [517]	Newark Air Museum, Winthorpe	
TG528	HP Hastings C1A	Skyfame Collection, Duxford	
TG568	HP Hastings C1A	RAE Bedford Fire Section	
TJ118	DH Mosquito TT35	Mosquito Aircraft Museum, St Albans	
TJ138	DH Mosquito B35 (7607M) [V-O]	RAF Museum Store, Swinderby	
TJ343	Auster 5 (G-AJXC)	Privately owned, Popham	
TJ472	Auster AOP5 (BAPC 70)	Royal Scottish Museum of Flight, East Fortune	
TJ569	Auster 5 (G-AKOW)	Museum of Army Flying, Middle Wallop	
TJ672	Auster 5 (G-ANIJ)	Privately owned, Thruxton	
TK777	GAL Hamilcar	Museum of Army Flying, Middle Wallop	
TL615	Airspeed Horsa II	Mosquito Aircraft Museum, London Colney	
TL659	Airspeed Horsa (BAPC 80) [74]	Museum of Army Flying, Middle Wallop	
TV959	DH Mosquito T3 [AF-V]	Imperial War Museum, Lambeth	
TW117	DH Mosquito T3 (7805M)	Bomber Command Museum, Hendon	
TW439	Auster 5 (G-ANRP)	Warnham War Museum, Horsham	
TW511	Auster 5 (G-APAF)	Privately owned, Gamston	
TW536	Auster AOP6 (7704M)	Museum of Army Flying, Middle Wallop	
TW641	Auster AOP6 (G-ATDN)	Privately owned, Biggin Hill	
TX183	Avro Anson C19	Privately owned, Arbroath	
TX213	Avro Anson C19 (G-AWRS)	North East Aircraft Museum, Usworth	
TX214	Avro Anson C19 (7817M)	RAF Cosford Aerospace Museum	
TX226	Avro Anson C19 (7865M)	Imperial War Museum, Duxford	
TX228	Avro Anson C19	City of Norwich Aviation Museum	
TX235	Avro Anson C19	Torbay Aircraft Museum, Paignton	
VF301	DH Vampire F1 (7060M) [RAL-B]	Midland Air Museum, Coventry	
VF516	Auster AOP6 (G-ASMZ)	Privately owned, Middle Wallop	
VH127	Fairey Firefly TT4	FAA Museum, RNAS Yeovilton	
VL348	Avro Anson C19 (G-AVVO)	Newark Air Museum, Winthorpe	
VL349	Avro Anson C19 (G-AWSA)	Norfolk & Suffolk Aviation Museum, Flixton	
VM325	Avro Anson C19	Midland Air Museum, Coventry	
VM360	Avro Anson C19 (G-APHV)	Royal Scottish Museum of Flight, East Fortune	
VM791	Slingsby Cadet TX3 (really XA312)	No 132 Redhill & Reigate Sqn, ATC, RAF Kenley	
VN148	Grunau Baby	Russavia Collection, Duxford	
VP293	Avro Shackleton T4	Strathallan Aircraft Collection	
VP519	Avro Anson C19 nose only (G-AVVR)	Privately owned, Stockport	
VP952	DH Devon C2 (8820M)	RAF Cosford Aerospace Museum	
VP953	DH Devon C2	CTE, RAF Manston	

Notes	Serial	Type (alternative identity)	Owner, Operator or Location
	VP955	DH Devon C2 (G-DVON)	Privately owned, Staverton
	VP956	DH Devon C2	No 1404 Sqn ATC, RAF Manston
	VP957	DH Devon C2 (8822M)	RAF BDRT, Bishop's Court, NI (at Aldergrove)
	VP958	DH Devon C2 [DC] (8795M)	RAF CTTS, St Athan
	VP959	DH Devon C2 [L]	MoD(PE) RAE Farnborough
	VP960	DH Devon C2	CTE, RAF Manston
	VP961	DH Devon C2 (G-ALFM)	Privately owned, Leavesden
	VP962	DH Devon C2 (G-BLRB)	Privately owned, RAF Kemble
	VP963	DH Devon C2	CTE, RAF Manston
	VP965	DH Devon C2 [DE] (8823M)	RAF Manston Fire Section
	VP967	DH Devon C2 (G-KOOL)	East Surrey Technical College, Redhill
	VP968	DH Devon C2	MoD(PE) A&AEE Boscombe Down
	VP971	DH Devon C2 (8824M)	RAF FF&SS, Catterick
	VP975	DH Devon C2 [M]	MoD(PE) RAE Farnborough
	VP976	DH Devon C2 (8784M)	RAF Northolt Fire Section
	VP977	DH Devon C2 (G-ALTS)	RAE West Freugh Fire Section
	VP981	DH Devon C2	RAF Battle of Britain Flight, Coningsby
	VR137	Westland Wyvern TF1	FAA Museum, RNAS Yeovilton
	VR192	Pervical Prentice T1 (G-APIT)	Second World War Aircraft Preservation Society, Lasham
	VR249	Percival Prentice T1 (G-APIY) [FA-EL]	Newark Air Museum, Winthorpe
	VR930	Hawker Sea Fury FB11 (8382M)	FAA Museum store, Wroughton
	VS356	Percival Prentice T1 (G-AOLU)	Scottish Aircraft Collection Trust, Perth
	VS562	Avro Anson T21 (8012M)	Privately owned, Southampton
	VS610	Percival Prentice T1 (G-AOKL) [K-L]	Privately owned, Southend
	VS623	Percival Prentice T1 (G-AOKZ)	Midland Air Museum, Coventry
	VT229	Gloster Meteor F4 (7151M) [60]	Newark Air Museum, Winthorpe
	VT260	Gloster Meteor F4 [67]	Imperial War Museum, Duxford
	VT409	Fairey Firefly AS5	North East Aircraft Museum, Usworth
	VT745	Fairey Firefly AS5 (fuselage)	Privately owned, St Merryn
	VT812	DH Vampire F3 (7200M) [N]	RAF Museum, Hendon
	VT921	Grunau Baby	Privately owned, Honington
	VT935	Boulton Paul P111A	Midland Air Museum, Coventry
	VV106	VS510 (7175M)	RAF Cosford Aerospace Museum
	VV119	Supermarine S35 (nose only) (7285M)	Lincolnshire Aviation Museum, East Kirkby
	VV217	DH Vampire FB5 (7323M)	No 301 Sqn ATC, Bury St Edmunds
	VV901	Avro Anson T21	Pennine Aviation Museum, Bacup
	VW453	Gloster Meteor T7 (8703M)	Cotswold Aircraft Restoration Group, RAF Innsworth
	VW985	Auster AOP6 (G-ASEF)	Privately owned, Somerton, Oxon
	VX118	Auster 6A (G-ANSB)	Privately owned, Keevil
	VX250	DH Sea Hornet 21 [48]	Mosquito Aircraft Museum, London Colney
	VX272	Hawker P1052 (7174M)	RAF Cosford Aerospace Museum
	VX275	Slingsby Sedbergh TX1	RAF St Athan
	VX461	DH Vampire FB5 (7646M)	RAF Museum Store, Henlow
	VX573	Vickers Valetta C2 (8389M)	RAF Cosford Aerospace Museum
	VX577	Vickers Valetta C2	North East Aircraft Museum, Usworth
	VX580	Vickers Valetta C2	Norfolk & Suffolk Aviation Museum Flixton
	VX595	Westland Dragonfly HR1 [29]	RAF Museum Store, Henlow
	VX653	Hawker Sea Fury FB11	RAF Museum, Hendon
	VZ304	DH Vampire FB5 (7630M) [S]	Vintage Aircraft Team, Cranfield
	VZ462	Gloster Meteor F8	Second World War Aircraft Preservation Society, store
	VZ467	Gloster Meteor F8 [01]	RAF Shawbury store
	VZ477	Gloster Meteor F8 (nose only)	Kimbolton School CCF, Cambs
	VZ608	Gloster Meteor FR9	Newark Air Museum, Winthorpe
	VZ634	Gloster Meteor T7 (8657M)	Newark Air Museum, Winthorpe
	VZ638	Gloster Meteor T7 (G-JETM)	Brencham Historic Collection, Bournemouth
	VZ728	RS4 Desford Trainer (G-AGOS)	Scottish Aircraft Collection Trust, Perth
	VZ962	Westland Dragonfly HR1	Cornwall Aero Park, Helston
	VZ965	Westland Dragonfly HR5	FAA Museum, at RNAS Culdrose
	WA473	VS Attacker F1 [102/J]	FAA Museum, RNAS Yeovilton

Serial	Type (alternative identity)	Owner, Operator or Location	Notes
WA576	Bristol Sycamore 3 (G-ALSS/ 7900M)	Privately owned, East Fortune	
WA577	Bristol Sycamore 3 (G-ALST/ 7718M)	North East Aircraft Museum, Usworth	
WA591	Gloster Meteor T7 (7917M) [W]	RAF Woodvale, on display	
WA634	Gloster Meteor T7/8	RAF Cosford Aerospace Museum	
WA638	Gloster Meteor T7	Martin Baker Aircraft, Chalgrove	
WA662	Gloster Meteor T7	MoD(PE) RAE Llanbedr	
WA669	Gloster Meteor T7	RAF CFS, *Vintage Pair*, Scampton	
WA984	Gloster Meteor F8 [A]	Wessex Aviation Society, Wimborne	
WB188	Hawker Hunter F3 (7154M)	RAF Cosford Aerospace Museum	
WB271	Fairey Firefly AS5 [204/R]	RN Historic Flight, RNAS Yeovilton	
WB440	Fairey Firefly AS6	Greater Manchester Museum of Science and Industry	
WB491	Avro Ashton	Wales Aircraft Museum, Cardiff	
WB530	DH Devon C2 (8825M)	RAF Swinderby Fire Section	
WB531	DH Devon C2 (G-BLRN)	Privately owned, Staverton	
WB533	DH Devon C2 (G-DEVN) [DA]	British Air Reserve, Lympne	
WB534	DH Devon C2 (G-BLPZ) [DB]	Privately owned, Guernsey	
WB550	DH Chipmunk T10 [F]	RAF FSS, Swinderby	
WB560	DH Chipmunk T10	RAF No 4 AEF, Exeter	
WB565	DH Chipmunk T10 [X]	AAC BFWF, Middle Wallop	
WB567	DH Chipmunk T10	RAF No 12 AEF, Turnhouse	
WB569	DH Chipmunk T10 [2]	RAF No 1 AEF, Manston	
WB575	DH Chipmunk T10 [907]	RN Flying Grading Flt, Plymouth	
WB584	DH Chipmunk T10 PAX (7706M)	RAF No 12 AEF, Turnhouse	
WB586	DH Chipmunk T10 [A]	RAF No 6 AEF, Abingdon	
WB588	DH Chipmunk T10 (G-AOTD)	Shuttleworth Collection, Old Warden	
WB615	DH Chipmunk T10 [E]	AAC BFWF, Middle Wallop	
WB624	DH Chipmunk T10 PAX	The Aeroplane Collection, Warmingham	
WB627	DH Chipmunk T10 [N]	RAF No 5 AEF, Cambridge	
WB645	DH Chipmunk T10 PAX (8218M)	RAFGSA Bicester	
WB647	DH Chipmunk T10 [R]	AAC BFWF, Middle Wallop	
WB652	DH Chipmunk T10 [V]	RAF No 5 AEF, Cambridge	
WB654	DH Chipmunk T10 [14]	RAF No 10 AEF, Woodvale	
WB657	DH Chipmunk T10 [908]	RN Flying Grading Flt, Plymouth	
WB660	DH Chipmunk T10 (G-ARMB)	Privately owned, Fairoaks	
WB670	DH Chipmunk T10 (8361M)	Newark Air Museum, Winthorpe	
WB671	DH Chipmunk T10 [910]	RN Flying Grading Flt, Plymouth	
WB685	DH Chipmunk T10 PAX	Privately owned, Leeds	
WB693	DH Chipmunk T10 [S]	AAC BFWF, Middle Wallop	
WB697	DH Chipmunk T10 [O]	RAF No 3 AEF, Filton	
WB732	DH Chipmunk T10 (G-AOJZ/ 'G-ASTD')	Air Service Training, Perth	
WB739	DH Chipmunk T10 [8]	RAF No 8 AEF, Cosford	
WB754	DH Chipmunk T10 [H]	AAC BFWF, Middle Wallop	
WB758	DH Chipmunk T10 (7729M) [P]	Torbay Aircraft Museum, Paignton	
WB763	DH Chipmunk T10 (G-BBMR) [14]	Southall Technical College	
WB922	Slingsby Sedbergh TX1	RAF No 615 VGS, Kenley	
WB923	Slingsby Sedbergh TX1	RAF Cranwell Glider Flight	
WB924	Slingsby Sedbergh TX1	RAF store, Syerston	
WB927	Slingsby Sedbergh TX1	RAF No 615 VGS, Kenley	
WB932	Slingsby Sedbergh TX1	RAF No 1 MGSP, Halton	
WB934	Slingsby Sedbergh TX1 [A]	RAF No 618 VGS, West Malling	
WB935	Slingsby Sedbergh TX1	RAF No 634 VGS, St Athan	
WB937	Slingsby Sedbergh TX1	RAF No 615 VGS, Kenley	
WB938	Slingsby Sedbergh TX1	RAF Halton Glider Flight	
WB942	Slingsby Sedbergh TX1	RAF ACCGS/No 644 VGS, Syerston	
WB946	Slingsby Sedbergh TX1	RAF Sealand, stored	
WB958	Slingsby Sedbergh TX1	RAF No 621 VGS, Weston-super-Mare	
WB960	Slingsby Sedbergh TX1	RAF No 4 MGSP, Dishforth	
WB961	Slingsby Sedbergh TX1	RAF No 661 VGS, Kirknewton	
WB962	Slingsby Sedbergh TX1	RAF store, Syerston	
WB963	Slingsby Sedbergh TX1	RAF No 618 VGS, West Malling	
WB971	Slingsby Sedbergh TX1	RAF Sealand, stored	
WB972	Slingsby Sedbergh TX1	RAF No 626 VGS, Predannack	
WB973	Slingsby Sedbergh TX1	RAF No 634 VGS, St Athan	
WB974	Slingsby Sedbergh TX1	RAF No 663 VGS, Kinloss	

Notes	Serial	Type (alternative identity)	Owner, Operator or Location
	WB975	Slingsby Sedbergh TX1	RAF store, Syerston
	WB979	Slingsby Sedbergh TX1	RAF No 663 VGS, Kinloss
	WB980	Slingsby Sedbergh TX1	RAF No 1 MGSP, Halton
	WB981	Slingsby Sedbergh TX1	RAF Sealand, stored
	WB986	Slingsby Sedbergh TX1	RAF store, Syerston
	WB987	Slingsby Sedbergh TX1	RAF No 662 VGS, Arbroath
	WB989	Slingsby Sedbergh TX1	RAF Sealand, stored
	WB991	Slingsby Sedbergh TX1	RAF No 621 VGS, Weston-super-Mare
	WB992	Slingsby Sedbergh TX1	RAF store, Syerston
	WB993	Slingsby Sedbergh TX1	RAF Sealand, stored
	WD289	DH Chipmunk T10	RAF Gatow Station Flight, Berlin
	WD293	DH Chipmunk T10 PAX (7645M)	No 2308 Sqn ATC, Cwmbran
	WD310	DH Chipmunk T10 [H]	RAF FSS, Swinderby
	WD318	DH Chipmunk T10 PAX (8207M)	No 145 Sqn ATC, Timperley
	WD325	DH Chipmunk T10 [N]	AAC BFWF, Middle Wallop
	WD331	DH Chipmunk T10 [A]	RAF FSS, Swinderby
	WD355	DH Chipmunk T10 PAX	No 1955 Sqn ATC, Wells, Somerset
	WD356	DH Chipmunk T10 (7625M)	Privately owned, Huntingdon
	WD363	DH Chipmunk T10 (G-BCIH)	Privately owned, Stansted
	WD373	DH Chipmunk T10 [12]	RAF No 2 AEF, Hurn
	WD374	DH Chipmunk T10 [903]	RN Flying Grading Flt, Plymouth
	WD379	DH Chipmunk T10 (G-APLO) [K]	Privately owned, Jersey
	WD390	DH Chipmunk T10 [68]	RAF No 9 AEF, Finningley
	WD413	Avro Anson C 21 (G-BFIR/ 7881M)	Privately owned, Edinburgh
	WD496	HP Hastings C2	A&AEE Boscombe Down Fire Section
	WD646	Gloster Meteor TT20 (8189M) [R]	No 2030 Sqn ATC, Sheldon
	WD686	Gloster Meteor NF11	Imperial War Museum, Duxford
	WD790	Gloster Meteor NF11 (8743M) nose only	North East Aircraft Museum, Usworth
	WD889	Fairey Firefly AS6	North East Aircraft Museum, Usworth
	WD931	EE Canberra B2 nose only	No 425 Sqn ATC, Aldridge, W Midlands
	WD935	EE Canberra B2 (8440M)	RAF St Athan Historic Aircraft Collection
	WD954	EE Canberra B2 (nose only)	Lincolnshire Aviation Museum, East Kirkby
	WD955	EE Canberra T17 [EM]	RAF No 360 Sqn, Wyton
	WE113	EE Canberra B2 [BJ]	RAF No 231 OCU, Wyton
	WE122	EE Canberra TT18 [845]	RN FRADU, Yeovilton
	WE139	EE Canberra PR3 (8369M)	RAF Museum, Hendon
	WE146	EE Canberra PR3	RAE Llanbedr Fire Section
	WE168	EE Canberra PR3 (8049M)	RAF Manston, on display
	WE173	EE Canberra PR3 (8740M)	RAF Coltishall, BDRT
	WE188	EE Canberra T4	BAe Samlesbury, stored
	WE192	EE Canberra T4 [92]	BAe Samlesbury, stored
	WE569	Auster T7 (G-ASAJ)	Privately owned, Oakington
	WE600	Auster T7 (mod) (7602M)	RAF St Athan Historic Aircraft Collection
	WE925	Gloster Meteor F8	Wales Aircraft Museum, Cardiff
	WE982	Slingsby Prefect TX1 (8781M)	RAF Museum, Hendon
	WF122	Sea Prince T1 (A2673) [575/CU]	Cornwall Aero Park, Helston
	WF125	Sea Prince T1 (A2674)	RN Fire Section, Predannack
	WF128	Sea Prince T1 (8611M)	Norfolk & Suffolk Aviation Museum, Flixton
	WF137	Sea Prince C1	Second World War Aircraft Preservation Society, Lasham
	WF219	Hawker Sea Hawk F1 (A2439)	FAA Museum, RNAS Yeovilton
	WF225	Hawker Sea Hawk F1 (A2645) [CU]	RNAS Culdrose, at main gate
	WF259	Hawker Sea Hawk F2 (A2483) [171/A]	Royal Scottish Museum of Flight, East Fortune
	WF299	Hawker Sea Hawk FB3 (A2662/A2509/8164M)	Cornwall Aero Park, Helston
	WF369	Vickers Varsity T1 [F]	Newark Air Museum, Winthorpe
	WF372	Vickers Varsity T1 [T]	Nene Valley Aviation Society, Sibson
	WF376	Vickers Varsity T1	Bristol Airport Fire Section
	WF379	Vickers Varsity T1	RAE West Freugh, Fire Section

Serial	Type (alternative identity)	Owner, Operator or Location	Notes
WF408	Vickers Varsity T1 (8395M)	RAF Cosford Aerospace Museum	
WF410	Vickers Varsity T1 [F]	Bristol Airport Fire Section	
WF413	Vickers Varsity T1 [V]	CTE, RAF Manston	
WF425	Vickers Varsity T1	Imperial War Museum, Duxford	
WF643	Gloster Meteor F8 [X]	Norfolk & Suffolk Aviation Museum, Flixton	
WF784	Gloster Meteor T7 (7895M)	RAF Quedgeley, at main gate	
WF791	Gloster Meteor T7	RAF CFS, Scampton	
WF825	Gloster Meteor T7 (8359M) [Z]	No 2491 Sqn ATC, RAF Lyneham	
WF877	Gloster Meteor T7	Torbay Aircraft Museum, Paignton	
WF890	EE Canberra T17 [EJ]	RAF No 360 Sqn, Wyton	
WF911	EE Canberra B2 nose only	Pennine Aviation Museum, Bacup	
WF914	Gloster Meteor F8 [K] Really WK914	RAeS Medway Branch, Rochester	
WF916	EE Canberra T17 [EL]	RAF No 360 Sqn, Wyton	
WF922	EE Canberra PR3	Midland Air Museum, Coventry	
WG303	DH Chipmunk T10 PAX (8208M)	RAFGSA, Bicester	
WG307	DH Chipmunk 22 (G-BCYJ)	Privately owned, Lossiemouth	
WG308	DH Chipmunk T10	RAF No 7 AEF, Newton	
WG321	DH Chipmunk T10 [G]	AAC BFWF, Middle Wallop	
WG323	DH Chipmunk T10 [F]	AAC BFWF, Middle Wallop	
WG348	DH Chipmunk 22 (G-BBMV)	Privately owned, Booker	
WG350	DH Chipmunk 22 (G-BCYE)	Privately owned, Biggin Hill	
WG362	DH Chipmunk T10 PAX (8630M)	RAF FSS, Swinderby	
WG403	DH Chipmunk T10 [O]	AAC BFWF, Middle Wallop	
WG407	DH Chipmunk T10 [67]	RAF No 9 AEF, Finningley	
WG418	DH Chipmunk T10 PAX (8209M/G-ATDY)	RAF No 10 AEF, Woodvale	
WG419	DH Chipmunk T10 PAX (8206M)	No 1053 Sqn ATC, Armthorpe, S. Yorks	
WG422	DH Chipmunk 22 (G-BFAX/ 8394M) [16]	Privately owned, Coal Ashton	
WG430	DH Chipmunk T10 [1]	RAF No 1 AEF, Manston	
WG432	DH Chipmunk T10 [L]	AAC BFWF, Middle Wallop	
WG458	DH Chipmunk T10	RAF Shawbury store	
WG463	DH Chipmunk T10 PAX (8363M)	No 188 Sqn ATC, Ipswich	
WG464	DH Chipmunk T10 PAX (8364M)	No 131 Sqn ATC, Newcastle	
WG465	DH Chipmunk 22 (G-BCEY)	Privately owned, Debden	
WG466	DH Chipmunk T10	AAC, Shawbury store	
WG469	DH Chipmunk T10	RAF No 7 AEF, Newton	
WG471	DH Chipmunk T10 PAX (8210M)	RAF No 11 AEF, Leeming	
WG477	DH Chipmunk T10 PAX (8362M)	No 281 Sqn ATC, Birkdale	
WG478	DH Chipmunk T10 [J]	RAF Shawbury store	
WG479	DH Chipmunk T10 [K]	RAF FSS, Swinderby	
WG480	DH Chipmunk T10 [D]	RAF FSS, Swinderby	
WG486	DH Chipmunk T10	AAC, Shawbury store	
WG496	Slingsby Sedbergh TX1	RAF Halton Glider Flight	
WG498	Slingsby Sedbergh TX1	RAF store, Syerston	
WG511	Avro Shackleton T4 (nose only)	Cornwall Aero Park, Helston	
WG655	Hawker Sea Fury T20 [910/GN]	RN Historic Flight, RNAS Yeovilton	
WG677	EE Canberra B2 (nose only)	RNAS Yeovilton, Fire Section	
WG718	WS51 Dragonfly HR5 (A2531) [934/-]	Wales Aircraft Museum, Cardiff	
WG719	WS51 Dragonfly HR5 (G-BRMA) [902]	British Rotorcraft Museum, Weston-super-Mare	
WG724	WS51 Dragonfly HR5 [932]	North East Aircraft Museum, Usworth	
WG751	WS51 Dragonfly HR5	Privately owned, Ramsgreave, Lancs	
WG752	WS51 Dragonfly HR5	Imperial War Museum, Duxford	
WG760	English Electric P1A (7755M)	RAF Binbrook	
WG763	English Electric P1A (7816M)	Greater Manchester Museum of Science and Industry	
WG768	Short SB5 (8005M)	RAF Cosford Aerospace Museum	
WG774	BAC 221	Science Museum, RNAS Yeovilton	
WG777	Fairey FD2 (7986M)	RAF Cosford Aerospace Museum	
WG789	EE Canberra B2	MoD(PE) RAE Bedford	

Notes	Serial	Type (alternative identity)	Owner, Operator or Location
	WH132	Gloster Meteor T7 (7906M) [J]	No 276 Sqn ATC, Chelmsford
	WH166	Gloster Meteor T7 (8052M)	RAF Digby, at main gate
	WH291	Gloster Meteor F8	Second World War Aircraft Preservation Society, Lasham
	WH301	Gloster Meteor F8 (7930M) [T]	RAF Museum, Hendon
	WH364	Gloster Meteor F8 (8169M)	RAF Kemble, at main gate
	WH453	Gloster Meteor D16 [L]	MoD(PE) RAE Llanbedr
	WH646	EE Canberra T17 [EG]	RAF No 360 Sqn, Wyton
	WH657	EE Canberra B2	RFD Ltd, Godalming
	WH664	EE Canberra T17 [EH]	RAF No 360 Sqn, Wyton
	WH665	EE Canberra T17 (8763M) [J]	BAe Samlesbury
	WH670	EE Canberra B2 [CB]	RAF No 100 Sqn, Wyton
	WH699	EE Canberra B2T (8755M) (really WJ637)	RAFC Cranwell, Trenchard Hall on display
	WH703	EE Canberra B2 (8490M) [S]	RAF Abingdon, BDRF
	WH718	EE Canberra TT18 [CW]	RAF No 100 Sqn, Wyton
	WH725	EE Canberra B2	Imperial War Museum, Duxford
	WH734	EE Canberra TT2	Flight Refuelling Ltd, Hurn
	WH740	EE Canberra T17 (8762M) [K]	RAF No 2 SoTT, Cosford
	WH742	EE Canberra T19 (nose only)	RAF Shawbury Fire Section
	WH773	EE Canberra PR7 (8696M)	No 2331 Sqn ATC, RAF Wyton
	WH774	EE Canberra PR7	MoD(PE) RAE Farnborough, stored
	WH775	EE Canberra PR7 (8128M)	RAF St Athan, stored
	WH779	EE Canberra PR7 [CK]	RAF No 100 Sqn, Wyton
	WH780	EE Canberra T22 [853]	RN, St Athan store
	WH791	EE Canberra PR7 (8187M)	RAF Cottesmore, at main gate
	WH794	EE Canberra PR7 (8652M)	RAF FF&SS, Catterick
	WH796	EE Canberra PR7 (nose only)	Bomber County Museum, Cleethorpes
	WH797	EE Canberra T22 [851]	RN, St Athan store
	WH798	EE Canberra PR7	Wales Aircraft Museum, Cardiff
	WH801	EE Canberra T22 [850]	RN, St Athan store
	WH803	EE Canberra T22 [856]	RN, St Athan store
	WH840	EE Canberra T4 (8350M)	RAF Locking, at main gate
	WH844	EE Canberra T4	MoD(PE) RAE Farnborough, stored
	WH846	EE Canberra T4	BAe Samlesbury, stored
	WH848	EE Canberra T4 [BD]	RAF No 231 OCU, Wyton
	WH849	EE Canberra T4 [BE]	RAF No 231 OCU, Wyton
	WH850	EE Canberra T4	BAe Samlesbury, stored
	WH854	EE Canberra B2 nose only	Martin Baker Aircraft, Chalgrove
	WH856	EE Canberra TT18 (8742M) [849]	RAF Abingdon, BDRF
	WH863	EE Canberra T17 (8693M)	RAF Marham, BDRT
	WH869	EE Canberra B2 (8515M)	RAF AS&RU, Abingdon
	WH872	EE Canberra T17 [W]	RAE Bedford Fire Section
	WH876	EE Canberra D14	MoD(PE) Boscombe Down, store
	WH887	EE Canberra TT18 [847]	RN FRADU, Yeovilton
	WH902	EE Canberra T17 [EK]	RAF No 360 Sqn, Wyton
	WH903	EE Canberra B2 (8584M) nose only	RAF Exhibition Flight, Abingdon
	WH904	EE Canberra T19 [04]	Newark Air Museum, Winthorpe
	WH911	EE Canberra E15	Wales Aircraft Museum, Cardiff
	WH914	EE Canberra B2 (G-27-373) [U]	BAe Samlesbury, stored
	WH919	EE Canberra B2	RAF St Athan, stored
	WH946	EE Canberra B6 (Mod) (8185M)	Bomber County Aviation Museum, Cleethorpes
	WH952	EE Canberra B6	MoD(PE) RAE Bedford, for ground instruction
	WH953	EE Canberra B6	MoD(PE) RAE Bedford
	WH957	EE Canberra E15 [CX]	RAF St Athan, stored
	WH960	EE Canberra B15 (8344M) [A]	RAF No 2 SoTT, Cosford
	WH964	EE Canberra E15 [V]	RAF St Athan, stored
	WH972	EE Canberra E15 [CM]	RAF No 100 Sqn, Wyton
	WH981	EE Canberra E15 [CN]	RAF No 100 Sqn, Wyton
	WH983	EE Canberra E15 [CP]	RAF No 100 Sqn, Wyton
	WH984	EE Canberra B15 (8101M) [E]	RAF No 2 SoTT, Cosford
	WH991	WS51 Dragonfly HR5	Privately owned, Tattershall Thorpe
	WJ231	Hawker Sea Fury FB11 [115/0]	FAA Museum, RNAS Yeovilton

Serial	Type (alternative identity)	Owner, Operator or Location	Notes
WJ288	Hawker Sea Fury FB11 (G-SALY) [029]	Privately owned, Lympne	
WJ306	Slingsby Sedbergh TX1	RAF No 621 VGS, Weston-super-Mare	
WJ329	Handley Page Hastings C2	RAF Leeming Fire Section	
WJ349	Percival Sea Prince C2	No 11 Sqn ATC, Weybridge	
WJ350	Percival Sea Prince C2	Guernsey Airport Fire Section	
WJ358	Auster AOP6 (G-ARYD)	Museum of Army Flying, Middle Wallop	
WJ565	EE Canberra T17 [C]	RAF St Athan, stored	
WJ567	EE Canberra B2 [CC]	RAF No 100 Sqn, Wyton	
WJ573	EE Canberra B2 (7656M)	RAF Museum Store, Henlow	
WJ574	EE Canberra TT18 [844]	RAF St Athan, stored	
WJ576	EE Canberra T17	Wales Aircraft Museum, Cardiff	
WJ581	EE Canberra T17	Wales Aircraft Museum, Cardiff	
WJ603	EE Canberra B2 (8664M) [G]	RAF Wattisham, BDRT	
WJ607	EE Canberra T17 [EB]	RAF No 360 Sqn, Wyton	
WJ614	EE Canberra TT18 [846]	RN FRADU, Yeovilton	
WJ627	EE Canberra B2	RAE Bedford Fire Section	
WJ629	EE Canberra TT18 (8747M) [845]	RAF Chivenor, BDRT	
WJ630	EE Canberra T17 [ED]	RAF No 360 Sqn, Wyton	
WJ633	EE Canberra T17 [EF]	RAF No 360 Sqn, Wyton	
WJ635	EE Canberra B2	RAF St Mawgan Fire Section	
WJ636	EE Canberra TT18 [842]	RN FRADU, Yeovilton	
WJ639	EE Canberra TT18 [39]	BAe Samlesbury, stored	
WJ640	EE Canberra B2 (8722M) [L]	RAF No 2 SoTT, Cosford	
WJ676	EE Canberra B2 (7796M)	Princess Alexandra RAF Hospital Wroughton	
WJ677	EE Canberra B2 (nose only)	RNAS Yeovilton Fire Section	
WJ678	EE Canberra B2 [CF]	RAF Abingdon BDRF	
WJ680	EE Canberra TT18 [CT]	RAF No 100 Sqn, Wyton	
WJ681	EE Canberra B2T (8735M)	RAF Brawdy Fire Section	
WJ682	EE Canberra TT18 [CU]	RAF No 100 Sqn, Wyton	
WJ715	EE Canberra TT18 [CV]	RAF No 100 Sqn, Wyton	
WJ717	EE Canberra TT18 [841]	RN store, St Athan	
WJ721	EE Canberra TT18 [21]	BAe Samlesbury, stored	
WJ722	EE Canberra B2	Privately owned, Macclesfield	
WJ731	EE Canberra B2 [BK]	RAF No 231 OCU, Wyton	
WJ756	EE Canberra E15 [CL]	RAF No 100 Sqn, Wyton	
WJ775	EE Canberra B6 (8581M) [Z]	CSDE, RAF Swanton Morley	
WJ815	EE Canberra PR7 (8729M)	RAF Coningsby BDRT	
WJ817	EE Canberra PR7 (8695M)	RAF Wyton, BDRT	
WJ821	EE Canberra PR7 (8668M)	Bassingbourn, on display	
WJ825	EE Canberra PR7 (8697M)	RAF Honington, BDRT	
WJ861	EE Canberra T4 [BF]	RAF No 231 OCU, Wyton	
WJ863	EE Canberra T4 (nose only)	Cambridge Airport Fire Section	
WJ865	EE Canberra T4	RAE Apprentice School, Farnborough	
WJ866	EE Canberra T4 [BL]	RAF No 231 OCU, Wyton	
WJ867	EE Canberra T4 (8643M)	RAF Abingdon, BDRF	
WJ870	EE Canberra T4 (8683M)	RAF St Mawgan, BDRT	
WJ872	EE Canberra T4 (8492M) (nose only)	No 2408 Sqn ATC, Hornchurch	
WJ874	EE Canberra T4 [858]	RN FRADU, Yeovilton	
WJ876	EE Canberra T4 nose only	RAF Exhibition Flight, Abingdon	
WJ877	EE Canberra T4 [BG]	RAF No 231 OCU, Wyton	
WJ879	EE Canberra T4 [BH]	RAF No 231 OCU, Wyton	
WJ880	EE Canberra T4 (8491M) [39] nose only	Privately owned, Kilmarnock	
WJ893	Vickers Varsity T1	RAE Aberporth Fire Section	
WJ902	Vickers Varsity T1 [C]	RAF Wittering Fire Section	
WJ903	Vickers Varsity T1 [C]	Dumfries & Galloway Aviation Museum Tinwald Downs	
WJ907	Vickers Varsity T1 [G]	Norwich Airport Fire Section	
WJ944	Vickers Varsity T1 [Y]	Wales Aircraft Museum, Cardiff	
WJ945	Vickers Varsity T1 (G-BEDV) [21]	Duxford Aviation Society	
WJ975	EE Canberra T19 [S]	Bomber County Aviation Museum, Cleethorpes	
WJ977	EE Canberra T17 (8761M) [R]	RAF Wyton	
WJ981	EE Canberra T17 [EN]	RAF No 360 Sqn, Wyton	
WJ986	EE Canberra T17 [EP]	RAF No 360 Sqn, Wyton	
WJ992	EE Canberra T4	MoD(PE) RAE Bedford	

Notes	Serial	Type (alternative identity)	Owner, Operator or Location
	WK102	EE Canberra T17 [EQ] (8780M)	RAF No 2 SoTT, Cosford
	WK111	EE Canberra T17 [EA]	RAF No 360 Sqn, Wyton
	WK118	EE Canberra TT18 [CQ]	RAF No 100 Sqn, Wyton
	WK122	EE Canberra TT18 [22]	BAe Samlesbury, stored
	WK123	EE Canberra TT18 [840]	RN FRADU, Yeovilton
	WK124	EE Canberra TT18 [CR]	RAF No 100 Sqn, Wyton
	WK126	EE Canberra TT18 [843]	RAF St Athan, stored
	WK127	EE Canberra TT18 [CS]	RAF No 100 Sqn, Wyton
	WK128	EE Canberra B2	Flight Refuelling Ltd, Hurn
	WK142	EE Canberra TT18 [848]	RN FRADU, Yeovilton
	WK143	EE Canberra B2	Flight Refuelling Ltd, Hurn
	WK144	EE Canberra B2 (8689M) [W]	RAF St Athan, fire section
	WK145	EE Canberra B2	RAE Llanbedr Fire Section
	WK146	EE Canberra B2 nose only	RAF Exhibition Flt, Abingdon
	WK163	EE Canberra B6	MoD(PE) RAE Bedford
	WK198	VS Swift F4 (7428M)	North East Aircraft Museum, Usworth
	WK275	VS Swift F4	Privately owned, Upper Hill, nr Leominster
	WK277	VS Swift FR5 (7719M) [N]	Newark Air Museum, Winthorpe
	WK281	VS Swift FR5 (7712M) [S]	RAF St Athan Historic Aircraft Collection
	WK511	DH Chipmunk T10 [905]	RN, Shawbury store
	WK512	DH Chipmunk T10 [A]	AAC BFWF, Middle Wallop
	WK517	DH Chipmunk T10 [84]	RAF No 11 AEF, Leeming
	WK518	DH Chipmunk T10	RAF Battle of Britain Flight, Coningsby
	WK549	DH Chipmunk T10 [Y]	Privately owned, Currock Hill
	WK550	DH Chipmunk T10 [J]	RAF FSS, Swinderby
	WK554	DH Chipmunk T10	RAF Shawbury store
	WK559	DH Chipmunk T10 [M]	AAC BFWF, Middle Wallop
	WK562	DH Chipmunk T10 [T]	RAF No 3 AEF, Filton
	WK570	DH Chipmunk T10 PAX (8211M)	RAF No 358 Sqn ATC, Hurn
	WK572	DH Chipmunk T10 [X]	RAF No 3 AEF, Filton
	WK574	DH Chipmunk T10 [738/VL]	RNAS Yeovilton Station Flight
	WK575	DH Chipmunk T10 PAX [F]	No 301 Sqn ATC, Bury St Edmunds
	WK576	DH Chipmunk T10 PAX (8357M)	No 1206 Sqn ATC, Lichfield
	WK585	DH Chipmunk T10	RAF No 12 AEF, Turnhouse
	WK586	DH Chipmunk T10	RAF Shawbury store
	WK587	DH Chipmunk T10 PAX (8212M)	St Ignatius Coll, Enfield
	WK589	DH Chipmunk T10 [C]	RAF No 6 AEF, Abingdon
	WK590	DH Chipmunk T10 [69]	RAF No 9 AEF, Finningley
	WK608	DH Chipmunk T10 [906]	RN Flying Grading Flt, Plymouth
	WK609	DH Chipmunk T10 [L]	RAF No 3 AEF, Filton
	WK613	DH Chipmunk T10 [P]	Pennine Aviation Museum, Bacup
	WK620	DH Chipmunk T10 [T]	AAC BFWF, Middle Wallop
	WK624	DH Chipmunk T10 [12]	RAF No 10 AEF, Woodvale
	WK626	DH Chipmunk T10 PAX (8213M)	Privately owned, White Waltham
	WK630	DH Chipmunk T10 [11]	RAF No 2 AEF, Hurn
	WK633	DH Chipmunk T10 [B]	RAF FSS, Swinderby
	WK634	DH Chipmunk T10 [902]	RN Flying Grading Flt, Plymouth
	WK635	DH Chipmunk T10	RNAS Yeovilton, Station Flight
	WK638	DH Chipmunk T10 [83]	RAF Shawbury store
	WK639	DH Chipmunk T10 [10]	RAF No 10 AEF, Woodvale
	WK640	DH Chipmunk T10 [C]	RAF FSS, Swinderby
	WK642	DH Chipmunk T10	RAF No 1 AEF, Manston
	WK643	DH Chipmunk T10 [G]	RAF FSS, Swinderby
	WK654	Gloster Meteor F8 (8092M) [X]	RAF Neatishead, at main gate
	WK800	Gloster Meteor D16 [Z]	MoD(PE)/Marshalls, Cambridge
	WK935	Gloster Meteor Prone Pilot (7869M)	RAF Cosford Aerospace Museum
	WK968	Gloster Meteor F8 (8053M) [A]	RAF Odiham, at main gate
	WK991	Gloster Meteor F8 (7825M)	Imperial War Museum, Duxford
	WL168	Gloster Meteor F8 (7750M) [A]	RAF St Athan Historic Aircraft Collection
	WL181	Gloster Meteor F8 [X]	North East Aircraft Museum, Usworth
	WL332	Gloster Meteor T7	Wales Aircraft Museum, Cardiff

Serial	Type (alternative identity)	Owner, Operator or Location	Notes
WL345	Gloster Meteor T7	Privately owned, Hastings	
WL349	Gloster Meteor T7 [Z]	Staverton Airport, on display	
WL360	Gloster Meteor T7 (7920M) [G]	RAF Locking, at main gate	
WL375	Gloster Meteor T7	Dumfries & Galloway Aviation Museum, Tinwald Downs	
WL405	Gloster Meteor T7	North East Aircraft Museum, Usworth	
WL419	Gloster Meteor T7	Martin Baker Aircraft, Chalgrove	
WL505	DH Vampire FB9 (7705M)	RAF St Athan Historic Aircraft Collection	
WL626	Vickers Varsity T1 (G-BHDD) [P]	East Midlands Aeropark	
WL627	Vickers Varsity T1 (8488M) [D]	RAF Newton Fire Section	
WL635	Vickers Varsity T1	RAF Machrihanish Police School	
WL678	Vickers Varsity T1 [C]	Leeds-Bradford Airport Fire Section	
WL679	Vickers Varsity T1	MoD(PE) RAE Farnborough	
WL732	BP Sea Balliol T21	RAF Cosford, stored	
WL738	Avro Shackleton MR2C (8567M)	RAF Lossiemouth, at main gate	
WL741	Avro Shackleton AEW2 (8692M)	CTE, RAF Manston	
WL747	Avro Shackleton AEW2	RAF No 8 Sqn, Lossiemouth	
WL754	Avro Shackleton AEW2 (8665M) [54]	RAF Valley, fire section	
WL756	Avro Shackleton AEW2	RAF No 8 Sqn, Lossiemouth	
WL757	Avro Shackleton AEW2	RAF No 8 Sqn, Lossiemouth	
WL790	Avro Shackleton AEW2	RAF No 8 Sqn, Lossiemouth	
WL795	Avro Shackleton AEW2 (8753M)	RAF St Mawgan, on display	
WL798	Avro Shackleton MR2C (8114M) [Z]	RAF No 2 SoTT, Cosford	
WL801	Avro Shackleton MR2C (8629M) [01]	RAF No 2 SoTT, Cosford	
WL925	Slingsby Cadet TX3 (really WV925)	Air Cadet Recruiting Team, Cosford	
WM145	AW Meteor NF11 (nose only)	N. Yorks Recovery Group, Chop Gate	
WM167	AW Meteor TT20 (G-LOSM) [M]	Brencham Historic Collection, Hurn	
WM223	AW Meteor TT20	Second World War Aircraft Preservation Society, Lasham	
WM224	AW Meteor TT20 (8177M) [X]	Privately owned, North Weald	
WM292	AW Meteor TT20 [841]	Wales Aircraft Museum, Cardiff	
WM366	AW Meteor NF13 (4X-FNA)	Second World War Aircraft Preservation Society, store	
WM367	AW Meteor NF13	Privately owned, Powick, Hereford & Worcs	
WM571	DH Sea Venom FAW 21 [742/VL]	Wessex Aviation Society, Wimborne	
WM913	Hawker Sea Hawk FB5 (A2510/8162M) [616]	Newark Air Museum, Winthorpe	
WM961	Hawker Sea Hawk FB5 [J] (A2517)	Torbay Aircraft Museum, Paignton	
WM969	Hawker Sea Hawk FB5 (A2530)	Imperial War Museum, Duxford	
WM983	Hawker Sea Hawk FGA6 (really XE489)	Chilton Cantelo House School, Somerset	
WM993	Hawker Sea Hawk FB5 (A2522) [034]	Privately owned, Peasedown St John, Avon	
WM994	Hawker Sea Hawk FB5 (A2503/G-SEAH)	Brencham Historic Collection, Hurn	
WN108	Hawker Sea Hawk FB5 [033]	Shorts Apprentice School, Belfast	
WN149	BP Balliol T2 (nose only)	Pennine Aviation Museum, Bacup	
WN464	Fairey Gannet AS6 (A2540)	Cornwall Aero Park, Helston	
WN493	WS51 Dragonfly HR5	FAA Museum, RNAS Yeovilton	
WN499	WS51 Dragonfly HR5 [Y]	Torbay Aircraft Museum, Paignton	
WN516	BP Balliol T2	North East Aircraft Museum, Usworth	
WN534	BP Balliol T2 (nose only)	Pennine Aviation Museum, Bacup	
WN901	Hawker Hunter F2 (7543M)	RAF Newton Fire Section	
WN904	Hawker Hunter F2 (7544M) [3]	Imperial War Museum, Duxford	

Notes	Serial	Type (alternative identity)	Owner, Operator or Location
	WN907	Hawker Hunter F2 (7416M)	Staravia, Ascot
	WP180	Hawker Hunter F5 (7582M/ 8473M) [K] (really WP190)	RAF Stanbridge, at main gate
	WP185	Hawker Hunter F5 (7583M)	RAF Museum, Hendon
	WP232	DH Vampire NF10 (nose only)	Privately owned, Ecclesfield, S. Yorks
	WP250	DH Vampire NF10 (nose only)	Booker Air Museum
	WP270	EoN Eton TX1 (8598M)	Greater Manchester Museum of Science and Industry
	WP271	EoN Eton TX1	Stored Keevil
	WP309	Percival Sea Prince T1 [750/CU]	RNAS Yeovilton Fire Section
	WP314	Percival Sea Prince T1 (8634M) [573/CU]	RAF Police Dog School, Syerston
	WP320	Percival Sea Prince T1 [573/CU]	RAF Leuchars Fire Section
	WP321	Percival Sea Prince T1 (G-BRFC) [750/CU]	Privately owned, Bourn
	WP503	WS51 Dragonfly HR3 [901]	Privately owned, Storwood, South Yorks
	WP515	EE Canberra B2 [CD]	RAF No 100 Sqn, Wyton
	WP772	DH Chipmunk T10 [Q]	AAC BFWF, Middle Wallop
	WP776	DH Chipmunk T10 [817]	RNAS Culdrose Station Flight
	WP778	DH Chipmunk T10 (G-BBNF)	Privately owned, Botney, Essex
	WP786	DH Chipmunk T10 [D]	RAF Shawbury store
	WP788	DH Chipmunk 22 (G-BCHL)	Privately owned, Sleap
	WP790	DH Chipmunk 22 (G-BBNC) [T]	Mosquito Aircraft Museum, London Colney
	WP795	DH Chipmunk T10 [901]	RN Flying Grading Flt, Plymouth
	WP801	DH Chipmunk T10 [911]	RN Flying Grading Flt, Plymouth
	WP803	DH Chipmunk T10	RAF Shawbury store
	WP805	DH Chipmunk T10 [D]	RAF No 6 AEF, Abingdon
	WP808	DH Chipmunk 22 (G-BDEU)	Privately owned, Sibson
	WP809	DH Chipmunk T10 [912]	RNAS Yeovilton Station Flight
	WP833	DH Chipmunk T10	RAF No 4 AEF, Exeter
	WP837	DH Chipmunk T10 [L]	RAF No 5 AEF, Cambridge
	WP839	DH Chipmunk T10 [A]	RAF No 8 AEF, Shawbury
	WP840	DH Chipmunk T10 [9]	RAF No 2 AEF, Hurn
	WP843	DH Chipmunk 22 (G-BDBP)	Privately owned, Tollerton
	WP844	DH Chipmunk T10	RAF Shawbury store
	WP845	DH Chipmunk T10 PAX	No 1329 Sqn ATC, Stroud
	WP855	DH Chipmunk T10 [3]	RAF No 1 AEF, Manston
	WP856	DH Chipmunk T10 [904]	RN Flying Grading Flt, Plymouth
	WP857	DH Chipmunk 22 (G-BDRJ) [24]	Privately owned, Elstree
	WP859	DH Chipmunk T10 [E]	RAF No 8 AEF, Shawbury
	WP860	DH Chipmunk T10	RAF No 12 AEF, Turnhouse
	WP863	DH Chipmunk T10 PAX (8360M)	No 1304 Sqn ATC, Chippenham
	WP869	DH Chipmunk T10 PAX (8215M)	RAF No 8 AEF, Shawbury
	WP871	DH Chipmunk T10	RAF Shawbury store
	WP872	DH Chipmunk T10	AAC, Shawbury store
	WP896	DH Chipmunk T10 [11]	RAF No 10 AEF, Woodvale
	WP900	DH Chipmunk T10 [13]	RAF No 10 AEF, Woodvale
	WP901	DH Chipmunk T10 [B]	RAF No 6 AEF, Abingdon
	WP904	DH Chipmunk T10 [909]	RN Flying Grading Flt, Plymouth
	WP906	DH Chipmunk T10 [816]	RNAS Culdrose Station Flight
	WP907	DH Chipmunk T10 PAX (7970M)	Privately owned, RAF Abingdon
	WP912	DH Chipmunk T10 (8467M)	RAF Cosford Aerospace Museum
	WP914	DH Chipmunk T10 [E]	RAF No 6 AEF, Abingdon
	WP920	DH Chipmunk T10 [10]	RAF No 2 AEF, Hurn
	WP925	DH Chipmunk T10 [C]	AAC BFWF, Middle Wallop
	WP927	DH Chipmunk T10 PAX (8216M/G-ATJK)	No 1430 Sqn ATC, RAF Woodvale
	WP928	DH Chipmunk T10 [D]	AAC BFWF, Middle Wallop
	WP929	DH Chipmunk T10 [F]	RAF No 8 AEF, Shawbury
	WP930	DH Chipmunk T10 [J]	AAC BFWF, Middle Wallop
	WP962	DH Chipmunk T10 [V]	RAF No 3 AEF, Filton
	WP964	DH Chipmunk T10	AAC BFWF Middle Wallop
	WP967	DH Chipmunk T10	RAF No 12 AEF, Turnhouse
	WP970	DH Chipmunk T10 [T]	RAF No 5 AEF, Cambridge
	WP972	DH Chipmunk T10 PAX (8667M)	CSDE, RAF Swanton Morley
	WP974	DH Chipmunk T10 [N]	RAF No 3 AEF, Filton

Serial	Type (alternative identity)	Owner, Operator or Location	Notes
WP977	DH Chipmunk 22 (G-BHRD)	Privately owned, Leicester	
WP978	DH Chipmunk T10 PAX	RAF No 2 AEF, Hurn	
WP979	DH Cipmunk T10 [J]	CSDE, RAF Swanton Morley	
WP980	DH Chipmunk T10 [E]	RAF FSS, Swinderby	
WP981	DH Chipmunk T10	AAC, Shawbury store	
WP983	DH Chipmunk T10 [B]	AAC BFWF, Middle Wallop	
WP984	DH Chipmunk T10	RAF No 7 AEF, Newton	
WR410	DH Venom FB54 (J1790/G-BLKA)	Privately owned, Cranfield	
WR539	DH Venom FB4 (8399M) [F]	Wales Aircraft Museum, Cardiff	
WR960	Avro Shackleton AEW2 (8772M)	Greater Manchester Museum of Science and Industry	
WR963	Avro Shackleton AEW2	RAF No 8 Sqn, Lossiemouth	
WR965	Avro Shackleton AEW2	RAF No 8 Sqn, Lossiemouth	
WR967	Avro Shackleton MR2C (8398M)	RAF Lossiemouth, as a simulator	
WR971	Avro Shackleton MR3 (8119M) [Q]	RAF No 2 SoTT, Cosford	
WR974	Avro Shackleton MR3 (8117M) [K]	RAF Cosford Aerospace Museum	
WR977	Avro Shackleton MR3 (8186M) [B]	Newark Air Museum, Winthorpe	
WR982	Avro Shackleton MR3 (8106M) [J]	RAF No 2 SoTT, Cosford	
WR985	Avro Shackleton MR3 (8103M) [H]	RAF No 2 SoTT, Cosford	
WS103	Gloster Meteor T7 [709/VL]	FAA Museum store, Wroughton	
WS692	Gloster Meteor NF12 (7605M) [C]	Newark Air Museum, Winthorpe	
WS726	Gloster Meteor NF14 (7960M) [G]	No 1855 Sqn ATC, Royton	
WS739	Gloster Meteor NF14 (7961M)	Newark Air Museum, Winthorpe	
WS760	Gloster Meteor NF14 (7964M)	Privately owned, Cranfield	
WS774	Gloster Meteor NF14 (7959M)	RAF Hospital Ely, at main gate	
WS776	Gloster Meteor NF14 (7716M) [K]	RAF North Luffenham, at main gate	
WS792	Gloster Meteor NF14 (7965M) [K]	RAF Carlisle, at main gate	
WS807	Gloster Meteor NF14 (7973M) [N]	RAF Watton, at main gate	
WS832	Gloster Meteor NF14 [W]	Solway Aviation Society, Carlisle	
WS838	Gloster Meteor NF14	Midland Air Museum, Coventry	
WS840	Gloster Meteor NF14 (7969M)	Aldergrove Fire Section	
WS843	Gloster Meteor NF14 (7937M) [Y]	RAF St Athan Historic Aircraft Collection	
WS844	Gloster Meteor NF14 (7967M) [JCF] really WS788	RAF Leeming, at main gate	
WT121	Douglas Skyraider AEW1 [415/CU]	FAA Museum, RNAS Yeovilton	
WT301	EE Canberra B6 (Mod)	Defence School, Chattenden	
WT305	EE Canberra B6 (8511M) [X]	RAF Wyton, at main gate	
WT308	EE Canberra B(I)6	MoD(PE) RAE Farnborough, stored	
WT309	EE Canberra B(I)6	MoD(PE) A&AEE Boscombe Down	
WT327	EE Canberra B(I)8	MoD(PE) RAE Bedford	
WT333	EE Canberra B(I)8	MoD(PE) RAE Bedford	
WT339	EE Canberra B(I)8 (8198M)	RAF College Cranwell Fire Section	
WT346	EE Canberra B(I)8 (8197M)	RAF Cosford Aerospace Museum	
WT478	EE Canberra T4 [BA]	RAF No 231 OCU, Wyton	
WT480	EE Canberra T4 [BC]	RAF No 231 OCU, Wyton	
WT483	EE Canberra T4 [83]	BAe Samlesbury stored	
WT486	EE Canberra T4 (8102M) [C]	Aldergrove Fire Section	
WT488	EE Canberra T4	BAe Samlesbury stored	
WT507	EE Canberra PR7 (8548M) [44] nose only	No 384 Sqn ATC, Mansfield	
WT509	EE Canberra PR7 [CG]	RAF No 100 Sqn, Wyton	
WT510	EE Canberra T22 [854]	RN, St Athan store	
WT518	EE Canberra PR7 (8691M)	Wales Aircraft Museum, Cardiff	
WT519	EE Canberra PR7 [CH]	RAF No 100 Sqn, Wyton	
WT520	EE Canberra PR7 (8184M) [20]	RAF Swinderby, on display	
WT525	EE Canberra T22 [855]	RN, St Athan store	
WT532	EE Canberra PR7 (8728M)	MoD(PE) RAE Bedford	

Notes	Serial	Type (alternative identity)	Owner, Operator or Location
	WT534	EE Canberra PR7 (8549M) [43] nose only	No 489 Sqn ATC, Solihull
	WT535	EE Canberra T22 [852]	RN, St Athan store
	WT536	EE Canberra PR7 (8063M) [F]	RAF No 2 SoTT, Cosford
	WT537	EE Canberra PR7	BAe Samlesbury stored
	WT538	EE Canberra PR7 [CJ]	RAF No 100 Sqn, Wyton
	WT555	Hawker Hunter F1 (7499M)	RAF Cosford Aerospace Museum
	WT569	Hawker Hunter F1 (7491M)	No 2117 Sqn ATC, Kenfig Hill, Mid-Glamorgan
	WT612	Hawker Hunter F1 (7496M)	RAF Henlow on dipslay
	WT619	Hawker Hunter F1 (7525M)	Greater Manchester Museum of Science and Industry
	WT648	Hawker Hunter F1 (7530M) nose section	RAF St Athan Fire Section
	WT651	Hawker Hunter F1 (7532M) [C]	RAF Lawford Heath, Warwicks, on display
	WT660	Hawker Hunter F1 (7421M) [C]	RAF Carlisle, at main gate
	WT680	Hawker Hunter F1 (7533M) [Z]	No 1429 Sqn ATC at RAE Aberporth
	WT684	Hawker Hunter F1 (7422M)	RAF Brize Norton Fire Section
	WT694	Hawker Hunter F1 (7510M) [Y]	RAF Newton, at main gate
	WT711	Hawker Hunter GA11 [DD]	RNAS Culdrose, SAH
	WT722	Hawker Hunter T8C [878/VL]	RN FRADU, Yeovilton
	WT723	Hawker Hunter PR11 [866/VL]	RN FRADU, Yeovilton
	WT744	Hawker Hunter GA11 [868/VL]	RN FRADU, Yeovilton
	WT745	Hawker Hunter T8C	RN, Shawbury store
	WT746	Hawker Hunter F4 (7770M) [A]	RAF No 1 SoTT, Halton
	WT799	Hawker Hunter T8C [879/-]	RN, Shawbury store
	WT804	Hawker Hunter GA11 [DD]	RNAS Culdrose store, SAH
	WT806	Hawker Hunter GA11 [838/VL]	RN FRADU, Yeovilton
	WT809	Hawker Hunter GA11 [867/VL]	RN FRADU, Yeovilton
	WT868	Slingsby Cadet TX3	RAF No 643 VGS, Scampton
	WT869	Slingsby Cadet TX3	RAF No 618 VGS, West Malling
	WT870	Slingsby Cadet TX3	RAF store, Syerston
	WT877	Slingsby Cadet TX3	RAF store, Syerston
	WT898	Slingsby Cadet TX3	RAF No 662 VGS, Arbroath
	WT900	Slingsby Cadet TX3 [S]	RAF No 663 VGS, Kinloss
	WT903	Slingsby Cadet TX3	RAF store, Syerston
	WT906	Slingsby Cadet TX3	RAF No 643 VGS, Scampton
	WT908	Slingsby Cadet TX3	RAF No 662 VGS, Arbroath
	WT910	Slingsby Cadet TX3	RAF No 617 VGS, Manston
	WT913	Slingsby Cadet TX3	RAF No 615 VGS, Kenley
	WT917	Slingsby Cadet TX3	RAF store, Syerston
	WT918	Slingsby Cadet TX3	RAF No 644 VGS, Syerston
	WT919	Slingsby Cadet TX3	RAF No 661 VGS, Kirknewton
	WT933	Bristol Sycamore 3 (G-ALSW/7709M)	Newark Air Museum, Winthorpe
	WV106	Douglas Skyraider AEW1 [427/C]	Cornwall Aero Park, Helston
	WV198	S55 Whirlwind HAR21 (G-BJWY/A2576) [K]	Privately owned, Heysham, Lancs
	WV256	Hawker Hunter GA11 [862/VL]	RN FRADU, Yeovilton
	WV267	Hawker Hunter GA11 [836/VL]	RN FRADU, Yeovilton
	WV276	Hawker Hunter F4 (7847M) [D]	RAF No 1 SoTT, Halton
	WV318	Hawker Hunter T7B [ZS]	RAF No 208 Sqn, Lossiemouth
	WV322	Hawker Hunter T8B [ZC]	RAF No 237 OCU, Lossiemouth
	WV332	Hawker Hunter .... (nose only)	No 1254 Sqn ATC, Godalming
	WV363	Hawker Hunter T8C [872/VL]	RN FRADU, Yeovilton
	WV372	Hawker Hunter T7 [877/VL]	RN FRADU, Yeovilton
	WV381	Hawker Hunter GA11 [732]	UKAEA, Culham, Oxon
	WV382	Hawker Hunter GA11	RN AES, Lee-on-Solent
	WV383	Hawker Hunter T7	MoD(PE) RAE Farnborough
	WV396	Hawker Hunter T8C [871/VL]	RN, St Athan store
	WV483	Percival Provost T1 (7693M) [N-E]	Warbirds of GB, Bitteswell
	WV486	Percival Provost T1 (7694M) [N-D]	Privately owned, Grately, Berks
	WV493	Percival Provost T1 (G-BDYG/7696M) [29]	Royal Scottish Museum of Flight, East Fortune

Serial	Type (alternative identity)	Owner, Operator or Location	Notes
WV495	Percival Provost T1 (7697M) [P-C]	Booker Air Museum	
WV499	Percival Provost T1 (7698M) [P-G]	RAF St Athan Historic Aircraft Collection	
WV544	Percival Provost T1 (7700M)	AAC Netheravon Fire Section	
WV562	Percival Provost T1 (7606M) [P-C]	RAF Cosford Aerospace Museum	
WV605	Percival Provost T1 [T-B]	Norfolk & Suffolk Aviation Museum, Flixton	
WV606	Percival Provost T1 (7622M) [P-B]	Newark Air Museum, Winthorpe	
WV679	Percival Provost T1 (7615M) [O-J]	Torbay Aircraft Museum, Paignton	
WV686	Percival Provost T1 (7621M) (G-BLFT) [O-P]	Privately owned, Slough	
WV701	Percival Pembroke C1	RAF No 60 Sqn, Wildenrath	
WV703	Percival Pembroke C1 (8108M/ G-IIIM)	Privately owned, Tattershall Thorpe	
WV705	Percival Pembroke C1	Marine Aircraft Preservation Group, Wimborne	
WV740	Percival Pembroke C1	RAF No 60 Sqn, Wildenrath	
WV746	Percival Pembroke C1	RAF No 60 Sqn, Wildenrath	
WV753	Percival Pembroke C1 (8113M)	Wales Aircraft Museum, Cardiff	
WV781	Bristol Sycamore HR12 (G-ALTD/7839M)	RAF SAREW, Finningley, for display	
WV783	Bristol Sycamore HR12 (G-ALSP/7841M)	RAF Museum Store, Henlow	
WV787	EE Canberra B2/8 (8799M)	Newark Air Museum, Winthorpe	
WV795	Hawker Sea Hawk FGA6 (A2661/8151M)	Privately owned, Peasedown St John, Avon	
WV797	Hawker Sea Hawk FGA4 (A2637/8155M)	Midland Air Museum, Coventry	
WV798	Hawker Sea Hawk FGA6 (A2557) [028/CU]	Second World War Aircraft Preservation Society, Lasham	
WV826	Hawker Sea Hawk FGA6 (A2532) [147/CU]	Wales Aircraft Museum, Cardiff	
WV843	Hawker Sea Hawk FGA4 nose only	Torbay Aircraft Museum, Paignton	
WV856	Hawker Sea Hawk FGA6 [163]	FAA Museum, RNAS Yeovilton	
WV903	Hawker Sea Hawk FGA6 (A2632/8153M) [128/C] [SAH-8]	RNAS Lee-on-Solent	
WV908	Hawker Sea Hawk FGA6 (A2660/8154M) [188/A]	RN Historic Flight, RNAS Yeovilton	
WV911	Hawker Sea Hawk FGA4 (A2526) [115/C]	RN AES, Lee-on-Solent	
WW138	DH Sea Venom FAW21 [229/O]	FAA Museum, RNAS Yeovilton	
WW145	DH Sea Venom FAW21 [680/LM]	Royal Scottish Museum of Flight, East Fortune	
WW217	DH Sea Venom FAW22 [736]	Newark Air Museum, Winthorpe	
WW388	Percival Provost T1 (7616M) [O-F]	Wales Aircraft Museum, Cardiff	
WW397	Percival Provost T1 (8060M/ G-BKHP) [N-E]	Privately owned, RAF Lyneham	
WW421	Percival Provost T1 (7688M) [O]	Lincolnshire Aviation Museum, East Kirkby	
WW442	Percival Provost T1 (7618M)	Privately owned, St Merryn	
WW444	Percival Provost T1 [D]	Privately owned, Coventry	
WW447	Percival Provost T1	Privately owned, Grately, Berks	
WW453	Percival Provost T1 [B-P]	Air Service Training, Perth	
WW654	Hawker Hunter GA11 [833/VL]	RN FRADU, Yeovilton	
WX788	DH Venom NF3	Wales Aircraft Museum, Cardiff	
WX853	DH Venom NF3 (7443M)	Mosquito Aircraft Museum, London Colney	
WX905	DH Venom NF3 (7458M)	RAF Museum Store, Henlow	
WZ415	DH Vampire T11 [72]	Vintage Aircraft Team, Bushey	
WZ425	DH Vampire T11	Wales Aircraft Museum, Cardiff	
WZ450	DH Vampire T11 [23]	No 2371 Sqn ATC, Tile Cross	

Notes	Serial	Type (alternative identity)	Owner, Operator or Location
	WZ464	DH Vampire T11 (N62430) [40]	Vintage Aircraft Team, Cranfield
	WZ476	DH Vampire T11	Mosquito Aircraft Museum, London Colney
	WZ507	DH Vampire T11 (G-VTII)	Privately owned, Cranfield
	WZ514	DH Vampire T11	Privately owned, Meols, Merseyside
	WZ515	DH Vampire T11 [60]	Skyfame Collection, Duxford
	WZ518	DH Vampire T11	North East Aircraft Museum, Usworth
	WZ544	DH Vampire T11 (pod only) (7652M)	MoD, Spitalgate
	WZ549	DH Vampire T11 (8118M) [F]	Lincolnshire Aviation Museum, East Kirkby
	WZ550	DH Vampire T11 (7902M) [R]	Booker Aircraft Museum
	WZ553	DH Vampire T11 [40]	Phoenix Aviation Museum Store, Leics
	WZ557	DH Vampire T11	N Yorks Recovery Group, Chop Gate
	WZ576	DH Vampire T11 (8174M)	No 2192 Sqn ATC, Appleby
	WZ581	DH Vampire T11 [77]	Privately owned, Ruislip
	WZ584	DH Vampire T11 [U]	St Albans College of FE
	WZ589	DH Vampire T11 [19]	Lashenden Air Warfare Museum, Headcorn
	WZ590	DH Vampire T11 [19]	Imperial War Museum, Duxford
	WZ608	DH Vampire T11 [56] (nose only)	Privately owned, Bruntingthorpe
	WZ616	DH Vampire T11 [60]	Vintage Aircraft Team, Cranfield
	WZ662	Auster AOP9 (G-BKVK)	Privately owned, Swanton Morley
	WZ672	Auster AOP9 (G-BDER)	Privately owned, Sibson
	WZ706	Auster AOP9 (7851M)	Royal Military College of Science, Shrivenham
	WZ711	Auster 9/Beagle E3 (G-AVHT)	Privately owned, Middle Wallop
	WZ721	Auster AOP9	Museum of Army Flying, Middle Wallop
	WZ724	Auster AOP9 (7432M/WZ670)	AAC Middle Wallop, at main gate
	WZ736	Avro 707A (7868M)	Greater Manchester Museum of Science and Industry
	WZ744	Avro 707C (7932M)	RAF Cosford Aerospace Museum
	WZ753	Slingsby Grasshopper TX1	Emanuel School CCF, London SW11
	WZ754	Slingsby Grasshopper TX1	Strathallan School CCF, Fordangenny, nr Perth
	WZ755	Slingsby Grasshopper TX1	King's School CCF, Bruton, Somerset
	WZ756	Slingsby Grasshopper TX1	RAF No 2 MGSP, Locking
	WZ757	Slingsby Grasshopper TX1	RAF No 2 MGSP, Locking
	WZ758	Slingsby Grasshopper TX1	King's School CCF, Grantham, Lincs
	WZ760	Slingsby Grasshopper TX1	RAF No 2 MGSP, Locking
	WZ762	Slingsby Grasshopper TX1	RAF No 3 MGSP, Cosford
	WZ765	Slingsby Grasshopper TX1	Radley College CCF, Abingdon
	WZ767	Slingsby Grasshopper TX1	North East Aircraft Museum, Usworth
	WZ768	Slingsby Grasshopper TX1	Warwick School CCF
	WZ769	Slingsby Grasshopper TX1	RAF No 2 MGSP, Locking
	WZ772	Slingsby Grasshopper TX1	RAF No 1 MGSP, Halton
	WZ773	Slingsby Grasshopper TX1	Edinburgh Academy CCF, Lothian
	WZ778	Slingsby Grasshopper TX1	RAF No 4 MGSP, Dishforth
	WZ779	Slingsby Grasshopper TX1	Ratcliffe College CCF, Syston, Leics
	WZ780	Slingsby Grasshopper TX1	Clifton College CCF, Bristol
	WZ781	Slingsby Grasshopper TX1	RAF No 4 MGSP, Dishforth
	WZ782	Slingsby Grasshopper TX1	Charterhouse School CCF, Godalming
	WZ784	Slingsby Grasshopper TX1	RAF No 4 MGSP, Dishforth
	WZ785	Slingsby Grasshopper TX1	Wellingborough School CCF, Northants
	WZ787	Slingsby Grasshopper TX1	RAF No 4 MGSP, Dishforth
	WZ789	Slingsby Grasshopper TX1	RAF No 3 MGSP, Cosford
	WZ791	Slingsby Grasshopper TX1	RAF No 1 MGSP, Halton
	WZ792	Slingsby Grasshopper TX1	RAF No 4 MGSP, Dishforth
	WZ793	Slingsby Grasshopper TX1	Lord Wandsworth College CCF, Basingstoke
	WZ794	Slingsby Grasshopper TX1	RAF No 1 MGSP, Halton
	WZ795	Slingsby Grasshopper TX1	RAF No 1 MGSP, Halton
	WZ796	Slingsby Grasshopper TX1	Eastbourne College CCF, East Sussex
	WZ797	Slingsby Grasshopper TX1	Canford School CCF, Dorset
	WZ798	Slingsby Grasshopper TX1	RAF No 2 MGSP, Locking
	WZ816	Slingsby Grasshopper TX1	RAF No 2 MGSP, Locking
	WZ817	Slingsby Grasshopper TX1	RAF No 4 MGSP, Dishforth
	WZ818	Slingsby Grasshopper TX1	Oakham School CCF, Leics
	WZ819	Slingsby Grasshopper TX1	RAF No 4 MGSP, Dishforth
	WZ820	Slingsby Grasshopper TX1	Whitgift School CCF, Croydon
	WZ822	Slingsby Grasshopper TX1	Robertsbridge Aviation Society, E. Sussex

Serial	*Type (alternative identity)*	*Owner, Operator or Location*	*Notes*
WZ824	Slingsby Grasshopper TX1	St Bees School CCF, Cumbria	
WZ825	Slingsby Grasshopper TX1	Bradfield College CCF, Reading, Berks	
WZ826	Slingsby Grasshopper TX1	Dulwich College CCF, London	
WZ827	Slingsby Grasshopper TX1	RAF ACCGS, Syerston	
WZ828	Slingsby Grasshopper TX1	Heles School CCF, Exeter, Devon	
WZ829	Slingsby Grasshopper TX1	Launceston College CCF, Cornwall	
WZ831	Slingsby Grasshopper TX1	RAF No 1 MGSP, Halton	
WZ845	DH Chipmunk T10 [2]	RAF No 1 AEF, Manston	
WZ847	DH Chipmunk T10 [F]	RAF No 6 AEF, Abingdon	
WZ849	DH Chipmunk T10 PAX (8439M)	No 1404 Sqn ATC, Chatham	
WZ856	DH Chipmunk T10	RAF No 7 AEF, Newton	
WZ862	DH Chipmunk T10	RAF Gatow Station Flight, Berlin	
WZ866	DH Chipmunk T10 PAX (8217M)	No 498 Sqn ATC, Carluke, Strathclyde	
WZ868	DH Chipmunk 22 (G-BCIW)	Privately owned, Duxford	
WZ869	DH Chipmunk T10 PAX (8019M) [R]	No 391 Sqn ATC, Handforth	
WZ872	DH Chipmunk T10 [E]	RAF No 5 AEF, Cambridge	
WZ877	DH Chipmunk T10 [G]	RAF No 6 AEF, Abingdon	
WZ878	DH Chipmunk T10 [E]	RAF No 11 AEF, Leeming	
WZ879	DH Chipmunk T10 [L]	RAF FSS, Swinderby	
WZ882	DH Chipmunk T10 [K]	AAC BFWF, Middle Wallop	
WZ884	DH Chipmunk T10 [P]	AAC BFWF, Middle Wallop	
XA109	DH Sea Vampire T22	Royal Scottish Museum of Flight, East Fortune	
XA129	DH Sea Vampire T22	—	
XA225	Slingsby Grasshopper TX1	Churchers College CCF, Petersfield	
XA228	Slingsby Grasshopper TX1	Glenalmond Trinity College CCF, Tayside	
XA229	Slingsby Grasshopper TX1	RAF No 3 MGSP, Cosford	
XA230	Slingsby Grasshopper TX1	Uppingham School CCF, Leics	
XA231	Slingsby Grasshopper TX1	Kimbolton School CCF, Cambs	
XA233	Slingsby Grasshopper TX1	RAF No 1 MGSP, Halton	
XA237	Slingsby Grasshopper TX1	Queen Victoria School CCF, Dunblane	
XA239	Slingsby Grasshopper TX1	Perse School CCF, Cambridge	
XA240	Slingsby Grasshopper TX1	Radley College CCF, Abingdon	
XA241	Slingsby Grasshopper TX1	Trinity School CCF, Croydon	
XA243	Slingsby Grasshopper TX1	Bournemouth School CCF, Dorset	
XA244	Slingsby Grasshopper TX1	RAF No 3 MGSP, Cosford	
XA282	Slingsby Cadet TX3	RAF store, Syerston	
XA286	Slingsby Cadet TX3	RAF No 1 MGSP, Halton	
XA288	Slingsby Cadet TX3	RAF No 636 VGS, Swansea	
XA290	Slingsby Cadet TX3	RAF No 661 VGS, Kirknewton	
XA292	Slingsby Cadet TX3	RAF No 615 VGS, Kenley	
XA293	Slingsby Cadet TX3	RAF ACCGS/644 VGS, Syerston	
XA295	Slingsby Cadet TX3	RAF store, Syerston	
XA308	Slingsby Cadet TX3	RAF store, Syerston	
XA309	Slingsby Cadet TX3	RAF store, Syerston	
XA454	Fairey Gannet COD4	RNAS Yeovilton Fire Section	
XA459	Fairey Gannet ECM6 (A2608) [E/-]	Wales Aircraft Museum, Cardiff	
XA460	Fairey Gannet ECM6 [768/BY]	Kelsterton College of Technology, Connah's Quay	
XA466	Fairey Gannet COD4 [777/LM]	FAA Museum, RNAS Yeovilton	
XA508	Fairey Gannet T2 (A2472) [627/GN]	Midland Air Museum, Coventry	
XA536	EE Canberra T19 (8605M)	RAF Abingdon Fire Section	
XA549	Gloster Javelin FAW1 (7717M) [E]	RAF Museum Store, Swinderby	
XA553	Gloster Javelin FAW1 (7470M)	RAF Stanmore Park, on display	
XA564	Gloster Javelin FAW1 (7464M)	RAF Cosford Aerospace Museum	
XA571	Gloster Javelin FAW1 (nose only)	Nene Valley Aviation Society, Sibson	
XA634	Gloster Javelin FAW4 (7641M) [L]	RAF Leeming, at main gate	
XA699	Gloster Javelin FAW9 (7809M)	Midland Air Museum, Coventry	
XA801	Gloster Javelin FAW2 (7739M)	RAF Stafford, at main gate	
XA847	English Electric PIB (8371M)	RAF Museum, Hendon	
XA862	WS55 Whirlwind HAR1 (A2542/G-AMJT)	Midland Air Museum, Coventry	
XA864	WS55 Whirlwind HAR1	FAA Museum, RNAS Yeovilton	
XA868	WS55 Whirlwind HAR1 (A2551)	Privately owned, Horsham	

Notes	Serial	Type (alternative identity)	Owner, Operator or Location
	XA870	WS55 Whirlwind HAR1 (A2543)	Cornwall Aero Park, Helston
	XA880	DH Devon C2	MoD(PE) RAE Llanbedr
	XA893	Avro Vulcan B1 (8591M) nose only	RAF Exhibition Flight, Abingdon
	XA900	Avro Vulcan B1 (7896M)	RAF Cosford Aerospace Museum
	XA903	Avro Vulcan B1 (nose only)	Wales Aircraft Museum, Cardiff
	XA917	HP Victor B1 (7827M) nose only	RAF Marham, ground instruction
	XA932	HP Victor K1 (8517M)	RAF Museum, on display Marham
	XB259	Blackburn Beverley C1 (G-AOAI)	Museum of Army Transport, Beverley
	XB261	Blackburn Beverley C1	Southend Airport Hotel
	XB288	Blackburn Beverley C1	Privately owned, Worminghall, Bucks
	XB446	Grumman Avenger ECM6B [992/C]	FAA Museum, RNAS Yeovilton
	XB480	Hiller HT1 (A2577) [537]	FAA Museum, RNAS Yeovilton
	XB833	NA Sabre 4	Privately owned, Duxford
	XD145	SARO SR53	RAF Cosford Aerospace Museum
	XD163	WS55 Whirlwind HAR10 (8645M) [X]	British Rotorcraft Museum, Wroughton
	XD165	WS55 Whirlwind HAR10 (8673M)	RAF No 1 SoTT, Halton
	XD182	WS55 Whirlwind HAR10 (8612M)	RAF Odiham Fire Section
	XD186	WS55 Whirlwind HAR10 (8730M)	RAF Chivenor, on display
	XD220	VS Scimitar F1	FAA Museum store, RNAY Wroughton
	XD317	VS Scimitar F1 [112/R]	FAA Museum, RNAS Yeovilton
	XD332	VS Scimitar F1 (A2574) [616]	Cornwall Aero Park, Helston
	XD375	DH Vampire T11 (7887M)	City of Norwich Aviation Museum
	XD377	DH Vampire T11 (8203M)	RAF Cosford Aerospace Museum
	XD382	DH Vampire T11 (8033M)	RAF Shawbury, at main gate
	XD425	DH Vampire T11 [16]	Dumfries & Galloway Aviation Museum, Tinwald Downs
	XD429	DH Vampire T11 (7604M) [28] (really XD542)	RAF Cranwell, at main gate
	XD434	DH Vampire T11 [25]	Manchester University, Barton
	XD435	DH Vampire T11 [26]	No 480 Sqn ATC, Kenilworth, Warwicks
	XD445	DH Vampire T11 [51]	Bomber County Aviation Museum, Cleethorpes
	XD447	DH Vampire T11 [50]	Lincolnshire Aviation Museum, East Kirkby
	XD452	DH Vampire T11 (7990M) [66]	Mosquito Aircraft Museum, London Colney
	XD453	DH Vampire T11 (7890M)	No 1010 Sqn ATC, Old Sarum
	XD459	DH Vampire T11 [63]	Vintage Aircraft Team, Cranfield
	XD463	DH Vampire T11 (8023M)	No 1360 Sqn ATC, Stapleford, Notts
	XD506	DH Vampire T11 (7983M) [E]	RAF Swinderby, on display
	XD515	DH Vampire T11 (7998M)	Newark Air Museum, Winthorpe
	XD527	DH Vampire T11 [46]	CTE, RAF Manston
	XD528	DH Vampire T11 (8159M)	No 2415 Sqn ATC, Penkridge, Staffs
	XD534	DH Vampire T11 [41]	Military Aircraft Preservation Group, Ashley, Cheshire
	XD535	DH Vampire T11	Friends of Biggin Hill
	XD536	DH Vampire T11 (7734M)	No 2287 Sqn ATC, Reading
	XD547	DH Vampire T11 [Z]	Strathallan Aircraft Collection
	XD593	DH Vampire T11 [50]	Newark Air Museum, Winthorpe
	XD596	DH Vampire T11 (7939M) [V2]	No 424 Sqn ATC, Testwood, Hants
	XD599	DH Vampire T11 [A]	Snowdonia National Park, Carnarvon
	XD601	DH Vampire T11 (7878M) [32]	Lincoln Field Vintage & HAC, Bushey
	XD602	DH Vampire T11 (7737M)	No 495 Sqn ATC, Wylde Green, W Midlands
	XD613	DH Vampire T11 (8122M) [M]	RAF Cosford, on parade ground
	XD616	DH Vampire T11 [56]	No 1239 Sqn ATC, Hoddesdon, Herts
	XD622	DH Vampire T11 (8160M)	No 2214 Sqn ATC, Usworth
	XD624	DH Vampire T11 [O]	Macclesfield Technical College
	XD626	DH Vampire T11 [Q]	Midland Air Museum, Coventry

Serial	Type (alternative identity)	Owner, Operator or Location	Notes
XD674	Hunting Jet Provost T1 (7570M) [T]	RAF Cosford Aerospace Museum	
XD818	Vickers Valiant B(K)1 (7894M)	Bomber Command Museum, Hendon	
XD826	Vickers Valiant B(K)I (7872M) (nose only)	Imperial War Museum, Duxford	
XD875	Vickers Valiant B(K)I (nose only)	No 163 Sqn ATC, Coventry	
XE317	Bristol Sycamore HR14 (G-AMWO) [S-N]	Newark Air Museum, Winthorpe	
XE327	Hawker Sea Hawk FGA6 (A2556) [644/LH]	RN Llangennech, Dyfed, on display	
XE339	Hawker Sea Hawk FGA6 (8156M/A2635) [149/E] [SAH-7]	RNAS Lee-on-Solent BDRT	
XE340	Hawker Sea Hawk FGA6 [131/Z]	Strathallan Aircraft Collection	
XE364	Hawker Sea Hawk FGA6 (really WM983) (G-JETH)	Brencham Historic Collection, Hurn	
XE368	Hawker Sea Hawk FGA6 (A2534) [200/J]	Cornwall Aero Park, Helston	
XE369	Hawker Sea Hawk FGA6 (A2580/8158M/A2633)	RNAS Yeovilton Fire Section	
XE587	Hawker Hunter F6 [7]	MoD(PE) RAE Farnborough	
XE597	Hawker Hunter FGA9 [F]	RAF Brawdy	
XE601	Hawker Hunter FGA9	MoD(PE) ETPS Boscombe Down	
XE624	Hawker Hunter FGA9 [G]	RAF Brawdy	
XE627	Hawker Hunter F6A	RAF Brawdy	
XE643	Hawker Hunter FGA9 (8586M) nose only	RAF Exhibition Flight, Abingdon	
XE650	Hawker Hunter FGA9 (G-9-449)	Lovaux Ltd, Macclesfield	
XE653	Hawker Hunter F6A (8829M) [D]	RAF TMTS, Scampton	
XE656	Hawker Hunter F6 (8678M)	RAF No 1 SoTT, Halton	
XE665	Hawker Hunter T8C [876]	RN FRADU, Yeovilton	
XE668	Hawker Hunter GA11 [832/DD]	RN SAH, Culdrose	
XE670	Hawker Hunter F4 (8585M) nose only	RAF Exhibition Flight, Abingdon	
XE673	Hawker Hunter GA11 (8846M) (tail from XE689)	RAF Bawdsy, BDRT	
XE677	Hawker Hunter F4	Loughborough University of Technology	
XE682	Hawker Hunter GA11 [835/VL]	RN store, Shawbury	
XE685	Hawker Hunter GA11 [861/VL]	RN FRADU, Yeovilton	
XE689	Hawker Hunter GA11 [864/VL]	RN FRADU, Yeovilton	
XE707	Hawker Hunter GA11 [865/VL]	RN FRADU, Yeovilton	
XE712	Hawker Hunter GA11	RN AES Lee-on-Solent	
XE785	Slingsby Cadet TX3	RAF No 663 VGS, Kinloss	
XE786	Slingsby Cadet TX3	RAF No 643 VGS, Scampton	
XE789	Slingsby Cadet TX3	RAF No 662 VGS, Arbroath	
XE790	Slingsby Cadet TX3	RAF store, Syerston	
XE793	Slingsby Cadet TX3 (8666M)	RAF St Athan	
XE794	Slingsby Cadet TX3	RAF No 4 MGSP, Dishforth	
XE795	Slingsby Cadet TX3	RAF No 643 VGS, Scampton	
XE797	Slingsby Cadet TX3 PAX	RAF No 645 VGS, Catterick	
XE799	Slingsby Cadet TX3	RAF store, Syerston	
XE801	Slingsby Cadet TX3	RAF No 617 VGS, Manston	
XE807	Slingsby Cadet TX3	RAF No 615 VGS, Kenley	
XE808	Slingsby Cadet TX3	RAF No 617 VGS, Manston	
XE849	DH Vampire T11 (7928M) [V3]	No 936 Sqn ATC, Ware, Herts	
XE852	DH Vampire T11 [60]	BAe Apprentice School, Hawarden	
XE855	DH Vampire T11	Midland Air Museum, Coventry	
XE856	DH Vampire T11	Second World War Aircraft Preservation Society, Lasham	
XE860	DH Vampire T11 [69]	Privately owned, Markfield, Leics	
XE864	DH Vampire T11	No 480 Sqn, ATC, Studley, Warwicks	
XE872	DH Vampire T11 [62]	Midland Air Museum, Coventry	
XE874	DH Vampire T11 (8582M) [61]	RAF Valley	
XE897	DH Vampire T11 (really XD403)	Strathallan Aircraft Collection	
XE920	DH Vampire T11 (8196M) [D]	RAF Museum Store, Henlow	
XE921	DH Vampire T11 [64]	Privately owned, Keevil	
XE928	DH Vampire T11 [76]	Privately owned, Keevil	
XE935	DH Vampire T11 [30]	Nene Valley Aviation Society, Sibson	

Notes	Serial	Type (alternative identity)	Owner, Operator or Location
	XE946	DH Vampire T11 (7473M) nose only	RAF Museum store, Cardington
	XE950	DH Vampire T11 (8175M)	Gordon School CCF, Chobham
	XE956	DH Vampire T11 [N]	St Albans College of FE
	XE979	DH Vampire T11 [54]	Privately owned, Stonehouse, Glos
	XE982	DH Vampire T11 (7564M)	No 124 Sqn ATC, Hereford
	XE995	DH Vampire T11 [53]	Torbay Aircraft Museum, Paignton
	XE998	DH Vampire T11 [36]	No 723 Sqn ATC, Wigan
	XF113	VS Swift F7 (nose only) [19]	Privately owned, Peasedown St John, Avon
	XF114	VS Swift F7	Kelsterton College of Technology, Connah's Quay
	XF274	Gloster Meteor T7	RAE/AIU on display, Farnborough
	XF289	Hawker Hunter T8C [875/VL]	RN FRADU, Yeovilton
	XF300	Hawker Hunter GA11 [860/VL]	RN FRADU, Yeovilton
	XF301	Hawker Hunter GA11 [834/VL]	RN FRADU, Yeovilton
	XF310	Hawker Hunter T7 [869/VL]	RN FRADU, Yeovilton
	XF319	Hawker Hunter F4 (7849M) [B]	RAF No 1 SoTT, Halton
	XF321	Hawker Hunter T7	RNEC Manadon
	XF357	Hawker Hunter T8C [877/VL]	RN Shawbury store
	XF358	Hawker Hunter T8C [870]	RN FRADU, Yeovilton
	XF368	Hawker Hunter GA11 [863/VL]	RN FRADU, Yeovilton
	XF375	Hawker Hunter F6 (8736M) [05]	RAFC Cranwell, Engineering Wing
	XF382	Hawker Hunter F6A [15]	RAF No 1 TWU, Brawdy
	XF383	Hawker Hunter F6 (8706M) [V]	RAF Wittering, BDRF
	XF383	Hawker Hunter F51 (really E-409) [71]	Wales Aircraft Museum, Cardiff
	XF386	Hawker Hunter F6 (8707M) [75]	RAF Coltishall, BDRT
	XF419	Hawker Hunter FGA9 [C]	RAF Brawdy
	XF431	Hawker Hunter FGA9 [O]	RAF store, St Athan
	XF435	Hawker Hunter FGA9 [52]	RAF store, St Athan
	XF445	Hawker Hunter FGA9 (8715M) [T] (really XG264)	RAF Brawdy, BDRT
	XF509	Hawker Hunter F6 (8708M) [73]	RAF Chivenor, at main gate
	XF515	Hawker Hunter F6A (8830M) [C]	RAF TMTS, Scampton
	XF516	Hawker Hunter F6A (8685M) [66]	RAFC Cranwell, Engineering Wing
	XF526	Hawker Hunter F6 (8679M)	RAF St Athan Fire Section
	XF527	Hawker Hunter F6 (8680M) [70]	RAF No 1 SoTT, Halton
	XF545	Percival Provost T1 (7957M) [O-K]	RAF Linton-on-Ouse, at main gate
	XF597	Percival Provost T1 (G-BKFW) [G]	Privately owned, Oakington
	XF603	Percival Provost T1 [H]	Rolls-Royce Tech Coll, Filton
	XF690	Percival Provost T1 (G-BGKA/ 8041M)	Leicester Aircraft Preservation Group, RAF Newton
	XF708	Avro Shackleton MR3 [C]	Imperial War Museum, Duxford
	XF730	Avro Shackleton MR3 [F]	RAF Kinloss Fire Section
	XF785	Bristol 173 (G-ALBN/7648M)	RAF Museum Store, Henlow
	XF799	Percival Pembroke C1	RAF No 60 Sqn, Wildenrath
	XF836	Percival Provost T1 (8043M/ G-AWRY) [JG]	Privately owned, Thruxton
	XF844	Percival Provost T1 [30]	RAE Farnborough Apprentice School
	XF877	Percival Provost T1 (G-AWVF) [JX]	Privately owned, Bourn
	XF898	Percival Provost T1 [Z]	Booker Air Museum
	XF914	Percival Provost T1	Vintage Aircraft Team, Cranfield
	XF926	Bristol 188 (8368M)	RAF Cosford Aerospace Museum
	XF967	Hawker Hunter T8C [XC]	RAF No 237 OCU, Lossiemouth
	XF974	Hawker Hunter F4 (7949M) [C]	RAF No 1 SoTT, Halton
	XF985	Hawker Hunter T8C [873/VL]	RN FRADU, Yeovilton
	XF990	Hawker Hunter F6 (8007M) nose only	RAF FF&SS, Catterick
	XF994	Hawker Hunter T8C [874/VL]	RN FRADU, Yeovilton
	XF995	Hawker Hunter T8B [XF]	RAF No 12 Sqn, Lossiemouth

Serial	Type (alternative identity)	Owner, Operator or Location	Notes
XG151	Hawker Hunter FGA9 (8798M)	RAF Lossiemouth, BDRT	
XG154	Hawker Hunter FGA9 [54]	RAF store, St Athan	
XG158	Hawker Hunter F6A (8686M) [21]	RAE Farnborough Apprentice School	
XG160	Hawker Hunter F6A [B] (8831M)	RAF TMTS, Scampton	
XG164	Hawker Hunter F6 (8681M)	RAF No 1 SoTT, Halton	
XG172	Hawker Hunter F6A [A] (8832M)	RAF No 2 SoTT, Cosford	
XG194	Hawker Hunter FGA9 [55] (8839M)	RAF No 2 SoTT, Cosford	
XG195	Hawker Hunter FGA9	Bomber County Aviation Museum, Cleethorpes	
XG196	Hawker Hunter F6A (8702M)	RAF Bracknell, on gate	
XG209	Hawker Hunter F6 (8709M)	RAF No 1 SoTT, Halton	
XG210	Hawker Hunter F6	BAe, Hatfield/Dunsfold	
XG225	Hawker Hunter F6A (8713M) [S]	RAF No 2 SoTT, Cosford	
XG226	Hawker Hunter F6A (8800M) [28] (nose only)	RAF FF&SS, Catterick	
XG228	Hawker Hunter FGA9 [56]	RAF store, St Athan	
XG252	Hawker Hunter FGA9 (8840M) [U]	RAF No 2 SoTT, Cosford	
XG254	Hawker Hunter FGA9 [57]	RAF store, St Athan	
XG274	Hawker Hunter F6 (8710M) [71]	RAF No 1 SoTT, Halton	
XG290	Hawker Hunter F6 (8711M) [74]	RAF No 1 SoTT, Halton	
XG297	Hawker Hunter FGA9 (nose only)	Pennine Aviation Museum, Bacup	
XG327	EE Lightning F1 (8188M)	RAF Manston, Fire Section	
XG329	EE Lightning F1 (8050M)	RAFC Cranwell, Engineering Wing	
XG337	EE Lightning F1 (8056M) [M]	RAF Cosford Aerospace Museum	
XG452	Westland Belvedere HC1 (G-BRMB/7997M)	British Rotorcraft Museum, Weston-super-Mare	
XG454	Westland Belvedere HC1 (8366M)	Greater Manchester Museum of Science and Industry	
XG474	Westland Belvedere HC1 (8367M) [O]	RAF Museum, Hendon	
XG496	DH Devon C2 (G-ANDX) [K]	MoD(PE) RAE Farnborough	
XG502	Bristol Sycamore HR14	Museum of Army Flying, Middle Wallop	
XG504	Bristol Sycamore HR14	Privately owned, Causewayhead, Dunblane	
XG506	Bristol Sycamore HR14 (7852M)	Bomber County Aviation Museum, Cleethorpes	
XG518	Bristol Sycamore HR14 (8009M) [S-E]	North East Aircraft Museum, Usworth	
XG540	Bristol Sycamore HR14 (7899M/8345M) [Y-S]	RAF Shawbury at main gate	
XG544	Bristol Sycamore HR14	Torbay Aircraft Museum, Paignton	
XG547	Bristol Sycamore HR14 (G-HAPR/8010M) [S-T]	British Rotorcraft Museum, Weston-super-Mare	
XG573	WS55 Whirlwind HAR3	CDE, Porton Down, Wilts	
XG574	WS55 Whirlwind HAR3 (A2575) [752/PO]	FAA Museum store, Wroughton	
XG577	WS55 Whirlwind HAR3 (A2571)	Imperial War Museum, Duxford	
XG592	WS55 Whirlwind HAS7 [54]	Wales Aircraft Museum, Cardiff	
XG594	WS55 Whirlwind HAS7 [517]	Strathallan Aircraft Collection	
XG596	WS55 Whirlwind HAS7 (A2651) [66]	British Rotorcraft Museum, Weston-super-Mare	
XG613	DH Sea Venom FAW21	Imperial War Museum, Duxford	
XG629	DH Sea Venom FAW22	Torbay Aircraft Museum, Paignton	
XG680	DH Sea Venom FAW22 [735/VL]	North East Aircraft Museum, Usworth	
XG691	DH Sea Venom FAW22 [493]	Cornwall Aero Park, Helston	
XG692	DH Sea Venom FAW22	Ulster Aviation Society, Castlereagh	
XG730	DH Sea Venom FAW22 [499/A]	Mosquito Aircraft Museum, London Colney	
XG734	DH Sea Venom FAW22	Ulster Aviation Society, Castlereagh	
XG736	DH Sea Venom FAW22	Ulster Aviation Society, Castlereagh	
XG737	DH Sea Venom FAW22 [220]	Wales Aircraft Museum, Cardiff	

Notes	Serial	Type (alternative identity)	Owner, Operator or Location
	XG743	DH Sea Vampire T22 [789-BY]	Imperial War Museum, Duxford
	XG797	Fairey Gannet ECM6 [766/BY]	Imperial War Museum, Duxford
	XG831	Fairey Gannet ECM6 (A2539) [396]	Cornwall Aero Park, Helston
	XG882	Fairey Gannet T5 (8754M) [771/LM]	RAF Lossiemouth on display
	XG883	Fairey Gannet T5 [773/BY]	Wales Aircraft Museum, Cardiff
	XG888	Fairey Gannet T5	RNAS Lee-on-Solent
	XG900	Short SC1	Science Museum store, Hayes
	XG905	Short SC1	Ulster Folk & Transport Museum, County Down
	XH124	Blackburn Beverley C1 (8025M)	RAF Museum, Hendon
	XH132	Short SC9 Canberra	MoD(PE) RS&RE Bedford
	XH134	EE Canberra PR9	RAF No 1 PRU, Wyton
	XH135	EE Canberra PR9	RAF No 1 PRU, Wyton
	XH136	EE Canberra PR9 (8782M)	RAF No 2 SoTT, Cosford
	XH165	EE Canberra PR9 [AK]	RAF No 1 PRU, Wyton
	XH169	EE Canberra PR9 [AQ]	RAF No 1 PRU, Wyton
	XH170	EE Canberra PR9 (8739M)	RAF Wyton, on gate
	XH171	EE Canberra PR9 (8746M)	RAF No 2 SoTT, Cosford
	XH174	EE Canberra PR9	RAF No 1 PRU, Wyton
	XH175	EE Canberra PR9 [AP]	RAF No 1 PRU, Wyton
	XH274	DH Vampire 11	RAF Ternhill Fire Section
	XH278	DH Vampire T11 (8595M/ 7866M)	No 2482 Sqn ATC, RAF Henlow
	XH304	DH Vampire T11	RAF CFS *Vintage Pair*, Scampton
	XH312	DH Vampire T11 [18]	Privately owned, Chester
	XH313	DH Vampire T11 [E]	St Albans College of FE
	XH318	DH Vampire T11 (7761M) [64]	No 424 Sqn ATC, Hants
	XH328	DH Vampire T11 [66]	Privately owned, Croxley Green
	XH329	DH Vampire T11 [70]	Privately owned, Keevil
	XH330	DH Vampire T11 [40]	Vintage Aircraft Team, Cranfield
	XH537	Avro Vulcan B2 MRR (8749M)	RAF Abingdon, on display
	XH539	Avro Vulcan B2	RAF Waddington, rescue training
	XH558	Avro Vulcan B2	RAF Waddington
	XH560	Avro Vulcan K2	RAF Marham
	XH563	Avro Vulcan B2 MRR (8744M)	RAF Scampton, preserved
	XH567	EE Canberra B6(mod)	MoD(PE) RAE Bedford
	XH568	EE Canberra B6(mod)	MoD(PE) RAE Bedford
	XH583	EE Canberra T4 (G-27-374)	BAe Samlesbury, stored
	XH590	HP Victor K1A	CTE, RAF Manston,
	XH592	HP Victor B1A (8429M) [L]	RAF Aerospace Museum
	XH593	HP Victor B1A (8428M) [T]	RAF No 2 SoTT, Cosford
	XH648	HP Victor K1A	Imperial War Museum, Duxford
	XH669	HP Victor K2	RAF No 57 Sqn, Marham
	XH670	HP Victor SR2 (nose only)	Lincolnshire Aviation Museum, East Kirkby
	XH671	HP Victor K2	RAF No 57 Sqn, Marham
	XH672	HP Victor K2	RAF No 57 Sqn, Marham
	XH673	HP Victor K2	RAF No 57 Sqn, Marham
	XH675	HP Victor K2	RAF No 55 Sqn, Marham
	XH764	Gloster Javelin FAW9 (7972M)	RAF Manston on display
	XH767	Gloster Javelin FAW9 (7955M) [K]	No 187 Sqn ATC, Worcester
	XH837	Gloster Javelin FAW7 (8032M) nose only	RAF Northolt Fire Section
	XH892	Gloster Javelin FAW9 (7982M) [B]	Norfolk & Suffolk Aviation Museum, Flixton
	XH897	Gloster Javelin FAW9	Imperial War Museum, Duxford
	XH903	Gloster Javelin FAW9 (7938M)	RAF Innsworth, at main gate
	XH980	Gloster Javelin FAW9 (7867M) [A]	RAF West Raynham, at main gate
	XH992	Gloster Javelin FAW9 (7829M) [P]	Newark Air Museum, Winthorpe
	XJ314	RR Thrust Measuring Rig	Science Museum, Strathallan

Serial	Type (alternative identity)	Owner, Operator or Location	Notes
XJ319	DH Sea Devon C20 (G-AMXP)	RNAS Culdrose Station Flight	
XJ324	DH Sea Devon C20 (G-AMXZ)	RN Kemble, store	
XJ348	DH Sea Devon C20 (G-AMXX/ G-NAVY)	Privately owned, Shoreham	
XJ380	Bristol Sycamore HR14 (8628M)	RAF Finningley, for display	
XJ389	Fairey Jet Gyrodyne (G-AJJP)	RAF Cosford Aerospace Museum	
XJ393	WS55 Whirlwind HAR3 (A2538)	Torbay Aircraft Museum, Paignton	
XJ402	WS55 Whirlwind HAR3 (A2572) [61]	FAA Museum Store, RNAS Yeovilton	
XJ407	WS55 Whirlwind HAR10 (G-BKHB)	Privately owned, Tattershall Thorpe	
XJ409	WS55 Whirlwind HAR10	Wales Aircraft Museum, Cardiff	
XJ411	WS55 Whirlwind HAR10 [Z]	RAE Farnborough Fire Section	
XJ430	WS55 Whirlwind HAR10	CTE, RAF Manston	
XJ435	WS55 Whirlwind HAR10 (8671M) [V]	RAF No 1 SoTT, Halton	
XJ445	WS55 Whirlwind HAR5	CDE, Porton Down, Wilts	
XJ476	DH Sea Vixen FAW1 nose section	Southampton Hall of Aviation	
XJ481	DH Sea Vixen FAW1 [VL]	Britannia Leisure Park, Ilkeston	
XJ482	DH Sea Vixen FAW1 (A2598) [713/VL]	Norfolk & Suffolk Aviation Museum, Flixton	
XJ494	DH Sea Vixen FAW2	Privately owned, Kings Langley, Herts	
XJ560	DH Sea Vixen FAW2 (8142M) [242]	Newark Air Museum, Winthorpe	
XJ565	DH Sea Vixen FAW2 [127/E]	Mosquito Aircraft Museum, London Colney	
XJ571	DH Sea Vixen FAW2 (8140M) [133/E]	RAF No 2 SoTT, Cosford	
XJ572	DH Sea Vixen FAW2 (8803M)	RAF FF&SS, Catterick	
XJ575	DH Sea Vixen FAW2 (A2611) [-/VL] [SAH-13]	Cornwall Aero Park, Helston	
XJ580	DH Sea Vixen FAW2 [131/E]	Christchurch Memorial Group	
XJ582	DH Sea Vixen FAW2 (8139M) [702]	RAF Cottesmore Fire Section	
XJ584	DH Sea Vixen FAW2 (A2621) [SAH-16]	Cornwall Aero Park, Helston	
XJ604	DH Sea Vixen FAW2 (8222M)	RAF No 1 SoTT, Halton	
XJ607	DH Sea Vixen FAW2 (8171M) [701]	RAF No 2 SoTT, Cosford	
XJ608	DH Sea Vixen FAW2 (8802M)	EOD, North Luffenham, ground instr	
XJ609	DH Sea Vixen FAW2 (8172M) painted 8171M [702/VL]	RAF Abingdon BDRF	
XJ634	Hawker Hunter F6A (8684M) [29]	RAFC Cranwell, Engineering Wing	
XJ639	Hawker Hunter F6A (8687M) [31]	RAFC Cranwell, Engineering Wing	
XJ676	Hawker Hunter F6A [32] (8844M)	RAF Lyneham Fire Section	
XJ683	Hawker Hunter FGA9	RAF Brawdy	
XJ690	Hawker Hunter FGA9 (composite with XG195)	Bomber County Aviation Museum, Cleethorpes	
XJ695	Hawker Hunter FGA9 (8677M/ 8738M) [J]	RAF Manston Fire School	
XJ723	WS55 Whirlwind HAR10	OPITB, Montrose	
XJ726	WS55 Whirlwind HAR10 [F]	Nene Valley Aviation Society, Sibson	
XJ727	WS55 Whirlwind HAR10 (8661M) [L]	RAF No 1 SoTT, Halton	
XJ729	WS55 Whirlwind HAR10 (8732M)	RAF Finningley, for display	
XJ763	WS55 Whirlwind HAR10 (G-BKHA)	Privately owned, Biggin Hill	
XJ772	DH Vampire T11 [H]	Brooklands Technical College	
XJ782	Avro Vulcan B2 MRR (8766M)	RAF Finningley on display	
XJ823	Avro Vulcan B2	Privately owned, Carlisle Airport	
XJ824	Avro Vulcan B2	Imperial War Museum, Duxford	
XJ825	Avro Vulcan K2 (8810M)	RAF Waddington BDRT	
XJ917	Bristol Sycamore HR14 [S-H]	Cornwall Aero Park, Helston	
XJ918	Bristol Sycamore HR14 (8190M)	RAF Cosford Aerospace Museum	

Notes	Serial	Type (alternative identity)	Owner, Operator or Location
	XK149	Hawker Hunter F6A (8714M) [34]	RAFC Cranwell, Engineering Wing
	XK412	Auster AOP9	Privately owned, Wootton Bassett
	XK416	Auster AOP9 (G-AYUA/ 7855M)	Vintage Aircraft Team, Cranfield
	XK417	Auster AOP9 (G-AVXY)	Privately owned, Leicester
	XK418	Auster AOP9 (7976M)	Second World War Aircraft Preservation Society, Lasham
	XK421	Auster AOP9 (8365M)	Cotswold Aircraft Restoration Group, RAF Innsworth
	XK482	Saro Skeeter AOP12 (7840M/ G-BJWC) [C]	Privately owned, Heysham, Lancs
	XK488	Blackburn Buccaneer S1	FAA Museum, RNAS Yeovilton
	XK526	Blackburn Buccaneer S2 (8648M)	RAF Honington, at main gate
	XK530	Blackburn Buccaneer S2	RAE Bedford
	XK531	Blackburn Buccaneer S1 (8403M)	Defence School, Winterbourne Gunner
	XK532	Blackburn Buccaneer S1 (A2581) [632/LM]	RAF Lossiemouth, on display
	XK533	Blackburn Buccaneer S1 (nose only)	Museum of Flight, East Fortune
	XK590	DH Vampire T11 [V]	Wellesbourne Aviation Group
	XK623	DH Vampire T11 [56]	Snowdonia National Park, Carnarvon
	XK624	DH Vampire T11 [32]	Norfolk & Suffolk Aviation Museum, Flixton
	XK625	DH Vampire T11 [12]	Privately owned, North Weald
	XK627	DH Vampire T11	Pennine Aviation Museum, Bacup
	XK632	DH Vampire T11 [67]	Lincoln Field Vintage & HAC, Bushey
	XK637	DH Vampire T11 [56]	No 1855 Sqn ATC, Royton, Manchester
	XK655	DH Comet 2R (G-AMXA)	Strathallan Aircraft Collection
	XK659	DH Comet 2 nose only	Privately owned, Elland, W. Yorks
	XK695	DH Comet 2R (G-AMXH)	Imperial War Museum, Duxford
	XK697	DH Comet 2R (G-AMXJ) [D]	Air Scouts, RAF Wyton
	XK699	DH Comet C2 (G-AMXM/ 7971M)	RAF Museum Store, Henlow
	XK724	Folland Gnat F1 (7715M)	RAFC Cranwell, Engineering Wing
	XK740	Folland Gnat F1 (8396M)	RAF Cosford Aerospace Museum
	XK741	Folland Gnat F1	Midland Air Museum, Coventry
	XK776	ML Utility I	Museum of Army Flying, Middle Wallop
	XK788	Slingsby Grasshopper TX1	RAF No 1 MGSP, Halton
	XK789	Slingsby Grasshopper TX1	RAF No 3 MGSP, Cosford
	XK819	Slingsby Grasshopper TX1	Malvern College CCF, Great Malvern
	XK820	Slingsby Grasshopper TX1	RAF No 2 MGSP, Locking
	XK822	Slingsby Grasshopper TX1	Kings College School CCF, Wimbledon
	XK824	Slingsby Grasshopper TX1	Wycliffe School CCF, Stonehouse, Glos
	XK884	Percival Pembroke C1	RAF No 60 Sqn, Wildenrath
	XK895	DH Sea Devon C20	RNAS Culdrose Station Flight
	XK906	WS55 Whirlwind HAS7	AAC Netheravon Fire Section
	XK907	WS55 Whirlwind HAS7 [9]	Midland Air Museum, Coventry
	XK911	WS55 Whirlwind HAS7 (A2603) [519/PO]	RN store, Wroughton
	XK912	WS55 Whirlwind HAS7 [60/CU]	Privately owned, Crudwell, Wilts
	XK936	WS55 Whirlwind HAS7 [62]	Imperial War Museum, Duxford
	XK943	WS55 Whirlwind HAS7 (A2653/8796M) [57]	RAF Abingdon, BDRF
	XK944	WS55 Whirlwind HAS7 (A2607)	Brunel Technical College, Bristol
	XK968	WS55 Whirlwind HAR10 (8445M) [E]	RAF Manston, on display
	XK969	WS55 Whirlwind HAR10 (8646M)	RAF Odiham, BDRT
	XK987	WS55 Whirlwind HAR10 (8393M)	MoD Swynnerton, Staffs
	XK988	WS55 Whirlwind HAR10 (A2646) [N]	Museum of Army Flying, Middle Wallop
	XL158	HP Victor K2	RAF No 55 Sqn, Marham
	XL160	HP Victor K2	RAF No 55 Sqn, Marham
	XL161	HP Victor K2	RAF No 55 Sqn, Marham
	XL162	HP Victor K2	RAF No 57 Sqn, Marham
	XL163	HP Victor K2	RAF No 55 Sqn, Marham

Serial	Type (alternative identity)	Owner, Operator or Location	Notes
XL164	HP Victor K2	RAF No 55 Sqn, Marham	
XL188	HP Victor K2	RAF No 55 Sqn, Marham	
XL189	HP Victor K2	RAF No 55 Sqn, Marham	
XL190	HP Victor K2	RAF No 55 Sqn, Marham	
XL191	HP Victor K2	RAF No 57 Sqn, Marham	
XL192	HP Victor K2	RAF No 57 Sqn, Marham	
XL231	HP Victor K2	RAF No 57 Sqn, Marham	
XL233	HP Victor K2	RAF No 55 Sqn, Marham	
XL318	Avro Vulcan B2 (8733M)	Bomber Command Museum, Hendon	
XL319	Avro Vulcan B2	North East Aircraft Museum, Usworth	
XL321	Avro Vulcan B2 (8759M)	RAF FF&SS Catterick	
XL360	Avro Vulcan B2	Midland Air Museum, Coventry	
XL384	Avro Vulcan B2 (nose only) (8670M)	Lincolnshire Aviation Museum, East Kirkby	
XL386	Avro Vulcan B2 (8760M)	RAF Manston Fire Section	
XL391	Avro Vulcan B2	Privately owned, Blackpool	
XL392	Avro Vulcan B2 (8745M)	RAF Valley Fire Section	
XL426	Avro Vulcan B2	Vulcan Memorial Flight, RAF Scampton	
XL427	Avro Vulcan B2 (8756M)	RAF Machrihanish Fire Section	
XL445	Avro Vulcan K2 (8811M)	RAF Lyneham Fire Section	
XL449	Fairey Gannet AEW3	Wales Aircraft Museum, Cardiff	
XL471	Fairey Gannet AEW3 [043/R]	MoD(PE) RAE Farnborough	
XL472	Fairey Gannet AEW3 [044/R]	A&AEE Boscombe Down, derelict	
XL497	Fairey Gannet AEW3 [041/R]	HMS *Gannet*, Prestwick, at gate	
XL500	Fairey Gannet AEW3 (A2701)	RN Lee-on-Solent, stored	
XL502	Fairey Gannet AEW3 (8610M)	RAF Leuchars BDRT	
XL503	Fairey Gannet AEW3 [070/E]	FAA Museum, RNAS Yeovilton	
XL511	HP Victor K2	RAF No 57 Sqn, Marham	
XL512	HP Victor K2	RAF No 55 Sqn, Marham	
XL563	Hawker Hunter T7	MoD(PE) RAE/IAM Farnborough	
XL564	Hawker Hunter T7 [4]	MoD(PE) ETPS Boscombe Down	
XL565	Hawker Hunter T7	MoD(PE) IAM/RAE Farnborough	
XL566	Hawker Hunter T7 [86]	RAF Shawbury store	
XL567	Hawker Hunter T7 (8723M) [84]	RAF Chivenor Fire Section	
XL568	Hawker Hunter T7B [ZF]	RAF No 12 Sqn, Lossiemouth	
XL569	Hawker Hunter T7 (8833M) [80]	RAF TMTS, Scampton	
XL572	Hawker Hunter T7 (8834M) [83]	RAF TMTS, Scampton	
XL573	Hawker Hunter T7 [WC]	RAF No 237 OCU, Lossiemouth	
XL576	Hawker Hunter T7 (8835M) [81]	RAF TMTS, Scampton	
XL577	Hawker Hunter T7 (8676M) [01]	RAFC Cranwell, Engineering Wing	
XL578	Hawker Hunter T7 [77]	RAF store, St Athan	
XL580	Hawker Hunter T8M [719/VL]	RN No 899 Sqn, Yeovilton	
XL583	Hawker Hunter T7 [84]	RAF Brawdy Dog Pound	
XL586	Hawker Hunter T7 [85]	MoD(PE) BAe Warton	
XL587	Hawker Hunter T7 (8807M) [Z]	RAF TMTS, Scampton	
XL591	Hawker Hunter T7 [VC]	RAF No 237 OCU, Lossiemouth	
XL592	Hawker Hunter T7 (8836M) [Y]	RAF TMTS, Scampton	
XL595	Hawker Hunter T7 [78]	RAF store, St Athan	
XL598	Hawker Hunter T8C [880/VL]	RN FRADU, Yeovilton	
XL600	Hawker Hunter T7 [FL]	RNAY Fleetlands Apprentice School	
XL601	Hawker Hunter T7 [879/VL]	RN FRADU, Yeovilton	
XL602	Hawker Hunter T8M	MoD(PE) BAe Dunsfold	
XL603	Hawker Hunter T8M [720]	RN No 899 Sqn, Yeovilton	
XL609	Hawker Hunter T7 [YF]	RAF No 12 Sqn, Lossiemouth	
XL612	Hawker Hunter T7 [2]	MoD(PE) ETPS Boscombe Down	
XL613	Hawker Hunter T7 [UC]	RAF No 237 OCU, Lossiemouth	
XL614	Hawker Hunter T7B [YC]	RAF No 237 OCU, Lossiemouth	
XL616	Hawker Hunter T7 [YS]	RAF No 208 Sqn, Lossiemouth	
XL617	Hawker Hunter T7 (8837M) [89]	RAF TMTS, Scampton	
XL618	Hawker Hunter T7 [05]	RAF Shawbury store	
XL621	Hawker Hunter T7	MoD(PE) RAE Bedford	
XL623	Hawker Hunter T7 (8770M) [90]	RAF No 2 SoTT, Cosford	
XL629	EE Lightning T4	A&AEE Boscombe Down, at main gate	
XL703	SAL Pioneer CC1 (8034M)	Greater Manchester Museum of Science and Industry	
XL714	DH Tiger Moth (G-AOGR)	Privately owned, Shipdham	
XL717	DH Tiger Moth (G-AOXG) [LM]	FAA Museum, RNAS Yeovilton	
XL728	Westland Wessex HAS1	MoD(PE) RAE Farnborough	
XL735	Saro Skeeter AOP12	No 1404 Sqn ATC, Manston	
XL738	Saro Skeeter AOP12 (7860M)	Southampton Hall of Aviation	

Notes	Serial	Type (alternative identity)	Owner, Operator or Location
	XL762	Saro Skeeter AOP12 (8017M)	Royal Scottish Museum of Flight, East Fortune
	XL763	Saro Skeeter AOP12	Southall Technical College
	XL764	Saro Skeeter AOP12 (7940M)	Newark Air Museum, Winthorpe
	XL765	Saro Skeeter AOP12	Midland Air Museum, Coventry
	XL770	Saro Skeeter AOP12 (8046M)	Royal Military College of Science, Shrivenham
	XL809	Saro Skeeter AOP12 (PH-HOF)	The Old Training Plane Co, Shobdon
	XL811	Saro Skeeter AOP12 [157]	The Aircraft Collection, Warmingham
	XL812	Saro Skeeter AOP12 (G-SARO)	Privately owned, Dalcross
	XL813	Saro Skeeter AOP12	Museum of Army Flying, Middle Wallop
	XL814	Saro Skeeter AOP12	AAC Historic Aircraft Flight, Middle Wallop
	XL824	Bristol Sycamore HR14 (8021M)	Greater Manchester Museum of Science and Industry
	XL829	Bristol Sycamore HR14	Bristol Industrial Museum
	XL836	WS55 Whirlwind HAS7 (A2642) [65/FL]	RN Predannack Fire Section
	XL839	WS55 Whirlwind HAR9 (A2665) [588/CU]	RNAS Lee-on-Solent Fire Section
	XL840	WS55 Whirlwind HAS7 [56]	Nene Valley Aviation Society, Sibson
	XL846	WS55 Whirlwind HAS7 (A2625) [85]	RNAS Yeovilton, fire section
	XL847	WS55 Whirlwind HAS7 (A2626) [83]	AAC, BDRT Middle Wallop
	XL853	WS55 Whirlwind HAS7 (A2630)	Museum of Army Flying, Andover store
	XL875	WS55 Whirlwind HAR9	Air Service Training, Perth
	XL880	WS55 Whirlwind HAR9 (A2714) [433/ED]	RN AES Lee-on-Solent
	XL898	WS55 Whirlwind HAR9 (8654M) [30/ED]	Boscombe Down Fire Section
	XL899	WS55 Whirlwind HAR9 [587/CU]	RN Predannack Fire School
	XL929	Percival Pembroke C1	RAF No 60 Sqn, Wildenrath
	XL954	Percival Pembroke C1	RAF No 60 Sqn, Wildenrath
	XL993	SAL Twin Pioneer CC1 (8388M)	RAF Cosford Aerospace Museum
	XM135	BAC Lightning F1 [135]	Imperial War Museum, Duxford
	XM139	BAC Lightning F1 (8411M) [F]	RAF Wattisham
	XM144	BAC Lightning F1 (8417M) [J]	RAF Leuchars, at main gate
	XM147	BAC Lightning F1 (8412M) [J]	RAF Wattisham
	XM169	BAC Lightning F1A (8422M) [W]	RAF Leuchars Fire Section
	XM172	BAC Lightning F1A (8427M) [B]	RAF Coltishall, at main gate
	XM173	BAC Lightning F1A (8414M) [A]	RAF Bentley Priory, at main gate
	XM178	BAC Lightning F1A (8418M) [Y]	RAF Leuchars Fire Section
	XM181	BAC Lightning F1A (8415M)	RAF Binbrook
	XM183	BAC Lightning F1A (8416M)	RAF Binbrook
	XM191	BAC Lightning F1A (8590M) (nose only)	RAF Exhibition Flight, Abingdon
	XM192	BAC Lightning F1A (8413M) [K]	RAF Wattisham, at main gate
	XM223	DH Devon C2 [J]	MoD(PE) RAE Farnborough
	XM275	EE Canberra B(I)8 (nose only)	RAF Wattisham Fire Section
	XM279	EE Canberra B(I)8 (nose only)	South Yorkshire APS, Firbeck
	XM296	DH Heron C4	RN FONAC, RNAS Yeovilton
	XM300	Westland Wessex HAS1	Wales Aircraft Museum, Cardiff
	XM326	Westland Wessex HAS1 [515]	RNAS Portland Fire Section
	XM327	Westland Wessex HAS3 [401/KE]	College of Nautical Studies, Warsash
	XM328	Westland Wessex HAS3	RNAS Culdrose, SAH
	XM329	Westland Wessex HAS1 (A2609)	RN AES Lee-on-Solent
	XM330	Westland Wessex HAS1	MoD(PE) RAE Farnborough

Serial	Type (alternative identity)	Owner, Operator or Location	Notes
XM331	Westland Wessex HAS3 [653/PO]	RNAS Lee-on-Solent Fire Section	
XM349	Hunting Jet Provost T3A [H]	RAF CFS, Scampton	
XM350	Hunting Jet Provost T3A [89]	RAF No 7 FTS, Church Fenton	
XM351	Hunting Jet Provost T3 (8078M) [05]	RAF No 2 SoTT, Cosford	
XM352	Hunting Jet Provost T3A [92]	RAF No 7 FTS, Church Fenton	
XM355	Hunting Jet Provost T3 (8229M) [D]	RAF No 1 SoTT, Halton	
XM357	Hunting Jet Provost T3A [45]	RAF No 1 FTS, Linton-on-Ouse	
XM358	Hunting Jet Provost T3A [53]	RAF No 1 FTS, Linton-on-Ouse	
XM362	Hunting Jet Provost T3 (8230M)	RAF No 1 SoTT, Halton	
XM365	Hunting Jet Provost T3A [37]	RAF No 1 FTS, Linton-on-Ouse	
XM367	Hunting Jet Provost T3 (8083M) [04]	RAF No 2 SoTT, Cosford	
XM369	Hunting Jet Provost T3 (8084M) [07]	RAF No 1 SoTT, Halton	
XM370	Hunting Jet Provost T3A [93]	RAF No 7 FTS, Church Fenton	
XM371	Hunting Jet Provost T3A [K]	RAF CFS, Scampton	
XM372	Hunting Jet Provost T3A [55]	RAF No 1 FTS, Linton-on-Ouse	
XM374	Hunting Jet Provost T3A [83]	RAF No 7 FTS, Church Fenton	
XM375	Hunting Jet Provost T3 (8231M) [B]	RAF No 1 SoTT, Halton	
XM376	Hunting Jet Provost T3A [97]	RAF No 7 FTS, Church Fenton	
XM378	Hunting Jet Provost T3A	RAF St Athan, hack	
XM379	Hunting Jet Provost T3	Army Apprentice College, Arborfield	
XM381	Hunting Jet Provost T3 (8232M) [O]	RAF No 1 SoTT, Halton	
XM383	Hunting Jet Provost T3A [90]	RAF No 7 FTS, Church Fenton	
XM386	Hunting Jet Provost T3 (8076M) [08]	RAF No 1 SoTT, Halton	
XM387	Hunting Jet Provost T3A [I]	RAF CFS, Scampton	
XM401	Hunting Jet Provost T3A [17]	RAF No 1 FTS, Linton-on-Ouse	
XM402	Hunting Jet Provost T3 (8055AM) [J]	RAF No 1 SoTT, Halton	
XM403	Hunting Jet Provost T3A [A]	RAF CFS, Scampton	
XM404	Hunting Jet Provost T3 (8055BM) [24]	RAF No 1 SoTT, Halton	
XM405	Hunting Jet Provost T3A [42]	RAF No 1 FTS, Linton-on-Ouse	
XM408	Hunting Jet Provost T3 (8233M) [P]	RAF No 1 SoTT, Halton	
XM409	Hunting Jet Provost T3 (8082M) [A]	RAF No 1 SoTT, Halton	
XM410	Hunting Jet Provost T3 (8054AM) [C]	RAF No 1 SoTT, Halton	
XM411	Hunting Jet Provost T3 (8434M) [L]	RAF No 1 SoTT, Halton	
XM412	Hunting Jet Provost T3A [41]	RAF No 1 FTS, Linton-on-Ouse	
XM413	Hunting Jet Provost T3	Army Apprentice College, Arborfield	
XM414	Hunting Jet Provost T3A [101]	RAF No 7 FTS, Church Fenton	
XM415	Hunting Jet Provost T3 (nose only)	Southampton Hall of Aviation	
XM417	Hunting Jet Provost T3 (8054BM) [D]	RAF No 1 SoTT, Halton	
XM419	Hunting Jet Provost T3A [102]	RAF No 7 FTS, Church Fenton	
XM424	Hunting Jet Provost T3A [30]	RAF No 1 FTS, Linton-on-Ouse	
XM425	Hunting Jet Provost T3A [88]	RAF No 7 FTS, Church Fenton	
XM426	Hunting Jet Provost T3 (nose only)	No 1151 Sqn ATC, Wallsend-on-Tyne	
XM455	Hunting Jet Provost T3A [F]	RAF CFS, Scampton	
XM458	Hunting Jet Provost T3A [B]	RAF CFS, Scampton	
XM459	Hunting Jet Provost T3A [104]	RAF No 7 FTS, Church Fenton	
XM461	Hunting Jet Provost T3A [11]	RAF No 1 FTS, Linton-on-Ouse	
XM463	Hunting Jet Provost T3A [38]	RAF No 1 FTS, Linton-on-Ouse	
XM464	Hunting Jet Provost T3A [23]	RAF No 1 FTS, Linton-on-Ouse	
XM465	Hunting Jet Provost T3A [85]	RAF No 7 FTS, Church Fenton	
XM466	Hunting Jet Provost T3A [31]	RAF No 1 FTS, Linton-on-Ouse	
XM467	Hunting Jet Provost T3 (8085M) [06] [69]	RAF No 1 SoTT, Halton	
XM468	Hunting Jet Provost T3 (8081M) [B]	RAF No 1 SoTT, Halton	
XM470	Hunting Jet Provost T3A [M]	RAF CFS, Scampton	
XM471	Hunting Jet Provost T3A [10]	RAF No 1 FTS, Linton-on-Ouse	

Notes	Serial	Type (alternative identity)	Owner, Operator or Location
	XM472	Hunting Jet Provost T3A [22]	RAF No 1 FTS, Linton-on-Ouse
	XM473	Hunting Jet Provost T3A [19]	RAF No 1 FTS, Linton-on-Ouse
	XM475	Hunting Jet Provost T3A [96]	RAF No 7 FTS, Church Fenton
	XM478	Hunting Jet Provost T3A [33]	RAF No 1 FTS, Linton-on-Ouse
	XM479	Hunting Jet Provost T3A [54]	RAF No 1 FTS, Linton-on-Ouse
	XM480	Hunting Jet Provost T3 (8080M)	RAF No 1 SoTT, Halton
	XM529	Saro Skeeter AOP12 (7979M/ G-BDNS)	Privately owned, Handforth
	XM553	Saro Skeeter AOP12 (G-AWSV)	Privately owned, Middle Wallop
	XM555	Saro Skeeter AOP12 (8027M)	RAF Cosford Aerospace Museum
	XM556	Saro Skeeter AOP12 (G-HELI/7870M) [V]	British Rotorcraft Museum, Weston-super-Mare
	XM561	Saro Skeeter AOP12 (7980M)	Lincolnshire Aviation Museum, East Kirkby
	XM564	Saro Skeeter AOP12	Royal Armoured Corps, Bovington
	XM569	Avro Vulcan B2	Wales Aircraft Museum, Cardiff
	XM594	Avro Vulcan B2	Newark Air Museum, Winthorpe
	XM597	Avro Vulcan B2	Royal Scottish Museum of Flight, East Fortune
	XM598	Avro Vulcan B2 (8778M)	RAF Cosford Aerospace Museum
	XM602	Avro Vulcan B2 (8771M)	RAF St Athan Historic Aircraft Collection
	XM603	Avro Vulcan B2	BAe Woodford
	XM607	Avro Vulcan B2 (8779M)	RAF Waddington, on display
	XM612	Avro Vulcan B2	City of Norwich Aviation Museum
	XM652	Avro Vulcan B2 (nose only)	Privately owned, Burntwood, Staffs
	XM655	Avro Vulcan B2 (G-VULC/ N655AV)	Privately owned, Wellesbourne Mountford
	XM656	Avro Vulcan B2 (8757M) (nose only)	RAF Cottesmore Fire Section
	XM657	Avro Vulcan B2 (8734M)	RAF Manston Fire School
	XM660	WS55 Whirlwind HAS7 [78]	North East Aircraft Museum, Usworth
	XM665	WS55 Whirlwind HAS7	Booker Air Museum
	XM667	WS55 Whirlwind HAS7 (A2629) [556/CU]	RNAS Lee-on-Solent, BDRT
	XM685	WS55 Whirlwind HAS7 (G-AYZJ) [518/PO]	Newark Air Museum, Winthorpe
	XM693	HS Gnat T1 (7891M)	BAe Hamble on display
	XM694	HS Gnat T1	RAE Bedford Apprentice School
	XM697	HS Gnat T1	No 1349 Sqn ATC, Woking
	XM698	HS Gnat T1 (8090M/8497M)	RAF Cosford Aerospace Museum
	XM706	HS Gnat T1 (8572M) [12]	RAF No 1 SoTT, Halton
	XM708	HS Gnat T1 (8573M)	RAF No 1 SoTT, Halton
	XM709	HS Gnat T1 (8617M) [67]	RAF No 1 SoTT, Halton
	XM715	HP Victor K2	RAF No 55 Sqn, Marham
	XM717	HP Victor K2	RAF No 57 Sqn, Marham
	XM832	Westland Wessex HAS1	RN NASU, Yeovilton
	XM833	Westland Wessex HAS3	Second World War Aircraft Preservation Society, Lasham
	XM836	Westland Wessex HAS3 [651/PO]	RNAY Fleetlands, instructional use
	XM838	Westland Wessex HAS3 [405/LN]	RNAS Lee-on-Solent, BDRT
	XM843	Westland Wessex HAS1 (A2693) [527/CU]	RN AES Lee-on-Solent
	XM845	Westland Wessex HAS1 (A2682) [530/PO]	RNAS Yeovilton Fire Section
	XM868	Westland Wessex HAS1 (A2706) [517/PO]	RN AES Lee-on-Solent
	XM870	Westland Wessex HAS3 [652/PO]	RN AES Lee-on-Solent
	XM874	Westland Wessex HAS1 (A2689) [521/PO]	RNAS Culdrose, SAH
	XM916	Westland Wessex HAS3 [666/PO]	Fire Section, Wroughton
	XM917	Westland Wessex HAS1 (A2692) [528/CU]	RN AES Lee-on-Solent
	XM919	Westland Wessex HAS3 [55]	RNAS Yeovilton Fire Section
	XM923	Westland Wessex HAS3	RNAY Fleetlands
	XM926	Westland Wessex HAS1	MoD(PE) RAE Farnborough
	XM927	Westland Wessex HAS3 (8814M) [660/PO]	RAF Shawbury, BDRT

Serial	Type (alternative identity)	Owner, Operator or Location	Notes
XM969	BAC Lightning T4 (8592M)	RAF Binbrook Fire Section	
XM987	BAC Lightning T4	RAF Coningsby, BDRT	
XM997	BAC Lightning T4	RAF FF&SS, Catterick	
XN126	WS55 Whirlwind HAR10 (8655M) [S]	RAF No 1 SoTT, Halton	
XN132	Sud Alouette AH2	AAC UNFICYP, Nicosia	
XN137	Hunting Jet Provost T3 [95] nose only	No 95 Sqn ATC, Crewe, Cheshire	
XN148	Slingsby Sedbergh TX1	RAF ACCGS, Syerston	
XN150	Slingsby Sedbergh TX1	RAF No 636 VGS, Swansea	
XN155	Slingsby Sedbergh TX1	RAF No 617 VGS, Manston	
XN157	Slingsby Sedbergh TX1	RAF Sealand, stored	
XN185	Slingsby Sedbergh TX1	RAF No 643 VGS, Syerston	
XN186	Slingsby Sedbergh TX1	RAF No 634 VGS, St Athan	
XN187	Slingsby Sedbergh TX1	RAF No 662 VGS, Arbroath	
XN195	Slingsby Cadet TX3 (7845M)	RAF No 611 VGS, Swanton Morley, instruction use	
XN198	Slingsby Cadet TX3	RAF No 663 VGS, Kinloss	
XN239	Slingsby Cadet TX3	RAF store, Syerston	
XN240	Slingsby Cadet TX3	RAF store, Syerston	
XN241	Slingsby Cadet TX3	RAF No 661 VGS, Kirknewton	
XN244	Slingsby Cadet TX3	RAF store, Syerston	
XN246	Slingsby Cadet TX3 [A]	RAF No 617 VGS, Manston	
XN252	Slingsby Cadet TX3	RAF store, Syerston	
XN258	WS55 Whirlwind HAR9 [589/CU]	Cornwall Aero Park, Helston	
XN261	WS55 Whirlwind HAS7 (A2652) [61]	RNAS Lee-on-Solent, dumped	
XN263	WS55 Whirlwind HAS7	Royal Military College of Science, Shrivenham	
XN264	WS55 Whirlwind HAS7 [53]	Privately owned, Grovesend, Avon	
XN297	WS55 Whirlwind HAR9 (really XN311) (A2643)	RNAY Fleetlands Apprentice Training School	
XN298	WS55 Wirlwind HAR9 [810/LS]	Linwood School, Winton, nr Bournemouth	
XN299	WS55 Whirlwind HAS7 [758]	Torbay Aircraft Museum, Paignton	
XN302	WS55 Whirlwind HAS7 (A2654) [LS]	RNAS Lee-on-Solent Fire Section	
XN304	WS55 Whirlwind HAS7 [64]	Norfolk & Suffolk Aviation Museum, Flixton	
XN306	WS55 Whirlwind HAR9 [434/ED]	RNAS Portland Fire Section	
XN308	WS55 Whirlwind HAS7 (A2605) [510/PO]	RNAS Lee-on-Solent, BDRT	
XN309	WS55 Whirlwind HAR9 (A2663) [590/CU]	Second World War Aircraft Preservation Society, Lasham	
XN314	WS55 Whirlwind HAS7 (A2614)	RN Predannack Fire School	
XN332	Saro P531 (G-APNV/A2579) [759]	FAA Museum, RNAS Yeovilton	
XN334	Saro P531 (A2525)	British Rotorcraft Museum, at Yeovilton	
XN341	Saro Skeeter AOP12 (8022M)	RAF St Athan Historic Aircraft Collection	
XN344	Saro Skeeter AOP12 (8018M)	Science Museum, South Kensington	
XN351	Saro Skeeter AOP12 (G-BKSC)	Privately owned, Shobdon	
XN359	WS55 Whirlwind HAR9 (A2712) [434/ED]	RNAS Lee-on-Solent, BDRT	
XN380	WS55 Whirlwind HAS7 [67]	Lashenden Air Warfare Museum, Headcorn	
XN382	WS55 Whirlwind HAS7	Privately owned, Thruxton	
XN385	WS55 Whirlwind HAS7	RN Historic Flight, stored Wroughton	
XN386	WS55 Whirlwind HAR9 [435/ED] (A2713)	RN AES Lee-on-Solent	
XN387	WS55 Whirlwind HAR9 (8564M)	RAF Odiham, BDRT	
XN435	Auster AOP9 (G-BGBU)	Privately owned, Egham	
XN437	Auster AOP9 (G-AXWA)	Privately owned, Welling, Kent	
XN441	Auster AOP9 (G-BGKT)	Privately owned, Reymerston Hall	
XN453	DH Comet 2e	RAE Farnborough Fire Section	
XN458	Hunting Jet Provost T3 (8234M) [H]	—	

Notes	Serial	Type (alternative identity)	Owner, Operator or Location
	XN459	Hunting Jet Provost T3A [20]	RAF No 1 FTS, Linton-on-Ouse
	XN461	Hunting Jet Provost T3A [28]	RAF No 1 FTS, Linton-on-Ouse
	XN462	Hunting Jet Provost T3A [87]	RAF No 7 FTS, Church Fenton
	XN466	Hunting Jet Provost T3A [29]	RAF No 1 FTS, Linton-on-Ouse
	XN467	Hunting Jet Provost T4 (8559M) [F]	RAF No 1 SoTT, Halton
	XN470	Hunting Jet Provost T3A [84]	RAF No 7 FTS, Church Fenton
	XN471	Hunting Jet Provost T3A [24]	RAF No 1 FTS, Linton-on-Ouse
	XN472	Hunting Jet Provost T3A [32]	RAF No 1 FTS, Linton-on-Ouse
	XN473	Hunting Jet Provost T3A (8862M) [98]	RAF Church Fenton Fire Section
	XN492	Hunting Jet Provost T3 (8079M) [08]	RAF No 2 SoTT, Cosford
	XN493	Hunting Jet Provost T3 nose only	RAF Exhibition Flight, Abingdon
	XN494	Hunting Jet Provost T3A [43]	RAF No 1 FTS, Linton-on-Ouse
	XN495	Hunting Jet Provost T3A [102] (8786M)	RAF Abingdon, BDRF
	XN497	Hunting Jet Provost T3A [52]	RAF No 1 FTS, Linton-on-Ouse
	XN498	Hunting Jet Provost T3A [16]	RAF No 1 FTS, Linton-on-Ouse
	XN499	Hunting Jet Provost T3A [L]	RAF CFS, Scampton
	XN500	Hunting Jet Provost T3A [80]	RAF No 7 FTS, Church Fenton
	XN501	Hunting Jet Provost T3A [G]	RAF CFS, Scampton
	XN502	Hunting Jet Provost T3A [D]	RAF CFS, Scampton
	XN503	Hunting Jet Provost T3 nose only	RAF Exhibition Flight, Abingdon
	XN505	Hunting Jet Provost T3A [25]	RAF No 1 FTS, Linton-on-Ouse
	XN506	Hunting Jet Provost T3A [81]	RAF No 7 FTS, Church Fenton
	XN508	Hunting Jet Provost T3A [98]	RAF No 7 FTS, Church Fenton
	XN509	Hunting Jet Provost T3A [50]	RAF No 1 FTS, Linton-on-Ouse
	XN510	Hunting Jet Provost T3A [40]	RAF No 1 FTS, Linton-on-Ouse
	XN511	Hunting Jet Provost T3 [21] (nose only)	No 177 Sqn ATC, Blackpool Airport
	XN512	Hunting Jet Provost T3 (8435M)	RAF No 1 SoTT, Halton
	XN547	Hunting Jet Provost T3A [48]	RAF No 1 FTS, Linton-on-Ouse
	XN548	Hunting Jet Provost T3A [103]	RAF No 7 FTS, Church Fenton
	XN549	Hunting Jet Provost T3 (8235M) [R]	RAF No 1 SoTT, Halton
	XN551	Hunting Jet Provost T3A [100]	RAF No 7 FTS, Church Fenton
	XN552	Hunting Jet Provost T3A [86]	RAF No 7 FTS, Church Fenton
	XN553	Hunting Jet Provost T3A [34]	RAF No 1 FTS, Linton-on-Ouse
	XN554	Hunting Jet Provost T3 (8436M) [K]	RAF No 1 SoTT, Halton
	XN574	Hunting Jet Provost T3A [21]	RAF No 1 FTS, Linton-on-Ouse
	XN577	Hunting Jet Provost T3A [18]	RAF No 1 FTS, Linton-on-Ouse
	XN579	Hunting Jet Provost T3A [14]	RAF No 1 FTS, Linton-on-Ouse
	XN581	Hunting Jet Provost T3A [C]	RAF CFS, Scampton
	XN582	Hunting Jet Provost T3A [95]	RAF No 7 FTS, Church Fenton
	XN584	Hunting Jet Provost T3A [E]	RAF CFS, Scampton
	XN585	Hunting Jet Provost T3A [12]	RAF Linton-on-Ouse, Fire Section
	XN586	Hunting Jet Provost T3A [91]	RAF No 7 FTS, Church Fenton
	XN589	Hunting Jet Provost T3A [46]	RAF No 1 FTS, Linton-on-Ouse
	XN592	Hunting Jet Provost T3 (nose only)	No 1105 Sqn ATC, Winchester
	XN593	Hunting Jet Provost T3A [27]	RAF No 1 FTS, Linton-on-Ouse
	XN594	Hunting Jet Provost T3 (8077M) [09]	RAF No 2 SoTT, Cosford
	XN595	Hunting Jet Provost T3A [82]	RAF No 7 FTS, Church Fenton
	XN597	Hunting Jet Provost T3 (7984M) [11] (nose only)	Brencham Historic Aircraft, Hurn
	XN602	Hunting Jet Provost T3 (8088M)	RAF Manston Fire Section
	XN605	Hunting Jet Provost T3A [J]	RAF CFS, Scampton
	XN606	Hunting Jet Provost T3A [36]	RAF No 1 FTS, Linton-on-Ouse
	XN629	Hunting Jet Provost T3A [39]	RAF No 1 FTS, Linton-on-Ouse
	XN632	Hunting Jet Provost T3 (8352M)	RAF St Athan, CTTS
	XN634	Hunting Jet Provost T3A [94]	RAF No 7 FTS, Church Fenton
	XN635	Hunting Jet Provost T3 [575]	RN Predannack Fire School
	XN636	Hunting Jet Provost T3A [15]	RAF No 1 FTS, Linton-on-Ouse
	XN637	Hunting Jet Provost T3 (G-BKOU)	Vintage Aircraft Team, Cranfield
	XN640	Hunting Jet Provost T3A [99]	RAF No 7 FTS, Church Fenton

Serial	Type (alternative identity)	Owner, Operator or Location	Notes
XN641	Hunting Jet Provost T3A [47]	RAF Newton Fire Section	
XN643	Hunting Jet Provost T3A (8704M) [26]	RAF Abingdon, BDRF	
XN647	DH Sea Vixen FAW2 (A2610)	Cornwall Aero Park, Helston	
XN649	DH Sea Vixen FAW2 [126]	MoD(PE) RAE Farnborough store	
XN650	DH Sea Vixen FAW2 (A2639)	Wales Aircraft Museum, Cardiff	
XN651	DH Sea Vixen FAW2 (A2616) (nose only)	Privately owned, Pucklechurch, Avon	
XN652	DH Sea Vixen D3 (8817M)	Flight Refuelling Ltd, Hurn	
XN657	DH Sea Vixen D3	MoD(PE) RAE Llanbedr Fire Section	
XN685	DH Sea Vixen FAW2 (8173M)	RAF No 2 SoTT, Cosford	
XN691	DH Sea Vixen FAW2 (8143M) [N]	RAF No 2 SoTT, Cosford	
XN692	DH Sea Vixen FAW2 (A2624) [SAH-17] [254/H]	RNAS Yeovilton for display	
XN694	DH Sea Vixen FAW2	Flight Refuelling Ltd, Hurn	
XN696	DH Sea Vixen FAW2 [751]	Privately owned, Suffolk	
XN699	DH Sea Vixen FAW2 (8224M)	RAF No 1 SoTT, Halton	
XN714	Hunting H126	RAF Cosford Aerospace Museum	
XN724	BAC Lightning F2A [F]	North East Aircraft Museum, Usworth	
XN728	BAC Lightning F2A (8546M) [V]	Privately owned, Balderton, Notts	
XN734	BAC Lightning F2 (8346M/ G-27-239)	BAe Warton	
XN769	BAC Lightning F2 (8402M) [Z]	London ATCC, West Drayton	
XN774	BAC Lightning F2A (8551M) [F]	RAF Coningsby	
XN776	BAC Lightning F2A [B] (8535M)	Royal Scottish Museum of Flight, East Fortune	
XN781	BAC Lightning F2A (8538M) [B]	RAF Leuchars Fire Section	
XN816	AW Argosy E1 (8489M) [G]	RAF No 2 SoTT, Cosford	
XN817	AW Argosy C1	MoD(PE) RAE West Freugh	
XN819	AW Argosy C1 (8205M)	RAF Finningley Fire Section	
XN855	AW Argosy E1 (8556M)	CTE, RAF Manston	
XN923	HS Buccaneer S1	MoD(PE) A&AEE Boscombe Down	
XN925	HS Buccaneer S1 (8087M/ A2602)	RAF FF&SS Catterick	
XN928	HS Buccaneer S1 (8179M)	Wales Aircraft Museum, Cardiff	
XN929	HS Buccaneer S1 (8051M) (nose only)	RAF Lossiemouth procedures trainer	
XN930	HS Buccaneer S1 (8180M) [632/LM]	RAF Honington, BDRT	
XN934	HS Buccaneer S1 (A2600) [631/LS]	RN Predannack Fire School	
XN953	HS Buccaneer S1 (A2655/ 8182M) [SAH-23]	RNAS Culdrose, SAH	
XN957	HS Buccaneer S1 [630/LM]	FAA Museum, RNAS Yeovilton	
XN962	HS Buccaneer S1 (8183M) (nose only)	RAF Exhibition Flight, Abingdon	
XN964	HS Buccaneer S1 [613/LM]	Phoenix Aviation Museum, Bruntingthorpe	
XN965	HS Buccaneer S1 [636]	MoD(PE) RAE Farnborough	
XN967	HS Buccaneer S1 (A2627) [103-E]	Cornwall Aero Park, Helston	
XN974	HS Buccaneer S2A	MoD(PE) BAe Warton	
XN976	HS Buccaneer S2B [NF]	RAF No 12 Sqn, Lossiemouth	
XN977	HS Buccaneer S2B [G]	RAF Shawbury store	
XN979	HS Buccaneer S2 (nose only)	Cranfield Institute of Technology	
XN981	HS Buccaneer S2B [FS]	RAF No 208 Sqn, Lossiemouth	
XN982	HS Buccaneer S2A	MoD(PE) BAe Brough	
XN983	HS Buccaneer S2B [PF]	RAF No 12 Sqn, Lossiemouth	
XP110	Westland Wessex HAS3 [655/PO]	RNAY Fleetlands Apprentice School	
XP116	Westland Wessex HAS3 (A2618) [520]	RN AES Lee-on-Solent	
XP117	Westland Wessex HAS1 (A2681) [521/PO]	RNAS Culdrose Fire Section	
XP137	Westland Wessex HAS3 [665/PO]	RN AES Lee-on-Solent	
XP139	Westland Wessex HAS3	RN Culdrose Fire Section	

Notes	Serial	Type (alternative identity)	Owner, Operator or Location
	XP140	Westland Wessex HAS3 (8806M) [653/PO]	RAF Chilmark, BDRT
	XP142	Westland Wessex HAS3	FAA Museum, RNAS Yeovilton
	XP149	Westland Wessex HAS1 (A2669) [533/CU]	RNAS Lee-on-Solent Fire Section
	XP150	Westland Wessex HAS3 [406/AN]	RN AES Lee-on-Solent
	XP151	Westland Wessex HAS1 (A2684) [047/R]	RN AES Lee-on-Solent
	XP155	Westland Wessex HAS1 (A2640)	RNAS Culdrose Fire Section
	XP157	Westland Wessex HAS1 (A2680)	RN AES Lee-on-Solent
	XP158	Westland Wessex HAS1 (A2688) [522/CU]	RNAS Culdrose, SAH
	XP159	Westland Wessex HAS1 [047/R]	No 2407 Sqn ATC, Fleet, Hants
	XP160	Westland Wessex HAS1 (A2650) [521/CU] [SAH-24]	RNAS Culdrose, Fire Section
	XP165	Westland Scout AH1	British Rotorcraft Museum, Weston-super-Mare
	XP166	Westland Scout AH1 (G-APVL)	MoD(PE) RAE Farnborough, in store
	XP190	Westland Scout AH1	Army Apprentice College, Arborfield
	XP191	Westland Scout AH1	Royal Military College of Science, Shrivenham
	XP226	Fairey Gannet AEW3 (A2667) [073/E]	Newark Air Museum, Winthorpe
	XP241	Auster AOP9	Tagmore Nurseries, Rabley Heath, Herts
	XP242	Auster AOP9	Museum of Army Flying, Middle Wallop
	XP244	Auster AOP9 (7864M)	Army Apprentice College, Arborfield
	XP248	Auster AOP9 (7822M)	No 2293 Sqn ATC, Marlborough
	XP279	Auster AOP9 (G-BWKK)	Privately owned, Derby
	XP280	Auster AOP9	Leicester Museum of Technology store
	XP281	Auster AOP9	Imperial War Museum, Duxford
	XP282	Auster AOP9 (G-BGTC)	Privately owned, Swanton Morley
	XP283	Auster AOP9 (7859M)	Privately owned, Middle Wallop
	XP286	Auster AOP9 (8044M)	Privately owned, Thruxton
	XP299	WS55 Whirlwind HAR10 (8726M)	RAF Cosford Aerospace Museum
	XP328	WS55 Whirlwind HAR10 (G-BKHC)	Privately owned, Tattershall Thorpe
	XP330	WS55 Whirlwind HAR10	CAA Fire School, Teesside Airport
	XP333	WS55 Whirlwind HAR10 (8650M) [G]	RAF Odiham Fire Section
	XP338	WS55 Whirlwind HAR10 (8647M) [N]	RAF No 2 SoTT, Cosford
	XP339	WS55 Whirlwind HAR10	Bomber County Aviation Museum, Cleethorpes
	XP341	WS55 Whirlwind HAR10 (8340M) [E]	RAFC Cranwell Fire Section
	XP344	WS55 Whirlwind HAR10 (8764M) [X]	RAFC Cranwell, Engineering Wing
	XP350	WS55 Whirlwind HAR10	Cornwall Aero Park, Helston
	XP351	WS55 Whirlwind HAR10 (8672M) [Z]	RAF Shawbury, BDRT
	XP352	WS55 Whirlwind HAR10 (8701M)	RAF Abingdon, BDRF
	XP354	WS55 Whirlwind HAR10 (8721M)	RAF No 1 SoTT, Halton
	XP355	WS55 Whirlwind HAR10 (8463M/G-BEBC) [A]	City of Norwich Aviation Museum
	XP356	WS55 Whirlwind HAR10	RAE Farnborough Fire Section
	XP357	WS55 Whirlwind HAR10 (8499M)	RAF Manston Fire Section
	XP359	WS55 Whirlwind HAR10 (8447M)	RAF Exhibition Flight, Abingdon
	XP360	WS55 Whirlwind HAR10 [V]	Second World War Aircraft Preservation Society, Lasham
	XP361	WS55 Whirlwind HAR10 (8731M)	RAF Valley, preserved at gate
	XP393	WS55 Whirlwind HAR10 [U]	RAE Farnborough Fire Section
	XP394	WS55 Whirlwind HAR10 [C]	RAF Manston Fire Section

Serial	Type (alternative identity)	Owner, Operator or Location	Notes
XP395	WS55 Whirlwind HAR10 (8674M)	RAF No 1 SoTT, Halton	
XP399	WS55 Whirlwind HAR10	Privately owned, Tor View Garage, Glastonbury, Som	
XP400	WS55 Whirlwind HAR10 (8444M) [N]	RAF Manston Fire Section	
XP404	WS55 Whirlwind HAR10 (8682M)	RAF SAREW, Finningley	
XP405	WS55 Whirlwind HAR10 (8656M) [Y]	RAF No 1 SoTT, Halton	
XP409	AW Argosy C1 (8221M)	Defence School, Winterbourne Gunner	
XP411	AW Argosy C1 (8442M) [C]	RAF No 2 SoTT, Cosford	
XP439	AW Argosy E1 (8558M)	RAF Lossiemouth Fire Section	
XP442	AW Argosy T2 (8454M) [442]	RAF No 1 SoTT, Halton	
XP444	AW Argosy C1 (8455M) [D]	RAF No 2 SoTT, Cosford	
XP454	Slingsby Grasshopper TX1	Kimbolton School CCF, Cambs	
XP459	Slingsby Grasshopper TX1	Woodbridge School CCF, Suffolk	
XP462	Slingsby Grasshopper TX1	RAF No 1 MGSP, Halton	
XP463	Slingsby Grasshopper TX1	William Parker School CCF, East Sussex	
XP464	Slingsby Grasshopper TX1	Sherborne School CCF, Dorset	
XP487	Slingsby Grasshopper TX1	RAF No 1 MGSP, Halton	
XP490	Slingsby Grasshopper TX1	RAF ACCGS, Syerston	
XP492	Slingsby Grasshopper TX1	King's College CCF, Taunton	
XP493	Slingsby Grasshopper TX1	RAF ACCGS, Syerston	
XP494	Slingsby Grasshopper TX1	Stamford School, Lincs	
XP502	HS Gnat T1 (8576M) [02]	RAF St Athan Fire Section	
XP503	HS Gnat T1 (8568M) [73]	RAF No 1 SoTT, Halton	
XP504	HS Gnat T1 (8618M) [68] [04]	RAF No 1 SoTT, Halton	
XP505	HS Gnat T1 [05]	Science Museum, South Kensington	
XP511	HS Gnat T1 (8619M) [65]	RAF No 1 SoTT, Halton	
XP514	HS Gnat T1 (8635M)	RAF No 2 SoTT, Cosford	
XP515	HS Gnat T1 (8614M) [59]	RAF Wattisham, BDRT	
XP516	HS Gnat T1 (8580M) [16]	MoD(PE) RAE Farnborough	
XP530	HS Gnat T1 (8606M) [60]	RAF No 1 SoTT, Halton	
XP531	HS Gnat T1 (nose only)	RAF Coltishall, BDRT	
XP532	HS Gnat T1 (8577M/8615M) [32]	MoD(PE) RAE Farnborough	
XP533	HS Gnat T1 (8632M) [74]	RAF No 1 SoTT, Halton	
XP534	HS Gnat T1 (8620M) [64]	RAF No 1 SoTT, Halton	
XP535	HS Gnat T1 (A2679) [SAH-1]	RNAS Culdrose, SAH	
XP538	HS Gnat T1 (8607M) [61]	RAF No 1 SoTT, Halton	
XP540	HS Gnat T1 (8608M) [62]	RAF No 1 SoTT, Halton	
XP541	HS Gnat T1 (8616M) [41]	RAF Abingdon, BDRF	
XP542	HS Gnat T1 (8575M) [42]	RAF St Athan, CTTS	
XP547	Hunting Jet Provost T4 [03]	RAF No 1 TWU/79 Sqn, Brawdy	
XP556	Hunting Jet Provost T4 [B]	RAF CATCS, Shawbury	
XP557	Hunting Jet Provost T4 (8494M)	RAF No 1 SoTT, Halton	
XP558	Hunting Jet Provost T4 (8627M/A2628) [20]	RAF St Athan	
XP563	Hunting Jet Provost T4 [C]	RAF CATCS, Shawbury	
XP564	Hunting Jet Provost T4 [04]	RAF Brawdy Dog Pound	
XP567	Hunting Jet Provost T4 (8510M) [23]	RAF No 1 SoTT, Halton	
XP573	Hunting Jet Provost T4 (8236M) [19]	RAF No 1 SoTT, Halton	
XP585	Hunting Jet Provost T4 (8407M) [24]	RAF No 1 SoTT, Halton	
XP627	Hunting Jet Provost T4	North East Aircraft Museum, Usworth	
XP629	Hunting Jet Provost T4 [P]	RAF CATCS, Shawbury	
XP638	Hunting Jet Provost T4 [A]	RAF CATCS, Shawbury	
XP640	Hunting Jet Provost T4 (8501M) [E]	RAF No 1 SoTT, Halton	
XP672	Hunting Jet Provost T4 (8458M) [27]	RAF No 1 SoTT, Halton	
XP677	Hunting Jet Provost T4 (8587M) (nose only)	RAF Exhibition Flight, Abingdon	
XP680	Hunting Jet Provost T4 (8460M)	RAF St Athan	
XP686	Hunting Jet Provost T4 (8401M/8502M) [G]	RAF No 1 SoTT, Halton	
XP688	Hunting Jet Provost T4 [E]	RAF CATCS, Shawbury	
XP693	BAC Lightning F6 [M]	MoD(PE) BAe Warton	
XP694	BAC Lightning F3 [BO]	RAF Binbrook store	

Notes	Serial	Type (alternative identity)	Owner, Operator or Location
	XP695	BAC Lightning F3 (8808M)	RAF Binbrook, BDRT
	XP701	BAC Lightning F3 [AR]	RAF store Binbrook
	XP702	BAC Lightning F3	RAF Binbrook, store
	XP706	BAC Lightning F3 [DD]	RAF Binbrook store
	XP707	BAC Lightning F3	RAF Binbrook, store
	XP741	BAC Lightning F3 [DD]	RAF Binbrook, store
	XP745	BAC Lightning F3 (8453M) [H]	RAF Boulmer, at main gate
	XP748	BAC Lightning F3 (8446M) [M]	RAF Binbrook, at main gate
	XP749	BAC Lightning F3 [DB]	RAF LTF Binbrook
	XP750	BAC Lightning F3 [DE]	RAF LTF, Binbrook
	XP751	BAC Lightning F3 [DB]	RAF store Binbrook
	XP761	BAC Lightning F3 (8438M) [N]	RAF Binbrook Fire Section
	XP764	BAC Lightning F3	RAF Binbrook, store
	XP769	DHC Beaver AL1	AAC, Aldergrove
	XP771	DHC Beaver AL1	AAC, Aldergrove
	XP772	DHC Beaver AL1	Museum of Army Transport, Beverley
	XP774	DHC Beaver AL1	AAC, Shawbury store
	XP775	DHC Beaver AL1	AAC, Shawbury store
	XP778	DHC Beaver AL1	AAC Beaver Training Flt, Middle Wallop
	XP779	DHC Beaver AL1	AAC Beaver Training Flt, Middle Wallop
	XP780	DHC Beaver AL1	AAC, Shawbury store
	XP804	DHC Beaver AL1	AAC, Shawbury store
	XP808	DHC Beaver AL1	AAC, Shawbury store
	XP810	DHC Beaver AL1	AAC, Shawbury store
	XP814	DHC Beaver AL1	AAC, Shawbury store
	XP816	DHC Beaver AL1	AAC, Shawbury sstore
	XP817	DHC Beaver AL1	Britannia Leisure Park, Ilkeston
	XP818	DHC Beaver AL1	AAC, Shawbury store
	XP820	DHC Beaver AL1	AAC Beaver Training Flt, Middle Wallop
	XP821	DHC Beaver AL1	Museum of Army Flying, Middle Wallop
	XP822	DHC Beaver AL1	AAC, Shawbury store
	XP823	DHC Beaver AL1	AAC, Shawbury store
	XP825	DHC Beaver AL1	AAC, Aldergrove
	XP826	DHC Beaver AL1 [L]	AAC No 29 Flt, Alberta, Canada
	XP827	DHC Beaver AL1	AAC, Shawbury store
	XP831	Hawker P1127 (8406M)	RAF Museum, Hendon
	XP841	Handley Page HP115	FAA Museum, RNAS Yeovilton
	XP846	Westland Scout AH1 [B]	AAC No 660 Sqn, Sek Kong
	XP847	Westland Scout AH1	Museum of Army Flying, Middle Wallop
	XP848	Westland Scout AH1	AAC AETW, Middle Wallop
	XP849	Westland Scout AH1	MoD(PE) ETPS Boscombe Down
	XP850	Westland Scout AH1	AAC store, Wroughton
	XP852	Westland Scout AH1	AAC store, Wroughton
	XP853	Westland Scout AH1	AAC AETW, Middle Wallop
	XP854	Westland Scout AH1 (7898M/ TAD043)	AAC AETW, Middle Wallop
	XP855	Westland Scout AH1	AAC store, Wroughton
	XP856	Westland Scout AH1	AAC AETW, Middle Wallop
	XP857	Westland Scout AH1	AAC Middle Wallop, BDRT
	XP883	Westland Scout AH1	AAC, store Wroughton
	XP884	Westland Scout AH1	AAC AETW, Middle Wallop
	XP885	Westland Scout AH1 [Y]	AAC ATS, Middle Wallop
	XP886	Westland Scout AH1	AAC store, Wroughton
	XP887	Westland Scout AH1 [C]	AAC No 660 Sqn, Sek Kong
	XP888	Westland Scout AH1	AAC AETW, Middle Wallop
	XP890	Westland Scout AH1	AAC store, Wroughton
	XP891	Westland Scout AH1 [Z]	AAC store, Wroughton
	XP893	Westland Scout AH1 [S]	AAC store, Wroughton
	XP894	Westland Scout AH1 [D]	AAC No 660 Sqn, Sek Kong
	XP897	Westland Scout AH1	AAC store, Wroughton
	XP898	Westland Scout AH1	AAC store, Wroughton
	XP899	Westland Scout AH1 [D]	Army Apprentice College, Arborfield
	XP900	Westland Scout AH1 [Z]	AAC ATS, Middle Wallop
	XP901	Westland Scout AH1 [E]	AAC No 660 Sqn, Sek Kong
	XP902	Westland Scout AH1 [T]	AAC store, Wroughton
	XP903	Westland Scout AH1	AAC store, Wroughton
	XP905	Westland Scout AH1	AAC AETW, Middle Wallop
	XP907	Westland Scout AH1	AAC Garrison Air Sqn, Falklands
	XP909	Westland Scout AH1	AAC AETW, Middle Wallop
	XP910	Westland Scout AH1	AAC store, Wroughton
	XP915	DH Comet 3B (G-ANLO)	BAe Woodford

Serial	Type (alternative identity)	Owner, Operator or Location	Notes
XP919	DH Sea Vixen FAW2 (8163M) [706/VL]	City of Norwich Aviation Museum	
XP921	DH Sea Vixen FAW2 (8226M)	RAF No 1 SoTT, Halton	
XP924	DH Sea Vixen D3	Flight Refuelling Ltd, Hurn	
XP967	Sud Alouette AH2	AAC No 16 Flt, Dhekelia	
XP976	Hawker Kestrel FGA1	RAF Wittering Fire Section	
XP980	Hawker Kestrel FGA1 (A2700)	RNAS Culdrose, SAH	
XP984	Hawker Kestrel FGA1 (A2658)	RNEC Manadon, for instruction	
XR107	AW Argosy T2 (8441M) [B]	RAF No 2 SoTT, Cosford	
XR137	AW Argosy E1	RAF Northolt Fire Section	
XR140	AW Argosy E1 (8579M) [140]	RAF No 1 SoTT, Halton	
XR220	BAC TSR2 (7933M)	RAF Cosford Aerospace Museum	
XR222	BAC TSR2	Imperial War Museum, Duxford	
XR232	Sud Alouette AH2 (F-WEIP)	AAC UNFICYP, Nicosia	
XR240	Auster AOP9 (G-BDFH)	Privately owned, Booker	
XR241	Auster AOP9 (G-AXRR)	Privately owned, Duxford	
XR243	Auster AOP9 (8057M)	RAF St Athan Historic Aircraft Collection	
XR244	Auster AOP9	AAC Historic Aircraft Flight, Middle Wallop	
XR246	Auster AOP9 (7862M/ G-AZBU)	Privately owned, Reymerston Hall	
XR267	Auster AOP9 (G-BJXR)	Cotswold Aircraft Restoration Group, RAF Innsworth	
XR269	Auster AOP9 (G-BDXY)	Privately owned, Eaglescott, Devon	
XR271	Auster AOP9	Museum of Artillery, Woolwich	
XR376	Sud Alouette AH2	AAC UNFICYP, Nicosia	
XR378	Sud Alouette AH2	AAC No 16 Flt, Dhekelia	
XR379	Sud Alouette AH2	AAC No 16 Flt, Dhekelia	
XR382	Sud Alouette AH2	AAC UNFICYP, Nicosia	
XR385	Sud Alouette AH2	AAC No 16 Flt, Dhekelia	
XR386	Sud Alouette AH2	AAC UNFICYP, Nicosia	
XR436	Saro P531/2	AAC Middle Wallop BDRT	
XR441	DH Sea Heron C1 (G-AORG)	RNAS Yeovilton, Station Flight	
XR442	DH Sea Heron C1 (G-AORH)	RNAS Yeovilton, Station Flight	
XR443	DH Sea Heron C1 (G-ARKU)	RNAS Yeovilton, Station Flight	
XR445	DH Sea Heron C1 (G-ARKW)	RNAS Yeovilton, Station Flight	
XR455	WS55 Whirlwind HAR10 (8219M) [J]	CTE, RAF Manston	
XR458	WS55 Whirlwind HAR10 (8662M) [H]	RAF No 1 SoTT, Halton	
XR478	WS55 Whirlwind HAR10 [P]	Defence School, Winterbourne Gunner	
XR479	WS55 Whirlwind HAR10 [A]	RAE Farnborough Fire Section	
XR481	WS55 Whirlwind HAR10	RAF store, Wroughton	
XR482	WS55 Whirlwind HAR10 [G]	Defence School, Winterbourne Gunner	
XR483	WS55 Whirlwind HAR10	RAF store, Wroughton	
XR485	WS55 Whirlwind HAR10 [Q]	Norfolk & Suffolk Aviation Museum, Flixton	
XR486	WS55 Whirlwind HCC12 (8727M)	RAF St Athan Historic Aircraft Collection	
XR493	SARO P531 (G-APVM/8040M)	MoD(PE) Farnborough	
XR497	Westland Wessex HC2	RAF No 22 Sqn SAR*	

Note: * No 22 Sqn SAR and the SAREW are based at RAF Finningley with detached Flights at: A Flt — RAF Chivenor; B Flt — RAF Leuchars; C Flt and SARTF — RAF Valley; D Flt — RAF Leconfield; E Flt — RAF Manston.

Serial	Type (alternative identity)	Owner, Operator or Location	Notes
XR498	Westland Wessex HC2 [X]	RAF No 72 Sqn, Aldergrove	
XR499	Westland Wessex HC2 [W]	RAF No 72 Sqn, Aldergrove	
XR501	Westland Wessex HC2	RAF No 22 Sqn SAR*	
XR502	Westland Wessex HC2 [Z]	RAF No 72 Sqn, Aldergrove	
XR503	Westland Wessex HC2	MoD(PE) RAE Bedford	
XR504	Westland Wessex HC2	RAF No 22 Sqn SAR*	
XR505	Westland Wessex HC2 [WA]	RAF No 2 FTS, Shawbury	
XR506	Westland Wessex HC2 [V]	RAF No 72 Sqn, Aldergrove	
XR507	Westland Wessex HC2	RAF No 22 Sqn SAR*	
XR508	Westland Wessex HC2 [D]	RAF No 28 Sqn, Sek Kong	
XR509	Westland Wessex HC2 (8752M)	RAF Benson, for crash rescue training	
XR511	Westland Wessex HC2 [L]	RAF No 72 Sqn, Aldergrove	
XR515	Westland Wessex HC2 [B]	RAF No 28 Sqn, Sek Kong	
XR516	Westland Wessex HC2 [WB]	RAF No 2 FTS, Shawbury	
XR517	Westland Wessex HC2 [N]	RAF No 72 Sqn, Aldergrove	
XR518	Westland Wessex HC2	RAF No 22 Sqn SAR*	

Notes	Serial	Type (alternative identity)	Owner, Operator or Location
	XR519	Westland Wessex HC2 [WC]	RAF No 2 FTS, Shawbury
	XR520	Westland Wessex HC2	RAF No 22 Sqn SAR*
	XR521	Westland Wessex HC2 [WD]	RAF No 2 FTS, Shawbury
	XR522	Westland Wessex HC2 [I]	RAF No 28 Sqn, Sek Kong
	XR523	Westland Wessex HC2 [M]	RAF No 72 Sqn, Aldergrove
	XR524	Westland Wessex HC2 [F]	RAF No 72 Sqn, Aldergrove
	XR525	Westland Wessex HC2 [G]	RAF No 72 Sqn, Aldergrove
	XR526	Westland Wessex HC2 (8147M)	Westlands, Sherborne
	XR527	Westland Wessex HC2 [C]	RAF No 28 Sqn, Sek Kong
	XR528	Westland Wessex HC2 [A]	RAF No 28 Sqn, Sek Kong
	XR529	Westland Wessex HC2 [E]	RAF No 72 Sqn, Aldergrove
	XR534	HS Gnat T1 (8578M) [65]	RAF Valley
	XR535	HS Gnat T1 (8569M) [05]	RAF No 1 SoTT, Halton
	XR537	HS Gnat T1 (8642M)	RAF No 2 SoTT, Cosford
	XR538	HS Gnat T1 (8621M) [69]	RAF No 1 SoTT, Halton
	XR540	HS Gnat T1 (8636M/A2708) [SAH-5]	RNAS Culdrose, SAH
	XR541	HS Gnat T1 (8602M)	RAF St Athan, CTTS
	XR569	HS Gnat T1 (8560M) [08]	RAF No 1 SoTT, Halton
	XR571	HS Gnat T1 (8493M) [23]	RAF *Red Arrows* Scampton on display
	XR572	HS Gnat T1 (A2676) [SAH-3]	RNAS Culdrose, SAH
	XR574	HS Gnat T1 (8631M) [72]	RAF No 1 SoTT, Halton
	XR588	Westland Wessex HC2	RAF No 22 Sqn SAR*
	XR595	Westland Scout AH1	AAC store, Wroughton
	XR597	Westland Scout AH1	AAC Exhibition Unit, Middle Wallop
	XR600	Westland Scout AH1 [B]	AAC store, Wroughton
	XR601	Westland Scout AH1	Army Apprentice College, Arborfield
	XR602	Westland Scout AH1	AAC store, Wroughton
	XR603	Westland Scout AH1 [A]	AAC store, Wroughton
	XR604	Westland Scout AH1	AAC Middle Wallop, BDRT
	XR627	Westland Scout AH1	AAC Garrison Air Sqn, Falklands
	XR629	Westland Scout AH1	AAC store, Wroughton
	XR630	Westland Scout AH1	AAC AETW, Middle Wallop
	XR632	Westland Scout AH1	AAC store, Wroughton
	XR635	Westland Scout AH1	AAC AETW, Middle Wallop
	XR637	Westland Scout AH1	AAC store, Wroughton
	XR639	Westland Scout AH1 [X]	AAC store, Wroughton
	XR643	Hunting Jet Provost T4 (8516M) [26]	RAF No 1 SoTT, Halton
	XR650	Hunting Jet Provost T4 (8459M) [28]	RAF No 1 SoTT, Halton
	XR651	Hunting Jet Provost T4 (8431M) [A]	RAF No 1 SoTT, Halton
	XR653	Hunting Jet Provost T4 [H]	RAF CATCS, Shawbury
	XR654	Hunting Jet Provost T4 [34]	Hunter One Ltd, Hurn
	XR658	Hunting Jet Provost T4 (8192M)	RAF Exhibition Flight, Abingdon
	XR662	Hunting Jet Provost T4 (8410M) [25]	RAF No 1 SoTT, Halton
	XR669	Hunting Jet Provost T4 (8062M) [02] (nose only)	RAF No 1 SoTT, Halton
	XR670	Hunting Jet Provost T4 (8498M)	RAF No 1 SoTT, Halton
	XR672	Hunting Jet Provost T4 (8495M) [C] [73]	RAF No 1 SoTT, Halton
	XR673	Hunting Jet Provost T4 [L]	RAF CATCS, Shawbury
	XR674	Hunting Jet Provost T4 [D]	RAF CATCS, Shawbury
	XR679	Hunting Jet Provost T4 [04]	RAF No 1 TWU/79 Sqn Brawdy
	XR681	Hunting Jet Provost T4 (8588M) (nose only)	RAF Exhibition Flight, Abingdon
	XR700	Hunting Jet Provost T4 (8589M) (nose only)	RAF Exhibition Flight, Aldergrove
	XR701	Hunting Jet Provost T4 [K]	RAF CATCS, Shawbury
	XR704	Hunting Jet Provost T4 (8506M) [30]	RAF No 1 SoTT, Halton
	XR713	EE Lightning F3 [DD]	RAF LTF, Binbrook
	XR716	EE Lightning F3 [AS]	RAF Binbrook store
	XR717	EE Lightning F3	A&AEE Boscombe Down Fire Section
	XR718	EE Lightning F3	RAF LTF, Binbrook
	XR720	EE Lightning F3 [DA]	RAF Binbrook store
	XR724	EE Lightning F6	RAF Binbrook store
	XR725	EE Lightning F6 [BA]	RAF No 11 Sqn, Binbrook
	XR726	EE Lightning F6 [BE]	RAF No 11 Sqn, Binbrook

Serial	Type (alternative identity)	Owner, Operator or Location	Notes
XR727	EE Lightning F6 [AB]	RAF No 5 Sqn, Binbrook	
XR728	EE Lightning F6 [BF]	RAF No 11 Sqn, Binbrook	
XR747	EE Lightning F6 [AL]	RAF No 5 Sqn, Binbrook	
XR749	EE Lightning F3 [DA]	RAF LTF, Binbrook	
XR751	EE Lightning F3	RAF Binbrook store	
XR752	EE Lightning F6 [BL]	RAF No 11 Sqn, Binbrook	
XR753	EE Lightning F6 [AC]	RAF No 5 Sqn, Binbrook	
XR754	EE Lightning F6 [AE]	RAF No 5 Sqn, Binbrook	
XR755	EE Lightning F6	RAF Binbrook store	
XR756	EE Lightning F6 [BH]	RAF No 11 Sqn, Binbrook	
XR757	EE Lightning F6 [BA]	RAF Binbrook store	
XR758	EE Lightning F6 [AH]	RAF No 5 Sqn, Binbrook	
XR759	EE Lightning F6 [BJ]	RAF No 11 Sqn, Binbrook	
XR760	EE Lightning F6 [BD]	RAF Binbrook store	
XR763	EE Lightning F6 [AN]	RAF No 5 Sqn, Binbrook	
XR769	EE Lightning F6 [BG]	RAF No 11 Sqn, Binbrook	
XR770	EE Lightning F6 [AJ]	RAF No 5 Sqn, Binbrook	
XR771	EE Lightning F6 [BA]	RAF Binbrook store	
XR773	EE Lightning F6 [DF]	RAF Binbrook store	
XR777	Westland Scout AH1 (really XT625)	St George's Barracks, Sutton Coldfield	
XR806	BAC VC10 C1	RAF No 10 Sqn, Brize Norton	
XR807	BAC VC10 C1	RAF No 10 Sqn, Brize Norton	
XR808	BAC VC10 C1	RAF No 10 Sqn, Brize Norton	
XR810	BAC VC10 C1	RAF No 10 Sqn, Brize Norton	
XR951	HS Gnat T1 (8603M) [26]	RAF No 1 SoTT, Halton	
XR953	HS Gnat T1 (8609M) [63]	RAF No 1 SoTT, Halton	
XR954	HS Gnat T1 (8570M) [30]	RAF No 1 SoTT, Halton	
XR955	HS Gnat T1 (A2678) [SAH-2]	RNAS Culdrose, SAH	
XR977	HS Gnat T1 (8640M)	RAF Cosford Aerospace Museum	
XR980	HS Gnat T1 (8622M) [70]	RAF No 1 SoTT, Halton	
XR984	HS Gnat T1 (8571M)	RAF No 1 SoTT, Halton	
XR987	HS Gnat T1 (8641M) [10]	RAF No 2 SoTT, Cosford	
XR991	HS Gnat T1 (8637M/ A2709)	RNAS Culdrose, SAH	
XR993	HS Gnat T1 (A2677) [SAH-4]	RNAS Culdrose, SAH	
XR998	HS Gnat T1 (8623M) [71]	RAF No 1 SoTT, Halton	
XS100	HS Gnat T1 (8561M) [57]	RAF No 1 SoTT, Halton	
XS101	HS Gnat T1 (8638M) (G-GNAT)	Privately owned, Cranfield	
XS102	HS Gnat T1 (8624M) [66]	RAF No 1 SoTT, Halton	
XS104	HS Gnat T1 (8604M) [44]	RAF No 2 SoTT, Cosford	
XS105	HS Gnat T1 (8625M) [35]	RAF No 2 SoTT, Cosford	
XS107	HS Gnat T1 (8639M)	RAF No 2 SoTT, Cosford	
XS109	HS Gnat T1 (8626M) [75]	RAF No 1 SoTT, Halton	
XS110	HS Gnat T1 (8562M) [20]	RAF No 1 SoTT, Halton	
XS119	Westland Wessex HAS3 [655/PO]	RN AES Lee-on-Solent	
XS120	Westland Wessex HAS1 (8653M) [520/CU]	RAF Abingdon Fire Section	
XS122	Westland Wessex HAS3 (A2707) [655/PO]	RNEC Manadon, for instruction	
XS125	Westland Wessex HAS1 (A2648) [517/PO]	RNAS Yeovilton Fire Section	
XS127	Westland Wessex HAS3	RN Predannack Fire Section	
XS128	Westland Wessex HAS1 (A2670) [437/PO]	RN AES Lee-on-Solent	
XS149	Westland Wessex HAS3 [661/GL]	RN store, Wroughton	
XS150	Westland Wessex HAS1 [593/CU]	RN AES Lee-on-Solent	
XS153	Westland Wessex HAS3 [662/PO]	RN AES Lee-on-Solent	
XS176	Hunting Jet Provost T4 (8514M) [N]	RAF No 1 SoTT, Halton	
XS177	Hunting Jet Provost T4 [N]	RAF CATCS, Shawbury	
XS178	Hunting Jet Provost T4 [05]	RAF No 1 TWU/79 Sqn, Brawdy	
XS179	Hunting Jet Provost T4 (8237M) [20]	RAF No 1 SoTT, Halton	
XS180	Hunting Jet Provost T4 (8238M) [21]	RAF No 1 SoTT, Halton	
XS181	Hunting Jet Provost T4 [F]	RAF CATCS, Shawbury	

Notes	Serial	Type (alternative identity)	Owner, Operator or Location
	XS186	Hunting Jet Provost T4 (8408M) [M]	RAF No 1 SoTT, Halton
	XS209	Hunting Jet Provost T4 (8409M) [29]	RAF No 1 SoTT, Halton
	XS210	Hunting Jet Provost T4 (8239M) [22]	RAF No 1 SoTT, Halton
	XS215	Hunting Jet Provost T4 (8507M) [17]	RAF No 1 SoTT, Halton
	XS216	Hunting Jet Provost T4 [Q]	RAF Finningley, for rescue training
	XS217	Hunting Jet Provost T4 [O]	RAF CATCS, Shawbury
	XS218	Hunting Jet Provost T4 (8508M) [18]	RAF No 1 SoTT, Halton
	XS219	Hunting Jet Provost T4 [06]	RAF No 1 TWU/79 Sqn, Brawdy
	XS230	BAC Jet Provost T5P	MoD(PE) ETPS Boscombe Down
	XS231	BAC Jet Provost T5 (G-ATAJ)	RAF Shawbury store
	XS235	HS Comet 4C	MoD(PE) A&AEE Boscombe Down
	XS241	Westland Wessex HU5	MoD(PE) RAE Farnborough
	XS416	EE Lightning T5 [AZ]	RAF No 5 Sqn, Binbrook
	XS417	EE Lightning T5 [DZ]	RAF LTF, Binbrook
	XS418	EE Lightning T5 (8531M)	RAF Binbrook
	XS419	EE Lightning T5 [DV]	RAF LTF, Binbrook
	XS420	EE Lightning T5 [DU]	RAF Binbrook store
	XS422	EE Lightning T5	MoD(PE) ETPS Boscombe Down
	XS423	EE Lightning T5 (8532M)	RAF Binbrook
	XS449	EE Lightning T5 (8533M)	RAF Binbrook
	XS450	EE Lightning T5 (8534M) [X]	RAF Binbrook Fire Section
	XS451	EE Lightning T5 (8503M)	RAF Newton, for ground instruction
	XS452	EE Lightning T5 [BT]	RAF No 11 Sqn, Binbrook
	XS454	EE Lightning T5 (8535M) [Y]	RAF Binbrook
	XS456	EE Lightning T5	RAF Binbrook store
	XS457	EE Lightning T5 [AT]	RAF Binbrook store
	XS458	EE Lightning T5 [DX]	RAF LTF, Binbrook
	XS459	EE Lightning T5 [DW]	RAF LTF, Binbrook
	XS463	Westland Wasp HAS1 (A2647)	RN Predannack Fire School
	XS463	Westland Wasp HAS1 (really XT431)	British Rotorcraft Museum, Weston-super-Mare
	XS479	Westland Wessex HU5 [XF] (8819M)	RAF JATE, Brize Norton
	XS481	Westland Wessex HU5	RN store, Wroughton
	XS482	Westland Wessex HU5 [A-D]	MoD(PE) A&AEE Boscombe Down
	XS483	Westland Wessex HU5 [T]	RN No 845 Sqn, Yeovilton
	XS484	Westland Wessex HU5 [821/CU]	RN No 771 Sqn, Culdrose
	XS485	Westland Wessex HU5C	RAF No 84 Sqn, Akrotiri
	XS486	Westland Wessex HU5 [ZH]	RN NASU, Yeovilton
	XS488	Westland Wessex HU5 [XK]	RN store, Wroughton
	XS489	Westland Wessex HU5 [R]	RN store, Wroughton
	XS491	Westland Wessex HU5 [XM]	RN store, Wroughton
	XS492	Westland Wessex HU5 [623/PO]	RN No 772 Sqn, Portland
	XS493	Westland Wessex HU5 [VE]	RN Exhibition Unit, Fleetlands
	XS496	Westland Wessex HU5 [625/PO]	RN No 772 Sqn, Portland
	XS498	Westland Wessex HU5C	RAF No 84 Sqn, Akrotiri
	XS506	Westland Wessex HU5 [XE]	RN store, Wroughton
	XS507	Westland Wessex HU5 [RN]	RN Presentation Team, No 845 Sqn, Yeovilton
	XS508	Westland Wessex HU5 [ZP]	RN No 707 Sqn, Yeovilton
	XS509	Westland Wessex HU5 (A2597)	MoD(PE) ETPS Boscombe Down
	XS510	Westland Wessex HU5 [626]	RN No 772 Sqn, Portland
	XS511	Westland Wessex HU5 [M]	RN No 845 Sqn, Yeovilton
	XS513	Westland Wessex HU5 [E]	RN No 845 Sqn, Yeovilton
	XS514	Westland Wessex HU5 [L]	RN No 845 Sqn, Yeovilton
	XS515	Westland Wessex HU5 [N]	RN No 845 Sqn, Yeovilton
	XS516	Westland Wessex HU5 [Q]	RN No 845 Sqn, Yeovilton
	XS517	Westland Wessex HU5C	RAF No 84 Sqn, Akrotiri
	XS518	Westland Wessex HU5C	RAF No 84 Sqn, Akrotiri
	XS520	Westland Wessex HU5 [F]	RN No 845 Sqn, Yeovilton
	XS521	Westland Wessex HU5 [B]	RN No 845 Sqn, Ascension Is
	XS522	Westland Wessex HU5 [ZL]	RN store, Wroughton
	XS523	Westland Wessex HU5 [824/CU]	RN No 771 Sqn, Culdrose

Serial	Type (alternative identity)	Owner, Operator or Location	Notes
XS527	Westland Wasp HAS1	RN No 829 Sqn, Portland	
XS529	Westland Wasp HAS1 [461]	RN No 829 Sqn, Portland	
XS535	Westland Wasp HAS1 [500]	RAOC, West Moors, Dorset	
XS537	Westland Wasp HAS1 (A2672) [582]	RN store, Wroughton	
XS538	Westland Wasp HAS1 [451]	RN No 829 Sqn, Portland	
XS539	Westland Wasp HAS1 [435]	RN No 829 Sqn, Portland	
XS541	Westland Wasp HAS1 [602]	RN No 829 Sqn, Portland	
XS545	Westland Wasp HAS1 (A2702) [645]	RNAS Lee-on-Solent, at gate	
XS562	Westland Wasp HAS1 [611]	RN No 829 Sqn, Portland	
XS565	Westland Wasp HAS1 [445]	MoD(PE) RAE Farnborough	
XS566	Westland Wasp HAS1 [607]	RN No 829 Sqn, Portland	
XS567	Westland Wasp HAS1 [434]	RN No 829 Sqn, Portland	
XS568	Westland Wasp HAS1 [441]	RNAY Fleetlands Apprentice School	
XS569	Westland Wasp HAS1	RNAY Fleetlands Apprentice School	
XS570	Westland Wasp HAS1 (A2699) [AP]	—	
XS572	Westland Wasp HAS1 [414]	RN store, Wroughton	
XS576	DH Sea Vixen FAW2 [125/E]	Imperial War Museum, Duxford	
XS577	DH Sea Vixen D3	Flight Refuelling Ltd, Hurn	
XS587	DH Sea Vixen FAW(TT)2 (G-VIXN/8828M)	The Sea Vixen Co, Hurn	
XS590	DH Sea Vixen FAW2 [131/E]	FAA Museum, RNAS Yeovilton	
XS595	HS Andover C1 [A]	RAF Brize Norton Fire Section	
XS596	HS Andover C1	RAF No 115 Sqn, Benson	
XS597	HS Andover C1	RAF No 32 Sqn, Northolt	
XS598	HS Andover C1 [E]	RAF AMS, Brize Norton	
XS603	HS Andover E3	RAF No 115 Sqn, Benson	
XS605	HS Andover E3	RAF No 115 Sqn, Benson	
XS606	HS Andover C1	MoD(PE) ETPS Boscombe Down	
XS607	HS Andover C1	MoD(PE) RAE West Freugh	
XS610	HS Andover E3	RAF No 115 Sqn, Benson	
XS637	HS Andover C1	RAF No 32 Sqn, Northolt	
XS639	HS Andover E3A	RAF No 115 Sqn, Benson	
XS640	HS Andover E3	RAF No 115 Sqn, Benson	
XS641	HS Andover E3A	RAF No 115 Sqn, Benson	
XS642	HS Andover C1 [C] (8785M)	RAF Benson Fire Section	
XS643	HS Andover E3A	RAF No 115 Sqn, Benson	
XS644	HS Andover C1 (Mod)	RAF EWAU, Wyton	
XS646	HS Andover C1	MoD(PE) RAE Farnborough	
XS647	HS Andover C1	British Aerospace, Woodford	
XS650	Slingsby Swallow TX1 (8801M)	RAF St Athan Historic Aircraft Collection	
XS674	Westland Wessex HC2 [R]	RAF No 72 Sqn, Aldergrove	
XS675	Westland Wessex HC2	RAF No 22 Sqn SAR*	
XS676	Westland Wessex HC2 [WJ]	RAF No 2 FTS, Shawbury	
XS677	Westland Wessex HC2 [WK]	RAF No 2 FTS, Shawbury	
XS679	Westland Wessex HC2 [WG]	RAF No 2 FTS, Shawbury	
XS695	HS Kestrel FGA1 (A2619) [SAH-6]	RNAS Culdrose, SAH	
XS709	HS Dominie T1 [M]	RAF No 6 FTS, Finningley	
XS710	HS Dominie T1 [O]	RAF No 6 FTS, Finningley	
XS711	HS Dominie T1 [L]	RAF No 6 FTS, Finningley	
XS712	HS Dominie T1 [A]	RAF No 6 FTS, Finningley	
XS713	HS Dominie T1 [C]	RAF No 6 FTS, Finningley	
XS714	HS Dominie T1 [P]	RAF No 6 FTS, Finningley	
XS726	HS Dominie T1 [T]	RAF No 6 FTS, Finningley	
XS727	HS Dominie T1 [D]	RAF No 6 FTS, Finningley	
XS728	HS Dominie T1 [E]	RAF No 6 FTS, Finningley	
XS729	HS Dominie T1 [G]	RAF No 6 FTS, Finningley	
XS730	HS Dominie T1 [H]	RAF No 6 FTS, Finningley	
XS731	HS Dominie T1 [J]	RAF No 6 FTS, Finningley	
XS732	HS Dominie T1 [B]	RAF No 6 FTS, Finningley	
XS733	HS Dominie T1 [Q]	RAF No 6 FTS, Finningley	
XS734	HS Dominie T1 [N]	RAF No 6 FTS, Finningley	
XS735	HS Dominie T1 [R]	RAF No 6 FTS, Finningley	
XS736	HS Dominie T1 [S]	RAF No 6 FTS, Finningley	
XS737	HS Dominie T1 [K]	RAF No 6 FTS, Finningley	
XS738	HS Dominie T1 [U]	RAF No 6 FTS, Finningley	
XS739	HS Dominie T1 [F]	RAF No 6 FTS, Finningley	
XS743	Beagle Basset CC1	MoD(PE) ETPS Boscombe Down	
XS765	Beagle Basset CC1	MoD(PE) A&AEE Boscombe Down	
XS770	Beagle Basset CC1	MoD(PE) A&AEE Boscombe Down	

Notes	Serial	Type (alternative identity)	Owner, Operator or Location
	XS789	HS Andover CC2	RAF Queen's Flight, Benson
	XS790	HS Andover CC2	RAF Queen's Flight, Benson
	XS791	HS Andover CC2	RAF No 32 Sqn, Northolt
	XS792	HS Andover CC2	RAF No 32 Sqn, Northolt
	XS793	HS Andover CC2	RAF Queen's Flight, Benson
	XS794	HS Andover CC2	RAF No 32 Sqn, Northolt
	XS862	Westland Wessex HAS3 [650/PO]	RNAS Lee-on-Solent, at gate
	XS863	Westland Wessex HAS1	Imperial War Museum, Duxford
	XS865	Westland Wessex HAS1 (A2694) [529/CU]	RN AES Lee-on-Solent
	XS866	Westland Wessex HAS1 (A2705) [520/CU]	RN AES Lee-on-Solent
	XS867	Westland Wessex HAS1 (A2671)	RNAS Lee-on-Solent Fire Section
	XS868	Westland Wessex HAS1 (A2691)	RNAY Fleetlands, on gate
	XS869	Westland Wessex HAS1 (A2649) [508/PO]	RN Air Medical School, Seafield Park, rescue training
	XS870	Westland Wessex HAS1 (A2697) [-/PO]	RN AES Lee-on-Solent
	XS871	Westland Wessex HAS1 (8457M) [AI]	RAF Odiham Fire Section
	XS872	Westland Wessex HAS1 (A2666) [572/CU]	RNAY Fleetlands Apprentice School
	XS873	Westland Wessex HAS1 (A2686) [525/CU]	RN AES Lee-on-Solent
	XS876	Westland Wessex HAS1 (A2695) [523/CU]	RN AES Lee-on-Solent
	XS877	Westland Wessex HAS1 (A2687) [516/PO]	RNAS Culdrose, SAH
	XS878	Westland Wessex HAS1 (A2683)	RN AES Lee-on-Solent
	XS881	Westland Wessex HAS1 (A2675) [046/CU]	Scottish Aircraft Collection Trust, Perth
	XS882	Westland Wessex HAS1 (A2696) [524/CU]	RN AES Lee-on-Solent
	XS885	Westland Wessex HAS1 (A2668) [512/PO]	RNAS Culdrose, SAH
	XS886	Westland Wessex HAS1 (A2685) [527/CU]	RN AES Lee-on-Solent
	XS887	Westland Wessex HAS1 (A2690) [514/PO]	RNAS Culdrose, SAH
	XS888	Westland Wessex HAS1 [521]	RN Exhibition Unit, Fleetlands
	XS895	EE Lightning F6 [BC]	RAF No 11 Sqn, Binbrook
	XS897	EE Lightning F6 [BD]	RAF Binbrook store
	XS898	EE Lightning F6 [AB]	RAF Binbrook store
	XS899	EE Lightning F6 [AJ]	RAF No 5 Sqn, Binbrook
	XS901	EE Lightning F6 [BH]	RAF Binbrook store
	XS903	EE Lightning F6 [AM]	RAF No 5 Sqn, Binbrook
	XS904	EE Lightning F6 [BM]	RAF No 11 Sqn, Binbrook
	XS919	EE Lightning F6 [BN]	RAF No 11 Sqn, Binbrook
	XS922	EE Lightning F6 [AG]	RAF No 5 Sqn, Binbrook
	XS923	EE Lightning F6 [AA]	RAF No 5 Sqn, Binbrook
	XS925	EE Lightning F6 [BD]	RAF No 11 Sqn, Binbrook
	XS927	EE Lightning F6 [BB]	RAF No 11 Sqn, Binbrook
	XS928	EE Lightning F6 [AH]	RAF No 5 Sqn, Binbrook
	XS929	EE Lightning F6 [DG]	RAF LTF, Binbrook
	XS932	EE Lightning F6 [AC]	RAF Binbrook store
	XS933	EE Lightning F6 [BE]	RAF Binbrook store
	XS935	EE Lightning F6 [AK]	RAF No 5 Sqn, Binbrook
	XS936	EE Lightning F6 [AS]	RAF No 5 Sqn, Binbrook
	XT108	Agusta-Bell Sioux AH1 [U]	Museum of Army Flying, Middle Wallop
	XT131	Agusta-Bell Sioux AH1 [B]	AAC Historic Aircraft Flight, Middle Wallop
	XT133	Agusta-Bell Sioux AH1 (7923M)	Royal Engineers' Museum, Chatham
	XT140	Agusta-Bell Sioux AH1	Air Service Training, Perth
	XT141	Agusta-Bell Sioux AH1 (8509M)	RAF AMS, Brize Norton
	XT150	Agusta-Bell Sioux AH1 (7883M) [R]	Wessex Aviation Society, Wimborne

Serial	Type (alternative identity)	Owner, Operator or Location	Notes
XT151	Westland Sioux AH1	Royal Military College of Science, Shrivenham	
XT175	Westland Sioux AH1 (TAD175)	CSE Oxford for ground instruction	
XT176	Westland Sioux AH1 [C]	FAA Museum, RNAS Yeovilton	
XT190	Westland Sioux AH1	Museum of Army Flying, Middle Wallop	
XT199	Westland Sioux AH1 [C]	Privately owned, Fairoaks	
XT200	Westland Sioux AH1 [F]	Newark Air Museum, Winthorpe	
XT236	Westland Sioux AH1	Museum of Army Flying, Middle Wallop	
XT242	Westland Sioux AH1 (really XW179)	Wessex Aviation Society, Wimborne	
XT248	Westland Sioux AH1 (G-BKNF)	Privately owned, Cranfield	
XT255	Westland Wessex HAS3 (8751M)	RAF No 14 MU, Carlisle	
XT256	Westland Wessex HAS3 (A2615)	RN AES Lee-on-Solent	
XT257	Westland Wessex HAS3 (8719M)	RAF No 1 SoTT, Halton	
XT270	HS Buccaneer S2B [C]	RAF Shawbury store	
XT271	HS Buccaneer S2A [C]	RAF store, St Athan	
XT272	HS Buccaneer S2	MoD(PE) RAE Bedford	
XT273	HS Buccaneer S2A [D]	RAF store, St Athan	
XT274	HS Buccaneer S2A (8856M) [E]	RAF Abingdon, BDRF	
XT275	HS Buccaneer S2B [B]	RAF Shawbury store	
XT276	HS Buccaneer S2B [S]	RAF Shawbury store	
XT277	HS Buccaneer S2A (8853M)	RAF No 2 SoTT, Cosford	
XT279	HS Buccaneer S2B [C]	RAF store, St Athan	
XT280	HS Buccaneer S2B [NS]	RAF No 208 Sqn, Lossiemouth	
XT281	HS Buccaneer S2B (8705M) [ET]	RAF Lossiemouth, ground instruction	
XT283	HS Buccaneer S2A [GC]	RAF No 237 OCU, Lossiemouth	
XT284	HS Buccaneer S2A (8855M) [H]	RAF Abingdon, BDRF	
XT286	HS Buccaneer S2B [W]	RAF store, St Athan	
XT287	HS Buccaneer S2B	RAF No 208 Sqn, Lossiemouth	
XT288	HS Buccaneer S2B	MoD(PE) A&AEE Boscombe Down	
XT415	Westland Wasp HAS1 [FIR3]	RN No 829 Sqn, Portland	
XT416	Westland Wasp HAS1 [442]	RNAY Fleetlands	
XT420	Westland Wasp HAS1 [604]	RN No 829 Sqn, Portland	
XT421	Westland Wasp HAS1 [433]	RN No 829 Sqn, Portland	
XT422	Westland Wasp HAS1 [326]	RN store, Wroughton	
XT423	Westland Wasp HAS1 [434]	RN No 829 Sqn, Portland	
XT426	Westland Wasp HAS1 [455]	RN No 829 Sqn, Portland	
XT427	Westland Wasp HAS1 [606]	FAA Museum, RNAS Yeovilton	
XT429	Westland Wasp HAS1 [445]	RN No 829 Sqn, Portland	
XT430	Westland Wasp HAS1 [444]	Defence School, Winterbourne Gunner	
XT431	Westland Wasp HAS1	RN No 829 Sqn, Portland	
XT432	Westland Wasp HAS1 [415]	RN No 829 Sqn, Portland	
XT434	Westland Wasp HAS1 [600]	RN No 829 Sqn, Portland	
XT437	Westland Wasp HAS1 [426]	RN No 829 Sqn, Portland	
XT439	Westland Wasp HAS1 [605]	RN No 829 Sqn, Portland	
XT441	Westland Wasp HAS1 (A2703) [337]	RN Wroughton Fire Section	
XT443	Westland Wasp HAS1 [422]	RN No 829 Sqn, Portland	
XT449	Westland Wessex HU5 [C]	RN No 845 Sqn, Yeovilton	
XT450	Westland Wessex HU5 [V]	RN Predannack Fire Section	
XT451	Westland Wessex HU5 [XN]	RN store, Wroughton	
XT453	Westland Wessex HU5 [A]	RN No 845 Sqn, Yeovilton	
XT455	Westland Wessex HU5 [U]	RN No 845 Sqn, Yeovilton	
XT456	Westland Wessex HU5 [XZ]	RN store, Wroughton	
XT458	Westland Wessex HU5 [622/PO]	RN No 772 Sqn, Portland	
XT459	Westland Wessex HU5 [D]	RNAS Lee-on-Solent Fire Section	
XT460	Westland Wessex HU5 [K]	RN No 845 Sqn, Yeovilton	
XT461	Westland Wessex HU5 [W]	RN No 845 Sqn, Yeovilton	
XT463	Westland Wessex HU5C	RAF No 84 Sqn, Akrotiri	
XT466	Westland Wessex HU5 [XV]	RN store, Wroughton	
XT467	Westland Wessex HU5	RN store, Wroughton	
XT468	Westland Wessex HU5 [628]	RN No 772 Sqn, Portland	
XT469	Westland Wessex HU5 [XN]	RN store, Wroughton	
XT470	Westland Wessex HU5 [A]	AAC Netheravon, Fire Section	

Notes	Serial	Type (alternative identity)	Owner, Operator or Location
	XT471	Westland Wessex HU5 [826]	RN No 771 Sqn, Culdrose
	XT472	Westland Wessex HU5 [X-C]	RAF Hullavington for instruction
	XT474	Westland Wessex HU5 [820/CU]	RN No 771 Sqn, Culdrose
	XT475	Westland Wessex HU5 [624/PO]	RN No 772 Sqn, Portland
	XT479	Westland Wessex HU5C	RAF No 84 Sqn, Akrotiri
	XT480	Westland Wessex HU5 [XQ]	RN store, Wroughton
	XT481	Westland Wessex HU5 [XF]	RN store, Wroughton
	XT482	Westland Wessex HU5 [ZM]	RN store, Wroughton
	XT484	Westland Wessex HU5 [H]	RN No 845 Sqn, Yeovilton
	XT485	Westland Wessex HU5 [621/PO]	RN No 772 Sqn, Portland
	XT486	Westland Wessex HU5 [XR]	RN store, Wroughton
	XT487	Westland Wessex HU5 (A2723) [815/LS]	RN AES Lee-on-Solent
	XT548	Westland Sioux AH1 [D]	AAC Middle Wallop
	XT550	Westland Sioux AH1 [D]	Museum of Army Flying, Middle Wallop
	XT567	Westland Sioux AH1	Privately owned, Fairoaks
	XT575	Vickers Viscount (OE-LAG)	MoD(PE) RS&RE Bedford
	XT595	McD Phantom FG1 (fuselage etc) (8851M)	RAF St Athan, BDRT
	XT595	McD Phantom FG1 (nose only) (8550M)	RAF Exhibition Flight, Abingdon
	XT596	McD Phantom FG1	MoD(PE) BAe Scampton
	XT597	McD Phantom FG1	MoD(PE) A&AEE Boscombe Down
	XT601	Westland Wessex HC2	RAF No 22 Sqn SAR*
	XT602	Westland Wessex HC2	RAF No 22 Sqn SAR*
	XT603	Westland Wessex HC2 [WF]	RAF No 2 FTS, Shawbury
	XT604	Westland Wessex HC2	RAF No 22 Sqn SAR*
	XT605	Westland Wessex HC2 [E]	RAF No 28 Sqn, Sek Kong
	XT606	Westland Wessex HC2	RAF No 22 Sqn SAR*
	XT607	Westland Wessex HC2 [P]	RAF No 72 Sqn, Aldergrove
	XT614	Westland Scout AH1 [G]	AAC No 660 Sqn, Sek Kong
	XT616	Westland Scout AH1 [W]	AAC store, Wroughton
	XT617	Westland Scout AH1	AAC store, Wroughton
	XT618	Westland Scout AH1 [K]	AAC No 660 Sqn, Sek Kong
	XT620	Westland Scout AH1 [B]	AAC store, Wroughton
	XT621	Westland Scout AH1	AAC store, Wroughton
	XT623	Westland Scout AH1	AAC store, Wroughton
	XT624	Westland Scout AH1 [W]	AAC ATS, Middle Wallop
	XT626	Westland Scout AH1	AAC store, Wroughton
	XT627	Westland Scout AH1 [H]	AAC No 660 Sqn, Sek Kong
	XT628	Westland Scout AH1 [J]	AAC No 660 Sqn, Sek Kong
	XT630	Westland Scout AH1 [F]	AAC store, Wroughton
	XT631	Westland Scout AH1 [D]	MoD(PE) A&AEE Boscombe Down
	XT632	Westland Scout AH1	AAC Garrison Air Sqn, Falklands
	XT633	Westland Scout AH1	AAC store, Wroughton
	XT634	Westland Scout AH1	AAC store, Wroughton
	XT636	Westland Scout AH1 [X]	AAC ATS, Middle Wallop
	XT637	Westland Scout AH1	AAC store, Wroughton
	XT638	Westland Scout AH1	AAC store, Wroughton
	XT639	Westland Scout AH1 [Y]	AAC store, Wroughton
	XT640	Westland Scout AH1	AAC AETW, Middle Wallop
	XT642	Westland Scout AH1 [W]	AAC No 656 Sqn, Netheravon
	XT643	Westland Scout AH1	AAC No 660 Sqn, Sek Kong
	XT644	Westland Scout AH1	AAC store, Wroughton
	XT645	Westland Scout AH1	AAC No 656 Sqn, Netheravon
	XT646	Westland Scout AH1	AAC store, Wroughton
	XT648	Westland Scout AH1	AAC store, Wroughton
	XT649	Westland Scout AH1	AAC store, Wroughton
	XT657	BHC SR.N6 Winchester 5	British Hovercraft Corpn
	XT661	Vickers Viscount (9G-AAV)	MoD(PE) RS&RE Bedford
	XT667	Westland Wessex HC2 [F]	RAF No 28 Sqn, Sek Kong
	XT668	Westland Wessex HC2 [S]	RAF No 72 Sqn, Aldergrove
	XT669	Westland Wessex HC2 [T]	RAF Aldergrove Fire Section
	XT670	Westland Wessex HC2	RAF No 22 Sqn SAR*
	XT671	Westland Wessex HC2 [D]	RAF No 72 Sqn, Aldergrove
	XT672	Westland Wessex HC2 [WE]	RAF No 2 FTS, Shawbury
	XT673	Westland Wessex HC2 [G]	RAF No 28 Sqn, Sek Kong
	XT674	Westland Wessex HC2	RAF No 22 Sqn SAR*
	XT675	Westland Wessex HC2	RAF No 28 Sqn, Sek Kong
	XT676	Westland Wessex HC2 [I]	RAF No 72 Sqn, Aldergrove
	XT678	Westland Wessex HC2 [H]	RAF No 28 Sqn, Sek Kong
	XT680	Westland Wessex HC2	RAF No 22 Sqn SAR*

Serial	Type (alternative identity)	Owner, Operator or Location	Notes
XT681	Westland Wessex HC2 [U]	RAF No 72 Sqn, Aldergrove	
XT752	Fairey Gannet T5 [-/LM] (G-APYO/WN365)	RNAS Lee-on-Solent	
XT755	Westland Wessex HU5 [V]	RN store, Wroughton	
XT756	Westland Wessex HU5 [ZJ]	RN store, Wroughton	
XT757	Westland Wessex HU5 [XH] (A2722)	RN AES Lee-on-Solent	
XT759	Westland Wessex HU5 [XY]	RN store, Wroughton	
XT760	Westland Wessex HU5	RN NASU, Yeovilton	
XT761	Westland Wessex HU5 [P]	RN NASU, Yeovilton	
XT762	Westland Wessex HU5	MoD(PE) RS&RE Bedford	
XT764	Westland Wessex HU5 [G]	RN store, Wroughton	
XT765	Westland Wessex HU5 [J]	RN No 845 Sqn, Yeovilton	
XT766	Westland Wessex HU5 [822/CU]	RN No 771 Sqn, Culdrose	
XT768	Westland Wessex HU5	RN store, Wroughton	
XT769	Westland Wessex HU5 [823/CU]	RN No 771 Sqn, Culdrose	
XT770	Westland Wessex HU5 [P]	RN store, Wroughton	
XT771	Westland Wessex HU5 [620/PO]	RN No 772 Sqn, Portland	
XT772	Westland Wessex HU5 (8805M)	RAF SARTF, Valley	
XT773	Westland Wessex HU5	RN NASU, Yeovilton	
XT778	Westland Wasp HAS1 [430]	RN No 829 Sqn, Portland	
XT779	Westland Wasp HAS1 [456]	RN No 829 Sqn, Portland	
XT780	Westland Wasp HAS1 [636]	RNAY Fleetlands Apprentice School	
XT782	Westland Wasp HAS1 [324]	RN No 829 Sqn, Portland	
XT783	Westland Wasp HAS1 [470]	RN No 829 Sqn, Portland	
XT784	Westland Wasp HAS1 [FIR1]	RN No 829 Sqn, Portland	
XT785	Westland Wasp HAS1 [462]	RN No 829 Sqn, Portland	
XT786	Westland Wasp HAS1 [441]	RN store, Wroughton	
XT788	Westland Wasp HAS1 [442]	RN store, Wroughton	
XT790	Westland Wasp HAS1 [603]	RN No 829 Sqn, Portland	
XT791	Westland Wasp HAS1 [433]	RN No 829 Sqn, Portland	
XT793	Westland Wasp HAS1 [440]	RN No 829 Sqn, Portland	
XT795	Westland Wasp HAS1 [476]	RN No 829 Sqn, Portland	
XT803	Westland Sioux AH1 [Y]	Privately owned, Panshanger	
XT827	Westland Sioux AH1 [D]	Army Apprentice College, Arborfield	
XT847	Westland Sioux AH1	Privately owned, Fairoaks	
XT852	McD Phantom FGR2	MoD(PE) BAe Scampton	
XT853	McD Phantom FGR2	MoD(PE) BAe Scampton	
XT857	McD Phantom FG1 [C]	RAF No 111 Sqn, Leuchars	
XT858	McD Phantom FG1	MoD(PE) BAe Brough (structures test)	
XT859	McD Phantom FG1 [K]	RAF No 111 Sqn, Leuchars	
XT860	McD Phantom FG1 [L]	RAF No 43 Sqn, Leuchars	
XT861	McD Phantom FG1 [C]	RAF No 43 Sqn, Leuchars	
XT863	McD Phantom FG1 [G]	RAF No 111 Sqn, Leuchars	
XT864	McD Phantom FG1 [J]	RAF No 111 Sqn, Leuchars	
XT865	McD Phantom FG1 [U]	RAF No 111 Sqn, Leuchars	
XT867	McD Phantom FG1 [H]	RAF No 111 Sqn, Leuchars	
XT870	McD Phantom FG1 [S]	RAF No 111 Sqn, Leuchars	
XT872	McD Phantom FG1 [T]	RAF No 111 Sqn, Leuchars	
XT873	McD Phantom FG1 [A]	RAF No 111 Sqn, Leuchars	
XT874	McD Phantom FG1 [E]	RAF No 111 Sqn, Leuchars	
XT875	McD Phantom FG1 [K]	RAF No 43 Sqn, Leuchars	
XT891	McD Phantom FGR2 [Z]	RAF No 228 OCU, Coningsby	
XT892	McD Phantom FGR2 [V]	RAF No 228 OCU, Coningsby	
XT893	McD Phantom FGR2 [Q]	RAF No 228 OCU, Coningsby	
XT894	McD Phantom FGR2 [P]	RAF No 228 OCU, Coningsby	
XT895	McD Phantom FGR2 [H]	RAF No 228 OCU, Coningsby	
XT896	McD Phantom FGR2 [Y]	RAF No 228 OCU, Coningsby	
XT897	McD Phantom FGR2 [M]	RAF No 228 OCU, Coningsby	
XT898	McD Phantom FGR2 [E]	RAF No 228 OCU, Coningsby	
XT899	McD Phantom FGR2 [K]	RAF No 19 Sqn, Wildenrath	
XT900	McD Phantom FGR2 [O]	RAF No 228 OCU, Coningsby	
XT901	McD Phantom FGR2 [Y]	RAF No 56 Sqn, Wattisham	
XT902	McD Phantom FGR2 [M]	RAF No 29 Sqn, Coningsby	
XT903	McD Phantom FGR2 [R]	RAF No 228 OCU, Coningbsy	
XT905	McD Phantom FGR2 [U]	RAF No 228 OCU, Coningsby	
XT906	McD Phantom FGR2 [X]	RAF No 56 Sqn, Wattisham	
XT907	McD Phantom FGR2 [T]	RAF No 228 OCU, Coningsby	
XT908	McD Phantom FGR2 [T]	RAF No 92 Sqn, Wildenrath	
XT909	McD Phantom FGR2 [T]	RAF No 29 Sqn, Coningsby	

Notes	Serial	Type (alternative identity)	Owner, Operator or Location
	XT910	McD Phantom FGR2 [Z]	RAF No 56 Sqn, Wattisham
	XT911	McD Phantom FGR2 [K]	RAF No 92 Sqn, Wildenrath
	XT914	McD Phantom FGR2 [N]	RAF No 228 OCU, Coningsby
	XV101	BAC VC10 C1	RAF No 10 Sqn, Brize Norton
	XV102	BAC VC10 C1	RAF No 10 Sqn, Brize Norton
	XV103	BAC VC10 C1	RAF No 10 Sqn, Brize Norton
	XV104	BAC VC10 C1	RAF No 10 Sqn, Brize Norton
	XV105	BAC VC10 C1	RAF No 10 Sqn, Brize Norton
	XV106	BAC VC10 C1	RAF No 10 Sqn, Brize Norton
	XV107	BAC VC10 C1	RAF No 10 Sqn, Brize Norton
	XV108	BAC VC10 C1	RAF No 10 Sqn, Brize Norton
	XV109	BAC VC10 C1	RAF No 10 Sqn, Brize Norton
	XV118	Westland Scout AH1	AAC store, Wroughton
	XV119	Westland Scout AH1	AAC store, Wroughton
	XV121	Westland Scout AH1	AAC No 658 Sqn, Netheravon
	XV122	Westland Scout AH1 [A]	AAC No 660 Sqn, Sek Kong
	XV123	Westland Scout AH1	AAC store, Wroughton
	XV124	Westland Scout AH1	AAC store, Wroughton
	XV126	Westland Scout AH1	AAC store, Wroughton
	XV127	Westland Scout AH1	AAC store, Wroughton
	XV128	Westland Scout AH1	AAC D&TS, Middle Wallop
	XV129	Westland Scout AH1	AAC store, Wroughton
	XV130	Westland Scout AH1	AAC store, Wroughton
	XV131	Westland Scout AH1 [X]	AAC No 660 Sqn, Brunei
	XV134	Westland Scout AH1	AAC No 658 Sqn, Netheravon
	XV135	Westland Scout AH1	AAC store, Wroughton
	XV136	Westland Scout AH1	AAC store, Wroughton
	XV137	Westland Scout AH1 [Z]	AAC No 658 Sqn, Netheravon
	XV138	Westland Scout AH1	AAC No 658 Sqn, Netheravon
	XV139	Westland Scout AH1	AAC store, Wroughton
	XV140	Westland Scout AH1	AAC No 656 Sqn, Netheravon
	XV141	Westland Scout AH1	Army Apprentice College, Arborfield
	XV147	HS Nimrod MR1 (Mod)	MoD(PE) RAE Farnborough
	XV148	HS Nimrod MR1 (Mod)	MoD(PE) BAe Woodford
	XV152	HS Buccaneer S2A (8776M) [A]	RAF CSDE, Swanton Morley
	XV154	HS Buccaneer S2A (8854M) [A]	RAF Wattisham, BDRT
	XV155	HS Buccaneer S2B (8716M)	BAe Brough
	XV156	HS Buccaneer S2A (8773M)	RAF St Athan Fire Section
	XV157	HS Buccaneer S2B	RAF Shawbury store
	XV161	HS Buccaneer S2B [AF]	RAF No 12 Sqn, Lossiemouth
	XV163	HS Buccaneer S2A [B]	RAF St Athan store
	XV165	HS Buccaneer S2B [BF]	RAF No 12 Sqn, Lossiemouth
	XV168	HS Buccaneer S2B [VS]	RAF No 208 Sqn, Lossiemouth
	XV176	Lockheed Hercules C3	RAF Lyneham Transport Wing
	XV177	Lockheed Hercules C3	RAF Lyneham Transport Wing
	XV178	Lockheed Hercules C1	RAF Lyneham Transport Wing
	XV179	Lockheed Hercules C1P	RAF Lyneham Transport Wing
	XV181	Lockheed Hercules C1	RAF Lyneham Transport Wing
	XV182	Lockheed Hercules C1	RAF Lyneham Transport Wing
	XV183	Lockheed Hercules C3	RAF Lyneham Transport Wing
	XV184	Lockheed Hercules C3	RAF Lyneham Transport Wing
	XV185	Lockheed Hercules C1P	RAF Lyneham Transport Wing
	XV186	Lockheed Hercules C1	RAF Lyneham Transport Wing
	XV187	Lockheed Hercules C1P	RAF Lyneham Transport Wing
	XV188	Lockheed Hercules C3	RAF Lyneham Transport Wing
	XV189	Lockheed Hercules C3	RAF Lyneham Transport Wing
	XV190	Lockheed Hercules C3	RAF Lyneham Transport Wing
	XV191	Lockheed Hercules C1P	RAF Lyneham Transport Wing
	XV192	Lockheed Hercules C1K	RAF Lyneham Transport Wing
	XV193	Lockheed Hercules C3	RAF Lyneham Transport Wing
	XV195	Lockheed Hercules C1P	RAF Lyneham Transport Wing
	XV196	Lockheed Hercules C1P	RAF Lyneham Transport Wing
	XV197	Lockheed Hercules C3	RAF Lyneham Transport Wing
	XV199	Lockheed Hercules C3	RAF Lyneham Transport Wing
	XV200	Lockheed Hercules C1P	RAF Lyneham Transport Wing
	XV201	Lockheed Hercules C1K	RAF Lyneham Transport Wing/ 1312 Flt, Stanley
	XV202	Lockheed Hercules C3	RAF Lyneham Transport Wing
	XV203	Lockheed Hercules C1K	RAF Lyneham Transport Wing
	XV204	Lockheed Hercules C1K	RAF Lyneham Transport Wing/ 1312 Flt, Stanley
	XV205	Lockheed Hercules C1P	RAF Lyneham Transport Wing/ 1312 Flt, Stanley

Serial	Type (alternative identity)	Owner, Operator or Location	Notes
XV206	Lockheed Hercules C1P	RAF Lyneham Transport Wing	
XV207	Lockheed Hercules C3	RAF Lyneham Transport Wing	
XV208	Lockheed Hercules W2	MoD(PE) RAE Farnborough	
XV209	Lockheed Hercules C3	RAF Lyneham Transport Wing	
XV210	Lockheed Hercules C1P	MoD(PE) A&AEE Boscombe Down	
XV211	Lockheed Hercules C1P	RAF Lyneham Transport Wing	
XV212	Lockheed Hercules C3	RAF Lyneham Transport Wing	
XV213	Lockheed Hercules C1K	RAF Lyneham Transport Wing	
XV214	Lockheed Hercules C3	RAF Lyneham Transport Wing	
XV215	Lockheed Hercules C1	RAF Lyneham Transport Wing	
XV217	Lockheed Hercules C3	RAF Lyneham Transport Wing	
XV218	Lockheed Hercules C1P	RAF Lyneham Transport Wing	
XV219	Lockheed Hercules C3	RAF Lyneham Transport Wing	
XV220	Lockheed Hercules C3	RAF Lyneham Transport Wing	
XV221	Lockheed Hercules C3	RAF Lyneham Transport Wing	
XV222	Lockheed Hercules C3	RAF Lyneham Transport Wing	
XV223	Lockheed Hercules C3	RAF Lyneham Transport Wing	
XV226	HS Nimrod MR1	RAF No 42 Sqn, St Mawgan	
XV227	HS Nimrod MR2P	RAF Kinloss MR Wing	
XV228	HS Nimrod ER2P	RAF Kinloss MR Wing	
XV229	HS Nimrod MR2	RAF No 42 Sqn, St Mawgan	
XV230	HS Nimrod MR2P	RAF Kinloss MR Wing	
XV231	HS Nimrod MR2	RAF No 42 Sqn, St Mawgan	
XV232	HS Nimrod MR2P	RAF Kinloss MR Wing	
XV233	HS Nimrod MR2	RAF No 42 Sqn, St Mawgan	
XV234	HS Nimrod MR2P	RAF Kinloss MR Wing	
XV235	HS Nimrod MR2	RAF No 42 Sqn, St Mawgan	
XV236	HS Nimrod MR2P	RAF No 42 Sqn, St Mawgan	
XV237	HS Nimrod MR2P	RAF Kinloss MR Wing	
XV238	HS Nimrod MR2P	RAF Kinloss MR Wing	
XV239	HS Nimrod MR2P	RAF Kinloss MR Wing	
XV240	HS Nimrod MR2	RAF Kinloss MR Wing	
XV241	HS Nimrod MR2	MoD(PE) A&AEE Boscombe Down	
XV242	HS Nimrod MR2	RAF No 42 Sqn, St Mawgan	
XV243	HS Nimrod MR2P	RAF No 42 Sqn, St Mawgan	
XV244	HS Nimrod MR2	RAF Kinloss MR Wing	
XV245	HS Nimrod MR2	MoD(PE) BAe Woodford	
XV246	HS Nimrod MR2	RAF Kinloss MR Wing	
XV247	HS Nimrod MR2P	RAF Kinloss MR Wing	
XV248	HS Nimrod MR2P	RAF Kinloss MR Wing	
XV249	HS Nimrod MR2	RAF Kinloss MR Wing	
XV250	HS Nimrod MR2	RAF No 42 Sqn, St Mawgan	
XV251	HS Nimrod MR2	MoD(PE) BAe Woodford	
XV252	HS Nimrod MR2	RAF Kinloss MR Wing	
XV253	HS Nimrod MR2P	RAF Kinloss MR Wing	
XV254	HS Nimrod MR2P	RAF Kinloss MR Wing	
XV255	HS Nimrod MR2P	RAF Kinloss MR Wing	
XV257	HS Nimrod MR2	RAF St Mawgan on rebuild	
XV258	HS Nimrod MR2	RAF Kinloss MR Wing	
XV259	BAe Nimrod AEW3	MoD(PE) BAe Woodford	
XV260	HS Nimrod MR2P	RAF Kinloss MR Wing	
XV261	BAe Nimrod AEW3	MoD(PE) BAe Woodford	
XV262	BAe Nimrod AEW3	MoD(PE) BAe Woodford	
XV263	BAe Nimrod AEW3	MoD(PE) BAe Woodford	
XV268	DHC Beaver AL1	AAC Beaver Training Flight, Middle Wallop	
XV269	DHC Beaver AL1 (8011M)	AAC AETW, Middle Wallop	
XV270	DHC Beaver AL1	AAC, Aldergrove	
XV271	DHC Beaver AL1	AAC, Aldergrove	
XV272	DHC Beaver AL1	AAC Shawbury store	
XV277	HS Harrier GR1	MoD(PE) Rolls-Royce, Filton	
XV281	HS Harrier GR1 [B]	MoD(PE) RAE Farnborough	
XV290	Lockheed Hercules C3	RAF Lyneham Transport Wing	
XV291	Lockheed Hercules C1P	RAF Lyneham Transport Wing	
XV292	Lockheed Hercules C1P	RAF Lyneham Transport Wing	
XV293	Lockheed Hercules C1	RAF Lyneham Transport Wing	
XV294	Lockheed Hercules C3	RAF Lyneham Transport Wing	
XV295	Lockheed Hercules C1	RAF Lyneham Transport Wing	
XV296	Lockheed Hercules C1K	RAF Lyneham Transport Wing	
XV297	Lockheed Hercules C1	RAF Lyneham Transport Wing	
XV298	Lockheed Hercules C1P	RAF Lyneham Transport Wing	
XV299	Lockheed Hercules C3	RAF Lyneham Transport Wing	
XV300	Lockheed Hercules C1P	RAF Lyneham Transport Wing	
XV301	Lockheed Hercules C3	RAF Lyneham Transport Wing	

Notes	Serial	Type (alternative identity)	Owner, Operator or Location
	XV302	Lockheed Hercules C3	RAF Lyneham Transport Wing
	XV303	Lockheed Hercules C3	RAF Lyneham Transport Wing
	XV304	Lockheed Hercules C3	RAF Lyneham Transport Wing
	XV305	Lockheed Hercules C3	RAF Lyneham Transport Wing
	XV306	Lockheed Hercules C1	RAF Lyneham Transport Wing
	XV307	Lockheed Hercules C3	RAF Lyneham Transport Wing
	XV328	EE Lightning T5 [DU]	RAF LTF, Binbrook
	XV332	HS Buccaneer S2B [RS]	RAF No 208 Sqn, Lossiemouth
	XV333	HS Buccaneer S2B [DF]	RAF No 12 Sqn, Lossiemouth
	XV334	HS Buccaneer S2B [D]	RAF Shawbury store
	XV336	HS Buccaneer S2A	RAF Shawbury store
	XV337	HS Buccaneer S2C (8852M)	RAF Abingdon BDRF
	XV338	HS Buccaneer S2A (fuselage etc) (8774M)	RAF St Athan (for RAF Honington ground instruction)
	XV338	HS Buccaneer S2A (nose only)	RAF Exhibition Flight, Abingdon
	XV342	HS Buccaneer S2B [T]	RAF store, St Athan
	XV344	HS Buccaneer S2C	MoD(PE) RAE Farnborough
	XV349	HS Buccaneer S2B	RAF Shawbury store
	XV350	HS Buccaneer S2B	MoD(PE) BAe Brough
	XV352	HS Buccaneer S2B [TS]	RAF No 208 Sqn, Lossiemouth
	XV353	HS Buccaneer S2B [LS]	RAF No 208 Sqn, Lossiemouth
	XV355	HS Buccaneer S2A [AC]	RAF No 237 OCU, Lossiemouth
	XV356	HS Buccaneer S2A [B]	RAF Shawbury store
	XV359	HS Buccaneer S2C [CF]	RAF No 12 Sqn, Lossiemouth
	XV361	HS Buccaneer S2C [FF]	RAF No 12 Sqn, Lossiemouth
	XV370	Sikorsky SH-3D (G-ATYU)	MoD(PE) ETPS Boscombe Down
	XV371	Westland Sea King HAS1	MoD(PE) RAE Farnborough
	XV372	Westland Sea King HAS1	Westland Helicopters, Yeovil
	XV373	Westland Sea King HAS1	MoD(PE) A&AEE Boscombe Down
	XV393	McD Phantom FGR2 [A]	RAF No 228 OCU, Coningsby
	XV394	McD Phantom FGR2 [C]	RAF No 228 OCU, Coningsby
	XV396	McD Phantom FGR2 [D]	RAF No 228 OCU, Coningsby
	XV398	McD Phantom FGR2 [I]	RAF No 228 OCU, Coningsby
	XV399	McD Phantom FGR2 [L]	RAF No 56 Sqn, Wattisham
	XV400	McD Phantom FGR2 [D]	RAF No 56 Sqn, Wattisham
	XV401	McD Phantom FGR2 [L]	RAF No 29 Sqn, Coningsby
	XV402	McD Phantom FGR2 [A]	RAF No 23 Sqn, Stanley
	XV404	McD Phantom FGR2 [E]	RAF No 29 Sqn, Coningsby
	XV406	McD Phantom FGR2 [K]	RAF No 228 OCU, Coningsby
	XV407	McD Phantom FGR2 [X]	RAF No 29 Sqn, Coningbsy
	XV408	McD Phantom FGR2 [P]	RAF No 29 Sqn, Coningsby
	XV409	McD Phantom FGR2 [A]	RAF No 29 Sqn, Coningsby
	XV410	McD Phantom FGR2 [E]	RAF No 56 Sqn, Wattisham
	XV411	McD Phantom FGR2 [Q]	RAF No 92 Sqn, Wildenrath
	XV412	McD Phantom FGR2 [S]	RAF No 29 Sqn, Coningsby
	XV414	McD Phantom FGR2 [R]	RAF Wattisham, BDRT
	XV415	McD Phantom FGR2 [O]	RAF No 92 Sqn, Wildenrath
	XV419	McD Phantom FGR2 [G]	RAF No 23 Sqn, Stanley
	XV420	McD Phantom FGR2 [B]	RAF No 23 Sqn, Stanley
	XV421	McD Phantom FGR2 [B]	RAF No 228 OCU, Coningsby
	XV422	McD Phantom FGR2 [J]	RAF No 19 Sqn, Wildenrath
	XV423	McD Phantom FGR2 [D]	RAF No 23 Sqn, Stanley
	XV424	McD Phantom FGR2 [W]	RAF No 92 Sqn, Wildenrath
	XV425	McD Phantom FGR2	RAF No 56 Sqn, Wattisham
	XV426	McD Phantom FGR2 [F]	RAF No 23 Sqn, Stanley
	XV428	McD Phantom FGR2 [I]	RAF No 56 Sqn, Wattisham
	XV429	McD Phantom FGR2 [K]	RAF No 56 Sqn, Wattisham
	XV430	McD Phantom FGR2 [A]	RAF No 19 Sqn, Wildenrath
	XV432	McD Phantom FGR2 [T]	RAF No 29 Sqn, Coningsby
	XV433	McD Phantom FGR2 [I]	RAF No 29 Sqn, Coningsby
	XV434	McD Phantom FGR2 [J]	RAF No 29 Sqn, Coningsby
	XV435	McD Phantom FGR2 [R]	RAF No 92 Sqn, Wildenrath
	XV436	McD Phantom FGR2 [E] (8850M)	RAF Abingdon BDRF
	XV437	McD Phantom FGR2 [B]	RAF No 19 Sqn, Wildenrath
	XV438	McD Phantom FGR2 [Y]	RAF No 29 Sqn, Coningsby
	XV439	McD Phantom FGR2 [D]	RAF No 19 Sqn, Wildenrath
	XV442	McD Phantom FGR2 [R]	RAF No 29 Sqn, Coningsby
	XV460	McD Phantom FGR2 [G]	RAF No 225 OCU, Coningsby
	XV461	McD Phantom FGR2 [G]	RAF No 56 Sqn, Wattisham
	XV462	McD Phantom FGR2 [U]	RAF No 92 Sqn, Wildenrath
	XV464	McD Phantom FGR2 [J]	RAF No 29 Sqn, Coningsby
	XV465	McD Phantom FGR2 [F]	RAF No 19 Sqn, Wildenrath
	XV466	McD Phantom FGR2 [E]	RAF No 23 Sqn, Stanley
	XV467	McD Phantom FGR2 [Q]	RAF No 92 Sqn, Wildenrath

Serial	Type (alternative identity)	Owner, Operator or Location	Notes
XV468	McD Phantom FGR2 [P]	RAF No 92 Sqn, Wildenrath	
XV469	McD Phantom FGR2 [T]	RAF No 56 Sqn, Wattisham	
XV470	McD Phantom FGR2 [S]	RAF No 19 Sqn, Wildenrath	
XV471	McD Phantom FGR2	RAF No 92 Sqn, Wildenrath	
XV472	McD Phantom FGR2 [E]	RAF No 19 Sqn, Wildenrath	
XV473	McD Phantom FGR2 [L]	RAF No 228 OCU, Coningsby	
XV474	McD Phantom FGR2	RAF No 29 Sqn, Coningsby	
XV475	McD Phantom FGR2 [Z]	RAF No 92 Sqn, Wildenrath	
XV476	McD Phantom FGR2 [V]	RAF No 92 Sqn, Wildenrath	
XV478	McD Phantom FGR2 [C]	RAF No 19 Sqn, Wildenrath	
XV480	McD Phantom FGR2 [X]	RAF No 92 Sqn, Wildenrath	
XV481	McD Phantom FGR2 [H]	RAF No 19 Sqn, Wildenrath	
XV482	McD Phantom FGR2 [C]	RAF No 56 Sqn, Wattisham	
XV485	McD Phantom FGR2 [N]	RAF No 19 Sqn, Wildenrath	
XV486	McD Phantom FGR2 [N]	RAF No 29 Sqn, Coningsby	
XV487	McD Phantom FGR2 [Q]	RAF No 29 Sqn, Coningsby	
XV488	McD Phantom FGR2	RAF No 228 OCU, Coningsby	
XV489	McD Phantom FGR2 [A]	RAF No 56 Sqn, Wattisham	
XV490	McD Phantom FGR2 [S]	RAF No 92 Sqn, Wildenrath	
XV492	McD Phantom FGR2 [U]	RAF No 56 Sqn, Wattisham	
XV494	McD Phantom FGR2 [M]	RAF No 56 Sqn, Wattisham	
XV495	McD Phantom FGR2 [C]	RAF No 23 Sqn, Stanley	
XV496	McD Phantom FGR2 [L]	RAF No 19 Sqn, Wildenrath	
XV497	McD Phantom FGR2	RAF No 29 Sqn, Coningsby	
XV498	McD Phantom FGR2 [N]	RAF No 92 Sqn, Wildenrath	
XV499	McD Phantom FGR2 [F]	RAF No 228 OCU, Coningsby	
XV500	EcD Phantom FGR2 [J]	RAF No 56 Sqn, Wattisham	
XV501	McD Phantom FGR2 [B]	RAF No 56 Sqn, Wattisham	
XV555	HS Harrier GR1 (8566M) (really XV279)	RAF Wittering, for instructional use	
XV567	McD Phantom FG1 [I]	RAF No 43 Sqn, Leuchars	
XV568	McD Phantom FG1 [T]	RAF No 43 Sqn, Leuchars	
XV569	McD Phantom FG1 [Q]	RAF No 111 Sqn, Leuchars	
XV570	McD Phantom FG1 [N]	RAF No 111 Sqn, Leuchars	
XV571	McD Phantom FG1 [A]	RAF No 43 Sqn, Leuchars	
XV572	McD Phantom FG1 [N]	RAF No 43 Sqn, Leuchars	
XV573	McD Phantom FG1 [D]	RAF No 111 Sqn, Leuchars	
XV574	McD Phantom FG1 [Z]	RAF No 111 Sqn, Leuchars	
XV575	McD Phantom FG1 [S]	RAF No 43 Sqn, Leuchars	
XV576	McD Phantom FG1 [D]	RAF No 43 Sqn, Leuchars	
XV577	McD Phantom FG1 [M]	RAF No 43 Sqn, Leuchars	
XV579	McD Phantom FG1 [R]	RAF No 43 Sqn, Leuchars	
XV581	McD Phantom FG1 [E]	RAF No 43 Sqn, Leuchars	
XV582	McD Phantom FG1 [F]	RAF No 43 Sqn, Leuchars	
XV583	McD Phantom FG1 [B]	RAF No 111 Sqn, Leuchars	
XV584	McD Phantom FG1 [F]	RAF No 111 Sqn, Leuchars	
XV585	McD Phantom FG1 [P]	RAF No 43 Sqn, Leuchars	
XV586	McD Phantom FG1 [J]	RAF No 43 Sqn, Leuchars	
XV587	McD Phantom FG1 [G]	RAF No 43 Sqn, Leuchars	
XV590	McD Phantom FG1 [X]	RAF No 43 Sqn, Leuchars	
XV591	McD Phantom FG1 [M]	RAF No 111 Sqn, Leuchars	
XV592	McD Phantom FG1 [L]	RAF No 111 Sqn, Leuchars	
XV615	BHC SR.N6 Winchester 2	RN Hong Kong	
XV623	Westland Wasp HAS1 [601]	RN No 829 Sqn, Portland	
XV624	Westland Wasp HAS1 [FIR4]	RN Wroughton	
XV625	Westland Wasp HAS1 [471/PB]	RNEC Manadon, for instruction	
XV626	Westland Wasp HAS1 [323]	RN No 829 Sqn, Portland	
XV629	Westland Wasp HAS1	AAC, BDRT Middle Wallop	
XV631	Westland Wasp HAS1 [617]	MoD(PE), RAE Farnborough	
XV632	Westland Wasp HAS1 [610]	RN No 829 Sqn, Portland	
XV634	Westland Wasp HAS1 [423]	RN No 829 Sqn, Portland	
XV636	Westland Wasp HAS1 [606]	RN No 829 Sqn, Portland	
XV638	Westland Wasp HAS1 [A430] (8826M)	RAF AMS, Brize Norton	
XV639	Westland Wasp HAS1 [612]	RN No 829 Sqn, Portland	
XV642	Westland Sea King HAS2A	MoD(PE) Westlands, Yeovil	
XV643	Westland Sea King HAS5 [705/PW]	RNAY Fleetlands	
XV644	Westland Sea King HAS1 (A2664) [64]	RN AES Lee-on-Solent	
XV647	Westland Sea King HAS5 [265]	RN No 814 Sqn, Culdrose	

Notes	Serial	Type (alternative identity)	Owner, Operator or Location
	XV648	Westland Sea King HAS5 [587]	RN No 706 Sqn, Culdrose
	XV649	Westland Sea King AEW2	RNAY Fleetlands
	XV650	Westland Sea King AEW2 [164]	RN No 849 Sqn, Culdrose
	XV651	Westland Sea King HAS5 [131]	RN No 826 Sqn, Culdrose
	XV652	Westland Sea King HAS5 [582]	RN No 706 Sqn, Culdrose
	XV653	Westland Sea King HAS5 [509]	RN No 810 Sqn, Culdrose
	XV654	Westland Sea King HAS5 [588]	RN No 706 Sqn, Culdrose
	XV655	Westland Sea King HAS5 [534]	RN No 826 Sqn, Culdrose
	XV656	Westland Sea King AEW2 [186]	RN No 849 Sqn, Culdrose
	XV657	Westland Sea King AEW2	RN NASU, Culdrose
	XV659	Westland Sea King HAS2A [584]	RN No 706 Sqn, Culdrose
	XV660	Westland Sea King HAS5 [507]	RN No 810 Sqn, Culdrose
	XV661	Westland Sea King HAS5 [502]	RN No 810 Sqn, Culdrose
	XV663	Westland Sea King HAS5 [703]	RN No 819 Sqn, Prestwick
	XV664	Westland Sea King HAS2A [581]	RN No 706 Sqn, Culdrose
	XV665	Westland Sea King HAS5 [508]	RN No 810 Sqn, Culdrose
	XV666	Westland Sea King HAS5 [598]	RNAY Fleetlands
	XV668	Westland Sea King HAS5 [586]	RN No 706 Sqn, Culdrose
	XV669	Westland Sea King HAS1 (A2659) [410/BL]	RNAS Culdrose, Engineering Training School
	XV670	Westland Sea King HAS5 [592]	RN No 706 Sqn, Culdrose
	XV671	Westland Sea King AEW2 [185]	RN No 849 Sqn, Culdrose
	XV672	Westland Sea King AEW2	RNAY Fleetlands
	XV673	Westland Sea King HAS5 [512]	RN No 810 Sqn, Culdrose
	XV674	Westland Sea King HAS2A [706/PW]	RN No 819 Sqn, Prestwick
	XV675	Westland Sea King HAS5 [274]	RN No 814 Sqn, Culdrose
	XV676	Westland Sea King HAS5 [266/L]	RN No 814 Sqn, Culdrose
	XV677	Westland Sea King HAS5 [705]	RN No 819 Sqn, Prestwick
	XV696	Westland Sea King HAS5 [503]	RN No 810 Sqn, Culdrose
	XV697	Westland Sea King AEW2	RN No 849 Sqn, Culdrose
	XV699	Westland Sea King HAS5 [272]	RN No 814 Sqn, Culdrose
	XV700	Westland Sea King AEW2 [362]	RN No 849 Sqn, Culdrose
	XV701	Westland Sea King HAS5 [706]	RN No 819 Sqn, Prestwick
	XV703	Westland Sea King HAS5 [596]	RN No 706 Sqn, Culdrose
	XV704	Westland Sea King AEW2 [363]	RN No 849 Sqn, Culdrose
	XV705	Westland Sea King HAS2A [596]	RN No 706 Sqn, Culdrose
	XV706	Westland Sea King HAS5 [597]	RN No 706 Sqn, Culdrose
	XV707	Westland Sea King HAS2A [707/PW]	RNAS Culdrose store
	XV708	Westland Sea King HAS2A [702/PW]	RN NASU, Culdrose
	XV709	Westland Sea King HAS5 [016/N]	RN No 820 Sqn, Culdrose
	XV710	Westland Sea King HAS2A [701/PW]	RN No 819 Sqn, Prestwick
	XV711	Westland Sea King HAS5 [011/N]	RN No 820 Sqn, Culdrose
	XV712	Westland Sea King HAS5 [270/L]	RN No 814 Sqn, Culdrose

Serial	Type (alternative identity)	Owner, Operator or Location	Notes
XV713	Westland Sea King HAS5 [536]	RN No 826 Sqn, Culdrose	
XV714	Westland Sea King AEW2 [187]	RN No 849 Sqn, Culdrose	
XV719	Westland Wessex HC2 [B]	RAF No 72 Sqn, Aldergrove	
XV720	Westland Wessex HC2	RAF No 22 Sqn SAR*	
XV721	Westland Wessex HC2 [H]	RAF No 72 Sqn Aldergrove	
XV722	Westland Wessex HC2 [WH]	RAF No 2 FTS, Shawbury	
XV723	Westland Wessex HC2 [Q]	RAF No 72 Sqn, Aldergrove	
XV724	Westland Wessex HC2	RAF No 22 Sqn SAR*	
XV725	Westland Wessex HC2 [C]	RAF No 72 Sqn, Aldergrove	
XV726	Westland Wessex HC2 [J]	RAF No 72 Sqn, Aldergrove	
XV728	Westland Wessex HC2 [A]	RAF No 72 Sqn, Aldergrove	
XV729	Westland Wessex HC2	RAF No 22 Sqn SAR*	
XV730	Westland Wessex HC2	RAF No 22 Sqn SAR*	
XV731	Westland Wessex HC2 [Y]	RAF No 72 Sqn, Aldergrove	
XV732	Westland Wessex HCC4	RAF Queen's Flight, Benson	
XV733	Westland Wessex HCC4	RAF Queen's Flight, Benson	
XV738	HS Harrier GR3 [B]	RAF No 4 Sqn, Gutersloh	
XV740	HS Harrier GR3 [05]	RAF No 1 Sqn, Wittering	
XV741	HS Harrier GR3 [A]	RAF No 233 OCU, Wittering	
XV744	HS Harrier GR3 [D]	RAF No 233 OCU, Wittering	
XV747	HS Harrier GR3 [G]	RAF No 233 OCU, Wittering	
XV748	HS Harrier GR3 [11]	RAF No 1 Sqn, Wittering	
XV751	HS Harrier GR3 [AU]	RAF No 3 Sqn, Gutersloh	
XV752	HS Harrier GR3 [AG]	RAF No 3 Sqn, Gutersloh	
XV753	HS Harrier GR3 [06]	RAF No 1 Sqn, Wittering	
XV755	HS Harrier GR3 [AK]	RAF No 3 Sqn, Gutersloh	
XV758	HS Harrier GR3 [J]	RAF No 233 OCU, Wittering	
XV759	HS Harrier GR3 [H]	RAF No 233 OCU, Wittering	
XV760	HS Harrier GR3 [C]	RAF No 4 Sqn, Gutersloh	
XV762	HS Harrier GR3 [09]	RAF SSF, Wittering	
XV778	HS Harrier GR3 [08]	RAF No 1 Sqn, Wittering	
XV779	HS Harrier GR3 [AA]	RAF No 3 Sqn, Gutersloh	
XV782	HS Harrier GR3 [F]	RAF No 4 Sqn, Gutersloh	
XV783	HS Harrier GR3 [AE]	RAF No 3 Sqn, Gutersloh	
XV784	HS Harrier GR3 [C]	RAF No 233 OCU, Wittering	
XV786	HS Harrier GR3 [E]	RAF No 4 Sqn, Gutersloh	
XV789	HS Harrier GR3 [07]	RAF No 1 Sqn, Wittering	
XV790	HS Harrier GR3 [AP]	RAF No 3 Sqn, Gutersloh	
XV793	HS Harrier GR3 [L]	RAF No 4 Sqn, Gutersloh	
XV804	HS Harrier GR3 [AD]	RAF No 3 Sqn, Gutersloh	
XV806	HS Harrier GR3 [AN]	RAF No 3 Sqn, Gutersloh	
XV808	HS Harrier GR3 [L]	RAF No 233 OCU, Wittering	
XV809	HS Harrier GR3 [AF]	RAF No 3 Sqn, Gutersloh	
XV810	HS Harrier GR3 [X]	RAF No 4 Sqn, Gutersloh	
XV814	HS Comet 4C (G-APDF)	MoD(PE) RAE Farnborough	
XV859	BHC SR.N6 Winchester 6	RN NHTU Lee-on-Solent	
XV863	HS Buccaneer S2B [CS]	RAF No 208 Sqn, Lossiemouth	
XV864	HS Buccaneer S2B [KF]	RAF No 12 Sqn, Lossiemouth	
XV865	HS Buccaneer S2B [BS]	RAF No 208 Sqn, Lossiemouth	
XV866	HS Buccaneer S2B [Y]	RAF Shawbury store	
XV867	HS Buccaneer S2B [EF]	RAF No 12 Sqn, Lossiemouth	
XV868	HS Buccaneer S2B [FS]	RAF No 208 Sqn, Lossiemouth	
XV869	HS Buccaneer S2B [MF]	RAF No 12 Sqn, Lossiemouth	
XW175	HS Harrier T4	MoD(PE) RAE Bedford/Cranfield Institute of Technology	
XW198	Westland Puma HC1 [DL]	RAF No 230 Sqn, Gutersloh	
XW199	Westland Puma HC1 [DU]	RAF No 230 Sqn, Gutersloh	
XW200	Westland Puma HC1 [FA]	RAF No 240 OCU, Odiham	
XW201	Westland Puma HC1 [FB]	RAF No 240 OCU, Odiham	
XW202	Westland Puma HC1 [FC]	RAF No 1563 Flt, Belize	
XW204	Westland Puma HC1 [CA]	RAF No 33 Sqn, Odiham	
XW206	Westland Puma HC1 [CC]	RAF No 33 Sqn, Odiham	
XW207	Westland Puma HC1 [CD]	RAF No 1563 Flt, Belize	
XW208	Westland Puma HC1 [DP]	RAF No 230 Sqn, Gutersloh	
XW209	Westland Puma HC1 [CF]	RAF No 1563 Flt, Belize	
XW210	Westland Puma HC1 [CG]	RAF No 33 Sqn, Odiham	
XW211	Westland Puma HC1 [CH]	RAF No 33 Sqn, Odiham	
XW212	Westland Puma HC1 [FD]	RAF No 240 OCU, Odiham	
XW213	Westland Puma HC1 [CJ]	RAF No 33 Sqn, Odiham	
XW214	Westland Puma HC1 [CK]	RAF No 33 Sqn, Odiham	
XW215	Westland Puma HC1 [DM]	RAF No 230 Sqn, Gutersloh	

Notes	Serial	Type (alternative identity)	Owner, Operator or Location
	XW216	Westland Puma HC1 [CL]	RAF No 33 Sqn, Odiham
	XW217	Westland Puma HC1 [DA]	RAF No 230 Sqn, Gutersloh
	XW218	Westland Puma HC1 [DT]	RAF No 230 Sqn, Gutersloh
	XW219	Westland Puma HC1 [DC]	RAF No 230 Sqn, Gutersloh
	XW220	Westland Puma HC1 [DD]	RAF No 230 Sqn, Gutersloh
	XW221	Westland Puma HC1 [DE]	RAF No 230 Sqn, Gutersloh
	XW222	Westland Puma HC1 [DF]	RAF No 230 Sqn, Gutersloh
	XW223	Westland Puma HC1 [DG]	RAF No 230 Sqn, Gutersloh
	XW224	Westland Puma HC1 [DH]	RAF No 230 Sqn, Gutersloh
	XW225	Westland Puma HC1 [FE]	RAF No 240 OCU, Odiham
	XW226	Westland Puma HC1 [DK]	RAF No 230 Sqn, Gutersloh
	XW227	Westland Puma HC1 [DN]	RAF No 230 Sqn, Gutersloh
	XW229	Westland Puma HC1 [DB]	RAF No 230 Sqn, Gutersloh
	XW231	Westland Puma HC1 [CM]	RAF No 33 Sqn, Odiham
	XW232	Westland Puma HC1 [DJ]	RAF No 230 Sqn, Gutersloh
	XW233	Westland Puma HC1 [CN]	RAF No 33 Sqn, Odiham
	XW234	Westland Puma HC1 [CO]	RAF No 33 Sqn, Odiham
	XW235	Westland Puma HC1 [CP]	RAF No 1563 Flt, Belize
	XW236	Westland Puma HC1 [CQ]	RAF No 33 Sqn, Odiham
	XW237	Westland Puma HC1 [CR]	RAF No 33 Sqn, Odiham
	XW241	Aerospatiale SA330 (F-ZJUX)	MoD(PE) RAE Bedford
	XW249	Cushioncraft CC7	Cornwall Aero Park, Helston
	XW255	BHC BH-7 Wellington	RN NHTU Lee-on-Solent
	XW265	HS Harrier T4A	MoD(PE) A&AEE Boscombe Down
	XW266	HS Harrier T4A [S]	RAF No 233 OCU, Wittering
	XW267	HS Harrier T4 [T]	RAF No 233 OCU, Wittering
	XW268	HS Harrier T4A [U]	RAF No 233 OCU, Wittering
	XW269	HS Harrier T4 [AY]	RAF No 3 Sqn, Gutersloh
	XW270	HS Harrier T4 [12]	RAF No 1 Sqn, Wittering
	XW271	HS Harrier T4 [R]	RAF No 233 OCU, Wittering
	XW272	HS Harrier T4 (8783M)	Cranfield Institute of Technology
	XW276	Aerospatiale SA341 (F-ZWRI)	Southampton Hall of Aviation
	XW280	Westland Scout AH1	AAC store, Wroughton
	XW281	Westland Scout AH1 [U]	AAC No 658 Sqn, Netheravon
	XW282	Westland Scout AH1	AAC store, Wroughton
	XW283	Westland Scout AH1 [W]	AAC No 658 Sqn, Netheravon
	XW284	Westland Scout AH1	AAC store, Wroughton
	XW287	BAC Jet Provost T5 [P]	RAF No 6 FTS, Finningley
	XW289	BAC Jet Provost T5A [31]	RAF College, Cranwell
	XW290	BAC Jet Provost T5A [41]	RAF College, Cranwell
	XW291	BAC Jet Provost T5 [N]	RAF No 6 FTS, Finningley
	XW292	BAC Jet Provost T5A [32]	RAF College, Cranwell
	XW293	BAC Jet Provost T5 [Z]	RAF No 6 FTS, Finningley
	XW294	BAC Jet Provost T5A [45]	RAF College, Cranwell
	XW295	BAC Jet Provost T5A [67]	RAF No 1 FTS, Linton-on-Ouse
	XW296	BAC Jet Provost T5 [Q]	RAF No 6 FTS, Finningley
	XW298	BAC Jet Provost T5 [O]	RAF No 6 FTS, Finningley
	XW299	BAC Jet Provost T5A [60]	RAF No 1 FTS, Linton-on-Ouse
	XW301	BAC Jet Provost T5A [63]	RAF No 1 FTS, Linton-on-Ouse
	XW302	BAC Jet Provost T5 [T]	RAF No 6 FTS, Finningley
	XW303	BAC Jet Provost T5A [127]	RAF No 7 FTS, Church Fenton
	XW304	BAC Jet Provost T5 [X]	RAF No 6 FTS, Finningley
	XW305	BAC Jet Provost T5A [42]	RAF College, Cranwell
	XW306	BAC Jet Provost T5 [Y]	RAF No 6 FTS, Finningley
	XW307	BAC Jet Provost T5 [S]	RAF No 6 FTS, Finningley
	XW309	BAC Jet Provost T5 [V]	RAF No 6 FTS, Finningley
	XW310	BAC Jet Provost T5A [37]	RAF College, Cranwell
	XW311	BAC Jet Provost T5 [W]	RAF No 6 FTS, Finningley
	XW312	BAC Jet Provost T5A [64]	RAF No 1 FTS, Linton-on-Ouse
	XW313	BAC Jet Provost T5A [30]	RAF College, Cranwell
	XW315	BAC Jet Provost T5A [63]	RAF No 3 FTS, Scampton
	XW316	BAC Jet Provost T5A [52]	RAF No 3 FTS, Scampton
	XW317	BAC Jet Provost T5A [25]	RAF College, Cranwell
	XW318	BAC Jet Provost T5A [12]	RAF College, Cranwell
	XW319	BAC Jet Provost T5A [57]	RAF No 3 FTS, Scampton
	XW320	BAC Jet Provost T5A [71]	RAF No 1 FTS, Linton-on-Ouse
	XW321	BAC Jet Provost T5A [132]	RAF No 7 FTS, Church Fenton
	XW322	BAC Jet Provost T5A [43]	RAF College, Cranwell
	XW323	BAC Jet Provost T5A [44]	RAF College, Cranwell
	XW324	BAC Jet Provost T5 [U]	RAF No 6 FTS, Finningley
	XW325	BAC Jet Provost T5A [33]	RAF College, Cranwell
	XW326	BAC Jet Provost T5A [120]	RAF No 7 FTS, Church Fenton
	XW327	BAC Jet Provost T5A [134]	RAF No 7 FTS, Church Fenton
	XW328	BAC Jet Provost T5A [22]	RAF College, Cranwell

Serial	Type (alternative identity)	Owner, Operator or Location	Notes
XW329	BAC Jet Provost T5A [48] (8741M)	RAF Church Fenton Fire Section	
XW330	BAC Jet Provost T5A [130]	RAF No 7 FTS, Church Fenton	
XW332	BAC Jet Provost T5A [34]	RAF College, Cranwell	
XW333	BAC Jet Provost T5A [36]	RAF College, Cranwell	
XW334	BAC Jet Provost T5A [131]	RAF No 7 FTS, Church Fenton	
XW335	BAC Jet Provost T5A [27]	RAF College, Cranwell	
XW336	BAC Jet Provost T5A [6]	RAF College, Cranwell	
XW351	BAC Jet Provost T5A [74]	RAF No 1 FTS, Linton-on-Ouse	
XW352	BAC Jet Provost T5 [R]	RAF No 6 FTS, Finningley	
XW353	BAC Jet Provost T5A [51]	RAF No 3 FTS, Scampton	
XW354	BAC Jet Provost T5A [7]	RAF College, Cranwell	
XW355	BAC Jet Provost T5A [20]	RAF College, Cranwell	
XW357	BAC Jet Provost T5A [5]	RAF College, Cranwell	
XW358	BAC Jet Provost T5A [18]	RAF College, Cranwell	
XW359	BAC Jet Provost T5A [128]	RAF No 7 FTS, Church Fenton	
XW360	BAC Jet Provost T5A [129]	RAF No 7 FTS, Church Fenton	
XW361	BAC Jet Provost T5A [21]	RAF College, Cranwell	
XW362	BAC Jet Provost T5A [17]	RAF College, Cranwell	
XW363	BAC Jet Provost T5A [68]	RAF No 1 FTS, Linton-on-Ouse	
XW364	BAC Jet Provost T5A [35]	RAF College, Cranwell	
XW365	BAC Jet Provost T5A [73]	RAF No 1 FTS, Linton-on-Ouse	
XW366	BAC Jet Provost T5A [75]	RAF No 1 FTS, Linton-on-Ouse	
XW367	BAC Jet Provost T5A [26]	RAF College, Cranwell	
XW368	BAC Jet Provost T5A [55]	RAF No 3 FTS, Scampton	
XW369	BAC Jet Provost T5A [9]	RAF College, Cranwell	
XW370	BAC Jet Provost T5A [72]	RAF No 1 FTS, Linton-on-Ouse	
XW372	BAC Jet Provost T5A [121]	RAF No 7 FTS, Church Fenton	
XW373	BAC Jet Provost T5A [11]	RAF College, Cranwell	
XW374	BAC Jet Provost T5A [38]	RAF College, Cranwell	
XW375	BAC Jet Provost T5A [10]	RAF College, Cranwell	
XW404	BAC Jet Provost T5A [77]	RAF No 1 FTS, Linton-on-Ouse	
XW405	BAC Jet Provost T5A [61]	RAF No 1 FTS, Linton-on-Ouse	
XW406	BAC Jet Provost T5A [23]	RAF College, Cranwell	
XW407	BAC Jet Provost T5A [122]	RAF No 7 FTS, Church Fenton	
XW408	BAC Jet Provost T5A [24]	RAF College, Cranwell	
XW409	BAC Jet Provost T5A [123]	RAF No 7 FTS, Church Fenton	
XW410	BAC Jet Provost T5A [80]	RAF No 1 FTS, Linton-on-Ouse	
XW411	BAC Jet Provost T5A [133]	RAF No 7 FTS, Church Fenton	
XW412	BAC Jet Provost T5A [15]	RAF College, Cranwell	
XW413	BAC Jet Provost T5A [69]	RAF No 1 FTS, Linton-on-Ouse	
XW415	BAC Jet Provost T5A [53]	RAF No 3 FTS, Scampton	
XW416	BAC Jet Provost T5A [19]	RAF College, Cranwell	
XW418	BAC Jet Provost T5A [54]	RAF No 3 FTS, Scampton	
XW419	BAC Jet Provost T5A [125]	RAF No 7 FTS, Church Fenton	
XW420	BAC Jet Provost T5A [8]	RAF College, Cranwell	
XW421	BAC Jet Provost T5A [60]	RAF No 3 FTS, Scampton	
XW422	BAC Jet Provost T5A [3]	RAF College, Cranwell	
XW423	BAC Jet Provost T5A [14]	RAF College, Cranwell	
XW424	BAC Jet Provost T5A [62]	Privately owned, Misson, Notts	
XW425	BAC Jet Provost T5A [61]	RAF No 3 FTS, Scampton	
XW427	BAC Jet Provost T5A [56]	RAF No 3 FTS, Scampton	
XW428	BAC Jet Provost T5A [70]	RAF No 1 FTS, Linton-on-Ouse	
XW429	BAC Jet Provost T5A [28]	RAF College, Cranwell	
XW430	BAC Jet Provost T5A [58]	RAF No 3 FTS, Scampton	
XW431	BAC Jet Provost T5A [59]	RAF No 3 FTS, Scampton	
XW432	BAC Jet Provost T5A [76]	RAF No 1 FTS, Linton-on-Ouse	
XW433	BAC Jet Provost T5A [124]	RAF No 7 FTS, Church Fenton	
XW434	BAC Jet Provost T5A [126]	RAF No 7 FTS, Church Fenton	
XW435	BAC Jet Provost T5A [4]	RAF College, Cranwell	
XW436	BAC Jet Provost T5A [62]	RAF No 3 FTS, Scampton	
XW437	BAC Jet Provost T5A [1]	RAF College, Cranwell	
XW438	BAC Jet Provost T5A [2]	RAF College, Cranwell	
XW527	HS Buccaneer S2B [GF]	RAF No 12 Sqn, Lossiemouth	
XW528	HS Buccaneer S2B (8861M) [C]	RAF Coningsby, BDRT	
XW529	HS Buccaneer S2B	MoD(PE) BAe Woodford	
XW530	HS Buccaneer S2B [HF]	RAF No 12 Sqn, Lossiemouth	
XW533	HS Buccaneer S2B [AS]	RAF No 208 Sqn, Lossiemouth	
XW534	HS Buccaneer S2B	MoD(PE) BAe Woodford	
XW538	HS Buccaneer S2B (8660M) [T]	RAF Lossiemouth Fire Section	
XW540	HS Buccaneer S2B [JF]	RAF No 12 Sqn, Lossiemouth	
XW541	HS Buccaneer S2B (8858M)	RAF Honington Fire Section	
XW542	HS Buccaneer S2B [KS]	RAF No 208 Sqn, Lossiemouth	

Notes	Serial	Type (alternative identity)	Owner, Operator or Location
	XW543	HS Buccaneer S2B [E]	RAF store St Athan
	XW544	HS Buccaneer S2B (8857M) [O]	RAF No 2 SoTT, Cosford
	XW545	HS Buccaneer S2B (8859M)	RAF Lossiemouth, BDRT
	XW546	HS Buccaneer S2B [E]	RAF ASF, Honington
	XW547	HS Buccaneer S2B [JS]	RAF No 208 Sqn, Lossiemouth
	XW549	HS Buccaneer S2B (8860M)	RAF Kinloss, BDRT
	XW550	HS Buccaneer S2B [X]	RAF St Athan store
	XW566	SEPECAT Jaguar T2	MoD(PE) RAE Farnborough store
	XW612	Westland Scout AH1 [X]	AAC No 658 Sqn, Netheravon
	XW613	Westland Scout AH1 [V]	AAC ATS, Middle Wallop
	XW614	Westland Scout AH1	AAC store, Wroughton
	XW615	Westland Scout AH1	AAC store, Wroughton
	XW616	Westland Scout AH1	AAC Falkland Islands
	XW626	HS Comet 4AEW (G-APDS)	MoD(PE) RAE Bedford
	XW630	HS Harrier GR3 [M]	RAF No 4 Sqn, Gutersloh
	XW635	Beagle D5/180 (G-AWSW)	RAF No 5 AEF, Teversham
	XW664	HS Nimrod R1P	RAF No 51 Sqn, Wyton
	XW665	HS Nimrod R1	RAF No 51 Sqn, Wyton
	XW666	HS Nimrod R1	RAF No 51 Sqn, Wyton
	XW750	HS748 Series 107 (G-ASJT)	MoD(PE) RAE Bedford
	XW763	HS Harrier GR3 [02]	RAF No 1 Sqn, Wittering
	XW764	HS Harrier GR3 [AC]	RAF No 3 Sqn, Gutersloh
	XW768	HS Harrier GR3 [01]	RAF No 1 Sqn, Wittering
	XW769	HS Harrier GR3 [A]	RAF No 4 Sqn, Gutersloh
	XW788	HS125 CC1	RAF No 32 Sqn, Northolt
	XW789	HS125 CC1	RAF No 32 Sqn, Northolt
	XW790	HS125 CC1	RAF No 32 Sqn, Northolt
	XW791	HS125 CC1	RAF No 32 Sqn, Northolt
	XW795	Westland Scout AH1	AAC No 658 Sqn, Detmold
	XW796	Westland Scout AH1 [W]	AAC No 660 Sqn, Sek Kong
	XW797	Westland Scout AH1 [T]	AAC SCF, Middle Wallop
	XW798	Westland Scout AH1 [U]	AAC SCF, Middle Wallop
	XW799	Westland Scout AH1 [V]	AAC No 658 Sqn, Netheravon
	XW836	Westland Lynx	Westlands, RNAS Yeovilton
	XW839	Westland Lynx	Rolls-Royce, Filton
	XW843	Westland Gazelle AH1	AAC No 2 Flt, Netheravon
	XW844	Westland Gazelle AH1	AAC No 661 Sqn, Hildesheim
	XW845	Westland Gazelle HT2	RN store, Wroughton
	XW846	Westland Gazelle AH1	MoD(PE) A&AEE, Westlands, Weston-super-Mare
	XW847	Westland Gazelle AH1	AAC D&TS, Middle Wallop
	XW848	Westland Gazelle AH1	AAC AETW, Middle Wallop
	XW849	Westland Gazelle AH1 [33B]	RM 3 CBAS, Yeovilton
	XW851	Westland Gazelle AH1 [33A]	RM 3 CBAS, Yeovilton
	XW852	Westland Gazelle HT3	RAF No 32 Sqn, Northolt
	XW853	Westland Gazelle HT2	RN store, Wroughton
	XW854	Westland Gazelle HT2 [46/CU]	RN No 705 Sqn, Culdrose
	XW855	Westland Gazelle HT3	RAF No 32 Sqn, Northolt
	XW856	Westland Gazelle HT2 [47/CU]	RN No 705 Sqn, Culdrose
	XW857	Westland Gazelle HT2 [55/CU]	RN No 705 Sqn, Culdrose
	XW858	Westland Gazelle HT3 [C]	RAF No 2 FTS, Shawbury
	XW860	Westland Gazelle HT2 [44/CU]	RN No 705 Sqn, Culdrose
	XW861	Westland Gazelle HT2 [59/CU]	RN No 705 Sqn, Culdrose
	XW862	Westland Gazelle HT3 [D]	RAF No 2 FTS, Shawbury
	XW863	Westland Gazelle HT2 [42/CU]	RN No 705 Sqn, Culdrose
	XW864	Westland Gazelle HT2 [54/CU]	RN No 705 Sqn, Culdrose
	XW865	Westland Gazelle AH1 [C]	AAC ARWS, Middle Wallop
	XW866	Westland Gazelle HT3 [E]	RAF No 2 FTS, Shawbury
	XW868	Westland Gazelle HT2 [50/CU]	RN No 705 Sqn, Culdrose
	XW870	Westland Gazelle HT3 [F]	RAF No 2 FTS, Shawbury
	XW871	Westland Gazelle HT2 [49/CU]	RN store, Wroughton
	XW884	Westland Gazelle HT2 [41/CU]	RN No 705 Sqn, Culdrose
	XW885	Westland Gazelle AH1 [B]	AAC ARWS, Middle Wallop

Serial	Type (alternative identity)	Owner, Operator or Location	Notes
XW886	Westland Gazelle HT2 [48/CU]	RN No 705 Sqn, Culdrose	
XW887	Westland Gazelle HT2 [57/CU]	RN store, Wroughton	
XW888	Westland Gazelle AH1	AAC AETW, Middle Wallop	
XW889	Westland Gazelle AH1 [D]	AAC ARWS, Middle Wallop	
XW890	Westland Gazelle HT2 [53/CU]	RN No 705 Sqn, Culdrose	
XW891	Westland Gazelle HT2 [49/CU]	RN No 705 Sqn, Culdrose	
XW892	Westland Gazelle AH1	AAC No 663 Sqn, Soest	
XW893	Westland Gazelle AH1	AAC Falkland Islands	
XW894	Westland Gazelle HT2 [52/CU]	RN No 705 Sqn, Culdrose	
XW895	Westland Gazelle HT2 [51/CU]	RN No 705 Sqn, Culdrose	
XW897	Westland Gazelle AH1	AAC No 664 Sqn, Minden	
XW898	Westland Gazelle HT3 [G]	RAF No 2 FTS, Shawbury	
XW899	Westland Gazelle AH1	AAC No 655 Sqn, Aldergrove	
XW900	Westland Gazelle AH1 (TAD-900)	AAC AETW, Middle Wallop	
XW902	Westland Gazelle HT3 [H]	RAF No 2 FTS, Shawbury	
XW903	Westland Gazelle AH1 [E]	AAC ARWS, Middle Wallop	
XW904	Westland Gazelle AH1	AAC No 664 Sqn, Minden	
XW906	Westland Gazelle HT3 [J]	RAF No 2 FTS, Shawbury	
XW907	Westland Gazelle HT2 [40/CU]	RN No 705 Sqn, Culdrose	
XW908	Westland Gazelle AH1	AAC D&TS, Middle Wallop	
XW909	Westland Gazelle AH1	AAC No 663 Sqn, Soest	
XW910	Westland Gazelle HT3 [K]	RAF No 2 FTS, Shawbury	
XW911	Westland Gazelle AH1 [I]	AAC ARWS, Middle Wallop	
XW912	Westland Gazelle AH1	RM 3 CBAS, Yeovilton	
XW913	Westland Gazelle AH1	AAC No 664 Sqn, Minden	
XW916	HS Harrier GR3 [W]	RAF No 4 Sqn, Gutersloh	
XW917	HS Harrier GR3 [AL]	RAF No 3 Sqn, Gutersloh	
XW919	HS Harrier GR3 [03]	RAF No 1 Sqn, Wittering	
XW921	HS Harrier GR3 [V]	RAF No 4 Sqn, Gutersloh	
XW922	HS Harrier GR3 [B]	RAF No 233 OCU, Wittering	
XW924	HS Harrier GR3 [G]	RAF No 4 Sqn, Gutersloh	
XW925	HS Harrier T4	RAF No 233 OCU, Wittering	
XW927	HS Harrier T4 [S]	RAF No 4 Sqn, Gutersloh	
XW930	HS125 (G-ATPC)	MoD(PE) RAE Bedford	
XW934	HS Harrier T4 [V]	RAF No 233 OCU, Wittering	
XW986	HS Buccaneer S2	MoD(PE) RAE Farnborough	
XW987	HS Buccaneer S2	MoD(PE) RAE West Freugh	
XW988	HS Buccaneer S2	MoD(PE) RAE Farnborough	
XX101	Cushioncraft CC7	British Rotorcraft Museum, Weston-super-Mare	
XX102	Cushioncraft CC7	Museum of Army Transport, Beverley	
XX105	BAC 1-11/201 (G-ASJD)	MoD(PE) RAE Bedford	
XX108	SEPECAT Jaguar GR1 (G27-313)	MoD(PE) BAe Warton	
XX109	SEPECAT Jaguar GR1	MoD(PE) BAe Warton	
XX110	SEPECAT Jaguar GR1 [EP]	RAF store, Shawbury	
XX110	SEPECAT Jaguar Replica (BAPC 169)	RAF No 1 SoTT, Halton	
XX112	SEPECAT Jaguar GR1A [EA]	RAF No 6 Sqn, Coltishall	
XX115	SEPECAT Jaguar GR1 (JI005) (8821M)	RAF No 1 SoTT, Halton	
XX116	SEPECAT Jaguar GR1A (JI008) [EE]	RAF No 6 Sqn, Coltishall	
XX117	SEPECAT Jaguar GR1A (JI004) [GG]	RAF No 54 Sqn, Coltishall	
XX119	SEPECAT Jaguar GR1	MoD(PE) A&AEE, Boscombe Down	
XX121	SEPECAT Jaguar GR1 [EQ]	RAF store, Shawbury	
XX139	SEPECAT Jaguar T2A [C]	RAF No 226 OCU, Lossiemouth	
XX140	SEPECAT Jaguar T2 [D]	RAF store, Shawbury	
XX141	SEPECAT Jaguar T2 [EU]	RAF No 6 Sqn, Coltishall	
XX143	SEPECAT Jaguar T2A (JI002) [B]	RAF No 226 OCU, Lossiemouth	
XX144	SEPECAT Jaguar T2A [I]	RAF No 226 OCU, Lossiemouth	
XX145	SEPECAT Jaguar T2	MoD(PE) A&AEE, Boscombe Down	
XX146	SEPECAT Jaguar T2A [GS]	RAF No 54 Sqn, Coltishall	

Notes	Serial	Type (alternative identity)	Owner, Operator or Location
	XX150	SEPECAT Jaguar T2 [AX]	RAF store, Shawbury
	XX154	HS Hawk T1 [1]	MoD(PE) RAE Llanbedr
	XX156	HS Hawk T1	MoD(PE) ETPS Boscombe Down
	XX157	HS Hawk T1	RAF No 2 TWU/63 Sqn, Chivenor
	XX158	HS Hawk T1A	RAF No 2 TWU/63 Sqn, Chivenor
	XX159	HS Hawk T1A	RAF No 1 TWU/234 Sqn Brawdy
	XX160	HS Hawk T1	MoD(PE) RAE Llanbedr
	XX161	HS Hawk T1	RAF No 4 FTS, Valley
	XX162	HS Hawk T1 replica (BAPC 152)	RAF Exhibition Flight, Abingdon
	XX162	HS Hawk T1	RAF No 4 FTS, Valley
	XX163	HS Hawk T1	RAF No 4 FTS, Valley
	XX164	HS Hawk T1	RAF No 4 FTS, Valley
	XX165	HS Hawk T1	RAF No 4 FTS, Valley
	XX167	HS Hawk T1	RAF No 4 FTS, Valley
	XX168	HS Hawk T1	RAF No 4 FTS, Valley
	XX169	HS Hawk T1	RAF No 4 FTS, Valley
	XX170	HS Hawk T1	RAF No 4 FTS, Valley
	XX171	HS Hawk T1	RAF No 4 FTS, Valley
	XX172	HS Hawk T1	RAF No 4 FTS, Valley
	XX173	HS Hawk T1	RAF No 4 FTS, Valley
	XX174	HS Hawk T1	RAF No 4 FTS, Valley
	XX175	HS Hawk T1	RAF No 4 FTS, Valley
	XX176	HS Hawk T1	RAF No 4 FTS, Valley
	XX177	HS Hawk T1	RAF No 4 FTS, Valley
	XX178	HS Hawk T1	RAF No 4 FTS, Valley
	XX179	HS Hawk T1	RAF No 4 FTS, Valley
	XX181	HS Hawk T1	RAF CFS, Valley
	XX182	HS Hawk T1	RAF No 4 FTS, Valley
	XX183	HS Hawk T1	RAF No 4 FTS, Valley
	XX184	HS Hawk T1	RAF No 4 FTS, Valley
	XX185	HS Hawk T1	RAF No 4 FTS, Valley
	XX186	HS Hawk T1A	RAF No 2 TWU/63 Sqn, Chivenor
	XX187	HS Hawk T1A [L]	RAF No 2 TWU/151 Sqn, Chivenor
	XX188	HS Hawk T1A	RAF No 1 TWU/234 Sqn, Brawdy
	XX189	HS Hawk T1A [J]	RAF No 2 TWU/151 Sqn, Chivenor
	XX190	HS Hawk T1A	RAF No 1 TWU/234 Sqn, Brawdy
	XX191	HS Hawk T1	RAF No 1 TWU/79 Sqn, Brawdy
	XX192	HS Hawk T1A	RAF No 1 TWU/79 Sqn, Brawdy
	XX193	HS Hawk T1A	RAF No 1 TWU/234 Sqn, Brawdy
	XX194	HS Hawk T1A	RAF No 1 TWU/234 Sqn, Brawdy
	XX195	HS Hawk T1	RAF No 2 TWU/63 Sqn, Chivenor
	XX196	HS Hawk T1A	RAF No 1 TWU/234 Sqn, Brawdy
	XX197	HS Hawk T1A	RAF No 1 TWU/79 Sqn, Brawdy
	XX198	HS Hawk T1A	RAF No 1 TWU/79 Sqn, Brawdy
	XX199	HS Hawk T1A	RAF No 1 TWU, Brawdy
	XX200	HS Hawk T1A	RAF No 1 TWU, Brawdy
	XX201	HS Hawk T1A [N]	RAF No 2 TWU/151 Sqn, Chivenor
	XX202	HS Hawk T1A [P]	RAF No 2 TWU/151 Sqn, Chivenor
	XX203	HS Hawk T1A	RAF No 2 TWU/63 Sqn, Chivenor
	XX204	HS Hawk T1A	RAF No 2 TWU/63 Sqn, Chivenor
	XX205	HS Hawk T1A	RAF No 2 TWU/63 Sqn, Chivenor
	XX217	HS Hawk T1	RAF No 2 TWU/63 Sqn, Chivenor
	XX218	HS Hawk T1A	RAF No 1 TWU/234 Sqn, Brawdy
	XX219	HS Hawk T1A	RAF No 2 TWU/63 Sqn, Chivenor
	XX220	HS Hawk T1	RAF No 1 TWU/234 Sqn, Brawdy
	XX221	HS Hawk T1A	RAF No 1 TWU/79 Sqn, Brawdy
	XX222	HS Hawk T1A	RAF No 1 TWU/79 Sqn, Brawdy
	XX223	HS Hawk T1	RAF CFS, Valley
	XX224	HS Hawk T1	RAF CFS, Valley
	XX225	HS Hawk T1	RAF No 4 FTS, Valley
	XX226	HS Hawk T1	RAF No 4 FTS, Valley
	XX227	HS Hawk T1	RAF Red Arrows, Scampton
	XX228	HS Hawk T1A [Q]	RAF No 2 TWU/151 Sqn, Chivenor
	XX230	HS Hawk T1A [M]	RAF No 2 TWU/151 Sqn, Chivenor
	XX231	HS Hawk T1	RAF No 4 FTS, Valley
	XX232	HS Hawk T1	RAF No 4 FTS, Valley
	XX233	HS Hawk T1	RAF No 4 FTS, Valley
	XX234	HS Hawk T1	RAF CFS, Valley
	XX235	HS Hawk T1	RAF No 4 FTS, Valley
	XX236	HS Hawk T1	RAF No 4 FTS, Valley
	XX237	HS Hawk T1A	RAF Red Arrows, Scampton
	XX238	HS Hawk T1	RAF No 4 FTS, Valley
	XX239	HS Hawk T1	RAF No 4 FTS, Valley

Serial	Type (alternative identity)	Owner, Operator or Location	Notes
XX240	HS Hawk T1	RAF No 4 FTS, Valley	
XX241	HS Hawk T1	RAF No 4 FTS, Valley	
XX242	HS Hawk T1	RAF No 4 FTS, Valley	
XX243	HS Hawk T1	RAF Red Arrows, Scampton	
XX244	HS Hawk T1	RAF No 4 FTS, Valley	
XX245	HS Hawk T1	RAF No 4 FTS, Valley	
XX246	HS Hawk T1A	RAF No 2 TWU/63 Sqn, Chivenor	
XX247	HS Hawk T1A	RAF No 2 TWU/63 Sqn, Chivenor	
XX248	HS Hawk T1A	RAF No 2 TWU/63 Sqn, Chivenor	
XX249	HS Hawk T1	RAF No 4 FTS, Valley	
XX250	HS Hawk T1	RAF No 4 FTS, Valley	
XX252	HS Hawk T1A	RAF Red Arrows, Scampton	
XX253	HS Hawk T1A	RAF Red Arrows, Scampton	
XX254	HS Hawk T1A	RAF No 2 TWU/63 Sqn, Chivenor	
XX255	HS Hawk T1A	RAF No 2 TWU/63 Sqn, Chivenor	
XX256	HS Hawk T1	RAF No 2 TWU/63 Sqn, Chivenor	
XX257	HS Hawk T1	RAF No 1 SoTT, Halton	
XX258	HS Hawk T1A	RAF No 1 TWU/79 Sqn, Brawdy	
XX259	HS Hawk T1	RAF Red Arrows, Scampton	
XX260	HS Hawk T1A	RAF Red Arrows, Scampton	
XX261	HS Hawk T1A	RAF No 1 TWU/234 Sqn, Brawdy	
XX262	HS Hawk T1 replica (BAPC171)	RAF Exhibition Flight, Abingdon	
XX263	HS Hawk T1A	RAF No 2 TWU/63 Sqn, Chivenor	
XX264	HS Hawk T1A	RAF Red Arrows, Scampton	
XX265	HS Hawk T1A [U]	RAF No 2 TWU/151 Sqn, Chivenor	
XX266	HS Hawk T1	RAF Red Arrows, Scampton	
XX278	HS Hawk T1A	RAF No 2 TWU/63 Sqn, Chivenor	
XX280	HS Hawk T1A	RAF No 1 TWU/79 Sqn, Brawdy	
XX281	HS Hawk T1A [O]	RAF No 2 TWU/151 Sqn, Chivenor	
XX282	HS Hawk T1A	RAF No 2 TWU/63 Sqn, Chivenor	
XX283	HS Hawk T1A	RAF No 2 TWU/63 Sqn, Chivenor	
XX284	HS Hawk T1A	RAF No 2 TWU/63 Sqn, Chivenor	
XX285	HS Hawk T1 [R]	RAF No 2 TWU/151 Sqn, Chivenor	
XX286	HS Hawc T1A	RAF No 1 TWU/79 Sqn, Brawdy	
XX287	HS Hawk T1A	RAF No 2 TWU/63 Sqn, Chivenor	
XX288	HS Hawk T1A	RAF No 2 TWU/63 Sqn, Chivenor	
XX289	HS Hawk T1A	RAF No 2 TWU/63 Sqn, Chivenor	
XX290	HS Hawk T1	RAF No 4 FTS, Valley	
XX291	HS Hawk T1	RAF No 4 FTS, Valley	
XX292	HS Hawk T1	RAF No 4 FTS, Valley	
XX293	HS Hawk T1	RAF Wattisham Fire Section	
XX294	HS Hawk T1	RAF No 4 FTS, Valley	
XX295	HS Hawk T1	RAF No 4 FTS, Valley	
XX296	HS Hawk T1	RAF No 4 FTS, Valley	
XX297	HS Hawk T1	RAF Red Arrows, Scampton	
XX299	HS Hawk T1	RAF No 4 FTS, Valley	
XX300	HS Hawk T1 [S] (8827M)	RAF Abingdon BDRF	
XX301	HS Hawk T1A	RAF No 1 TWU/79 Sqn, Brawdy	
XX302	HS Hawk T1A	RAF No 1 TWU/234 Sqn, Brawdy	
XX303	HS Hawk T1A	RAF No 1 TWU/234 Sqn, Brawdy	
XX304	HS Hawk T1A	RAF Red Arrows, Scampton	
XX306	HS Hawk T1A	RAF Red Arrows, Scampton	
XX307	HS Hawk T1	RAF No 4 FTS, Valley	
XX308	HS Hawk T1A	RAF Red Arrows, Scampton	
XX309	HS Hawk T1	RAF No 4 FTS, Valley	
XX310	HS Hawk T1	RAF CFS, Valley	
XX311	HS Hawk T1	RAF No 4 FTS, Valley	
XX312	HS Hawk T1	RAF CFS, Valley	
XX313	HS Hawk T1	RAF No 4 FTS, Valley	
XX314	HS Hawk T1	RAF No 4 FTS, Valley	
XX315	HS Hawk T1A	RAF No 1 TWU/234 Sqn, Brawdy	
XX316	HS Hawk T1A	RAF No 1 TWU/79 Sqn, Brawdy	
XX317	HS Hawk T1A	RAF No 1 TWU/234 Sqn, Brawdy	
XX318	HS Hawk T1A	RAF No 1 TWU/79 Sqn, Brawdy	
XX319	HS Hawk T1A	RAF No 1 TWU/79 Sqn, Brawdy	
XX320	HS Hawk T1A [V]	RAF No 2 TWU/151 Sqn, Chivenor	
XX321	HS Hawk T1A	RAF No 1 TWU/79 Sqn, Brawdy	
XX322	HS Hawk T1A [W]	RAF No 2 TWU/151 Sqn, Chivenor	
XX323	HS Hawk T1A	RAF No 1 TWU/234 Sqn, Brawdy	
XX324	HS Hawk T1A	RAF No 1 TWU/234 Sqn, Brawdy	
XX325	HS Hawk T1 [X]	RAF No 2 TWU/151 Sqn, Chivenor	
XX326	HS Hawk T1A [A]	RAF No 2 TWU/151 Sqn, Chivenor	
XX327	HS Hawk T1A [B]	RAF No 2 TWU/151 Sqn, Chivenor	

Notes	Serial	Type (alternative identity)	Owner, Operator or Location
	XX329	HS Hawk T1 [C]	RAF No 2 TWU/151 Sqn, Chivenor
	XX330	HS Hawk T1A [D]	RAF No 2 TWU/151 Sqn, Chivenor
	XX331	HS Hawk T1A [E]	RAF No 2 TWU/151 Sqn, Chivenor
	XX332	HS Hawk T1A [F]	RAF No 2 TWU/151 Sqn, Chivenor
	XX334	HS Hawk T1A [H]	RAF No 2 TWU/151 Sqn, Chivenor
	XX335	HS Hawk T1A [I]	RAF No 2 TWU/151 Sqn, Chivenor
	XX337	HS Hawk T1A [K]	RAF No 2 TWU/151 Sqn, Chivenor
	XX338	HS Hawk T1	RAF No 4 FTS, Valley
	XX339	HS Hawk T1A	RAF No 1 TWU/234 Sqn, Brawdy
	XX341	HS Hawk T1 ASTRA [1]	MoD(PE) Institute of Technology, Cranfield
	XX342	HS Hawk T1 [2]	MoD(PE) ETPS Boscombe Down
	XX343	HS Hawk T1 [3]	MoD(PE) ETPS Boscombe Down
	XX344	HS Hawk T1 (8847M)	RAF Abingdon, BDRF
	XX345	HS Hawk T1A [Y]	RAF No 2 TWU/151 Sqn, Chivenor
	XX346	HS Hawk T1A [T]	RAF No 2 TWU/151 Sqn, Chivenor
	XX347	HS Hawk T1	RAF No 4 FTS, Valley
	XX348	HS Hawk T1A	RAF No 1 TWU, Brawdy
	XX349	HS Hawk T1	RAF No 4 FTS, Valley
	XX350	HS Hawk T1A	RAF No 1 TWU/234 Sqn, Brawdy
	XX351	HS Hawk T1A	RAF No 1 TWU/234 Sqn, Brawdy
	XX352	HS Hawk T1A	RAF No 2 TWU/63 Sqn, Chivenor
	XX370	Westland Gazelle AH1 [A]	AAC ARWS, Middle Wallop
	XX371	Westland Gazelle AH1	AAC No 12 Flt, Wildenrath
	XX372	Westland Gazelle AH1 [B]	AAC No 658 Sqn, Netheravon
	XX373	Westland Gazelle AH1	AAC No 663 Sqn, Soest
	XX375	Westland Gazelle AH1 [C]	AAC No 658 Sqn, Netheravon
	XX376	Westland Gazelle AH1 [D]	RM 3 CBAS, Yeovilton
	XX377	Westland Gazelle AH1 [L]	RM 3 CBAS, Yeovilton
	XX378	Westland Gazelle AH1	Westlands, Yeovil, on rebuild
	XX379	Westland Gazelle AH1 [D]	AAC No 658 Sqn, Netheravon
	XX380	Westland Gazelle AH1 [33B]	RM 3 CBAS, Yeovilton
	XX381	Westland Gazelle AH1	AAC No 2 Flt, Netheravon
	XX382	Westland Gazelle HT3 [M]	RAF No 2 FTS, Shawbury
	XX383	Westland Gazelle AH1 [E]	AAC No 658 Sqn, Netheravon
	XX384	Westland Gazelle AH1	AAC No 2 Flt, Netheravon
	XX385	Westland Gazelle AH1	AAC No 661 Sqn, Hildesheim
	XX386	Westland Gazelle AH1	AAC No 12 Flt, Wildenrath
	XX387	Westland Gazelle AH1	AAC No 661 Sqn, Hildesheim
	XX388	Westland Gazelle AH1	AAC No 652 Sqn, Hildesheim
	XX389	Westland Gazelle AH1	AAC No 652 Sqn, Hildesheim
	XX391	Westland Gazelle HT2 [56/CU]	RN No 705 Sqn, Culdrose
	XX392	Westland Gazelle AH1 [W]	AAC ARWS, Middle Wallop
	XX393	Westland Gazelle AH1	AAC No 2 Flt, Netheravon
	XX394	Westland Gazelle AH1	AAC No 2 Flt, Netheravon
	XX395	Westland Gazelle AH1	AAC No 661 Sqn, Hildesheim
	XX396	Westland Gazelle HT3 [N] (8718M)	RAF Exhibition Flight, Abingdon
	XX398	Westland Gazelle AH1	AAC No 661 Sqn, Hildesheim
	XX399	Westland Gazelle AH1	RM 3 CBAS, Yeovilton
	XX403	Westland Gazelle AH1 [Y]	AAC ARWS, Middle Wallop
	XX405	Westland Gazelle AH1	AAC No 659 Sqn, Detmold
	XX406	Westland Gazelle HT3 [P]	RAF No 2 FTS, Shawbury
	XX407	Westland Gazelle AH1	AAC No 655 Sqn, Aldergrove
	XX408	Westland Gazelle AH1	AAC No 655 Sqn, Aldergrove
	XX409	Westland Gazelle AH1	AAC No 656 Sqn, Netheravon
	XX410	Westland Gazelle HT2 [58/CU]	RN AES Lee-on-Solent
	XX411	Westland Gazelle AH1 [X] tail only	FAA Museum, RNAS Yeovilton
	XX412	Westland Gazelle AH1 [33C]	RM 3 CBAS, Yeovilton
	XX413	Westland Gazelle AH1 [33D]	RM 3 CBAS, Yeovilton
	XX414	Westland Gazelle AH1	AAC No 663 Sqn, Soest
	XX416	Westland Gazelle AH1	AAC No 664 Sqn, Minden
	XX417	Westland Gazelle AH1 [A]	AAC No 653 Sqn, Soest
	XX418	Westland Gazelle AH1	AAC No 664 Sqn, Minden
	XX419	Westland Gazelle AH1	AAC No 664 Sqn, Minden
	XX431	Westland Gazelle HT2 [43/CU]	RN No 705 Sqn, Culdrose
	XX432	Westland Gazelle AH1	AAC No 664 Sqn, Minden
	XX433	Westland Gazelle AH1 [B]	AAC No 653 Sqn, Soest
	XX434	Westland Gazelle AH1	RAF Abingdon, BDRF
	XX435	Westland Gazelle AH1	AAC No 663 Sqn, Soest

Serial	*Type (alternative identity)*	*Owner, Operator or Location*	*Notes*
XX436	Westland Gazelle HT2 [39/CU]	RN No 705 Sqn, Culdrose	
XX437	Westland Gazelle AH1	AAC No 663 Sqn, Soest	
XX438	Westland Gazelle AH1	AAC No 664 Sqn, Minden	
XX439	Westland Gazelle AH1	AAC No 651 Sqn, Hildesheim	
XX440	Westland Gazelle AH1 (G-BCHN) [C]	AAC No 653 Sqn, Soest	
XX441	Westland Gazelle HT2 [38/CU]	RN No 705 Sqn, Culdrose	
XX442	Westland Gazelle AH1	AAC No 669 Sqn, Detmold	
XX443	Westland Gazelle AH1	AAC No 669 Sqn, Detmold	
XX444	Westland Gazelle AH1	AAC No 656 Sqn, Netheravon	
XX445	Westland Gazelle AH1	AAC No 659 Sqn, Detmold	
XX446	Westland Gazelle HT2 [57/CU]	RN No 705 Sqn, Culdrose	
XX447	Westland Gazelle AH1	AAC No 669 Sqn, Detmold	
XX448	Westland Gazelle AH1	AAC No 659 Sqn, Detmold	
XX449	Westland Gazelle AH1	AAC No 669 Sqn, Detmold	
XX450	Westland Gazelle AH1 [13B]	RM 3 CBAS, Yeovilton	
XX451	Westland Gazelle HT2 [58/CU]	RN No 705 Sqn, Culdrose	
XX452	Westland Gazelle AH1	AAC Fire Section Middle Wallop	
XX453	Westland Gazelle AH1	AAC No 659 Sqn, Detmold	
XX454	Westland Gazelle AH1	AAC No 659 Sqn, Detmold	
XX455	Westland Gazelle AH1	AAC No 663 Sqn, Soest	
XX456	Westland Gazelle AH1	AAC No 669 Sqn, Detmold	
XX457	Westland Gazelle AH1 [H]	AAC ARWS, Middle Wallop	
XX460	Westland Gazelle AH1	AAC No 652 Sqn, Hildesheim	
XX462	Westland Gazelle AH1	AAC No 661 Sqn, Hildesheim	
XX466	HS Hunter T66B/T7 [879/VL]	RN, Shawbury store	
XX467	HS Hunter T66B/T7 [86]	Air Service Training, Perth	
XX475	SA Jetstream T2 [572/CU] (N1036S)	RN No 750 Sqn, Culdrose	
XX476	SA Jetstream T2 [561/CU] (N1037S)	RN No 750 Sqn, Culdrose	
XX477	SA Jetstream T1 (8462M)	RAF Finningley — ground instruction	
XX478	SA Jetstream T2 [564/CU] (G-AXXT)	RN No 750 Sqn, Culdrose	
XX479	SA Jetstream T2 [563/CU] (G-AXUR)	RN No 750 Sqn, Culdrose	
XX480	SA Jetstream T2 [565/CU] (G-AXXU)	RN No 750 Sqn, Culdrose	
XX481	SA Jetstream T2 [560/CU] (G-AXUP)	RN No 750 Sqn, Culdrose	
XX482	SA Jetstream T1 [J]	RAF No 6 FTS, Finningley	
XX483	SA Jetstream T2 [562/CU]	RN No 750 Sqn, Culdrose	
XX484	SA Jetstream T2 [566/CU]	RN No 750 Sqn, Culdrose	
XX485	SA Jetstream T2 [567/CU]	RN No 750 Sqn, Culdrose	
XX486	SA Jetstream T2 [569/CU]	RN No 750 Sqn, Culdrose	
XX487	SA Jetstream T2 [568/CU]	RN No 750 Sqn, Culdrose	
XX488	SA Jetstream T2 [571/CU]	RN No 750 Sqn, Culdrose	
XX489	SA Jetstream T2 [575/CU]	RN No 750 Sqn, Culdrose	
XX490	SA Jetstream T2 [570/CU]	RN No 750 Sqn, Culdrose	
XX491	SA Jetstream T1 [K]	RAF No 6 FTS, Finningley	
XX492	SA Jetstream T1 [A]	RAF No 6 FTS, Finningley	
XX493	SA Jetstream T1 [L]	RAF No 6 FTS, Finningley	
XX494	SA Jetstream T1 [B]	RAF No 6 FTS, Finningley	
XX495	SA Jetstream T1 [C]	RAF No 6 FTS, Finningley	
XX496	SA Jetstream T1 [D]	RAF No 6 FTS, Finningley	
XX497	SA Jetstream T1 [E]	RAF No 6 FTS, Finningley	
XX498	SA Jetstream T1 [F]	RAF No 6 FTS, Finningley	
XX499	SA Jetstream T1 [G]	RAF No 6 FTS, Finningley	
XX500	SA Jetstream T1 [H]	RAF No 6 FTS, Finningley	
XX507	HS125 CC2	RAF No 32 Sqn, Northolt	
XX508	HS125 CC2	RAF No 32 Sqn, Northolt	
XX513	SA Bulldog T1 [A]	RAF No 1 FTS/RNEFTS, Topcliffe	
XX514	SA Bulldog T1 [B]	RAF No 1 FTS/RNEFTS, Topcliffe	
XX515	SA Bulldog T1 [7]	RAF CFS, Scampton	
XX516	SA Bulldog T1 [C]	RAF No 1 FTS/RNEFTS Topcliffe	
XX517	SA Bulldog T1 [8]	RAF CFS, Scampton	
XX518	SA Bulldog T1 [24]	RAF Shawbury store	
XX519	SA Bulldog T1 [I]	RAF No 1 FTS/RNEFTS, Topcliffe	
XX520	SA Bulldog T1 [2]	RAF CFS, Scampton	
XX521	SA Bulldog T1 [01]	RAF, East Lowlands UAS, Turnhouse	
XX522	SA Bulldog T1 [E]	RAF No 1 FTS/RNEFTS, Topcliffe	
XX523	SA Bulldog T1 [F]	RAF No 1 FTS/RNEFTS, Topcliffe	

Notes	Serial	Type (alternative identity)	Owner, Operator or Location
	XX524	SA Bulldog T1 [04]	RAF, London UAS, Abingdon
	XX525	SA Bulldog T1 [03]	RAF, East Lowlands UAS, Turnhouse
	XX526	SA Bulldog T1 [C]	RAF, Oxford UAS, Abingdon
	XX527	SA Bulldog T1 [G]	RAF No 1 FTS/RNEFTS, Topcliffe
	XX528	SA Bulldog T1 [D]	RAF, Oxford UAS, Abingdon
	XX529	SA Bulldog T1 [H]	RAF No 1 FTS/RNEFTS, Topcliffe
	XX530	SA Bulldog T1 [12]	CTE, RAF Manston
	XX531	SA Bulldog T1 [4]	RAF CFS, Scampton
	XX532	SA Bulldog T1 [5]	RAF CFS, Scampton
	XX533	SA Bulldog T1 [J]	RAF No 1 FTS/RNEFTS, Topcliffe
	XX534	SA Bulldog T1 [04]	RAF, East Lowlands UAS, Turnhouse
	XX535	SA Bulldog T1 [10]	RAF, London UAS, Abingdon
	XX536	SA Bulldog T1 [9]	RAF CFS, Scampton
	XX537	SA Bulldog T1 [02]	RAF, East Lowlands UAS, Turnhouse
	XX538	SA Bulldog T1 [E]	RAF Shawbury store
	XX539	SA Bulldog T1 [1]	RAF CFS, Scampton
	XX540	SA Bulldog T1 [K]	RAF No 1 FTS/RNEFTS, Topcliffe
	XX541	SA Bulldog T1 [L]	RAF No 1 FTS/RNEFTS, Topcliffe
	XX543	SA Bulldog T1 [F]	RAF, Yorkshire UAS, Finningley
	XX544	SA Bulldog T1 [01]	RAF, London UAS, Abingdon
	XX545	SA Bulldog T1 PAX [02]	RAF, East Lowlands UAS, Turnhouse
	XX546	SA Bulldog T1 [03]	RAF, London UAS, Abingdon
	XX547	SA Bulldog T1 [05]	RAF, London UAS, Abingdon
	XX548	SA Bulldog T1 [06]	RAF, London UAS, Abingdon
	XX549	SA Bulldog T1 [5]	RAF, Manchester UAS, Woodvale
	XX550	SA Bulldog T1 [8]	RAF Shawbury store
	XX551	SA Bulldog T1 [M]	RAF No 1 FTS/RNEFTS, Topcliffe
	XX552	SA Bulldog T1 [08]	RAF, London UAS, Abingdon
	XX553	SA Bulldog T1 [07]	RAF, London UAS, Abingdon
	XX554	SA Bulldog T1 [09]	RAF, London UAS, Abingdon
	XX555	SA Bulldog T1 [10]	RAF CFS, Scampton
	XX556	SA Bulldog T1 [S]	RAF, East Midlands UAS, Newton
	XX557	SA Bulldog T1 PAX	RAF Topcliffe, ground instruction
	XX558	SA Bulldog T1 [A]	RAF, Birmingham UAS, Cosford
	XX559	SA Bulldog T1	RAF, Glasgow & Strathclyde UAS, Glasgow
	XX560	SA Bulldog T1	RAF, Glasgow & Strathclyde UAS, Glasgow
	XX561	SA Bulldog T1 [A]	RAF, Aberdeen, Dundee & St Andrews UAS, Leuchars
	XX562	SA Bulldog T1 [S]	RAF, Queen's UAS, Sydenham
	XX611	SA Bulldog T1	RAF, Glasgow & Strathclyde UAS, Glasgow
	XX612	SA Bulldog T1 [05]	RAF, Wales UAS, St Athan
	XX613	SA Bulldog T1 [A]	RAF, Queen's UAS, Sydenham
	XX614	SA Bulldog T1 [1]	RAF Shawbury store
	XX615	SA Bulldog T1 [2]	RAF, Manchester UAS, Woodvale
	XX616	SA Bulldog T1 [3]	RAF, Manchester UAS, Woodvale
	XX617	SA Bulldog T1 [4]	RAF, Manchester UAS, Woodvale
	XX619	SA Bulldog T1 [B]	RAF, Yorkshire UAS, Finningley
	XX620	SA Bulldog T1 [C]	RAF, Yorkshire UAS, Finningley
	XX621	SA Bulldog T1 [D]	RAF, Yorkshire UAS, Finningley
	XX622	SA Bulldog T1 [E]	RAF, Yorkshire UAS, Finningley
	XX623	SA Bulldog T1 [M]	RAF, East Midlands UAS, Newton
	XX624	SA Bulldog T1 [G]	RAF, Yorkshire UAS, Finningley
	XX625	SA Bulldog T1 [01]	RAF, Wales UAS, St Athan
	XX626	SA Bulldog T1 [02]	RAF, Wales UAS, St Athan
	XX627	SA Bulldog T1 [03]	RAF, Wales UAS, St Athan
	XX628	SA Bulldog T1 [04]	RAF, Wales UAS, St Athan
	XX629	SA Bulldog T1 [V]	RAF, Northumbria UAS, Teesside
	XX630	SA Bulldog T1 [A]	RAF, Liverpool UAS, Woodvale
	XX631	SA Bulldog T1 [W]	RAF, Northumbria UAS, Teesside
	XX632	SA Bulldog T1 [D]	RAF, Bristol UAS, Filton
	XX633	SA Bulldog T1 [X]	RAF, Northumbria UAS, Teesside
	XX634	SA Bulldog T1 [C]	RAF, Cambridge UAS, Teversham
	XX635	SA Bulldog T1 (8767M) [S]	RAF St Athan CTTS
	XX636	SA Bulldog T1 [Y]	RAF, Northumbria UAS, Teesside
	XX637	SA Bulldog T1 [Z]	RAF, Northumbria UAS, Teesside
	XX638	SA Bulldog T1 [N]	RAF No 1 FTS/RNEFTS, Topcliffe
	XX639	SA Bulldog T1 [02]	RAF, London UAS, Abingdon
	XX640	SA Bulldog T1 [U]	RAF, Queen's UAS, Sydenham
	XX653	SA Bulldog T1 [E]	RAF, Bristol UAS, Filton
	XX654	SA Bulldog T1 [A]	RAF, Bristol UAS, Filton
	XX655	SA Bulldog T1 [B]	RAF, Bristol UAS, Filton

Serial	Type (alternative identity)	Owner, Operator or Location	Notes
XX656	SA Bulldog T1 [C]	RAF, Bristol UAS, Filton	
XX657	SA Bulldog T1 [U]	RAF, Cambridge UAS, Teversham	
XX658	SA Bulldog T1 [A]	RAF, Cambridge UAS, Teversham	
XX659	SA Bulldog T1 [S]	RAF, Cambridge UAS, Teversham	
XX661	SA Bulldog T1 [B]	RAF, Oxford UAS, Abingdon	
XX663	SA Bulldog T1 [B]	RAF, Aberdeen, Dundee & St Andrews UAS, Leuchars	
XX664	SA Bulldog T1 [05]	RAF, East Lowlands UAS, Turnhouse	
XX665	SA Bulldog T1 [E]	RAF, Aberdeen, Dundee & St Andrews UAS, Leuchars	
XX666	SA Bulldog T1 [C]	RAF, Aberdeen, Dundee & St Andrews UAS, Leuchars	
XX667	SA Bulldog T1 [D]	RAF, Aberdeen, Dundee & St Andrews UAS, Leuchars	
XX668	SA Bulldog T1 [P]	RAF No 1 FTS/RNEFTS, Topcliffe	
XX669	SA Bulldog T1 [B]	RAF, Birmingham UAS, Cosford	
XX670	SA Bulldog T1 [C]	RAF, Birmingham UAS, Cosford	
XX671	SA Bulldog T1 [D]	RAF, Birmingham UAS, Cosford	
XX672	SA Bulldog T1 [E]	RAF, Birmingham UAS, Cosford	
XX685	SA Bulldog T1 [L]	RAF, Liverpool UAS, Woodvale	
XX686	SA Bulldog T1 [U]	RAF, Liverpool UAS, Woodvale	
XX687	SA Bulldog T1 [A]	RAF, East Midlands UAS, Newton	
XX688	SA Bulldog T1 [S]	RAF, Liverpool UAS, Woodvale	
XX689	SA Bulldog T1 [3]	RAF CFS, Scampton	
XX690	SA Bulldog T1 [A]	RAF, Yorkshire UAS, Finningley	
XX691	SA Bulldog T1	RAF Shawbury store	
XX692	SA Bulldog T1	RAF Shawbury store	
XX693	SA Bulldog T1	RAF Kemble store	
XX694	SA Bulldog T1 [E]	RAF, East Midlands UAS, Newton	
XX695	SA Bulldog T1 [A]	RAF, Oxford UAS, Abingdon	
XX696	SA Bulldog T1	RAF Kemble store	
XX697	SA Bulldog T1 [Q]	RAF, Queen's UAS, Sydenham	
XX698	SA Bulldog T1 [D]	RAF No 1 FTS/RNEFTS, Topcliffe	
XX699	SA Bulldog T1 [Q]	RAF No 1 FTS/RNEFTS, Topcliffe	
XX700	SA Bulldog T1 [R]	RAF No 1 FTS/RNEFTS, Topcliffe	
XX701	SA Bulldog T1 [02]	RAF, Southampton UAS, Hurn	
XX702	SA Bulldog T1	RAF, Glasgow & Strathclyde UAS, Glasgow	
XX704	SA Bulldog T1 [U]	RAF, East Midlands UAS, Newton	
XX705	SA Bulldog T1 [05]	RAF, Southampton UAS, Hurn	
XX706	SA Bulldog T1 [01]	RAF, Southampton UAS, Hurn	
XX707	SA Bulldog T1 [04]	RAF, Southampton UAS, Hurn	
XX708	SA Bulldog T1 [03]	RAF, Southampton UAS, Hurn	
XX709	SA Bulldog T1 [33]	RAF Shawbury store	
XX710	SA Bulldog T1 [34]	RAF Shawbury store	
XX711	SA Bulldog T1 [E]	RAF No 13 AEF, Sydenham	
XX712	SA Bulldog T1 [D]	RAF No 1 FTS/RNEFTS, Topcliffe	
XX713	SA Bulldog T1 [6]	RAF CFS, Scampton	
XX714	SA Bulldog T1	MoD(PE) BAe Prestwick	
XX718	SEPECAT Jaguar Replica (BAPC150)	RAF Exhibition Flight, Abingdon	
XX719	SEPECAT Jaguar GR1 [EB]	RAF No 6 Sqn, Coltishall	
XX720	SEPECAT Jaguar GR1A [GQ]	RAF No 54 Sqn, Coltishall	
XX722	SEPECAT Jaguar GR1 [EF]	RAF store, Shawbury	
XX723	SEPECAT Jaguar GR1A [EQ]	RAF No 6 Sqn, Coltishall	
XX724	SEPECAT Jaguar GR1A [GA]	RAF No 54 Sqn, Coltishall	
XX725	SEPECAT Jaguar GR1A [EL]	RAF No 6 Sqn, Coltishall	
XX726	SEPECAT Jaguar GR1 [EB]	RAF store, Shawbury	
XX727	SEPECAT Jaguar GR1 [ER]	RAF store, Shawbury	
XX729	SEPECAT Jaguar GR1 [EJ]	RAF store, Shawbury	
XX730	SEPECAT Jaguar GR1 [EC]	RAF store, Shawbury	
XX732	SEPECAT Jaguar GR1A [03]	RAF No 226 OCU, Lossiemouth	
XX733	SEPECAT Jaguar GR1A [GL]	RAF No 54 Sqn, Coltishall	
XX734	SEPECAT Jaguar GR1 (JI014) (8816M)	RAF Coltishall, BDRT	
XX736	SEPECAT Jaguar GR1 (JI013)	BAe Warton	
XX737	SEPECAT Jaguar GR1 [EN] (JI015)	RAF JMU, Abingdon	
XX738	SEPECAT Jaguar GR1A (JI016) [GJ]	RAF No 54 Sqn, Coltishall	
XX739	SEPECAT Jaguar GR1 [I]	RAF store, Shawbury	
XX741	SEPECAT Jaguar GR1A [EJ]	RAF JMU, Abingdon	
XX743	SEPECAT Jaguar GR1 [EG]	RAF store, Shawbury	
XX744	SEPECAT Jaguar GR1 [DJ]	RAF store, Shawbury	

Notes	Serial	Type (alternative identity)	Owner, Operator or Location
	XX745	SEPECAT Jaguar GR1A [GN]	RAF No 54 Sqn, Coltishall
	XX746	SEPECAT Jaguar GR1 [AB]	RAF Coltishall
	XX747	SEPECAT Jaguar GR1 [B]	RAF store, Shawbury
	XX748	SEPECAT Jaguar GR1 [AA]	RAF Coltishall
	XX751	SEPECAT Jaguar GR1 [10]	RAF No 226 OCU, Lossiemouth
	XX752	SEPECAT Jaguar GR1A [GF]	RAF No 54 Sqn, Coltishall
	XX753	SEPECAT Jaguar GR1 [05]	RAF No 226 OCU, Lossiemouth
	XX754	SEPECAT Jaguar GR1 [23]	RAF No 226 OCU, Lossiemouth
	XX756	SEPECAT Jaguar GR1 [AM]	RAF Coltishall
	XX757	SEPECAT Jaguar GR1 [CU]	RAF store, Shawbury
	XX761	SEPECAT Jaguar GR1 (8600M) nose only	RAF Lossiemouth for ground instruction, BAe Warton
	XX763	SEPECAT Jaguar GR1 [24]	RAF store, Shawbury
	XX764	SEPECAT Jaguar GR1 [13]	RAF store, Shawbury
	XX765	SEPECAT Jaguar ACT	MoD(PE) BAe Warton
	XX766	SEPECAT Jaguar GR1A [GP]	RAF No 54 Sqn, Coltishall
	XX767	SEPECAT Jaguar GR1 [17]	RAF No 226 OCU, Lossiemouth
	XX818	SEPECAT Jaguar GR1 [DE]	RAF store, Shawbury
	XX819	SEPECAT Jaguar GR1 [CE]	RAF store, Shawbury
	XX821	SEPECAT Jaguar GR1 [P]	RAF No 41 Sqn, Coltishall
	XX824	SEPECAT Jaguar GR1 [AD]	RAF store, Shawbury
	XX824	SEPECAT Jaguar replica (BAPC 151)	RAF Exhibition Flight, Abingdon
	XX825	SEPECAT Jaguar GR1	RAF store, Shawbury
	XX826	SEPECAT Jaguar GR1 [34]	RAF store, Shawbury
	XX829	SEPECAT Jaguar T2 [ER]	RAF No 6 Sqn, Coltishall
	XX830	SEPECAT Jaguar T2	MoD(PE) ETPS Boscombe Down
	XX832	SEPECAT Jaguar T2 [S]	RAF No 226 OCU, Lossiemouth
	XX833	SEPECAT Jaguar T2 [AY]	—
	XX834	SEPECAT Jaguar T2A [34]	RAF No 2 Sqn, Laarbruch
	XX835	SEPECAT Jaguar T2	MoD(PE) RAE Farnborough
	XX836	SEPECAT Jaguar T2A [ER]	RAF No 6 Sqn, Coltishall
	XX837	SEPECAT Jaguar T2A [Z]	RAF No 226 OCU, Lossiemouth
	XX838	SEPECAT Jaguar T2A [X]	RAF No 226 OCU, Lossiemouth
	XX839	SEPECAT Jaguar T2 [Y]	RAF No 226 OCU, Lossiemouth
	XX840	SEPECAT Jaguar T2 [T]	RAF No 226 OCU, Lossiemouth
	XX841	SEPECAT Jaguar T2 [S]	RAF No 41 Sqn, Coltishall
	XX842	SEPECAT Jaguar T2 [T]	RAF No 41 Sqn, Coltishall
	XX843	SEPECAT Jaguar T2A [36]	RAF No 2 Sqn, Laarbruch
	XX844	SEPECAT Jaguar T2 [F]	RAF No 226 OCU, Lossiemouth
	XX845	SEPECAT Jaguar T2	RAF Coltishall
	XX846	SEPECAT Jaguar T2A [A]	RAF No 226 OCU, Lossiemouth
	XX847	SEPECAT Jaguar T2 [G]	RAF No 226 OCU, Lossiemouth
	XX885	HS Buccaneer S2B [BC]	RAF No 237 OCU, Lossiemouth
	XX886	HS Buccaneer S2B	RAF Honington, ASF
	XX887	HS Buccaneer S2B [N]	RAF store, Shawbury
	XX888	HS Buccaneer S2B [Z]	RAF store, Shawbury
	XX889	HS Buccaneer S2B [WS]	RAF No 208 Sqn, Lossiemouth
	XX892	HS Buccaneer S2B [FC]	RAF No 237 OCU, Lossiemouth
	XX893	HS Buccaneer S2B [DC]	RAF No 237 OCU, Lossiemouth
	XX894	HS Buccaneer S2B [HS]	RAF No 208 Sqn, Lossiemouth
	XX895	HS Buccaneer S2B	RAF No 237 OCU, Lossiemouth
	XX896	HS Buccaneer S2B	RAF Shawbury, store
	XX897	HS Buccaneer S2B	MoD(PE) RS&RE Bedford
	XX899	HS Buccaneer S2B [JC]	RAF No 237 OCU, Lossiemouth
	XX900	HS Buccaneer S2B [MS]	RAF No 208 Sqn, Lossiemouth
	XX901	HS Buccaneer S2B [GS]	RAF No 208 Sqn, Lossiemouth
	XX914	BAC VC10 srs 1103 (G-ATDJ/ 8777M)	RAF AMS, Brize Norton
	XX919	BAC 1-11/402 (PI-C 1121)	MoD(PE) RAE Farnborough
	XX946	Panavia Tornado (P02)	MoD(PE) BAe Warton
	XX947	Panavia Tornado (P03) (8797M)	RAF Marham for ground instruction
	XX948	Panavia Tornado (P06)	RAF No 2 SoTT, Cosford
	XX955	SEPECAT Jaguar GR1 [AN]	RAF Coltishall
	XX956	SEPECAT Jaguar GR1 [BE]	RAF store, Shawbury
	XX958	SEPECAT Jaguar GR1 [BK]	RAF store, Shawbury
	XX959	SEPECAT Jaguar GR1 [CJ]	RAF store, Shawbury
	XX962	SEPECAT Jaguar GR1 [BG]	RAF JMU, Abingdon
	XX965	SEPECAT Jaguar GR1A [GB]	RAF No 54 Sqn, Coltishall
	XX966	SEPECAT Jaguar GR1A [EL]	RAF JMU, Abingdon
	XX967	SEPECAT Jaguar GR1 [AC]	RAF store, Shawbury
	XX968	SEPECAT Jaguar GR1 [AJ]	RAF store, Shawbury
	XX969	SEPECAT Jaguar GR1 [01]	RAF No 226 OCU, Lossiemouth

Serial	Type (alternative identity)	Owner, Operator or Location	Notes
XX970	SEPECAT Jaguar GR1 [11]	RAF No 226 OCU, Lossiemouth	
XX974	SEPECAT Jaguar GR1A [EG]	RAF No 6 Sqn, Coltishall	
XX975	SEPECAT Jaguar GR1 [07]	RAF No 226 OCU, Lossiemouth	
XX976	SEPECAT Jaguar GR1	RAF store, Shawbury	
XX977	SEPECAT Jaguar GR1 [DL]	RAF store, Shawbury	
XX979	SEPECAT Jaguar GR1A	MoD(PE) A&AEE Boscombe Down	
XZ101	SEPECAT Jaguar GR1A [20]	RAF No 2 Sqn, Laarbruch	
XZ103	SEPECAT Jaguar GR1A [23]	RAF No 2 Sqn, Laarbruch	
XZ104	SEPECAT Jaguar GR1A [24]	RAF No 2 Sqn, Laarbruch	
XZ106	SEPECAT Jaguar GR1A [26]	RAF No 2 Sqn, Laarbruch	
XZ107	SEPECAT Jaguar GR1 [H]	RAF No 41 Sqn, Coltishall	
XZ108	SEPECAT Jaguar GR1A [28]	RAF No 2 Sqn, Laarbruch	
XZ109	SEPECAT Jaguar GR1A [29]	RAF No 2 Sqn, Laarbruch	
XZ111	SEPECAT Jaguar GR1A [31]	RAF No 2 Sqn, Laarbruch	
XZ112	SEPECAT Jaguar GR1A [32]	RAF No 2 Sqn, Laarbruch	
XZ113	SEPECAT Jaguar GR1A [30]	RAF No 2 Sqn, Laarbruch	
XZ114	SEPECAT Jaguar GR1 [B]	RAF No 41 Sqn, Coltishall	
XZ115	SEPECAT Jaguar GR1 [C]	RAF No 41 Sqn, Coltishall	
XZ116	SEPECAT Jaguar GR1 [D]	RAF No 41 Sqn, Coltishall	
XZ117	SEPECAT Jaguar GR1 [E]	RAF No 41 Sqn, Coltishall	
XZ118	SEPECAT Jaguar GR1 [F]	RAF No 41 Sqn, Coltishall	
XZ119	SEPECAT Jaguar GR1 [G]	RAF No 41 Sqn, Coltishall	
XZ129	HS Harrier GR3 [06]	RAF No 1 Sqn, Wittering	
XZ130	HS Harrier GR3 [AH]	RAF No 3 Sqn, Gutersloh	
XZ131	HS Harrier GR3 [02]	RAF No 1 Sqn, Wittering	
XZ132	HS Harrier GR3 [09]	RAF No 1 Sqn, Wittering	
XZ133	HS Harrier GR3 [10]	RAF No 1 Sqn, Wittering	
XZ135	HS Harrier GR3 [P] (8848M)	RAF Exhibition Flight, Abingdon	
XZ136	HS Harrier GR3	MoD(PE) A&AEE Boscombe Down	
XZ138	HS Harrier GR3 [02]	RAF No 1 Sqn, Wittering	
XZ145	HS Harrier T4 [T]	RAF No 233 OCU, Wittering	
XZ146	HS Harrier T4 [W]	RAF No 233 OCU, Wittering	
XZ147	HS Harrier T4A [Z]	RAF No 233 OCU, Wittering	
XZ170	Westland Lynx AH1	MoD(PE) Westlands, Yeovil	
XZ171	Westland Lynx AH1	MoD(PE)/Rolls-Royce, Filton	
XZ172	Westland Lynx AH1 [K]	AAC ARW/LCF, Middle Wallop	
XZ173	Westland Lynx AH1	AAC No 651 Sqn, Hildesheim	
XZ174	Westland Lynx AH1	AAC No 651 Sqn, Hildesheim	
XZ175	Westland Lynx AH1 [C]	AAC ARW/LCF, Middle Wallop	
XZ176	Westland Lynx AH1 [A]	AAC ATS, Middle Wallop	
XZ177	Westland Lynx AH1	AAC No 652 Sqn, Hildesheim	
XZ178	Westland Lynx AH1	AAC No 654 Sqn, Detmold	
XZ179	Westland Lynx AH1	MoD(PE) ETPS Boscombe Down	
XZ180	Westland Lynx AH1	MoD(PE) Westlands, Yeovil	
XZ181	Westland Lynx AH1	AAC No 654 Sqn, Detmold	
XZ182	Westland Lynx AH1 [23A]	RM 3 CBAS, Yeovilton	
XZ183	Westland Lynx AH1	AAC No 654 Sqn, Detmold	
XZ184	Westland Lynx AH1	AAC No 654 Sqn, Detmold	
XZ185	Westland Lynx AH1	AAC No 662 Sqn, Munster	
XZ186	Westland Lynx AH1	AAC No 662 Sqn, Munster	
XZ187	Westland Lynx AH1	AAC No 655 Sqn, Aldergrove	
XZ188	Westland Lynx AH1	AAC No 655 Sqn, Aldergrove	
XZ190	Westland Lynx AH1	AAC No 651 Sqn, Hildesheim	
XZ191	Westland Lynx AH1	AAC No 651 Sqn, Hildesheim	
XZ192	Westland Lynx AH1	AAC No 651 Sqn, Hildesheim	
XZ193	Westland Lynx AH1	AAC No 653 Sqn, Soest	
XZ194	Westland Lynx AH1	AAC No 663 Sqn, Soest	
XZ195	Westland Lynx AH1	AAC No 663 Sqn, Soest	
XZ196	Westland Lynx AH1	AAC No 653 Sqn, Soest	
XZ197	Westland Lynx AH1	AAC No 663 Sqn, Soest	
XZ198	Westland Lynx AH1	AAC No 653 Sqn, Soest	
XZ199	Westland Lynx AH1	AAC No 653 Sqn, Soest	
XZ203	Westland Lynx AH1 [B]	AAC ARW/LCF, Middle Wallop	
XZ204	Westland Lynx AH1	AAC No 662 Sqn, Munster	
XZ205	Westland Lynx AH1 [E]	AAC D&TS, Middle Wallop	
XZ206	Westland Lynx AH1	AAC No 655 Sqn, Aldergrove	
XZ207	Westland Lynx AH1	AAC No 655 Sqn, Aldergrove	
XZ208	Westland Lynx AH1	AAC No 659 Sqn, Detmold	
XZ209	Westland Lynx AH1	AAC No 662 Sqn, Munster	
XZ210	Westland Lynx AH1	AAC No 656 Sqn, Netheravon	
XZ211	Westland Lynx AH1	AAC No 659 Sqn, Detmold	
XZ212	Westland Lynx AH1	AAC No 659 Sqn, Detmold	
XZ213	Westland Lynx AH1	AAC No 659 Sqn, Detmold	

Notes	Serial	Type (alternative identity)	Owner, Operator or Location
	XZ214	Westland Lynx AH1	AAC store, Wroughton
	XZ215	Westland Lynx AH1	AAC AETW, Middle Wallop
	XZ216	Westland Lynx AH1	AAC No 662 Sqn, Munster
	XZ217	Westland Lynx AH1	AAC No 663 Sqn, Soest
	XZ218	Westland Lynx AH1	AAC No 662 Sqn, Munster
	XZ219	Westland Lynx AH1	AAC No 662 Sqn, Munster
	XZ220	Westland Lynx AH1	AAC No 654 Sqn, Detmold
	XZ221	Westland Lynx AH1	AAC No 657 Sqn, Oakington
	XZ222	Westland Lynx AH1	AAC ARW/LCF, Middle Wallop
	XZ227	Westland Lynx HAS2 [303/PO]	RN No 815 Sqn, Portland
	XZ228	Westland Lynx HAS2	RNAY Fleetlands
	XZ229	Westland Lynx HAS2 [302/PO]	RNAY Fleetlands
	XZ230	Westland Lynx HAS2 [301/PO]	RN No 815 Sqn, Portland
	XZ231	Westland Lynx HAS2 [645/PO]	RN No 702 Sqn, Portland
	XZ232	Westland Lynx HAS2 [647/PO]	RN No 702 Sqn, Portland
	XZ233	Westland Lynx HAS2 [334/SN]	RN No 815 Sqn, Portland
	XZ234	Westland Lynx HAS2 [335/CF]	RN No 815 Sqn, Portland
	XZ235	Westland Lynx HAS2	RN NASU, Yeovilton
	XZ236	Westland Lynx HAS2	MoD(PE) Westlands, Yeovil
	XZ237	Westland Lynx HAS2 [302]	RN No 815 Sqn, Portland
	XZ238	Westland Lynx HAS2 [646/PO]	RN No 702 Sqn, Portland
	XZ239	Westland Lynx HAS2 [376/XB]	RN No 815 Sqn, Portland
	XZ240	Westland Lynx HAS2	RN NASU, Yeovilton
	XZ241	Westland Lynx HAS2 [417/NM]	RN No 815 Sqn, Portland
	XZ243	Westland Lynx HAS2 [640/PO]	RN No 702 Sqn, Portland
	XZ244	Westland Lynx HAS2 [472/AM]	RN No 815 Sqn, Portland
	XZ245	Westland Lynx HAS2	RN NASU, Yeovilton
	XZ246	Westland Lynx HAS2 [306]	RN No 815 Sqn, Portland
	XZ248	Westland Lynx HAS2 [404/FF]	RN No 815 Sqn, Portland
	XZ249	Westland Lynx HAS2	RNEC Manadon
	XZ250	Westland Lynx HAS2 [648/PO]	RN No 702 Sqn, Portland
	XZ252	Westland Lynx HAS2 [644/PO]	RN No 702 Sqn, Portland
	XZ254	Westland Lynx HAS2 [327/AL]	RN No 815 Sqn, Portland
	XZ255	Westland Lynx HAS2 [450/SS]	RN No 815 Sqn, Portland
	XZ256	Westland Lynx HAS2 [403/BX]	RN No 815 Sqn, Portland
	XZ257	Westland Lynx HAS2	RN NASU, Yeovilton
	XZ280	BAe Nimrod AEW3	MoD(PE) BAe Woodford
	XZ281	BAe Nimrod AEW3	MoD(PE) BAe Woodford
	XZ282	BAe Nimrod AEW3	MoD(PE) BAe Woodford
	XZ283	BAe Nimrod AEW3	MoD(PE) BAe Woodford
	XZ284	HS Nimrod MR2	RAF No 42 Sqn, St Mawgan
	XZ285	BAe Nimrod AEW3	RAF JTU, Waddington
	XZ286	BAe Nimrod AEW3	MoD(PE) A&AEE Boscombe Down
	XZ287	BAe Nimrod AEW3	MoD(PE) BAe Woodford
	XZ290	Westland Gazelle AH1	AAC, RNAY Fleetlands
	XZ291	Westland Gazelle AH1	AAC No 12 Flt, Wildenrath
	XZ292	Westland Gazelle AH1	AAC No 662 Sqn, Munster
	XZ294	Westland Gazelle AH1	AAC No 664 Sqn, Minden
	XZ295	Westland Gazelle AH1	AAC No 12 Flt, Wildenrath
	XZ296	Westland Gazelle AH1	AAC No 663 Sqn, Soest
	XZ297	Westland Gazelle AH1	AAC No 661 Sqn, Hildesheim
	XZ298	Westland Gazelle AH1	AAC No 662 Sqn, Munster
	XZ299	Westland Gazelle AH1	AAC No 657 Sqn, Oakington
	XZ300	Westland Gazelle AH1	AAC No 664 Sqn, Minden
	XZ301	Westland Gazelle AH1	AAC No 664 Sqn, Minden
	XZ302	Westland Gazelle AH1	AAC No 655 Sqn, Aldergrove

Serial	Type (alternative identity)	Owner, Operator or Location	Notes
XZ303	Westland Gazelle AH1	AAC No 663 Sqn, Soest	
XZ304	Westland Gazelle AH1	AAC No 664 Sqn, Minden	
XZ305	Westland Gazelle AH1 [D]	AAC No 653 Sqn, Soest	
XZ307	Westland Gazelle AH1 [E]	AAC No 653 Sqn, Soest	
XZ308	Westland Gazelle AH1 [L]	AAC ARWS, Middle Wallop	
XZ309	Westland Gazelle AH1	AAC No 664 Sqn, Minden	
XZ310	Westland Gazelle AH1	AAC No 661 Sqn, Hildesheim	
XZ311	Westland Gazelle AH1	AAC No 664 Sqn, Minden	
XZ312	Westland Gazelle AH1	AAC No 2 Flt, Netheravon	
XZ314	Westland Gazelle AH1	AAC No 656 Sqn, Netheravon	
XZ315	Westland Gazelle AH1 [P]	AAC ARWS, Middle Wallop	
XZ316	Westland Gazelle AH1 [R]	AAC ARWS, Middle Wallop	
XZ317	Westland Gazelle AH1 [Q]	AAC ARWS, Middle Wallop	
XZ318	Westland Gazelle AH1 [U]	AAC ARWS, Middle Wallop	
XZ319	Westland Gazelle AH1 [S]	AAC ARWS, Middle Wallop	
XZ320	Westland Gazelle AH1 [D]	AAC D&TS, Middle Wallop	
XZ321	Westland Gazelle AH1	AAC No 655 Sqn, Ballykelly	
XZ322	Westland Gazelle AH1 [N]	AAC ARWS, Middle Wallop	
XZ323	Westland Gazelle AH1	AAC No 655 Sqn, Aldergrove	
XZ324	Westland Gazelle AH1	AAC No 655 Sqn, Aldergrove	
XZ325	Westland Gazelle AH1	AAC No 655 Sqn, Aldergrove	
XZ326	Westland Gazelle AH1 [C]	RM 3 CBAS, Yeovilton	
XZ327	Westland Gazelle AH1	AAC No 655 Sqn, Aldergrove	
XZ328	Westland Gazelle AH1	AAC No 657 Sqn, Oakington	
XZ329	Westland Gazelle AH1 [J]	AAC ARWS, Middle Wallop	
XZ330	Westland Gazelle AH1	AAC No 657 Sqn, Oakington	
XZ331	Westland Gazelle AH1	AAC No 657 Sqn, Oakington	
XZ332	Westland Gazelle AH1 [O]	AAC ARWS, Middle Wallop	
XZ333	Westland Gazelle AH1 [A]	AAC ARWS, Middle Wallop	
XZ334	Westland Gazelle AH1	AAC No 657 Sqn, Oakington	
XZ335	Westland Gazelle AH1	AAC No 3 Flt, Topcliffe	
XZ336	Westland Gazelle AH1	AAC No 3 Flt, Topcliffe	
XZ337	Westland Gazelle AH1	AAC No 669 Sqn, Detmold	
XZ338	Westland Gazelle AH1 [X]	AAC ARWS, Middle Wallop	
XZ339	Westland Gazelle AH1	MoD(PE) Westlands, Weston-super-Mare	
XZ340	Westland Gazelle AH1 [T]	AAC ARWS, Middle Wallop	
XZ341	Westland Gazelle AH1	AAC D&TS, Middle Wallop	
XZ342	Westland Gazelle AH1	AAC No 661 Sqn, Hildesheim	
XZ343	Westland Gazelle AH1	AAC No 12 Flt, Wildenrath	
XZ344	Westland Gazelle AH1	AAC No 656 Sqn, Netheravon	
XZ345	Westland Gazelle AH1	AAC No 3 Flt, Topcliffe	
XZ346	Westland Gazelle AH1	AAC No 3 Flt, Topcliffe	
XZ347	Westland Gazelle AH1	AAC No 3 Flt, Topcliffe	
XZ348	Westland Gazelle AH1	AAC No 2 Flt, Netheravon	
XZ349	Westland Gazelle AH1 [M]	AAC ARWS, Middle Wallop	
XZ355	SEPECAT Jaguar GR1 [J]	RAF No 41 Sqn, Coltishall	
XZ356	SEPECAT Jaguar GR1 [AH]	RAF store, Shawbury	
XZ357	SEPECAT Jaguar GR1 [K]	RAF No 41 Sqn, Coltishall	
XZ358	SEPECAT Jaguar GR1 [L]	RAF No 41 Sqn, Coltishall	
XZ359	SEPECAT Jaguar GR1 [M]	RAF No 41 Sqn, Coltishall	
XZ360	SEPECAT Jaguar GR1 [N]	RAF No 41 Sqn, Coltishall	
XZ361	SEPECAT Jaguar GR1A [25]	RAF No 2 Sqn, Laarbruch	
XZ362	SEPECAT Jaguar GR1A [27]	RAF No 2 Sqn, Laarbruch	
XZ363	SEPECAT Jaguar GR1 [A]	RAF No 41 Sqn, Coltishall	
XZ364	SEPECAT Jaguar GR1A [21]	RAF No 2 Sqn, Laarbruch	
XZ366	SEPECAT Jaguar GR1A [22]	RAF No 2 Sqn, Laarbruch	
XZ367	SEPECAT Jaguar GR1A [33]	RAF No 2 Sqn, Laarbruch	
XZ368	SEPECAT Jaguar GR1 [AG]	RAF No — Sqn, Coltishall	
XZ369	SEPECAT Jaguar GR1 [BF]	RAF store, Shawbury	
XZ370	SEPECAT Jaguar GR1	RAF store, Shawbury	
XZ371	SEPECAT Jaguar GR1 [AP]	RAF Coltishall	
XZ372	SEPECAT Jaguar GR1A [ED]	RAF No 6 Sqn, Coltishall	
XZ373	SEPECAT Jaguar GR1A [EC]	RAF No 6 Sqn, Coltishall	
XZ374	SEPECAT Jaguar GR1 [AD]	RAF Shawbury store	
XZ375	SEPECAT Jaguar GR1 [AK]	RAF Coltishall	
XZ377	SEPECAT Jaguar GR1A [02]	RAF No 226 OCU, Lossiemouth	
XZ378	SEPECAT Jaguar GR1A [EP]	RAF No 6 Sqn, Coltishall	
XZ381	SEPECAT Jaguar GR1	RAF store, Shawbury	
XZ382	SEPECAT Jaguar GR1 [AE]	RAF store, Shawbury	
XZ383	SEPECAT Jaguar GR1 [AF]	RAF Coltishall	
XZ384	SEPECAT Jaguar GR1 [BC]	RAF store, Shawbury	
XZ385	SEPECAT Jaguar GR1 [EK]	RAF No 6 Sqn, Coltishall	
XZ386	SEPECAT Jaguar GR1 [B]	RAF JMU, Abingdon	

Notes	Serial	Type (alternative identity)	Owner, Operator or Location
	XZ387	SEPECAT Jaguar GR1A [EB]	RAF No 6 Sqn, Coltishall
	XZ389	SEPECAT Jaguar GR1 [BL]	RAF store, Shawbury
	XZ390	SEPECAT Jaguar GR1A [35]	RAF No 2 Sqn, Laarbruch
	XZ391	SEPECAT Jaguar GR1A [GE]	RAF No 54 Sqn, Coltishall
	XZ392	SEPECAT Jaguar GR1A [GR]	RAF No 54 Sqn, Coltishall
	XZ394	SEPECAT Jaguar GR1	RAF store, Shawbury
	XZ395	SEPECAT Jaguar GR1A [GJ]	RAF AST, Coltishall
	XZ396	SEPECAT Jaguar GR1A [EM]	RAF No 6 Sqn, Coltishall
	XZ398	SEPECAT Jaguar GR1A [EF]	RAF No 6 Sqn, Coltishall
	XZ399	SEPECAT Jaguar GR1A [EN]	RAF No 6 Sqn, Coltishall
	XZ400	SEPECAT Jaguar GR1A [GA]	RAF JMU, Abingdon
	XZ431	HS Buccaneer S2B [PS]	RAF No 208 Sqn, Lossiemouth
	XZ432	HS Buccaneer S2B [HC]	RAF No 237 OCU, Lossiemouth
	XZ439	BAe Sea Harrier FRS1 [2]	MoD(PE) BAe Dunsfold
	XZ440	BAe Sea Harrier FRS1 [40]	MoD(PE) A&AEE Boscombe Down
	XZ445	BAe Harrier T4A [AQ]	RAF No 3 Sqn, Gutersloh
	XZ451	BAe Sea Harrier FRS1	RN No 801 Sqn, Yeovilton
	XZ455	BAe Sea Harrier FRS1 [127/L]	RN No 800 Sqn, Yeovilton
	XZ457	BAe Sea Harrier FRS1 [715]	RN No 899 Sqn, Yeovilton
	XZ459	BAe Sea Harrier FRS1 [001/N]	RN No 801 Sqn, Yeovilton
	XZ460	BAe Sea Harrier FRS1 [714]	RN No 899 Sqn, Yeovilton
	XZ491	BAe Sea Harrier FRS1 [000/N]	RN No 801 Sqn, Yeovilton
	XZ492	BAe Sea Harrier FRS1 [125/L]	RN No 800 Sqn, Yeovilton
	XZ493	BAe Sea Harrier FRS1 [713]	RN No 899 Sqn, Yeovilton
	XZ494	BAe Sea Harrier FRS1 [716]	RN No 899 Sqn, Yeovilton
	XZ495	BAe Sea Harrier FRS1 [003/N]	RN No 801 Sqn, Yeovilton
	XZ497	BAe Sea Harrier FRS1 [4]	MoD(PE) BAe Dunsfold
	XZ498	BAe Sea Harrier FRS1 [002/N]	RN No 801 Sqn, Yeovilton
	XZ499	BAe Sea Harrier FRS1	RN No 801 Sqn, Yeovilton
	XZ550	Slingsby Venture T2	RAF No 642 VGS, Linton-on-Ouse
	XZ551	Slingsby Venture T2	RAF ACCGS, Syerston
	XZ552	Slingsby Venture T2 [A]	RAF No 632 VGS, Ternhill
	XZ553	Slingsby Venture T2 [Q]	RAF No 616 VGS, Henlow
	XZ554	Slingsby Venture T2 [4]	RAF No 633 VGS, Cosford
	XZ555	Slingsby Venture T2	RAF ACCGS, Syerston
	XZ556	Slingsby Venture T2 [6]	RAF No 611 VGS, Swanton Morley
	XZ557	Slingsby Venture T2 [7]	RAF No 633 VGS, Cosford
	XZ558	Slingsby Venture T2 [8]	RAF No 613 VGS, Halton
	XZ559	Slingsby Venture T2 [3]	RAF No 616 VGS, Henlow
	XZ560	Slingsby Venture T2 [0]	RAF No 611 VGS, Swanton Morley
	XZ561	Slingsby Venture T2 [1]	RAF No 611 VGS, Swanton Morley
	XZ562	Slingsby Venture T2 [2]	RAF No 635 VGS, Samlesbury
	XZ563	Slingsby Venture T2 [3]	RAF No 635 VGS, Samlesbury
	XZ564	Slingsby Venture T2 [4]	RAF No 635 VGS, Samlesbury
	XZ570	Westland Sea King HAS5	MoD(PE) A&AEE Boscombe Down/ Yeovil
	XZ571	Westland Sea King HAS5 [526]	RN No 826 Sqn, Culdrose
	XZ574	Westland Sea King HAS5 [506]	RN No 810 Sqn, Culdrose
	XZ575	Westland Sea King HAS5 [135]	RN No 826 Sqn, Culdrose
	XZ576	Westland Sea King HAS5	MoD(PE) Westlands, Yeovil
	XZ577	Westland Sea King HAS5 [138]	RN No 826 Sqn, Culdrose
	XZ578	Westland Sea King HAS5 [501]	RN No 810 Sqn, Culdrose
	XZ579	Westland Sea King HAS2 [702/PW]	RN No 819 Sqn, Prestwick
	XZ580	Westland Sea King HAS5 [591]	RN No 706 Sqn, Culdrose
	XZ581	Westland Sea King HAS5	RN No 826 Sqn, Culdrose
	XZ582	Westland Sea King HAS2 [594/CU]	RN No 706 Sqn, Culdrose
	XZ585	Westland Sea King HAR3	RAF No 202 Sqn SAR*
	XZ586	Westland Sea King HAR3 [S]	RAF No 202 Sqn SAR*
	XZ587	Westland Sea King HAR3	RAF No 202 Sqn SAR*
	XZ588	Westland Sea King HAR3	RAF No 202 Sqn SAR*
	XZ589	Westland Sea King HAR3	RAF No 202 Sqn SAR*
	XZ590	Westland Sea King HAR3	RAF No 202 Sqn SAR*
	XZ591	Westland Sea King HAR3	RAF 1564 Flt, Falklands
	XZ592	Westland Sea King HAR3	RAF 1564 Flt, Falklands
	XZ593	Westland Sea King HAR3	RAF No 202 Sqn SAR*
	XZ594	Westland Sea King HAR3	RAF No 202 Sqn SAR*
	XZ595	Westland Sea King HAR3	RAF No 202 Sqn SAR*

Serial	Type (alternative identity)	Owner, Operator or Location	Notes
XZ596	Westland Sea King HAR3	RAF No 202 Sqn SAR*	
XZ597	Westland Sea King HAR3	RAF No 202 Sqn SAR*	
XZ598	Westland Sea King HAR3	RAF No 202 Sqn SAR*	
XZ599	Westland Sea King HAR3	RAF No 202 Sqn SAR*	
XZ605	Westland Lynx AH1 [23B]	RM 3 CBAS, Yeovilton	
XZ606	Westland Lynx AH1	AAC No 662 Sqn, Munster	
XZ607	Westland Lynx AH1	AAC No 654 Sqn, Detmold	
XZ608	Westland Lynx AH1	AAC No 654 Sqn, Detmold	
XZ609	Westland Lynx AH1	AAC No 654 Sqn, Detmold	
XZ610	Westland Lynx AH1	AAC No 654 Sqn, Detmold	
XZ611	Westland Lynx AH1 [H]	AAC ARW/LCF, Middle Wallop	
XZ612	Westland Lynx AH1 [23C]	RM 3 CBAS, Yeovilton	
XZ613	Westland Lynx AH1	AAC No 657 Sqn, Oakington	
XZ614	Westland Lynx AH1 [23D]	RM 3 CBAS, Yeovilton	
XZ615	Westland Lynx AH1	AAC No 651 Sqn, Hildesheim	
XZ616	Westland Lynx AH1	AAC No 655 Sqn, Aldergrove	
XZ617	Westland Lynx AH1	AAC, RNAY Fleetlands	
XZ630	Panavia Tornado	MoD(PE) A&AEE/BAe Warton	
XZ631	Panavia Tornado	RAF No 2 SoTT, Cosford	
XZ640	Westland Lynx AH1 [L]	AAC ARW/LCF, Middle Wallop	
XZ641	Westland Lynx AH1	AAC No 653 Sqn, Soest	
XZ642	Westland Lynx AH1 [X]	AAC No 653 Sqn, Soest	
XZ643	Westland Lynx AH1	AAC No 663 Sqn, Soest	
XZ644	Westland Lynx AH1	AAC No 657 Sqn, Oakington	
XZ645	Westland Lynx AH1	AAC No 657 Sqn, Oakington	
XZ646	Westland Lynx AH1	AAC No 654 Sqn, Detmold	
XZ647	Westland Lynx AH1	AAC No 669 Sqn, Detmold	
XZ648	Westland Lynx AH1 [D]	AAC ARW/LCF, Middle Wallop	
XZ649	Westland Lynx AH1 [E]	AAC ARW/LCF, Middle Wallop	
XZ650	Westland Lynx AH1	AAC No 659 Sqn, Detmold	
XZ651	Westland Lynx AH1	AAC No 659 Sqn, Detmold	
XZ652	Westland Lynx AH1	AAC No 659 Sqn, Detmold	
XZ653	Westland Lynx AH1	AAC No 669 Sqn, Detmold	
XZ654	Westland Lynx AH1	AAC No 652 Sqn, Detmold	
XZ655	Westland Lynx AH1	AAC No 652 Sqn, Hildesheim	
XZ661	Westland Lynx AH1	AAC No 652 Sqn, Detmold	
XZ662	Westland Lynx AH1	AAC No 652 Sqn, Hildesheim	
XZ663	Westland Lynx AH1	AAC No 656 Sqn, Netheravon	
XZ664	Westland Lynx AH1	AAC No 655 Sqn, Aldergrove	
XZ665	Westland Lynx AH1	AAC No 655 Sqn, Aldergrove	
XZ666	Westland Lynx AH1	AAC No 655 Sqn, Aldergrove	
XZ667	Westland Lynx AH1 [Y]	AAC No 653 Sqn, Soest	
XZ668	Westland Lynx AH1 [Z]	AAC No 653 Sqn, Soest	
XZ669	Westland Lynx AH1	AAC No 653 Sqn, Soest	
XZ670	Westland Lynx AH1	AAC No 663 Sqn, Soest	
XZ671	Westland Lynx AH1	AAC No 652 Sqn, Hildesheim	
XZ672	Westland Lynx AH1	AAC No 669 Sqn, Detmold	
XZ673	Westland Lynx AH1	AAC No 652 Sqn, Hildesheim	
XZ674	Westland Lynx AH1	AAC No 652 Sqn, Hildesheim	
XZ675	Westland Lynx AH1	AAC No 652 Sqn, Hildesheim	
XZ676	Westland Lynx AH1	AAC No 657 Sqn, Oakington	
XZ677	Westland Lynx AH1	AAC No 651 Sqn, Hildesheim	
XZ678	Westland Lynx AH1	AAC No 651 Sqn, Hildesheim	
XZ679	Westland Lynx AH1	AAC No 651 Sqn, Hildesheim	
XZ680	Westland Lynx AH1 [F]	AAC LCF, Middle Wallop	
XZ681	Westland Lynx AH1	AAC Middle Wallop BDRT	
XZ689	Westland Lynx HAS2 [407/YK]	RN No 815 Sqn, Portland	
XZ690	Westland Lynx HAS2 [330/BZ]	RN No 815 Sqn, Portland	
XZ691	Westland Lynx HAS2 [342/BT]	RN No 815 Sqn, Portland	
XZ692	Westland Lynx HAS2 [643/PO]	RN No 702 Sqn, Portland	
XZ693	Westland Lynx HAS2	RN NASU, Yeovilton	
XZ694	Westland Lynx HAS2 [344/GW]	RN No 815 Sqn, Portland	
XZ695	Westland Lynx HAS2 [466/AT]	RN No 815 Sqn, Portland	
XZ696	Westland Lynx HAS2 [642/PO]	RN No 702 Sqn, Portland	
XZ697	Westland Lynx HAS2 [341/AG]	RN No 815 Sqn, Portland	
XZ698	Westland Lynx HAS2 [424/MV]	RN No 815 Sqn, Portland	
XZ699	Westland Lynx HAS2 [300/PO]	RN No 815 Sqn, Portland	
XZ719	Westland Lynx HAS2 [443/JP]	RN No 815 Sqn, Portland	
XZ720	Westland Lynx HAS2 [475/HM]	RN No 815 Sqn, Portland	
XZ721	Westland Lynx HAS2	RN NASU Yeovilton	

Note: *No 202 Sqn SAR and the SAREW are based at RAF Finingley with detached Flights at: A Flt — RAF Boulmer; B Flt — RAF Brawdy; C Flt — RAF Coltishall; D Flt — RAF Lossiemouth; SKTF — RNAS Culdrose.

Notes	Serial	Type (alternative identity)	Owner, Operator or Location
	XZ722	Westland Lynx HAS2 [410/GC]	RN No 815 Sqn, Portland
	XZ723	Westland Lynx HAS2 [454/PN]	RN No 815 Sqn, Portland
	XZ724	Westland Lynx HAS2 [471/PB]	RN No 815 Sqn, Portland
	XZ725	Westland Lynx HAS2 [320/AZ]	RN No 815 Sqn, Portland
	XZ726	Westland Lynx HAS2 [464/DN]	RN No 815 Sqn, Portland
	XZ727	Westland Lynx HAS2 [305]	RN No 815 Sqn, Portland
	XZ728	Westland Lynx HAS2 [332/LP]	RN No 815 Sqn, Portland
	XZ729	Westland Lynx HAS2 [377]	RN No 815 Sqn, Portland
	XZ730	Westland Lynx HAS2 [326/AW]	RN No 815 Sqn, Portland
	XZ731	Westland Lynx HAS2 [307/PO]	RN No 815 Sqn, Portland
	XZ732	Westland Lynx HAS2 [641/PO]	RN No 702 Sqn, Portland
	XZ733	Westland Lynx HAS2 [420/EX]	RN No 815 Sqn, Portland
	XZ734	Westland Lynx HAS2 [431/CY]	RN No 815 Sqn, Portland
	XZ735	Westland Lynx HAS2	RN No 815 Sqn, Portland
	XZ736	Westland Lynx HAS2 [360/MC]	RN No 815 Sqn, Portland
	XZ916	Westland Sea King HAS5 [130]	RN No 826 Sqn, Stanley
	XZ918	Westland Sea King HAS5 [020/N]	RN No 820 Sqn, Culdrose
	XZ920	Westland Sea King HAS5 [510]	RN No 810 Sqn, Culdrose
	XZ921	Westland Sea King HAS5 [017/N]	RN No 820 Sqn, Culdrose
	XZ922	Westland Sea King HAS5 [500]	RN No 810 Sqn, Culdrose
	XZ930	Westland Gazelle HT3 [Q]	RAF No 2 FTS, Shawbury
	XZ931	Westland Gazelle HT3 [R]	RAF No 2 FTS, Shawbury
	XZ932	Westland Gazelle HT3 [S]	RAF No 2 FTS, Shawbury
	XZ933	Westland Gazelle HT3 [T]	RAF No 2 FTS, Shawbury
	XZ934	Westland Gazelle HT3 [U]	RAF No 2 FTS, Shawbury
	XZ935	Westland Gazelle HT3	RAF No 32 Sqn, Northolt
	XZ936	Westland Gazelle HT3	MoD(PE) ETPS Boscombe Down
	XZ937	Westland Gazelle HT3 [Y]	RAF No 2 FTS, Shawbury
	XZ938	Westland Gazelle HT2 [45/CU]	RN No 705 Sqn, Culdrose
	XZ939	Westland Gazelle HT3 [Z]	MoD(PE) ETPS Boscombe Down
	XZ940	Westland Gazelle HT3 [O]	RAF No 2 FTS, Shawbury
	XZ941	Westland Gazelle HT3 [B]	RAF No 2 FTS, Shawbury
	XZ942	Westland Gazelle HT3	RNAY Fleetlands
	XZ964	BAe Harrier GR3 [AW]	RAF No 3 Sqn, Gutersloh
	XZ965	BAe Harrier GR3 [AM]	RAF No 3 Sqn, Gutersloh
	XZ966	BAe Harrier GR3 [C]	RAF No 1417 Flt, Belize
	XZ967	BAe Harrier GR3 [AB]	RAF No 3 Sqn, Gutersloh
	XZ969	BAe Harrier GR3 [D]	RAF No 4 Sqn, Gutersloh
	XZ970	BAe Harrier GR3 [AR]	RAF No 3 Sqn, Gutersloh
	XZ971	BAe Harrier GR3 [N]	RAF No 233 OCU, Wittering
	XZ987	BAe Harrier GR3 [AX]	RAF No 3 Sqn, Gutersloh
	XZ990	BAe Harrier GR3 [H]	RAF No 4 Sqn, Gutersloh
	XZ991	BAe Harrier GR3 [A]	RAF No 233 OCU, Wittering
	XZ992	BAe Harrier GR3 [T]	RAF St Athan
	XZ993	BAe Harrier GR3 [04]	RAF No 1 Sqn, Wittering
	XZ994	BAe Harrier GR3 [F]	RAF No 233 OCU, Wittering
	XZ995	BAe Harrier GR3 [AO]	RAF No 3 Sqn, Gutersloh
	XZ996	BAe Harrier GR3	RAF No 233 OCU, Wittering
	XZ997	BAe Harrier GR3 [E]	RAF No 233 OCU, Wittering
	XZ998	BAe Harrier GR3 [F]	RAF No 233 OCU, Wittering
	XZ999	BAe Harrier GR3 [I]	RAF No 4 Sqn, Gutersloh
	ZA101	BAe Hawk T50 (G-HAWK)	BAe Dunsfold
	ZA105	Westland Sea King HAR3 [SD]	RAF No 1564 Flt, Falklands
	ZA110	BAe Jetstream T2 [573/CU] (G-AXUO)	RN No 750 Sqn, Culdrose
	ZA111	BAe Jetstream T2 [574/CU] (G-AXFV)	RN No 750 Sqn, Culdrose
	ZA126	Westland Sea King HAS5 [012/N]	RN No 820 Sqn, Culdrose
	ZA127	Westland Sea King HAS5 [511]	RN No 810 Sqn, Culdrose
	ZA128	Westland Sea King HAS5 [014/N]	RN No 820 Sqn, Culdrose
	ZA129	Westland Sea King HAS5 [527]	RN No 826 Sqn, Culdrose
	ZA130	Westland Sea King HAS5 [253]	RN No 824 Sqn, Culdrose
	ZA131	Westland Sea King HAS5 [533]	RN No 826 Sqn, Culdrose
	ZA133	Westland Sea King HAS5 [352]	RN No 824 Sqn, Culdrose

Serial	Type (alternative identity)	Owner, Operator or Location	Notes
ZA134	Westland Sea King HAS5	RNAY Fleetlands	
ZA135	Westland Sea King HAS5 [505]	RN No 810 Sqn, Culdrose	
ZA136	Westland Sea King HAS5 [264]	RN No 826 Sqn, Culdrose	
ZA137	Westland Sea King HAS5 [137]	RN No 826 Sqn, Culdrose	
ZA140	BAe VC10 K2 (G-ARVL) [A]	RAF No 101 Sqn, Brize Norton	
ZA141	BAe VC10 K2 (G-ARVG) [B]	RAF No 101 Sqn, Brize Norton	
ZA142	BAe VC10 K2 (G-ARVI) [C]	RAF No 101 Sqn, Brize Norton	
ZA143	BAe VC10 K2 (G-ARVK) [D]	RAF No 101 Sqn, Brize Norton	
ZA144	BAe VC10 K2 (G-ARVC) [E]	RAF No 101 Sqn, Brize Norton	
ZA147	BAe VC10 K3 (5H-MMT) [F]	RAF No 101 Sqn, Brize Norton	
ZA148	BAe VC10 K3 (5Y-ADA) [G]	MoD(PE) A&AEE Boscombe Down	
ZA149	BAe VC10 K3 (5X-UVJ) [H]	RAF No 101 Sqn, Brize Norton	
ZA150	BAe VC10 K3 (5H-MOG) [J]	RAF No 101 Sqn, Brize Norton	
ZA166	Westland Sea King HAS5 [010/N]	RN No 820 Sqn, Culdrose	
ZA167	Westland Sea King HAS5 [273/L]	RN No 814 Sqn, Culdrose	
ZA168	Westland Sea King HAS5 [267]	RN No 814 Sqn, Culdrose	
ZA169	Westland Sea King HAS5 [015/N]	RN No 820 Sqn, Culdrose	
ZA170	Westland Sea King HAS5 [504]	RN No 810 Sqn, Culdrose	
ZA175	BAe Sea Harrier FRS1	RN No 800 Sqn, Yeovilton	
ZA176	BAe Sea Harrier FRS1	RN No 899 Sqn, Yeovilton	
ZA190	BAe Sea Harrier FRS1 [126/L]	RN No 800 Sqn, Yeovilton	
ZA191	BAe Sea Harrier FRS1 [123/L]	RN No 800 Sqn, Yeovilton	
ZA193	BAe Sea Harrier FRS1	RN NASU, Yeovilton	
ZA195	BAe Sea Harrier FRS1	RN NASU, Yeovilton	
ZA250	BAe Harrier T52 (G-VTOL)	BAe Dunsfold	
ZA254	Panavia Tornado F2	MoD(PE) BAe Warton	
ZA267	Panavia Tornado F2	MoD(PE) BAe Warton	
ZA283	Panavia Tornado F2	MoD(PE) BAe Warton	
ZA291	Westland Sea King HC4 [VB]	RN No 846 Sqn, Yeovilton	
ZA292	Westland Sea King HC4 [VH]	RN No 846 Sqn, Yeovilton	
ZA293	Westland Sea King HC4 [VK]	RN No 846 Sqn, Yeovilton	
ZA295	Westland Sea King HC4 [ZC]	RN No 707 Sqn, Yeovilton	
ZA296	Westland Sea King HC4 [VF]	RN No 846 Sqn, Yeovilton	
ZA297	Westland Sea King HC4 [VG]	RN NASU, Culdrose	
ZA298	Westland Sea King HC4 [VA] (G-BJNM)	RN No 846 Sqn, Yeovilton	
ZA299	Westland Sea King HC4 [ZD]	RN No 707 Sqn, Yeovilton	
ZA310	Westland Sea King HC4 [VS]	RN No 846 Sqn, Yeovilton	
ZA312	Westland Sea King HC4 [ZB]	RN No 707 Sqn, Yeovilton	
ZA313	Westland Sea King HC4 [VZ]	RN No 846 Sqn, Yeovilton	
ZA314	Westland Sea King HC4	MoD(PE) A&AEE Boscombe Down	
ZA319	Panavia Tornado GR1T [B-11]	RAF TTTE, Cottesmore	
ZA320	Panavia Tornado GR1T [B-01]	RAF TTTE, Cottesmore	
ZA321	Panavia Tornado GR1 [B-58]	RAF TTTE, Cottesmore	
ZA322	Panavia Tornado GR1 [B-50]	RAF TTTE, Cottesmore	
ZA322	Panavia Tornado GR1 replica (BAPC 155) [B-50]	RAF Exhibition Flight, Abingdon	
ZA323	Panavia Tornado GR1T [B-14]	RAF TTTE, Cottesmore	
ZA324	Panavia Tornado GR1T [B-02]	RAF TTTE, Cottesmore	
ZA325	Panavia Tornado GR1T [B-03]	RAF TTTE, Cottesmore	
ZA326	Panavia Tornado GR1T	MoD(PE) RAE Bedford	
ZA327	Panavia Tornado GR1 [B-51]	RAF TTTE, Cottesmore	
ZA328	Panavia Tornado GR1	MoD(PE) A&AEE Boscombe Down	
ZA329	Panavia Tornado GR1 [B-52)	RAF TTTE, Cottesmore	
ZA330	Panavia Tornado GR1T [B-08]	RAF TTTE, Cottesmore	
ZA352	Panavia Tornado GR1T [B-04]	RAF TTTE, Cottesmore	
ZA353	Panavia Tornado GR1 [B-53)	RAF TTTE, Cottesmore	
ZA354	Panavia Tornado GR1	MoD(PE) BAe Warton	
ZA355	Panavia Tornado GR1 [B-54]	RAF TTTE, Cottesmore	
ZA356	Panavia Tornado GR1T [B-07]	RAF TTTE, Cottesmore	
ZA357	Panavia Tornado GR1T [B-05]	RAF TTTE, Cottesmore	
ZA358	Panavia Tornado GR1T [B-06]	RAF TTTE, Cottesmore	
ZA359	Panavia Tornado GR1 [B-55]	RAF TTTE, Cottesmore	
ZA360	Panavia Tornado GR1 [B-56]	RAF TTTE, Cottesmore	
ZA361	Panavia Tornado GR1 [B-57]	RAF TTTE, Cottesmore	
ZA362	Panavia Tornado GR1T [B-09]	RAF TTTE, Cottesmore	

Notes	Serial	Type (alternative identity)	Owner, Operator or Location
	ZA365	Panavia Tornado GR1T [14]	RAF No 27 Sqn, Marham
	ZA366	Panavia Tornado GR1T	RAF TWCU/45 Sqn, Honington
	ZA367	Panavia Tornado GR1T [T]	RAF No 617 Sqn, Marham
	ZA368	Panavia Tornado GR1T [Y]	RAF No 9 Sqn, Honington
	ZA369	Panavia Tornado GR1	RAF TWCU/45 Sqn, Honington
	ZA370	Panavia Tornado GR1	RAF TWCU/45 Sqn, Honington
	ZA371	Panavia Tornado GR1	RAF TWCU/45 Sqn, Honington
	ZA372	Panavia Tornado GR1	RAF TWCU/45 Sqn, Honington
	ZA373	Panavia Tornado GR1	RAF TWCU/45 Sqn, Honington
	ZA374	Panavia Tornado GR1	RAF TWCU/45 Sqn, Honington
	ZA375	Panavia Tornado GR1	RAF TWCU/45 Sqn, Honington
	ZA376	Panavia Tornado GR1 [E]	MoD(PE) TOEU Boscombe Down
	ZA392	Panavia Tornado GR1 [EK]	RAF No 15 Sqn, Laarbruch
	ZA393	Panavia Tornado GR1	RAF TWCU, Honington
	ZA394	Panavia Tornado GR1 [K]	RAF No 617 Sqn, Marham
	ZA395	Panavia Tornado GR1 [06]	RAF No 27 Sqn, Marham
	ZA396	Panavia Tornado GR1 [GE]	RAF No 20 Sqn, Laarbruch
	ZA397	Panavia Tornado GR1	RAF TWCU/45 Sqn, Honington
	ZA398	Panavia Tornado GR1	RAF TWCU/45 Sqn, Honington
	ZA399	Panavia Tornado GR1 [GA]	RAF No 20 Sqn, Laarbruch
	ZA400	Panavia Tornado GR1	RAF TWCU/45 Sqn, Honington
	ZA401	Panavia Tornado GR1	RAF TWCU/45 Sqn, Honington
	ZA402	Panavia Tornado GR1	MoD(PE) BAe Warton
	ZA403	Panavia Tornado GR1	MoD(PE) for RAF
	ZA404	Panavia Tornado GR1	RAF TWCU/45 Sqn, Honington
	ZA405	Panavia Tornado GR1	RAF TWCU/45 Sqn, Honington
	ZA406	Panavia Tornado GR1	RAF TWCU/45 Sqn, Honington
	ZA407	Panavia Tornado GR1	RAF TWCU/45 Sqn, Honington
	ZA409	Panavia Tornado GR1T [EW]	RAF No 15 Sqn, Laarbruch
	ZA410	Panavia Tornado GR1T [EX]	RAF No 15 Sqn, Laarbruch
	ZA411	Panavia Tornado GR1T [GY]	RAF No 20 Sqn, Laarbruch
	ZA412	Panavia Tornado GR1T [FZ]	RAF No 16 Sqn, Laarbruch
	ZA446	Panavia Tornado GR1 [EF]	RAF No 15 Sqn, Laarbruch
	ZA447	Panavia Tornado GR1 [EA]	RAF No 15 Sqn, Laarbruch
	ZA448	Panavia Tornado GR1 [EB]	RAF No 15 Sqn, Laarbruch
	ZA449	Panavia Tornado GR1	MoD(PE) BAe Warton
	ZA450	Panavia Tornado GR1 [EC]	RAF No 15 Sqn, Laarbruch
	ZA452	Panavia Tornado GR1 [GK]	RAF No 20 Sqn, Laarbruch
	ZA453	Panavia Tornado GR1 [EG]	RAF No 15 Sqn, Laarbruch
	ZA454	Panavia Tornado GR1 [EH]	RAF No 15 Sqn, Laarbruch
	ZA455	Panavia Tornado GR1 [EJ]	RAF No 15 Sqn, Laarbruch
	ZA456	Panavia Tornado GR1 [GB]	RAF No 20 Sqn, Laarbruch
	ZA457	Panavia Tornado GR1 [O]	MoD(PE) TOEU Boscombe Down
	ZA458	Panavia Tornado GR1 [FB]	RAF No 16 Sqn, Laarbruch
	ZA459	Panavia Tornado GR1 [EL]	RAF No 15 Sqn, Laarbruch
	ZA460	Panavia Tornado GR1 [FD]	RAF No 16 Sqn, Laarbruch
	ZA461	Panavia Tornado GR1	RAF St Athan
	ZA462	Panavia Tornado GR1 [EM]	RAF No 15 Sqn, Laarbruch
	ZA463	Panavia Tornado GR1 [GL]	RAF No 20 Sqn, Laarbruch
	ZA464	Panavia Tornado GR1 [GM]	RAF No 20 Sqn, Laarbruch
	ZA465	Panavia Tornado GR1 [FK]	RAF No 16 Sqn, Laarbruch
	ZA466	Panavia Tornado GR1 [FH]	RAF No 16 Sqn, Laarbruch
	ZA467	Panavia Tornado GR1 [FF]	RAF No 16 Sqn, Laarbruch
	ZA468	Panavia Tornado GR1 [FN]	RAF No 16 Sqn, Laarbruch
	ZA469	Panavia Tornado GR1 [GD]	RAF No 20 Sqn, Laarbruch
	ZA470	Panavia Tornado GR1 [FL]	RAF No 16 Sqn, Laarbruch
	ZA471	Panavia Tornado GR1 [FJ]	RAF No 16 Sqn, Laarbruch
	ZA472	Panavia Tornado GR1 [EE]	RAF No 15 Sqn, Laarbruch
	ZA473	Panavia Tornado GR1 [FM]	RAF No 16 Sqn, Laarbruch
	ZA474	Panavia Tornado GR1 [FG]	RAF No 16 Sqn, Laarbruch
	ZA475	Panavia Tornado GR1 [FC]	RAF No 16 Sqn, Laarbruch
	ZA490	Panavia Tornado GR1 [GG]	RAF No 20 Sqn, Laarbruch
	ZA491	Panavia Tornado GR1 [GC]	RAF No 20 Sqn, Laarbruch
	ZA492	Panavia Tornado GR1 [FE]	RAF No 16 Sqn, Laarbruch
	ZA493	Panavia Tornado GR1 [GH]	RAF No 20 Sqn, Laarbruch
	ZA540	Panavia Tornado GR1T [B-12]	RAF TTTE, Cottesmore
	ZA541	Panavia Tornado GR1T [S]	RAF No 617 Sqn, Marham
	ZA542	Panavia Tornado GR1 [04]	RAF No 27 Sqn, Marham
	ZA543	Panavia Tornado GR1	RAF TWCU/45 Sqn, Honington
	ZA544	Panavia Tornado GR1T	RAF TWCU/45 Sqn, Honington
	ZA545	Panavia Tornado GR1 [V]	RAF No 9 Sqn, Honington
	ZA546	Panavia Tornado GR1 [05]	RAF No 27 Sqn, Marham
	ZA547	Panavia Tornado GR1 [03]	RAF No 27 Sqn, Marham
	ZA548	Panavia Tornado GR1T [B-10]	RAF TTTE, Cottesmore

Serial	Type (alternative identity)	Owner, Operator or Location	Notes
ZA549	Panavia Tornado GR1T	RAF TWCU/45 Sqn, Honington	
ZA550	Panavia Tornado GR1 [08]	RAF No 27 Sqn, Marham	
ZA551	Panavia Tornado GR1T	RAF TWCU/45 Sqn, Honington	
ZA552	Panavia Tornado GR1T	RAF TWCU/45 Sqn, Honington	
ZA553	Panavia Tornado GR1 [01]	RAF No 27 Sqn, Marham	
ZA554	Panavia Tornado GR1 [11]	RAF No 27 Sqn, Marham	
ZA555	Panavia Tornado GR1T	RAF TWCU/45 Sqn, Honington	
ZA556	Panavia Tornado GR1	RAF TWCU/45 Sqn, Honington	
ZA557	Panavia Tornado GR1 [15]	RAF No 27 Sqn, Marham	
ZA559	Panavia Tornado GR1 [U]	RAF No 9 Sqn, Honington	
ZA560	Panavia Tornado GR1 [C]	RAF No 617 Sqn, Marham	
ZA561	Panavia Tornado GR1 [02]	RAF No 27 Sqn, Marham	
ZA562	Panavia Tornado GR1T [12]	RAF No 27 Sqn, Marham	
ZA563	Panavia Tornado GR1 [10]	RAF No 27 Sqn, Marham	
ZA564	Panavia Tornado GR1 [S]	RAF No 9 Sqn, Honington	
ZA585	Panavia Tornado GR1 [L]	RAF No 617 Sqn, Marham	
ZA587	Panavia Tornado GR1 [B]	RAF No 9 Sqn, Honington	
ZA588	Panavia Tornado GR1 [C]	RAF No 9 Sqn, Honington	
ZA589	Panavia Tornado GR1 [D]	RAF No 9 Sqn, Honington	
ZA590	Panavia Tornado GR1 [E]	RAF No 9 Sqn, Honington	
ZA591	Panavia Tornado GR1 [F]	RAF No 9 Sqn, Honington	
ZA592	Panavia Tornado GR1 [G]	RAF No 9 Sqn, Honington	
ZA593	Panavia Tornado GR1 [H]	RAF No 9 Sqn, Honington	
ZA594	Panavia Tornado GR1T	RAF TWCU/45 Sqn, Honington	
ZA595	Panavia Tornado GR1T	RAF TWCU/45 Sqn, Honington	
ZA596	Panavia Tornado GR1 [L]	RAF No 9 Sqn, Honington	
ZA597	Panavia Tornado GR1 [M]	RAF No 9 Sqn, Honington	
ZA598	Panavia Tornado GR1T	RAF TWCU/45 Sqn, Honington	
ZA599	Panavia Tornado GR1T [Z]	RAF No 9 Sqn, Honington	
ZA600	Panavia Tornado GR1 [07]	RAF No 27 Sqn, Marham	
ZA601	Panavia Tornado GR1 [M]	RAF No 617 Sqn, Marham	
ZA602	Panavia Tornado GR1T [B-13]	RAF TTTE, Cottesmore	
ZA604	Panavia Tornado GR1T	RAF TWCU/45 Sqn, Honington	
ZA605	Panavia Tornado GR1 [G]	RAF No 617 Sqn, Marham	
ZA606	Panavia Tornado GR1 [09]	RAF No 27 Sqn, Marham	
ZA607	Panavia Tornado GR1 [P]	RAF No 617 Sqn, Marham	
ZA608	Panavia Tornado GR1 [Z]	RAF No 617 Sqn, Marham	
ZA609	Panavia Tornado GR1 [J]	RAF No 617 Sqn, Marham	
ZA611	Panavia Tornado GR1 [A]	RAF No 617 Sqn, Marham	
ZA612	Panavia Tornado GR1T	RAF TWCU/45 Sqn, Honington	
ZA613	Panavia Tornado GR1 [N]	RAF No 617 Sqn, Marham	
ZA614	Panavia Tornado GR1 [E]	RAF No 617 Sqn, Marham	
ZA625	Slingsby Venture T2 [1]	RAF No 616 VGS, Henlow	
ZA626	Slingsby Venture T2 [C]	RAF No 632 VGS, Ternhill	
ZA627	Slingsby Venture T2	RAF No 612 VGS, Benson	
ZA628	Slingsby Venture T2 [B]	RAF No 637 VGS, Little Rissington	
ZA629	Slingsby Venture T2 [9]	RAF No 633 VGS, Cosford	
ZA630	Slingsby Venture T2	RAF No 642 VGS, Linton-on-Ouse	
ZA631	Slingsby Venture T2 [1]	RAF No 613 VGS, Halton	
ZA632	Slingsby Venture T2 [2]	RAF No 613 VGS, Halton	
ZA633	Slingsby Venture T2 [3]	RAF No 616 VGS, Henlow	
ZA634	Slingsby Venture T2 [C]	RAF No 635 VGS, Samlesbury	
ZA652	Slingsby Venture T2 [6]	RAF No 642 VGS, Linton-on-Ouse	
ZA653	Slingsby Venture T2 [1]	RAF No 612 VGS, Benson	
ZA654	Slingsby Venture T2 [2]	RAF No 612 VGS, Benson	
ZA655	Slingsby Venture T2 [V]	RAF No 644 VGS, Syerston	
ZA656	Slingsby Venture T2 [6]	RAF No 624 VGS, Chivenor	
ZA657	Slingsby Venture T2	RAF No 644 VGS, Syerston	
ZA658	Slingsby Venture T2	RAF ACCGS/644 VGS, Syerston	
ZA659	Slingsby Venture T2	RAF No 642 VGS, Linton-on-Ouse	
ZA660	Slingsby Venture T2 [6]	RAF No 612 VGS, Benson	
ZA661	Slingsby Venture T2 [3]	RAF No 637 VGS, Little Rissington	
ZA662	Slingsby Venture T2	RAF No 611 VGS, Swanton Morley	
ZA663	Slingsby Venture T2 [3]	RAF No 624 VGS, Chivenor	
ZA664	Slingsby Venture T2 [4]	RAF No 624 VGS, Chivenor	
ZA665	Slingsby Venture T2	RAF No 637 VGS, Little Rissington	
ZA666	Slingsby Venture T2	RAF No 613 VGS, Halton	
ZA670	B-V Chinook HC1 [BG]	RAF No 18 Sqn, Gutersloh	
ZA671	B-V Chinook HC1	MoD(PE) A&AEE Boscombe Down	
ZA672	B-V Chinook HC1 [BX]	RAF No 18 Sqn, Gutersloh	
ZA673	B-V Chinook HC1 [BQ]	RAF No 18 Sqn, Gutersloh	
ZA674	B-V Chinook HC1 [BA]	RAF No 18 Sqn, Gutersloh	
ZA675	B-V Chinook HC1 [BB]	RAF No 18 Sqn, Gutersloh	
ZA676	B-V Chinook HC1 [FG]	RAF, on rebuild RNAY Fleetlands	

Notes	Serial	Type (alternative identity)	Owner, Operator or Location
	ZA677	B-V Chinook HC1 [BR]	RAF No 18 Sqn, Gutersloh
	ZA678	B-V Chinook HC1 [FL]	RAF No 240 OCU, Odiham
	ZA679	B-V Chinook HC1 [BC]	RAF No 18 Sqn, Gutersloh
	ZA680	B-V Chinook HC1 [J]	RAF No 1310 Flt, Falklands
	ZA681	B-V Chinook HC1 [ES]	RAF No 7 Sqn, Odiham
	ZA682	B-V Chinook HC1 [BY]	RAF No 18 Sqn, Gutersloh
	ZA683	B-V Chinook HC1 [FI]	RAF No 240 OCU, Odiham
	ZA684	B-V Chinook HC1 [F]	RAF ASF, Odiham
	ZA704	B-V Chinook HC1 [BV]	RAF No 18 Sqn, Gutersloh
	ZA705	B-V Chinook HC1 [EZ]	RAF No 7 Sqn, Odiham
	ZA707	B-V Chinook HC1 [FH]	RAF No 240 OCU, Odiham
	ZA708	B-V Chinook HC1 [EV]	RAF No 7 Sqn, Odiham
	ZA709	B-V Chinook HC1 [A]	RAF No 1310 Flt, Falklands
	ZA710	B-V Chinook HC1 [EY]	RAF No 7 Sqn, Odiham
	ZA711	B-V Chinook HC1 [ET]	RAF No 7 Sqn, Odiham
	ZA712	B-V Chinook HC1 [ER]	RAF No 7 Sqn, Odiham
	ZA713	B-V Chinook HC1 [EN]	RAF No 7 Sqn, Odiham
	ZA714	B-V Chinook HC1 [EX]	RAF No 7 Sqn, Odiham
	ZA715	B-V Chinook HC1 [C]	RAF No 1310 Flt, Falklands
	ZA717	B-V Chinook HC1 [B]	RAF No 1310 Flt, Falklands
	ZA718	B-V Chinook HC1 [EQ]	RAF No 7 Sqn, Odiham
	ZA720	B-V Chinook HC1 [BN]	RAF No 18 Sqn, Gutersloh
	ZA721	B-V Chinook HC1 [EP]	RAF No 7 Sqn, Odiham
	ZA726	Westland Gazelle AH1	AAC No 663 Sqn, Soest
	ZA727	Westland Gazelle AH1	AAC No 661 Sqn, Hildesheim
	ZA728	Westland Gazelle AH1 [13A]	RM 3 CBAS, Yeovilton
	ZA729	Westland Gazelle AH1	AAC No 652 Sqn, Hildesheim
	ZA730	Westland Gazelle AH1 [F]	RM 3 CBAS, Yeovilton
	ZA731	Westland Gazelle AH1 [C]	AAC No 29 Flt, Suffield, Canada
	ZA732	Westland Gazelle AH1 [D]	AAC No 29 Flt, Suffield, Canada
	ZA733	Westland Gazelle AH1 [F]	AAC No 653 Sqn, Soest
	ZA734	Westland Gazelle AH1	AAC No 25 Flt, Belize
	ZA735	Westland Gazelle AH1	AAC No 25 Flt, Belize
	ZA736	Westland Gazelle AH1 [A]	AAC No 29 Flt, Suffield, Canada
	ZA737	Westland Gazelle AH1 [V]	AAC ARWS, Middle Wallop
	ZA765	Westland Gazelle AH1	AAC No 25 Flt, Belize
	ZA766	Westland Gazelle AH1	AAC No 663 Sqn, Soest
	ZA767	Westland Gazelle AH1	AAC No 25 Flt, Belize
	ZA768	Westland Gazelle AH1 [F]	AAC ARWS, Middle Wallop
	ZA769	Westland Gazelle AH1 [K]	AAC ARWS, Middle Wallop
	ZA771	Westland Gazelle AH1 [Z]	AAC ARWS, Middle Wallop
	ZA772	Westland Gazelle AH1	AAC No 656 Sqn, Netheravon
	ZA773	Westland Gazelle AH1	AAC No 664 Sqn, Minden
	ZA774	Westland Gazelle AH1	AAC No 655 Sqn, Aldergrove
	ZA775	Westland Gazelle AH1	AAC No 656 Sqn, Netheravon
	ZA776	Westland Gazelle AH1 [13D]	RM 3 CBAS, Yeovilton
	ZA777	Westland Gazelle AH1	AAC No 661 Sqn, Hildesheim
	ZA801	Westland Gazelle HT3 [V]	RAF Abingdon, BDRF
	ZA802	Westland Gazelle HT3 [W]	RAF No 2 FTS, Shawbury
	ZA803	Westland Gazelle HT3 [X]	RAF No 2 FTS, Shawbury
	ZA804	Westland Gazelle HT3 [I]	RAF No 2 FTS, Shawbury
	ZA934	Westland Puma HC1 [FC]	RAF No 240 OCU, Odiham
	ZA935	Westland Puma HC1 [CT]	RAF No 33 Sqn, Odiham
	ZA936	Westland Puma HC1 [CU]	RAF No 33 Sqn, Odiham
	ZA937	Westland Puma HC1 [CV]	RAF No 33 Sqn, Odiham
	ZA938	Westland Puma HC1 [CW]	RAF No 33 Sqn, Odiham
	ZA939	Westland Puma HC1 [CX]	RAF No 33 Sqn, Odiham
	ZA940	Westland Puma HC1 [CY]	RAF No 33 Sqn, Odiham
	ZA941	Westland Puma HC1	MoD(PE) RAE Farnborough
	ZA947	Douglas Dakota C3 (KG661)	MoD(PE) RAE Farnborough
	ZB500	Westland Lynx (G-LYNX)	Westlands Yeovil
	ZB506	Westland Sea King Mk 4X	MoD(PE) RAE Bedford
	ZB507	Westland Sea King Mk 4X	MoD(PE) RAE Farnborough
	ZB600	BAe Harrier T4A [R]	RAF No 4 Sqn, Gutersloh
	ZB601	BAe Harrier T4A [X]	RAF No 233 OCU, Wittering
	ZB602	BAe Harrier T4A [Y]	RAF No 233 OCU, Wittering
	ZB603	BAe Harrier T4A [AZ]	RAF No 3 Sqn, Gutersloh
	ZB604	BAe Harrier T4N [717/VL]	RN No 899 Sqn, Yeovilton
	ZB605	BAe Harrier T4N [718/VL]	RN No 899 Sqn, Yeovilton
	ZB615	SEPECAT Jaguar T2	MoD(PE) IAM Farnborough
	ZB625	Westland Gazelle HT3 [N]	RAF No 2 FTS, Shawbury
	ZB626	Westland Gazelle HT3 [L]	RAF No 2 FTS, Shawbury
	ZB627	Westland Gazelle HT3 [A]	RAF No 2 FTS, Shawbury

Serial	Type (alternative identity)	Owner, Operator or Location	Notes
ZB628	Westland Gazelle HT3 [V]	RAF No 2 FTS, Shawbury	
ZB629	Westland Gazelle HT3	RAF No 32 Sqn, Northolt	
ZB646	Westland Gazelle HT2 [CU]	RN store, Wroughton	
ZB647	Westland Gazelle HT2 [CU]	RN store, Wroughton	
ZB648	Westland Gazelle HT2	MoD(PE) RAE Farnborough	
ZB649	Westland Gazelle HT2 [CU]	RNAY Fleetlands	
ZB665	Westland Gazelle AH1	AAC store, Wroughton	
ZB666	Westland Gazelle AH1 [G]	AAC ARWS, Middle Wallop	
ZB667	Westland Gazelle AH1	AAC store, Wroughton	
ZB668	Westland Gazelle AH1	AAC store, Wroughton	
ZB669	Westland Gazelle AH1	AAC store, Wroughton	
ZB670	Westland Gazelle AH1	AAC No 655 Sqn, Aldergrove	
ZB671	Westland Gazelle AH1	AAC, RNAY Fleetlands	
ZB672	Westland Gazelle AH1	AAC, Falklands	
ZB673	Westland Gazelle AH1	AAC, Falklands	
ZB674	Westland Gazelle AH1	AAC, Falklands	
ZB675	Westland Gazelle AH1	AAC, Falklands	
ZB676	Westland Gazelle AH1	AAC No 655 Sqn, Aldergrove	
ZB677	Westland Gazelle AH1 [A]	AAC ARWS, Middle Wallop	
ZB678	Westland Gazelle AH1	AAC store, Wroughton	
ZB679	Westland Gazelle AH1	AAC, RNAY Fleetlands	
ZB680	Westland Gazelle AH1	AAC No 29 Flt, Suffield, Canada	
ZB681	Westland Gazelle AH1	AAC No 655 Sqn, Aldergrove	
ZB682	Westland Gazelle AH1	AAC store, Wroughton	
ZB683	Westland Gazelle AH1	AAC store, Wroughton	
ZB684	Westland Gazelle AH1	MoD(PE) for AAC	
ZB685	Westland Gazelle AH1	MoD(PE) for AAC	
ZB686	Westland Gazelle AH1	MoD(PE) for AAC	
ZB687	Westland Gazelle AH1	MoD(PE) for AAC	
ZB688	Westland Gazelle AH1	MoD(PE) for AAC	
ZB689	Westland Gazelle AH1	MoD(PE) for AAC	
ZB690	Westland Gazelle AH1	MoD(PE) for AAC	
ZB691	Westland Gazelle AH1	MoD(PE) for AAC	
ZB692	Westland Gazelle AH1	MoD(PE) for AAC	
ZB693	Westland Gazelle AH1	MoD(PE) for AAC	
ZD230	BAC Super VC10 (G-ASGA)	RAF Abingdon, store	
ZD231	BAC Super VC10 (G-ASGB)	RAF Abingdon, store	
ZD232	BAC Super VC10 (G-ASGD) (8699M)	RAF Brize Norton, JATE	
ZD233	BAC Super VC10 (G-ASGE)	RAF FF&SS, Catterick	
ZD234	BAC Super VC10 (G-ASGF) (8700M)	RAF Brize Norton	
ZD235	BAC Super VC10 (G-ASGG)	RAF Abingdon, store	
ZD236	BAC Super VC10 (G-ASGH)	RAF Abingdon, store	
ZD237	BAC Super VC10 (G-ASGI)	RAF Abingdon, store	
ZD238	BAC Super VC10 (G-ASGJ)	RAF Abingdon, store	
ZD239	BAC Super VC10 (G-ASGK)	RAF Abingdon, store	
ZD240	BAC Super VC10 (G-ASGL)	RAF Abingdon, store	
ZD241	BAC Super VC10 (G-ASGM)	RAF Abingdon, store	
ZD242	BAC Super VC10 (G-ASGP)	RAF Abingdon, store	
ZD243	BAC Super VC10 (G-ASGR)	RAF Abingdon, store	
ZD249	Westland Lynx HAS3	MoD(PE) A&AEE Boscombe Down	
ZD250	Westland Lynx HAS3 [630/PO]	RN No 702 Sqn, Portland	
ZD251	Westland Lynx HAS3 [631/PO]	RN No 702 Sqn, Portland	
ZD252	Westland Lynx HAS3 [301/PO]	RN No 815 Sqn, Portland	
ZD253	Westland Lynx HAS3 [304/PO]	RN No 815 Sqn, Portland	
ZD254	Westland Lynx HAS3 [632/PO]	RN No 702 Sqn, Portland	
ZD255	Westland Lynx HAS3 [479]	RN No 815 Sqn, Portland	
ZD256	Westland Lynx HAS3 [432/SC]	RN No 815 Sqn, Portland	
ZD257	Westland Lynx HAS3 [346/BW]	RN No 815 Sqn, Portland	
ZD258	Westland Lynx HAS3	RN No 815 Sqn (208 Flt), Gibraltar	
ZD259	Westland Lynx HAS3 [323/AB]	RN No 815 Sqn, Portland	
ZD260	Westland Lynx HAS3	RN NASU, Yeovilton	
ZD261	Westland Lynx HAS3	RN Portland	
ZD262	Westland Lynx HAS3	RN NASU, Yeovilton	
ZD263	Westland Lynx HAS3	RN NATIU, Lee-on-Solent	
ZD264	Westland Lynx HAS3 [411/ED]	RN No 815 Sqn, Portland	
ZD265	Westland Lynx HAS3	RN NASU, Yeovilton	
ZD266	Westland Lynx HAS3	MoD(PE) A&AEE Boscombe Down	

Notes	Serial	Type (alternative identity)	Owner, Operator or Location
	ZD267	Westland Lynx HAS3	MoD(PE) Westlands, Yeovil
	ZD268	Westland Lynx HAS3 [375/VB]	RN No 815 Sqn, Portland
	ZD272	Westland Lynx AH1	AAC No 656 Sqn, Netheravon
	ZD273	Westland Lynx AH1	AAC No 656 Sqn, Netheravon
	ZD274	Westland Lynx AH1	AAC No 656 Sqn, Netheravon
	ZD275	Westland Lynx AH1	AAC No 657 Sqn, Oakington
	ZD276	Westland Lynx AH1	AAC No 652 Sqn, Hildesheim
	ZD277	Westland Lynx AH1	AAC store, Wroughton
	ZD278	Westland Lynx AH1	AAC store, Wroughton
	ZD279	Westland Lynx AH1	AAC store, Wroughton
	ZD280	Westland Lynx AH1	AAC store, Wroughton
	ZD281	Westland Lynx AH1	AAC No 657 Sqn, Oakington
	ZD282	Westland Lynx AH1 [24A]	RM 3 CBAS, Yeovilton
	ZD283	Westland Lynx AH1 [M]	AAC ARW/LCF, Middle Wallop
	ZD284	Westland Lynx AH1 [24B]	RM 3 CBAS, Yeovilton
	ZD285	Westland Lynx AH5	MoD(PE) RAE Farnborough
	ZD318	BAe Harrier GR5	MoD(PE) BAe Dunsfold
	ZD319	BAe Harrier GR5	MoD(PE) BAe Dunsfold
	ZD320	BAe Harrier GR5	MoD(PE) BAe Dunsfold
	ZD476	Westland Sea King HC4 [ZA]	RN No 707 Sqn, Yeovilton
	ZD477	Westland Sea King HC4 [VC]	RN No 846 Sqn, Yeovilton
	ZD478	Westland Sea King HC4 [VE]	RN No 846 Sqn, Yeovilton
	ZD479	Westland Sea King HC4 [ZE]	RN No 707 Sqn, Yeovilton
	ZD480	Westland Sea King HC4 [VG]	RN No 846 Sqn, Yeovilton
	ZD485	FMA IA58 Pucara (A-515)	RAF Cosford Aerospace Museum
	ZD493	BAC VC10 (G-ARVJ)	RAF Brize Norton
	ZD559	Westland Lynx AH5	MoD(PE) RAE Bedford
	ZD560	Westland Lynx HAS3	MoD(PE) ETPS Boscombe Down
	ZD565	Westland Lynx HAS3	RN store, Wroughton
	ZD566	Westland Lynx HAS3	RN NASU, Yeovilton
	ZD567	Westland Lynx HAS3	RN NASU, Yeovilton
	ZD574	B-V Chinook HC1 [EW]	RAF No 7 Sqn, Odiham
	ZD575	B-V Chinook HC1 [FF]	RAF No 240 OCU, Odiham
	ZD576	B-V Chinook HC1 [FG]	RAF No 240 OCU, Odiham
	ZD578	BAe Sea Harrier FRS1 [711]	RN No 899 Sqn, Yeovilton
	ZD579	BAe Sea Harrier FRS1 [710]	RN No 899 Sqn, Yeovilton
	ZD580	BAe Sea Harrier FRS1 [004/N]	RN No 801 Sqn, Yeovilton
	ZD581	BAe Sea Harrier FRS1 [721]	RN No 899 Sqn, Yeovilton
	ZD582	BAe Sea Harrier FRS1 [124/L]	RN No 800 Sqn, Yeovilton
	ZD607	BAe Sea Harrier FRS1 [712]	RN No 899 Sqn, Yeovilton
	ZD608	BAe Sea Harrier FRS1	RN No — Sqn, Yeovilton
	ZD609	BAe Sea Harrier FRS1	RN No — Sqn, Yeovilton
	ZD610	BAe Sea Harrier FRS1	RN No — Sqn, Yeovilton
	ZD611	BAe Sea Harrier FRS1	RN No — Sqn, Yeovilton
	ZD612	BAe Sea Harrier FRS1	RN No — Sqn, Yeovilton
	ZD613	BAe Sea Harrier FRS1	RN No — Sqn, Yeovilton
	ZD614	BAe Sea Harrier FRS1	RN No — Sqn, Yeovilton
	ZD615	BAe Sea Harrier FRS1	RN No — Sqn, Yeovilton
	ZD620	BAe 125 CC3	RAF No 32 Sqn, Northolt
	ZD621	BAe 125 CC3	RAF No 32 Sqn, Northolt
	ZD625	Westland Sea King HC4 [ZF]	RN No 707 Sqn, Yeovilton
	ZD626	Westland Sea King HC4 [ZG]	RN No 707 Sqn, Yeovilton
	ZD627	Westland Sea King HC4 [ZH]	RN No 707 Sqn, Yeovilton
	ZD630	Westland Sea King HAS5 [013/N]	RN No 820 Sqn, Culdrose
	ZD631	Westland Sea King HAS5 [590]	RN No 706 Sqn, Culdrose
	ZD632	Westland Sea King HAS5 [591]	RN No 706 Sqn, Culdrose
	ZD633	Westland Sea King HAS5 [593]	RN No 706 Sqn, Culdrose
	ZD634	Westland Sea King HAS5 [702]	RN No 819 Sqn, Prestwick
	ZD636	Westland Sea King HAS5 [701]	RN No 819 Sqn, Prestwick
	ZD637	Westland Sea King HAS5 [704]	RN No 819 Sqn, Prestwick
	ZD643	Schleicher Vanguard TX1 (BGA2884)	RAF No 618 VGS, West Malling
	ZD644	Schleicher Vanguard TX1 (BGA2883)	RAF No 618 Sqn, West Malling
	ZD645	Schleicher Vanguard TX1 (BGA2885)	RAF No 618 Sqn, West Malling
	ZD646	Schleicher Vanguard TX1 (BGA2886)	RAF No 618 VGS, West Malling
	ZD647	Schleicher Vanguard TX1 (BGA2887)	RAF No 618 VGS, West Malling
	ZD648	Schleicher Vanguard TX1 (BGA2888)	RAF No 618 VGS, West Malling

Serial	Type (alternative identity)	Owner, Operator or Location	Notes
ZD649	Schleicher Vanguard TX1 (BGA2889)	RAF ACCGS, Syerston	
ZD650	Schleicher Vanguard TX1 (BGA2890)	RAF No 618 VGS, West Malling	
ZD651	Schleicher Vanguard TX1 (BGA2891)	RAF No 618 VGS, West Malling	
ZD652	Schleicher Vanguard TX1 (BGA2892)	RAF No 618 VGS, West Malling	
ZD657	Schleicher Valiant TX1 (BGA2893)	RAF ACCGS, Syerston	
ZD658	Schleicher Valiant TX1 (BGA2894)	RAF ACCGS, Syerston	
ZD659	Schleicher Valiant TX1 (BGA2895)	RAF No 618 VGS, West Malling	
ZD660	Schleicher Valiant TX1 (BGA2896)	RAF No 645 VGS, Catterick	
ZD661	Schleicher Valiant TX1 (BGA2897)	RAF ACCGS, Syerston	
ZD667	BAe Harrier GR3	MoD(PE) for RAF	
ZD668	BAe Harrier GR3	MoD(PE) for RAF	
ZD669	BAe Harrier GR3	MoD(PE) for RAF	
ZD670	BAe Harrier GR3	MoD(PE) for RAF	
ZD671	BAe Harrier T4	MoD(PE) for RAF	
ZD672	BAe Harrier T4	MoD(PE) for RAF	
ZD673	BAe Harrier T4	MoD(PE) for RAF	
ZD674	BAe Harrier T4	MoD(PE) for RAF	
ZD703	BAe 125 CC3	RAF No 32 Sqn, Northolt	
ZD704	BAe 125 CC3	RAF No 32 Sqn, Northolt	
ZD707	Panavia Tornado GR1 [BK]	RAF No 14 Sqn, Bruggen	
ZD708	Panavia Tornado GR1	RAF	
ZD709	Panavia Tornado GR1 [GJ]	RAF No 20 Sqn, Laarbruch	
ZD710	Panavia Tornado GR1 [BJ]	RAF No 14 Sqn, Bruggen	
ZD711	Panavia Tornado GR1T [DY]	RAF No 31 Sqn, Bruggen	
ZD712	Panavia Tornado GR1T [BY]	RAF No 14 Sqn, Bruggen	
ZD713	Panavia Tornado GR1T [DX]	RAF No 31 Sqn, Bruggen	
ZD714	Panavia Tornado GR1	MoD(PE) BAe Warton	
ZD715	Panavia Tornado GR1 [ED]	RAF No 15 Sqn, Laarbruch	
ZD716	Panavia Tornado GR1 [T]	MoD(PE) TOEU Boscombe Down	
ZD717	Panavia Tornado GR1 [CD]	RAF No 17 Sqn, Bruggen	
ZD718	Panavia Tornado GR1 [BH]	RAF No 14 Sqn, Bruggen	
ZD719	Panavia Tornado GR1 [BF]	RAF No 14 Sqn, Bruggen	
ZD720	Panavia Tornado GR1 [CK]	RAF No 17 Sqn, Bruggen	
ZD738	Panavia Tornado GR1 [DD]	RAF No 31 Sqn, Bruggen	
ZD739	Panavia Tornado GR1 [BE]	RAF No 14 Sqn, Bruggen	
ZD740	Panavia Tornado GR1 [DA]	RAF No 31 Sqn, Bruggen	
ZD741	Panavia Tornado GR1T [GT]	RAF No 20 Sqn, Laarbruch	
ZD742	Panavia Tornado GR1T [CY]	RAF No 17 Sqn, Bruggen	
ZD743	Panavia Tornado GR1T [CZ]	RAF No 17 Sqn, Bruggen	
ZD744	Panavia Tornado GR1 [BD]	RAF No 14 Sqn, Bruggen	
ZD745	Panavia Tornado GR1 [BB]	RAF No 14 Sqn, Bruggen	
ZD746	Panavia Tornado GR1 [DJ]	RAF No 31 Sqn, Bruggen	
ZD747	Panavia Tornado GR1 [DK]	RAF No 31 Sqn, Bruggen	
ZD748	Panavia Tornado GR1 [DG]	RAF No 31 Sqn, Bruggen	
ZD749	Panavia Tornado GR1 [U]	MoD(PE) TOEU Boscombe Down	
ZD788	Panavia Tornado GR1 [CB]	RAF No 17 Sqn, Bruggen	
ZD789	Panavia Tornado GR1 [CE]	RAF No 17 Sqn, Bruggen	
ZD790	Panavia Tornado GR1 [DL]	RAF No 31 Sqn, Bruggen	
ZD791	Panavia Tornado GR1 [BG]	RAF No 14 Sqn, Bruggen	
ZD792	Panavia Tornado GR1 [CF]	RAF No 17 Sqn, Bruggen	
ZD793	Panavia Tornado GR1 [CA]	RAF No 17 Sqn, Bruggen	
ZD808	Panavia Tornado GR1 [CJ]	RAF No 17 Sqn, Bruggen	
ZD809	Panavia Tornado GR1	RAF Bruggen, ASF	
ZD810	Panavia Tornado GR1 [CG]	RAF No 17 Sqn, Bruggen	
ZD811	Panavia Tornado GR1 [DF]	RAF No 31 Sqn, Bruggen	
ZD812	Panavia Tornado GR1T [FV]	RAF No 16 Sqn, Laarbruch	
ZD842	Panavia Tornado GR1T [BZ]	RAF No 14 Sqn, Bruggen	
ZD843	Panavia Tornado GR1 [DH]	RAF No 31 Sqn, Bruggen	
ZD844	Panavia Tornado GR1 [DE]	RAF No 31 Sqn, Bruggen	
ZD845	Panavia Tornado GR1 [BA]	RAF No 14 Sqn, Bruggen	
ZD846	Panavia Tornado GR1 [BL]	No 14 Sqn, Bruggen	
ZD847	Panavia Tornado GR1 [CH]	RAF No 17 Sqn, Bruggen	
ZD848	Panavia Tornado GR1 [BC]	RAF No 14 Sqn, Bruggen	
ZD849	Panavia Tornado GR1 [CC]	RAF No 17 Sqn, Bruggen	
ZD850	Panavia Tornado GR1 [CL]	RAF No 17 Sqn, Bruggen	

Notes	Serial	Type (alternative identity)	Owner, Operator or Location
	ZD851	Panavia Tornado GR1 [DC]	RAF No 31 Sqn, Bruggen
	ZD890	Panavia Tornado GR1	RAF
	ZD891	Panavia Tornado GR1	RAF
	ZD892	Panavia Tornado GR1	RAF
	ZD893	Panavia Tornado GR1 [GF]	RAF No 20 Sqn, Laarbruch
	ZD894	Panavia Tornado GR1	RAF
	ZD895	Panavia Tornado GR1	RAF
	ZD899	Panavia Tornado F2T	MoD(PE) A&AEE Boscombe Down
	ZD900	Panavia Tornado F2T	MoD(PE) A&AEE Boscombe Down
	ZD901	Panavia Tornado F2T [AA]	RAF No 229 OCU, Coningsby
	ZD902	Panavia Tornado F2T [AC]	RAF No 229 OCU, Coningsby
	ZD903	Panavia Tornado F2T [AB]	RAF No 229 OCU, Coningsby
	ZD904	Panavia Tornado F2T [AE]	RAF No 229 OCU, Coningsby
	ZD905	Panavia Tornado F2 [AV]	RAF No 229 OCU, Coningsby
	ZD906	Panavia Tornado F2 [AN]	RAF No 229 OCU, Coningsby
	ZD932	Panavia Tornado F2 [AM]	RAF No 229 OCU, Coningsby
	ZD933	Panavia Tornado F2 [AO]	RAF No 229 OCU, Coningsby
	ZD934	Panavia Tornado F2T [AD]	RAF No 229 OCU, Coningsby
	ZD935	Panavia Tornado F2T [AF]	RAF No 229 OCU, Coningsby
	ZD936	Panavia Tornado F2 [AP]	RAF No 229 OCU, Coningsby
	ZD937	Panavia Tornado F2 [AQ]	RAF No 229 OCU, Coningsby
	ZD938	Panavia Tornado F2 [AR]	RAF No 229 OCU, Coningsby
	ZD939	Panavia Tornado F2 [AS]	RAF No 229 OCU, Coningsby
	ZD940	Panavia Tornado F2 [AT]	RAF No 229 OCU, Coningsby
	ZD941	Panavia Tornado F2 [AU]	RAF No 229 OCU, Coningsby
	ZD948	Lockheed TriStar C1 (G-BFCA)	MoD(PE) Marshalls, Cambridge
	ZD949	Lockheed TriStar C1 (G-BFCB)	MoD(PE) Marshalls, Cambridge
	ZD950	Lockheed TriStar K2 (G-BFCC)	MoD(PE) A&AEE Boscombe Down
	ZD951	Lockheed TriStar C1 (G-BFCD)	MoD(PE) Marshalls, Cambridge
	ZD952	Lockheed TriStar C1 (G-BFCE)	MoD(PE) Marshalls, Cambridge
	ZD953	Lockheed TriStar C1 (G-BFCF)	MoD(PE) Marshalls, Cambridge
	ZD974	Schleicher Janus C (BGA2875)	RAF ACCGS, Syerston
	ZD975	Schleicher Janus C (BGA2876)	RAF ACCGS, Syerston
	ZD980	B-V Chinook HC1	MoD(PE) A&AEE Boscombe Down
	ZD981	B-V Chinook HC1 [BD]	RAF No 18 Sqn, Gutersloh
	ZD982	B-V Chinook HC1	RAF
	ZD983	B-V Chinook HC1	RAF
	ZD984	B-V Chinook HC1	RAF
	ZD996	Panavia Tornado GR1	BAe for Saudi Arabia
	ZD997	Panavia Tornado GR1	BAe for Saudi Arabia
	ZD998	Panavia Tornado GR1	BAe for Saudi Arabia
	ZE114	Panavia Tornado GR1	BAe for Saudi Arabia
	ZE115	Panavia Tornado GR1	BAe for Saudi Arabia
	ZE116	Panavia Tornado GR1	BAe for Saudi Arabia
	ZE117	Panavia Tornado GR1	BAe for Saudi Arabia
	ZE118	Panavia Tornado GR1	BAe for Saudi Arabia
	ZE119	Panavia Tornado GR1	BAe for Saudi Arabia
	ZE120	Panavia Tornado GR1	BAe for Saudi Arabia
	ZE121	Panavia Tornado GR1	BAe for Saudi Arabia
	ZE122	Panavia Tornado GR1	BAe for Saudi Arabia
	ZE123	Panavia Tornado GR1	BAe for Saudi Arabia
	ZE124	Panavia Tornado GR1	BAe for Saudi Arabia
	ZE125	Panavia Tornado GR1	BAe for Saudi Arabia
	ZE126	Panavia Tornado GR1	BAe for Saudi Arabia
	ZE144	Panavia Tornado GR1	BAe for Saudi Arabia
	ZE145	Panavia Tornado GR1	BAe for Saudi Arabia
	ZE146	Panavia Tornado GR1	BAe for Saudi Arabia
	ZE147	Panavia Tornado GR1	BAe for Saudi Arabia
	ZE154	Panavia Tornado F3T	MoD(PE), BAe Warton
	ZE155	Panavia Tornado F3	MoD(PE), BAe Warton
	ZE156	Panavia Tornado F3	MoD(PE), BAe Warton
	ZE157	Panavia Tornado F3T	MoD(PE), BAe Warton
	ZE158	Panavia Tornado F3	MoD(PE), BAe Warton
	ZE159	Panavia Tornado F3	MoD(PE), BAe Warton
	ZE160	Panavia Tornado F3T	MoD(PE), BAe Warton
	ZE161	Panavia Tornado F3	MoD(PE), BAe Warton
	ZE162	Panavia Tornado F3	MoD(PE), BAe Warton
	ZE163	Panavia Tornado F3T	MoD(PE), BAe Warton
	ZE164	Panavia Tornado F3	MoD(PE), BAe Warton
	ZE165	Panavia Tornado F3	MoD(PE), BAe Warton
	ZE166	Panavia Tornado F3T	MoD(PE), BAe Warton
	ZE167	Panavia Tornado F3	MoD(PE), BAe Warton
	ZE168	Panavia Tornado F3	MoD(PE), BAe Warton
	ZE199	Panavia Tornado F3T	MoD(PE), BAe Warton

Serial	Type (alternative identity)	Owner, Operator or Location	Notes
ZE200	Panavia Tornado F3	MoD(PE), BAe Warton	
ZE201	Panavia Tornado F3	MoD(PE), BAe Warton	
ZE202	Panavia Tornado F3T	MoD(PE), BAe Warton	
ZE203	Panavia Tornado F3	MoD(PE), BAe Warton	
ZE204	Panavia Tornado F3	MoD(PE), BAe Warton	
ZE205	Panavia Tornado F3T	MoD(PE), BAe Warton	
ZE206	Panavia Tornado F3	MoD(PE), BAe Warton	
ZE207	Panavia Tornado F3	MoD(PE), BAe Warton	
ZE208	Panavia Tornado F3T	MoD(PE), BAe Warton	
ZE209	Panavia Tornado F3	MoD(PE), BAe Warton	
ZE210	Panavia Tornado F3	MoD(PE), BAe Warton	
ZE250	Panavia Tornado F3T	MoD(PE), BAe Warton	
ZE251	Panavia Tornado F3	MoD(PE), BAe Warton	
ZE252	Panavia Tornado F3	MoD(PE), BAe Warton	
ZE253	Panavia Tornado F3T	MoD(PE), BAe Warton	
ZE254	Panavia Tornado F3	MoD(PE), BAe Warton	
ZE255	Panavia Tornado F3	MoD(PE), BAe Warton	
ZE256	Panavia Tornado F3T	MoD(PE), BAe Warton	
ZE257	Panavia Tornado F3	MoD(PE), BAe Warton	
ZE258	Panavia Tornado F3	MoD(PE), BAe Warton	
ZE287	Panavia Tornado F3T	MoD(PE), BAe Warton	
ZE288	Panavia Tornado F3	MoD(PE), BAe Warton	
ZE289	Panavia Tornado F3	MoD(PE), BAe Warton	
ZE290	Panavia Tornado F3T	MoD(PE), BAe Warton	
ZE291	Panavia Tornado F3	MoD(PE), BAe Warton	
ZE292	Panavia Tornado F3	MoD(PE), BAe Warton	
ZE293	Panavia Tornado F3T	MoD(PE), BAe Warton	
ZE294	Panavia Tornado F3	MoD(PE), BAe Warton	
ZE296	Panavia Tornado F3T	MoD(PE), BAe Warton	
ZE338	Panavia Tornado F3	MoD(PE), BAe Warton	
ZE339	Panavia Tornado F3	MoD(PE), BAe Warton	
ZE340	Panavia Tornado F3T	MoD(PE), BAe Warton	
ZE341	Panavia Tornado F3	MoD(PE), BAe Warton	
ZE342	Panavia Tornado F3	MoD(PE), BAe Warton	
ZE343	Panavia Tornado F3T	MoD(PE), BAe Warton	
ZE350	McD Phantom F3 [T]	RAF No 74 Sqn, Wattisham	
ZE351	McD Phantom F3 [I]	RAF No 74 Sqn, Wattisham	
ZE352	McD Phantom F3 [G]	RAF No 74 Sqn, Wattisham	
ZE353	McD Phantom F3 [E]	RAF No 74 Sqn, Wattisham	
ZE354	McD Phantom F3 [R]	RAF No 74 Sqn, Wattisham	
ZE355	McD Phantom F3 [S]	RAF No 74 Sqn, Wattisham	
ZE356	McD Phantom F3 [Q]	RAF No 74 Sqn, Wattisham	
ZE357	McD Phantom F3 [N]	RAF No 74 Sqn, Wattisham	
ZE358	McD Phantom F3 [H]	RAF No 74 Sqn, Wattisham	
ZE359	McD Phantom F3 [J]	RAF No 74 Sqn, Wattisham	
ZE360	McD Phantom F3 [O]	RAF No 74 Sqn, Wattisham	
ZE361	McD Phantom F3 [P]	RAF No 74 Sqn, Wattisham	
ZE362	McD Phantom F3 [V]	RAF No 74 Sqn, Wattisham	
ZE363	McD Phantom F3 [W]	RAF No 74 Sqn, Wattisham	
ZE364	McD Phantom F3 [Z]	RAF No 74 Sqn, Wattisham	
ZE368	Westland Sea King HAR3	RAF No 202 Sqn SAR*	
ZE369	Westland Sea King HAR3	RAF No 202 Sqn SAR*	
ZE370	Westland Sea King HAR3	RAF No 202 Sqn SAR*	
ZE375	Westland Lynx AH5	MoD(PE) Rolls-Royce, Filton	
ZE376	Westland Lynx AH5	AAC	
ZE377	Westland Lynx AH5	AAC	
ZE378	Westland Lynx AH5	AAC	
ZE379	Westland Lynx AH5	AAC	
ZE380	Westland Lynx AH5	AAC	
ZE381	Westland Lynx AH5	AAC	
ZE382	Westland Lynx AH5	AAC	
ZE383	Westland Lynx AH5	AAC	
ZE395	BAe 125 CC3	RAF No 32 Sqn, Northolt	
ZE396	BAe 125 CC3	RAF No 32 Sqn, Northolt	
ZE410	Agusta A109A (AE-334)	AAC 7 Regt HQ Flt, Netheravon	
ZE411	Agusta A109A (AE-331)	AAC 7 Regt HQ Flt, Netheravon	
ZE412	Agusta A109A	AAC 7 Regt HQ Flt, Netheravon	
ZE413	Agusta A109A	AAC 7 Regt HQ Flt, Netheravon	
ZE425	Westland Sea King HC4	RN NASU Culdrose	
ZE426	Westland Sea King HC4	RN NASU Culdrose	
ZE427	Westland Sea King HC4	RN NASU Culdrose	
ZE428	Westland Sea King HC4	RN NASU Culdrose	
ZE432	BAC 1-11/479 (DQ-FBV)	MoD(PE) ETPS Boscombe Down	
ZE433	BAC 1-11/479 (DQ-FBQ)	MoD(PE) RAE Bedford	

Notes	Serial	Type (alternative identity)	Owner, Operator or Location
	ZE438	BAe Jetstream T3	RN No 750 Sqn, Culdrose
	ZE439	BAe Jetstream T3	RN No 750 Sqn, Culdrose
	ZE440	BAe Jetstream T3	RN No 750 Sqn, Culdrose
	ZE441	BAe Jetstream T3	RN No 750 Sqn, Culdrose
	ZE472	HS Hawk T63 (104)	BAe/Abu Dhabi AF, Dunsfold
	ZE477	Westland Lynx 3	Westlands, Yeovil
	ZE495	Grob Viking TX1 (BGA3000)	RAF No 644 VGS, Syerston
	ZE496	Grob Viking TX1 (BGA3001)	RAF No 631 VGS, Sealand
	ZE497	Grob Viking TX1 (BGA3002)	RAF No 622 VGS, Upavon
	ZE498	Grob Viking TX1 (BGA3003)	RAF ACCGS, Syerston
	ZE499	Grob Viking TX1 (BGA3004)	RAF No 631 VGS, Sealand
	ZE500	Grob Viking TX1 (BGA3005)	RAF No 631 VGS, Sealand
	ZE501	Grob Viking TX1 (BGA3006)	RAF No 645 VGS, Catterick
	ZE502	Grob Viking TX1 (BGA3007)	RAF No 645 VGS, Catterick
	ZE503	Grob Viking TX1 (BGA3008)	RAF No 625 VGS, South Cerney
	ZE504	Grob Viking TX1 (BGA3009)	RAF No 645 VGS, Catterick
	ZE520	Grob Viking TX1 (BGA3010)	RAF No 645 VGS, Catterick
	ZE521	Grob Viking TX1 (BGA3011)	RAF No 662 VGS, Arbroath
	ZE522	Grob Viking TX1 (BGA3012)	RAF No 662 VGS, Arbroath
	ZE523	Grob Viking TX1 (BGA3013)	RAF No 631 VGS, Sealand
	ZE524	Grob Viking TX1 (BGA3014)	RAF Kemble store
	ZE525	Grob Viking TX1 (BGA3015)	RAF No 622 VGS, Upavon
	ZE526	Grob Viking TX1 (BGA3016)	RAF No 631 VGS, Sealand
	ZE527	Grob Viking TX1 (BGA3017)	RAF
	ZE528	Grob Viking TX1 (BGA3018)	RAF No 631 VGS, Sealand
	ZE529	Grob Viking TX1 (BGA3019)	RAF No 631 VGS, Sealand
	ZE530	Grob Viking TX1 (BGA3020)	RAF No 645 VGS, Catterick
	ZE531	Grob Viking TX1 (BGA3021)	RAF ACCGS, Syerston
	ZE532	Grob Viking TX1 (BGA3022)	RAF ACCGS, Syerston
	ZE533	Grob Viking TX1 (BGA3023)	RAF No 622 VGS, Upavon
	ZE534	Grob Viking TX1 (BGA3024)	RAF No 662 VGS, Arbroath
	ZE550	Grob Viking TX1 (BGA3025)	RAF No 622 VGS, Upavon
	ZE551	Grob Viking TX1 (BGA3026)	RAF store, Kemble
	ZE552	Grob Viking TX1 (BGA3027)	RAF No 662 VGS, Arbroath
	ZE553	Grob Viking TX1 (BGA3028)	RAF No 643 VGS, Scampton
	ZE554	Grob Viking TX1 (BGA3029)	RAF No 631 VGS, Sealand
	ZE555	Grob Viking TX1 (BGA3030)	RAF No 631 VGS, Sealand
	ZE556	Grob Viking TX1 (BGA3031)	RAF No 622 VGS, Upavon
	ZE557	Grob Viking TX1 (BGA3032)	RAF No 661 VGS, Kirknewton
	ZE558	Grob Viking TX1 (BGA3033)	RAF store, Shawbury
	ZE559	Grob Viking TX1 (BGA3034)	RAF No 661 VGS, Kirknewton
	ZE560	Grob Viking TX1 (BGA3035)	RAF store, Kemble
	ZE561	Grob Viking TX1 (BGA3036)	RAF No 661 VGS, Kirknewton
	ZE562	Grob Viking TX1 (BGA3037)	RAF store, Kemble
	ZE563	Grob Viking TX1 (BGA3038)	RAF store, Kemble
	ZE564	Grob Viking TX1 (BGA3039)	RAF No 661 VGS, Kirknewton
	ZE584	Grob Viking TX1 (BGA3040)	RAF store, Kemble
	ZE585	Grob Viking TX1 (BGA3041)	RAF No 614 VGS, Wethersfield
	ZE586	Grob Viking TX1 (BGA3042)	RAF No 625 VGS, South Cerney
	ZE587	Grob Viking TX1 (BGA3043)	RAF No 614 VGS, Wethersfield
	ZE588	Grob Viking TX1 (BGA3044)	RAF No 614 VGS, Wethersfield
	ZE589	Grob Viking TX1 (BGA3045)	RAF store, Shawbury
	ZE590	Grob Viking TX1 (BGA3046)	RAF store, Shawbury
	ZE591	Grob Viking TX1 (BGA3047)	RAF store, Shawbury
	ZE592	Grob Viking TX1 (BGA3048)	RAF No 614 VGS, Wethersfield
	ZE593	Grob Viking TX1 (BGA3049)	RAF No 614 VGS, Wethersfield
	ZE594	Grob Viking TX1 (BGA3050)	RAF No 661 VGS, Kirknewton
	ZE595	Grob Viking TX1 (BGA3051)	RAF No 625 VGS, South Cerney
	ZE600	Grob Viking TX1 (BGA3052)	RAF No 626 VGS, Predannack
	ZE601	Grob Viking TX1 (BGA3053)	RAF No 625 VGS, South Cerney
	ZE602	Grob Viking TX1 (BGA3054)	RAF store, Kemble
	ZE603	Grob Viking TX1 (BGA3055)	RAF Kemble store
	ZE604	Grob Viking TX1 (BGA3056)	RAF store, Kemble
	ZE605	Grob Viking TX1 (BGA3057)	RAF store, Shawbury
	ZE606	Grob Viking TX1 (BGA3058)	RAF No 626 VGS, Predannack
	ZE607	Grob Viking TX1 (BGA3059)	RAF store, Shawbury
	ZE608	Grob Viking TX1 (BGA3060)	RAF No 625 VGS, South Cerney
	ZE609	Grob Viking TX1 (BGA3061)	RAF No 626 VGS, Predannack
	ZE610	Grob Viking TX1 (BGA3062)	RAF No 621 VGS, Weston-super-Mare
	ZE611	Grob Viking TX1 (BGA3063)	RAF No 621 VGS, Weston-super-Mare
	ZE612	Grob Viking TX1 (BGA3064)	RAF No 621 VGS, Weston-super-Mare
	ZE613	Grob Viking TX1 (BGA3065)	RAF No 621 VGS, Weston-super-Mare
	ZE614	Grob Viking TX1 (BGA3066)	RAF No 621 VGS, Weston-super-Mare
	ZE625	Grob Viking TX1 (BGA3067)	RAF ACCGS, Syerston

Serial	Type (alternative identity)	Owner, Operator or Location	Notes
ZE626	Grob Viking TX1 (BGA3068)	RAF store, Kemble	
ZE627	Grob Viking TX1 (BGA3069)	RAF store, Kemble	
ZE628	Grob Viking TX1 (BGA3070)	RAF	
ZE629	Grob Viking TX1 (BGA3071)	RAF No 662 VGS, Arbroath	
ZE630	Grob Viking TX1 (BGA3072)	RAF store, Kemble	
ZE631	Grob Viking TX1 (BGA3073)	RAF No 643 VGS, Scampton	
ZE632	Grob Viking TX1 (BGA3074)	RAF store, Kemble	
ZE633	Grob Viking TX1 (BGA3075)	RAF store, Kemble	
ZE634	Grob Viking TX1 (BGA3076)	RAF	
ZE635	Grob Viking TX1 (BGA3077)	RAF	
ZE636	Grob Viking TX1 (BGA3078)	RAF	
ZE637	Grob Viking TX1 (BGA3079)	RAF	
ZE650	Grob Viking TX1 (BGA3080)	RAF	
ZE651	Grob Viking TX1 (BGA3081)	RAF	
ZE652	Grob Viking TX1 (BGA3082)	RAF ACCGS, Syerston	
ZE653	Grob Viking TX1 (BGA3083)	RAF	
ZE654	Grob Viking TX1 (BGA3084)	RAF	
ZE655	Grob Viking TX1 (BGA3085)	RAF	
ZE656	Grob Viking TX1 (BGA3086)	RAF	
ZE657	Grob Viking TX1 (BGA3087)	RAF	
ZE658	Grob Viking TX1 (BGA3088)	RAF ACCGS, Syerston	
ZE659	Grob Viking TX1 (BGA3089)	RAF ACCGS, Syerston	
ZE677	Grob Viking TX1 (BGA3090)	RAF	
ZE678	Grob Viking TX1 (BGA3091)	RAF	
ZE679	Grob Viking TX1 (BGA3092)	RAF	
ZE680	Grob Viking TX1 (BGA3093)	RAF	
ZE681	Grob Viking TX1 (BGA3094)	RAF	
ZE682	Grob Viking TX1 (BGA3095)	RAF	
ZE683	Grob Viking TX1 (BGA3096)	RAF	
ZE684	Grob Viking TX1 (BGA3097)	RAF	
ZE685	Grob Viking TX1 (BGA3098)	RAF	
ZE686	Grob Viking TX1 (BGA3099)	RAF	
ZE700	BAe 146 CC2	RAF Queen's Flight, Benson	
ZE701	BAe 146 CC2	RAF Queen's Flight, Benson	
ZE704	Lockheed TriStar (N508PA)	RAF No 216 Sqn, Brize Norton	
ZE705	Lockheed TriStar (N509PA)	RAF No 216 Sqn, Brize Norton	
ZE706	Lockheed TriStar (N503PA)	RAF No 216 Sqn, Brize Norton	
ZE728	Panavia Tornado F3T	MoD(PE), BAe Warton	
ZE729	Panavia Tornado F3	MoD(PE), BAe Warton	
ZE730	Panavia Tornado F3	MoD(PE), BAe Warton	
ZE731	Panavia Tornado F3	MoD(PE), BAe Warton	
ZE732	Panavia Tornado F3	MoD(PE), BAe Warton	
ZE733	Panavia Tornado F3	MoD(PE), BAe Warton	
ZE734	Panavia Tornado F3	MoD(PE), BAe Warton	
ZE735	Panavia Tornado F3T	MoD(PE), BAe Warton	
ZE736	Panavia Tornado F3	MoD(PE), BAe Warton	
ZE737	Panavia Tornado F3	MoD(PE), BAe Warton	
ZE755	Panavia Tornado F3	MoD(PE), BAe Warton	
ZE756	Panavia Tornado F3	MoD(PE), BAe Warton	
ZE757	Panavia Tornado F3	MoD(PE), BAe Warton	
ZE758	Panavia Tornado F3	MoD(PE), BAe Warton	
ZE759	Panavia Tornado F3T	MoD(PE), BAe Warton	
ZE760	Panavia Tornado F3	MoD(PE), BAe Warton	
ZE761	Panavia Tornado F3	MoD(PE), BAe Warton	
ZE762	Panavia Tornado F3	MoD(PE), BAe Warton	
ZE763	Panavia Tornado F3	MoD(PE), BAe Warton	
ZE764	Panavia Tornado F3	MoD(PE), BAe Warton	
ZE785	Panavia Tornado F3	MoD(PE), BAe Warton	
ZE786	Panavia Tornado F3T	MoD(PE), BAe Warton	
ZE787	Panavia Tornado F3	MoD(PE), BAe Warton	
ZE788	Panavia Tornado F3	MoD(PE), BAe Warton	
ZE789	Panavia Tornado F3	MoD(PE), BAe Warton	
ZE790	Panavia Tornado F3	MoD(PE), BAe Warton	
ZE791	Panavia Tornado F3	MoD(PE), BAe Warton	
ZE792	Panavia Tornado F3	MoD(PE), BAe Warton	
ZE793	Panavia Tornado F3T	MoD(PE), BAe Warton	
ZE794	Panavia Tornado F3	MoD(PE), BAe Warton	
ZE808	Panavia Tornado F3	MoD(PE), BAe Warton	
ZE809	Panavia Tornado F3	MoD(PE), BAe Warton	
ZE810	Panavia Tornado F3	MoD(PE), BAe Warton	
ZE811	Panavia Tornado F3	MoD(PE), BAe Warton	
ZE812	Panavia Tornado F3	MoD(PE), BAe Warton	
ZE830	Panavia Tornado F3T	MoD(PE), BAe Warton	
ZE831	Panavia Tornado F3	MoD(PE), BAe Warton	

Notes	Serial	Type (alternative identity)	Owner, Operator or Location
	ZE832	Panavia Tornado F3	MoD(PE), BAe Warton
	ZE833	Panavia Tornado F3	MoD(PE), BAe Warton
	ZE834	Panavia Tornado F3	MoD(PE), BAe Warton
	ZE835	Panavia Tornado F3	MoD(PE), BAe Warton
	ZE836	Panavia Tornado F3	MoD(PE), BAe Warton
	ZE837	Panavia Tornado F3T	MoD(PE), BAe Warton
	ZE838	Panavia Tornado F3	MoD(PE), BAe Warton
	ZE839	Panavia Tornado F3	MoD(PE), BAe Warton
	ZE858	Panavia Tornado F3	MoD(PE), BAe Warton
	ZE859	Panavia Tornado F3	MoD(PE), BAe Warton
	ZE860	Panavia Tornado F3	MoD(PE), BAe Warton
	ZE861	Panavia Tornado F3	MoD(PE), BAe Warton
	ZE862	Panavia Tornado F3T	MoD(PE), BAe Warton
	ZE882	Panavia Tornado F3	MoD(PE), BAe Warton
	ZE883	Panavia Tornado F3	MoD(PE), BAe Warton
	ZE884	Panavia Tornado F3	MoD(PE), BAe Warton
	ZE885	Panavia Tornado F3	MoD(PE), BAe Warton
	ZE886	Panavia Tornado F3	MoD(PE), BAe Warton
	ZE887	Panavia Tornado F3	MoD(PE), BAe Warton
	ZE888	Panavia Tornado F3T	MoD(PE), BAe Warton
	ZE889	Panavia Tornado F3	MoD(PE), BAe Warton
	ZE890	Panavia Tornado F3	MoD(PE), BAe Warton
	ZE891	Panavia Tornado F3	MoD(PE), BAe Warton
	ZF107	HS Hawk T64 (140)	BAe/Kuwait AF, Dunsfold
	ZF108	HS Hawk T64 (142)	BAe/Kuwait AF, Dunsfold
	ZF115	Westland Sea King HC4	MoD(PE) A&AEE Boscombe Down
	ZF116	Westland Sea King HC4	MoD(PE) for RN
	ZF117	Westland Sea King HC4	MoD(PE) for RN
	ZF118	Westland Sea King HC4	MoD(PE) for RN
	ZF119	Westland Sea King HC4	MoD(PE) for RN
	ZF120	Westland Sea King HC4	MoD(PE) for RN
	ZF121	Westland Sea King HC4	MoD(PE) for RN
	ZF122	Westland Sea King HC4	MoD(PE) for RN
	ZF123	Westland Sea King HC4	MoD(PE) for RN
	ZF124	Westland Sea King HC4	MoD(PE) for RN
	ZF130	BAe 125-600B (G-BLUW)	MoD(PE) BAe Woodford
	ZF444	BN2A Islander (G-WOTG)	RAF Parachute Association, Weston-on-the-Green
	ZF520	Piper PA-31 Navajo Chieftain (N35823/G-BLZK)	MoD(PE) RAE Farnborough
	ZF521	Piper PA-31 Navajo Chieftain (N27509)	MoD(PE) RAE Farnborough
	ZF522	Piper PA-31 Navajo Chieftain (N4261A/G-RNAV/N27728)	MoD(PE) RAE Farnborough
	ZF526	Westland Sea King 42B (IN513)	Westlands/Indian Navy, Yeovil
	ZF527	Westland Sea King 42B (IN514)	Westlands/Indian Navy, Yeovil
	ZF573	BN2T Turbo Islander (G-PBIN)	DoTI/FRL, Hurn
	ZF577	BAC Lightning F53	MoD(PE), BAe Warton
	ZF578	BAC Lightning F53	MoD(PE), BAe Warton
	ZF579	BAC Lightning F53	MoD(PE), BAe Warton
	ZF580	BAC Lightning F53	MoD(PE), BAe Warton
	ZF581	BAC Lightning F53	MoD(PE), BAe Warton
	ZF582	BAC Lightning F53	MoD(PE), BAe Warton
	ZF583	BAC Lightning F53	MoD(PE), BAe Warton
	ZF584	BAC Lightning F53	MoD(PE), BAe Warton
	ZF585	BAC Lightning F53	MoD(PE), BAe Warton
	ZF586	BAC Lightning F53	MoD(PE), BAe Warton
	ZF587	BAC Lightning F53	MoD(PE), BAe Warton
	ZF588	BAC Lightning F53	MoD(PE), BAe Warton
	ZF589	BAC Lightning F53	MoD(PE), BAe Warton
	ZF590	BAC Lightning F53	MoD(PE), BAe Warton
	ZF591	BAC Lightning F53	MoD(PE), BAe Warton
	ZF592	BAC Lightning F53	MoD(PE), BAe Warton
	ZF593	BAC Lightning F53	MoD(PE), BAe Warton
	ZF594	BAC Lightning F53	MoD(PE), BAe Warton
	ZF595	BAC Lightning T55	MoD(PE), BAe Warton
	ZF596	BAC Lightning T55	MoD(PE), BAe Warton
	ZF597	BAC Lightning T55	MoD(PE), BAe Warton
	ZF598	BAC Lightning T55	MoD(PE), BAe Warton

K2050 Hawker(Isaacs) Fury replica G-ASCM; privately owned at Stapleford. *PRM*

N6847 DH Tiger Moth G-APAL landing at Popham. *DJM*

JV928 PBY-5A Catalina G-BLSC operated by Plane Sailing Ltd. *PRM*

ML407 VS Spitfire T9 G-LFIX based at Middle Wallop. *PRM*

WA669 Gloster Meteor T7 is flown by the RAF's *Vintage Pair*. *PRM*

WD413 Avro Anson C21 G-BFIR is based at Edinburgh Airport. *PRM*

WH876 EE Canberra D14, from the A&AEE fleet. *APM*

WL679 Vickers Varsity T1 remains with the RAE. *PRM*

XL580 Hawker Hunter T8M carries No 899 Squadron markings. *PRM*

XV244 HS Nimrod MR2; RAF Kinloss Wing. *PRM*

XX343 BAe Hawk T1 from the Empire Test Pilots' School. *PRM*

XX482 SA Jetstream T1; No 6FTS RAF Finningley. *DJM*

ZA718 BV Chinook HC1 coded EQ with No 7 Squadron. *PRM*

ZA947 Douglas Dakota C3 flies from Farnborough. *PRM*

ZD932 Panavia Tornado F2 with No 229 OCU code AM and badge. *APM*

ZD950 Lockheed TriStar K2 is the first tanker for No 216 Squadron. *APM*

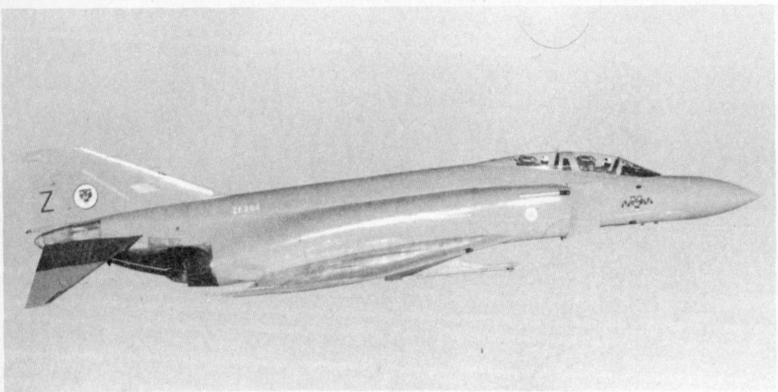

ZE364 McD F-4J Phantom F3 of No 74 Squadron. *PRM*

ZF586 BAC Lightning F53; MoD(PE), Bae Warton.

Deletions

The following serials of British aircraft which were shown in the sixth edition of *Military Aircraft Markings* have been deleted from the 1986 edition. The reason for the deletion has been given where possible.

Serial	*Type (alternative identity)*	*Owner, Operator or Location*	*Notes*
A2416	RAF SE5A Replica	To USA	
A3240	RAF SE5A Replica	To USA	
A5401	RAF SE5A Replica	To USA	
N9508	DH Tiger Moth	To Netherlands as PH-TGR	
BB731	DH Tiger Moth	To G-ADCG	
DE363	DH Tiger Moth	To G-ANFC	
PT229	NA Harvard IIB	To France	
FT323	NA Harvard IIB	To G-AZSC	
KH191	Consolidated Liberator	To Museum in Boston, Massachusetts	
MT818	VS Spitfire T8	To USA	
NH749	VS Spitfire XIV	To USA as N749DP	
NL750	DH Tiger Moth	To G-AHUF	
NM181	DH Tiger Moth	To G-AZGZ	
TG536	HP Hastings C1A	Burnt at Catterick	
TX192	Avro Anson C19	To Ailes Ancienne, nr Paris	
VP973	DH Devon C2	Scrapped at Northolt	
VX302	Hawker Sea Fury T20	To USA as N613RD	
VZ345	Hawker Sea Fury T20	Written off 17 April 1985	
WD480	HP Hastings C2	Burnt at Farnborough	
WD499	HP Hastings C2	Scrapped at Honington	
WD833	Fairy Firefly AS6	To USA	
WD948	EE Canberra B2	Burnt at Manston	
WG316	DH Chipmunk 22	To Spain	
WG611	EE Canberra B2	Scrapped at Aldergrove	
WH589	Hawker Sea Fury	To USA as N4434P	
WJ898	Vickers Varsity T1	Scrapped at Aldergove	
WJ916	Vickers Varsity T1	Scrapped at Lyneham	
WK162	EE Canberra B2	Written off 8 August 1985	
WL628	Vickers Varisty T1	Scrapped at Watton	
WP784	DH Chipmunk T10 PAX	Really WP907	
WP851	DH Chipmunk T10	To Netherlands	
WR981	Avro Shackleton MR3	Scrapped at Topcliffe	
WZ416	DH Vampire T11	Scrapped at Bushey	
XA866	WS55 Whirlwind HAR1	Scrapped at Donington Park	
XE606	Hawker Hunter F6A	To RAF Laarbruch as 8841M	
XF418	Hawker Hunter F6A	To RAF Germany as 8842M	
XG152	Hawker Hunter F6A	To RAF Gutersloh as 8843M	
XH228	EE Canberra B(I)8	Burnt at Catterick	
XH554	Avro Vulcan B2	Burnt at Catterick	
XH562	Avro Vulcan B2	Burnt at Catterick	
XH616	HP Victor K1A	Burnt at Manston	
XJ524	DH Sea Vixen FAW (TT)2	Burnt at Catterick	
XJ526	DH Sea Vixen FAW2	Burnt at Catterick	
XJ579	DH Sea Vixen FAW2	Scrapped at Farnborough	
XK885	Percival Pembroke C1	To USA as N46EA	
XL388	Avro Vulcan B2	Scrapped at Honington	
XL450	Fairy Gannet AEW3	To Air Classik, Moenchengladbach, W. Germany	
XL584	Hawker Hunter T8C	Written off 31 October 1984	
XM575	Avro Vulcan B2	To G-BLMC	
XM841	Westland Wessex HAS1	Burnt at Predannack	
XM842	Westland Wessex HAS1	Burnt at Predannack	
XN550	Hunting Jet Provost T3	Scrapped	
XN653	DH Sea Vixen FAW2	Scrapped at Farnborough	
XN688	DH Sea Vixen FAW2	Scrapped at Farnborough	
XN700	DH Sea Vixen FAW2	Scrapped at Farnborough	
XN705	DH Sea Vixen FAW2	Scrapped at Farnborough	
XN706	DH Sea Vixen FAW2	Scrapped at Farnborough	
XN707	DH Sea Vixen FAW2	Scrapped at Farnborough	
XP000	DHC Beaver AL1	To G-BMGE, then to the USA	

Deletions

Notes	Serial	Type (alternative identity)	Owner, Operator or Location
	XP105	Westland Wessex HAS3	Burnt at Lee-on-Solent
	XP118	Westland Wessex HAS3	Burnt at Predannock
	XP189	Westland Scout AH1	Scrapped at Farnborough
	XP353	WS55 Whirlwind HAR10	Burnt at Catterick
	XP513	HS Gnat T1	To USA
	XP583	Hunting Jet Provost T4	Burnt at Manston
	XP806	DHC Beaver AL1	To USA
	XP906	Westland Scout AH1	Written off 12 March 1985
	XP920	DH Sea Vixen FAW2	Scrapped at Farnborough
	XP925	DH Sea Vixen FAW2	Scrapped at Farnborough
	XP956	DH Sea Vixen FAW2	Scrapped at Farnborough
	XR772	EE Lightning F6	Written off 6 March 1985
	XS175	Hunting Jet Provost T4	Scrapped
	XS528	Westland Wasp HAS1	To R. New Zealand Navy as NZ3910
	XS532	Westland Wasp HAS1	To R. New Zealand Navy as NZ3909
	XS921	EE Lightning F6	Written off 19 September 1985
	XT428	Westland Wasp HAS1	To R. New Zealand Navy as NZ3911
	XT767	Westland Wessex HU5	Written off 3 December 1984
	XV125	Westland Scout AH1	Burnt at Manston
	XV278	HS Harrier GR1	To RAF Gutersloh as training aid
	XV341	HS Buccaneer S2B	Written off 14 June 1985
	XV672	Westland Sea King AEW2	Written off 14 October 1985
	XW179	Westland Scout AH1	Rebuilt into XT242
	XW933	HS Harrier T4	Written off 18 February 1985
	XX118	SEPECAT Jaguar GR1	To Foulness Range
	XX279	HS Hawk T1A	Written off 30 January 1985
	XX333	HS Hawk T1A	Written off 26 September 1985
	XX340	HS Hawk T1A	Written off 26 September 1985
	XX660	SA Bulldog T1	Written off 25 March 1985
	XX728	SEPECAT Jaguar GR1	Written off 7 October 1985
	XX731	SEPECAT Jaguar GR1	Written off 7 October 1985
	XX740	SEPECAT Jaguar GR1	To Oman AF as 225
	XZ365	SEPECAT Jaguar GR1A	Written off 9 July 1985
	XZ388	SEPECAT Jaguar GR1	Written off 1 April 1985
	XZ458	BAe Sea Harrier FRS1	Written off 1 December 1984
	XZ671	Westland Lynx AH1	Written off 4 January 1984
	XZ919	Westland Sea King HAS5	Written off 27 June 1985
	XZ968	BAe Harrier GR3	Written off 1 July 1984
	XZ989	BAe Harrier GR3	To 8849M Gutersloh for ground instruction
	ZA610	Panavia Tornado GR1	Written off 12 December 1985
	ZA770	Westland Gazelle AH1	Written off 22 June 1984
	ZB606	BAe Harrier T4N	Written off 7 February 1985
	ZD635	Westland Sea King HAS5	Written off 21 June 1985

The following gliders have been sold by the RAF:
Slingsby Sedbergh TX1s: WB919 (to BGA3174), WB920, WB926, WB939, WB941 (to BGA3160), WB947, WB976, WB978 (to BGA3189), WB983 (to BGA3175), WB985, WB988, WB990 (to BGA3148), WG497, WB499, XN151, XN156.
Slingsby Prefect TX1: WE990 (to BGA2583).
Slingsby Cadet TX3: WT867, WT871 (to BGA3149), WT899, WT901, WT902 (to BGA3147), WT904, WT905, WT909, WT911, WT914, WT915 (to BGA3181), XA284, XA289, XA302, XA310, XA311, XE791 (to BGA3185), XE798, XE800, XE802, XE806 (to BGA3135), XE810, XE812, XN238, XN243 (to BGA3145), XN253.
Slingsby Grasshopper TX1: WZ761, WZ764, XA228, XA236, XK790, XP455 (to BGA3143), XP458, XP488.
Slingsby Sky 1: XA876 (to RAFGSA as R76).
Slingsby Swallow TX1: XS651, XS652 (to BGA1107), XS859 (to BGA1136), XT653.

RAF Maintenance Command/ Support Command 'M' number cross-reference for serials listed in Military Aircraft Markings

1746M/K4972
4354M/BL614
5377M/EP120
5405M/LF738
5466M/LF751
5690M/MK356
5713M/BM597
5758M/DG202
6372M/EE549
6490M/LA255
6640M/RM694
6709M/TE356
6850M/TE184
6944M/RW386
6947M/RW388
6948M/DE673
6960M/MT847
7000M/TE392
7001M/TE356
7008M/EE549
7014M/N6720
7015M/NL985
7060M/VF301
7090M/EE531
7118M/LA198
7119M/LA226
7150M/PK683
7151M/VT229
7154M/WB188
7174M/VX272
7175M/VV106
7200M/VT812
7241M/TE311
7243M/TE462
7244M/TB382
7245M/RW382
7246M/TD248
7256M/TB752
7257M/TB252
7285M/VV119
7288M/PK724
7293M/RW393
7323M/VV217
7325M/R5868
7362M/475081
7416M/WN907
7421M/WT660
7422M/WT684
7428M/WK198
7432M/WZ724
7443M/WX853
7451M/TE476
7458M/WX905
7464M/XA564
7470M/XA553
7473M/XE946
7491M/WT569
7496M/WT612
7499M/WT555
7510M/WT694
7525M/WT619
7530M/WT648
7532M/WT651
7533M/WT680
7543M/WN901
7544M/WN904
7564M/XE982
7570M/XD674
7582M/WP180
7583M/WP185
7602M/WE600
7604M/XD542
7605M/WS692
7606M/WV562
7607M/TJ138
7615M/WV679
7616M/WW388
7618M/WW442
7621M/WV686
7622M/WV606
7625M/WD356
7630M/VZ304
7641M/XA634
7645M/WD293
7646M/VX461
7648M/XF785
7652M/WZ544
7656M/WJ573
7663M/XA571
7688M/WW421
7693M/WV483
7696M/WV493
7697M/WV495
7698M/WV499
7700M/WV544
7704M/TW536
7705M/WL505
7706M/WB584
7709M/WT933
7711M/PS915
7712M/WK281
7715M/XK724
7716M/WS776
7717M/XA549
7718M/WA577
7719M/WK277
7729M/WB758
7734M/XD536
7737M/XD602
7739M/XA801
7750M/WL168
7755M/WG760
7758M/PM651
7759M/PK664
7761M/XH318
7770M/WT746
7796M/WJ676
7805M/TW117
7806M/TA639
7809M/XA699
7814M/XD511
7816M/WG763
7817M/TX214
7822M/XP248
7825M/WK991
7827M/XA917
7829M/XH992
7839M/WV781
7840M/XK482
7841M/WV783
7845M/XN195
7847M/WV276
7849M/XF319
7851M/WZ706
7852M/XG506
7855M/XK416
7859M/XP283
7860M/XL738
7862M/XR246
7864M/XP244
7865M/TX226
7866M/XH278
7867M/XH980
7868M/WZ736
7869M/WK935
7870M/XM556
7878M/XD601
7881M/WD413
7883M/XT150
7887M/XD375
7890M/XD453
7891M/XM693
7894M/XD818
7895M/WF784
7896M/XA900
7898M/XP854
7899M/XG540
7900M/WA576
7902M/WZ550
7906M/WH132
7917M/WA591
7920M/WL360
7923M/XT133
7928M/XE849
7930M/WH301
7931M/RD253
7932M/WZ744
7933M/XR220
7937M/WS843
7938M/XH903
7939M/XD596
7940M/XL764
7949M/XF974
7955M/XH767
7957M/XF545
7959M/WS774
7960M/WS726
7961M/WS739
7964M/WS760
7965M/WS792
7967M/WS844
7969M/WS840
7970M/WP907
7971M/XK699
7972M/XH764
7973M/WS807
7976M/XK418
7979M/XM529
7980M/XM561
7982M/XH892
7983M/XD506
7984M/XN597
7986M/WG777
7990M/XD452
7997M/XG452
7998M/XD515
8005M/WG768
8007M/XF990
8009M/XG518
8010M/XG547
8011M/XV269
8012M/VS562
8017M/XL762
8018M/XN344
8019M/WZ869
8021M/XL824
8022M/XN341
8023M/XD463
8025M/XH124
8027M/XM555
8032M/XH837
8033M/XD382
8034M/XL703
8040M/XR493
8041M/XF690
8043M/XF836
8044M/XP286
8046M/XL770
8049M/WE168
8050M/XG329
8051M/XN929
8052M/WH166
8053M/WK968
8054AM/XM410
8054BM/XM417
8055AM/XM402
8055BM/XM404
8056M/XG337
8057M/XR243
8060M/WW397
8062M/XR669
8063M/WT536
8070M/EP120
8071M/TE476
8072M/PK624
8075M/RW382
8076M/XM386
8077M/XN594
8078M/XM351
8079M/XN492
8080M/XM480
8081M/XM468
8082M/XM409
8083M/XM367
8084M/XM369
8085M/XM467
8086M/TB752
8087M/XN925
8088M/XN602
8090M/XM698
8092M/WK654
8099M/WD355
8101M/WH984
8102M/WT486
8103M/WR985
8106M/WR982
8108M/WV703
8113M/WV753
8114M/WL798
8117M/WR974
8118M/WZ549
8119M/WR971
8121M/XM474
8122M/XD613
8128M/WH775
8139M/XJ582
8140M/XJ571
8142M/XJ560
8143M/XN691
8147M/XR526
8151M/WV795
8153M/WV903
8154M/WV908
8155M/WV797
8156M/XE339
8158M/XE369
8159M/XD528
8160M/XD622
8162M/WM913
8163M/XP919
8164M/WF299
8169M/WH364
8171M/XJ607
8172M/XJ609
8173M/XN685
8174M/WZ576
8175M/XE950
8177M/WM224
8179M/XN928
8180M/XN930

RAF Maintenance cross-reference

8182M/XN953
8183M/XN962
8184M/WT520
8186M/WR977
8187M/WH791
8188M/XG327
8189M/WD646
8190M/XJ918
8192M/XR658
8194M/XK862
8196M/XE920
8197M/WT346
8198M/WT339
8203M/XD377
8205M/XN819
8206M/WG419
8207M/WD318
8208M/WG303
8209M/WG418
8210M/WG471
8211M/WK570
8212M/WK587
8213M/WK626
8215M/WP869
8216M/WP927
8217M/WZ866
8218M/WB645
8219M/XR455
8221M/XP409
8222M/XJ604
8224M/XN699
8226M/XP921
8229M/XM355
8230M/XM362
8231M/XM375
8232M/XM381
8233M/XM408
8234M/XN458
8235M/XN549
8236M/XP573
8237M/XS179
8238M/XS180
8239M/XS210
8340M/XP341
8344M/WH960
8345M/XG540
8346M/XN734
8350M/WH840
8352M/XN632
8355M/KG374
/KN645
8357M/WK576
8359M/WF825
8360M/WP863
8361M/WB670
8362M/WG477
8363M/WG463
8364M/WG464
8365M/XK421
8366M/XG454
8367M/XG474
8368M/XF926
8369M/WE139
8370M/N1671
8371M/XA847
8372M/K8042
8373M/P2617
8375M/NX611
8376M/RF398
8377M/R9125
8378M/T9707
8379M/DG590
8380M/Z7197
8382M/VR930
8383M/K9942
8384M/X4590
8385M/N5912
8386M/NV778
8387M/T6296
8388M/XL993
8389M/VX573
8390M/SL542
8391M/SL574
8392M/SL674
8393M/XK987
8394M/WG422
8395M/WF408
8396M/XK740
8398M/WR967
8399M/WR539
8401M/XP686
8402M/XN769
8403M/XK531
8406M/XP831
8407M/XP585
8408M/XS186
8409M/XS209
8410M/XR662
8411M/XM139
8412M/XM147
8413M/XM192
8414M/XM173
8415M/XM181
8416M/XM183
8417M/XM144
8418M/XM178
8422M/XM169
8427M/XM172
8428M/XH593
8429M/XH592
8431M/XR651
8434M/XM411
8435M/XN512
8436M/XN554
8438M/XP761
8439M/WZ849
8440M/WD935
8441M/XR107
8442M/XP411
8444M/XP400
8445M/XK968
8446M/XP748
8447M/XP359
8453M/XP745
8454M/XP442
8455M/XP444
8457M/XS871
8458M/XP672
8459M/XR650
8460M/XP680
8462M/XX477
8463M/XP355
8465M/W1048
8466M/L-866
8467M/WP912
8473M/WP180
8484M/5439
8488M/WL627
8489M/XN816
8490M/WH703
8491M/WJ880
8492M/WJ872
8493M/XR571
8494M/XP557
8495M/XR672
8497M/XM698
8498M/XR670
8499M/XP357
8501M/XP640
8502M/XP686
8503M/XS451
8506M/XR704
8507M/XS215
8508M/XS218
8509M/XT141
8510M/XP567
8511M/WT305
8513M/XN724
8514M/XS176
8515M/WH869
8516M/XR643
8517M/XA932
8531M/XS418
8532M/XS423
8533M/XS449
8534M/XS450
8535M/XS454
8538M/XN781
8546M/XN728
8548M/WT507
8549M/WT534
8550M/XT595
8551M/XN774
8554M/TG511
8556M/XN855
8558M/XP439
8559M/XN467
8560M/XR569
8561M/XS100
8562M/XS110
8564M/XN387
8565M/E-408
8566M/XV279
8566M/XV555
8567M/WL738
8568M/XP503
8569M/XR535
8570M/XR954
8571M/XR984
8572M/XM706
8573M/XM708
8575M/XP542
8576M/XP502
8577M/XP532
8578M/XR534
8579M/XR140
8580M/XP516
8581M/WJ775
8582M/XE874
8584M/WH903
8585M/XE670
8586M/XE643
8587M/XP677
8588M/XR681
8589M/XR700
8590M/XM191
8591M/XA893
8592M/XM969
8595M/XH278
8598M/WP270
8600M/XX761
8602M/XR541
8603M/XR951
8604M/XS104
8605M/XA536
8606M/XP530
8607M/XP538
8608M/XP540
8609M/XR953
8610M/XL502
8611M/WF128
8612M/XD182
8613M/XJ724
8614M/XP515
8615M/XP532
8616M/XP541
8617M/XM709
8618M/XP504
8619M/XP511
8620M/XP534
8621M/XR538
8622M/XR980
8623M/XR998
8624M/XS102
8625M/XS105
8626M/XS109
8627M/XP558
8628M/XJ380
8629M/WL801
8630M/WG362
8631M/XR574
8632M/XP533
8634M/WP314
8635M/XP514
8636M/XR540
8637M/XR991
8638M/XS101
8639M/XS107
8640M/XR977
8641M/XR987
8642M/XR537
8643M/WJ867
8645M/XD163
8646M/XK969
8647M/XP338
8648M/XK526
8650M/XP333
8652M/WH794
8653M/XS120
8654M/XL898
8655M/XN126
8656M/XP405
8657M/VZ634
8660M/XW538
8661M/XJ727
8662M/XR458
8664M/WJ603
8665M/WL754
8666M/XE793
8667M/WP972
8668M/WJ821
8670M/XL384
8671M/XJ435
8672M/XP351
8673M/XD165
8674M/XP395
8676M/XL577
8677M/XJ695
8678M/XE656
8679M/XF526
8680M/XF527
8681M/XG164
8682M/XP404
8683M/WJ870
8684M/XJ634
8685M/XF516
8686M/XG158
8687M/XJ639
8689M/WK144
8691M/WT518
8692M/WL741
8693M/WH863
8695M/WJ817
8696M/WH773
8697M/WJ825
8699M/ZD232
8700M/ZD234
8701M/XP352
8702M/XG196
8703M/VW453
8704M/XN643
8705M/XT281
8706M/XF383
8707M/XF386
8708M/XF509
8709M/XG209
8710M/XG274
8711M/XG290
8712M/XF439
8713M/XG225
8714M/XK149
8715M/XG264
8716M/XV155
8718M/XX396
8719M/XT257
8721M/XP354
8722M/WJ640
8723M/XL567
8726M/XP299
8727M/XR486
8728M/WT532
8729M/WJ815
8730M/XD186
8731M/XP361
8732M/XJ729
8733M/XL318
8734M/XM657
8735M/WJ681
8736M/XF375
8738M/XJ695
8739M/XH170
8740M/WE173
8741M/XW329
8742M/WH856
8743M/WD790
8744M/XH563
8745M/XL392
8746M/XH171
8747M/WJ629
8749M/XH537
8751M/XT255
8752M/XR509
8753M/WL795
8754M/XG882
8755M/WH699
8755M/WJ637
8756M/XL427
8757M/XM656
8759M/XL321
8760M/XL386
8761M/WJ977
8762M/WH740
8763M/WH665
8764M/XP344
8766M/XJ782
8767M/XX635
8768M/A-522
8769M/A-528
8770M/XL623
8771M/XM602

8772M/WR960
8773M/XV156
8774M/XV338
8776M/XV152
8777M/XX914
8778M/XM598
8779M/XM607
8780M/WK102
8781M/WE982
8782M/XH136
8783M/XW272
8784M/VP976
8785M/XS642
8786M/XN495
8795M/VP958
8796M/XK943
8797M/XX947
8798M/XG151
8799M/WV787
8800M/XG226
8801M/XS650
8802M/XJ608
8803M/XJ572
8805M/XT772
8806M/XP140
8807M/XL587
8808M/XP695
8809M/XH561
8810M/XJ825
8811M/XL445
8813M/VT260
8814M/XM927
8816M/XX734
8817M/XN652
8818M/XK527
8819M/XS479
8820M/VP952
8821M/XX115
8822M/VP957
8823M/VP965
8824M/VP971
8825M/WB530
8826M/XV638
8827M/XX300
8828M/XS587
8829M/XE653
8830M/XF515
8831M/XG160
8832M/XG172
8833M/XL569
8834M/XL572
8835M/XL576
8836M/XL592
8837M/XL617
8838M/34037
8839M/XG194
8840M/XG252
8844M/XJ676
8845M/XS572
8846M/XE673
8847M/XX344
8848M/XZ135
8850M/XV436
8851M/XT595
8852M/XV337
8853M/XT277
8854M/XV154
8855M/XT284
8856M/XT274
8857M/XW544
8858M/XW541
8859M/XW545
8860M/XW549
8861M/XW528
8862M/XN473

RN engineerings 'A' airframe number cross-reference for serials listed in Military Aircraft Markings

A646/SX300
A680/DE373
A2001/W5984
A2055/SX336
A2127/DE373
A2439/WF219
A2472/XA508
A2483/WF259
A2503/WM994
A2509/WF299
A2510/WM913
A2511/WM983 (XE364)
A2517/WM961
A2522/WM993
A2525/XN334
A2526/WV911
A2530/WM969
A2531/WG718
A2532/WV826
A2534/XE368
A2538/XJ393
A2539/XG831
A2540/WN464
A2542/XA862
A2543/XA870
A2551/XA868
A2556/XE327
A2557/WV798
A2571/XG577
A2572/XJ402
A2574/XD332
A2575/XG574
A2576/WV198
A2577/XB480
A2579/XN332
A2580/XE369
A2581/XK532
A2597/XS509
A2598/XJ482
A2600/XN934
A2602/XN925
A2603/XK911
A2605/XN308
A2607/XK944
A2608/XA459
A2609/XM329
A2610/XN647
A2611/XJ575
A2614/XN314
A2615/XT256
A2616/XN651
A2618/XP116
A2619/XS695
A2621/XJ584
A2622/XJ602
A2623/XN697
A2624/XN692
A2625/XL846
A2626/XL847
A2627/XN967
A2628/XP558
A2629/XM667
A2630/XL853
A2632/WV903
A2633/XE369
A2635/XE339
A2637/WV797
A2639/XN650
A2640/XP155
A2642/XL836
A2643/XN311 (XN296)
A2645/WF225
A2646/XK988
A2647/XS463
A2648/XS125
A2649/XS869
A2650/XP160
A2651/XG596
A2652/XN261
A2653/XK943
A2654/XN302
A2655/XN953
A2658/XP984
A2659/XV669
A2660/WV908
A2661/WV795
A2662/WF299
A2663/XN309
A2664/XV644
A2665/XL839
A2666/XS872
A2667/XP226
A2668/XS885
A2669/XP149
A2670/XS128
A2671/XS867
A2672/XS537
A2673/WF122
A2674/WF125
A2675/XS881
A2676/XR572
A2677/XR993
A2678/XR955
A2679/XP535
A2680/XP157
A2681/XP117
A2682/XM845
A2683/XS878
A2684/XP151
A2685/XS886
A2686/XS873
A2687/XS877
A2688/XP158
A2689/XM874
A2690/XS887
A2691/XS868
A2692/XM917
A2693/XM843
A2694/XS865
A2695/XS876
A2696/XS882
A2697/XS870
A2699/XS570
A2700/XP980
A2701/XL500
A2702/XS545
A2703/XT441
A2705/XS866
A2706/XM868
A2707/XS122
A2708/XR540
A2709/XR991
A2710/
A2712/XN359
A2713/XN386
A2714/XL880
A2715
A2716
A2717
A2718
A2719
A2720
A2721
A2722/XT757
A2723/XT487

RAF Gliding and Soaring Association Markings

Notes	Identity	Type, Previous Identity and Competition Number	Club and Location
	R1	Schempp-Hirth Janus C (BGA2723)	Cranwell GC, RAF Cranwell
	R2	Schempp-Hirth-Janus C	RAFG&SA Centre, RAF Bicester
	R3	Schleicher ASK-13	RAFG&SA Centre, RAF Bicester
	R4	Schleicher ASK-13	Anglia GC, RAF Wattisham
	R5	Schleicher Ka-7	Four Counties GC, RAF Syerston
	R6	Grob G102 Astir	RAFG&SA Centre, RAF Bicester
	R7	Schleicher ASK-13	Clevelands GC, RAF Dishforth
	R9	Schleicher Janus B	Four Counties GC, RAF Syerston
	R10	Schempp-Hirth Discus B [R10]	RAFG&SA Centre, RAF Bicester
	R11	LET L-13 Blanik	RAFG&SA Centre, RAF Bicester
	R15	Schleicher Ka-7	Chilterns GC, RAF Halton
	R16	Schempp-Hirth Ventus [16]	Bannerdown GC, RAF Hullavington
	R18	Schleicher ASW-19 [R18]	Fenlands GC, RAF Marham
	R20	Schleicher ASK-21	Bannerdown GC, RAF Hullavington
	R21	Schleicher ASK-21	RAFG&SA Centre, RAF Bicester
	R22	Schleicher ASK-21	Wrekin GC, RAF Cosford
	R25	Schleicher ASK-21	Fulmar GC, RAF Kinloss
	R26	Schempp-Hirth Nimbus 3 [26]	RAFG&SA Centre, RAF Bicester
	R27	Schempp-Hirth Ventus [27]	RAFG&SA Centre, RAF Bicester
	R29	Schleicher Ka-7	Anglia GC, RAF Wattisham
	R30	Glaser-Dirks DG-300 [R30]	Humber GC, RAF Scampton
	R32	Schleicher ASK-18	Fulmar GC, RAF Kinloss
	R33	Schleicher ASK-18	RAFG&SA Centre, RAF Bicester
	R34	Schleicher ASK-21	Bannerdown GC, RAF Hullavington
	R36	Schleicher ASK-18	Four Counties GC, RAF Syerston
	R37	Schleicher ASK-13	Wrekin GC, RAF Cosford
	R40	Schleicher ASK-21	RAFG&SA Centre, RAF Bicester
	R42	Schleicher K-8b	Anglia GC, RAF Wattisham
	R43	Schleicher ASK-18	Wrekin GC, RAF Cosford
	R44	Schleicher K-8b	RAFG&SA Centre, RAF Bicester
	R45	Schleicher K-8b	Fulmar GC, RAF Kinloss
	R46	Schleicher ASK-13	Fenlands GC, RAF Marham
	R47	Schleicher K-8b	Cranwell GC, RAF Cranwell
	R49	Schleicher ASK-18	Bannerdown GC, RAF Hullavington
	R57	Grob G102 Astir	Four Counties GC, RAF Syerston
	R58	Grob G103a Twin Astir Acro	Four Counties GC, RAF Syerston
	R60	Grob G102 Astir	Clevelands GC, RAF Dishforth
	R63	Grob G102 Astir	Humber GC, RAF Scampton
	R66	Grob G102 Astir	Cranwell GC, RAF Cranwell
	R67	Grob G102 Astir	Anglia GC, RAF Wattisham
	R68	Grob G102 Astir	Wrekin GC, RAF Cosford
	R69	Grob G102 Astir	Fenlands GC, RAF Marham
	R74	LET L-13 Blanik	FAFG&SA Centre, RAF Bicester
	R75	Schleicher K-8b	Fenlands GC, RAF Marham
	R77	Grob G102 Astir	RAFG&SA Centre, RAF Bicester
	R78	Grob G102 Astir	Bannerdown GC, RAF Hullavington
	R82	Grob G102 Astir	Fulmar GC, RAF Kinloss
	R83	Grob G103 Twin Astir	Clevelands GC, RAF Dishforth
	R84	Grob G102 Astir	Chilterns GC, RAF Halton
	R85	Schleicher K-8b	Fenlands GC, RAF Marham
	R86	Schleicher ASK-13	Fenlands GC, RAF Marham
	R87	Schempp-Hirth Ventus [87]	Four Counties GC, RAF Syerston
	R88	Schleicher ASK-13	Humber GC, RAF Scampton
	R95	Schleicher K-8b	Clevelands GC, RAF Dishforth
	R96	Schleicher K-8b	Chilterns GC, RAF Halton
	R98	Schleicher K-8b	Humber GC, RAF Scampton
	232	Rolladen-Schneider LS4 [232]	Cranwell GC, RAF Cranwell

RN Landing Platform and Shore Station Code-letters

Sqn code	Tail code	Name and Pennant Number	Type/task	Notes
323	AB	HMS *Ambuscade* (F172)	Type 21	
430	AC	HMS *Achilles* (F12)	Leander	
455	AE	HMS *Ariadne* (F72)	Leander	
341	AG	HMS *Avenger* (F185)	Type 21	
421	AJ	HMS *Ajax* (F114)	Leander	
327	AL	HMS *Alacrity* (F174)	Type 21	
472	AM	HMS *Andromeda* (F57)	Leander	
470	AP	HMS *Apollo* (F70)	Leander	
426	AR	HMS *Arethusa* (F38)	Leander	
466	AT	HMS *Argonaut* (F56)	Leander	
422	AU	HMS *Aurora* (F10)	Leander	
322	AV	HMS *Active* (F171)	Type 21	
326	AW	HMS *Arrow* (F173)	Type 21	
320	AZ	HMS *Amazon* (F169)	Type 21	
—	BD	RFA *Sir Bedivere* (L3004)	Landing ship	
—	BE	RFA *Blue Rover* (A270)	Fleet tanker	
440	BK	HMS *Berwick* (F115)	Type 12	
333	BM	HMS *Birmingham* (D86)	Type 42	
334	BS	HMS *Bristol* (D23)	Type 82	
342	BT	HMS *Brilliant* (F90)	Type 22	
—	BV	HMS *Black Rover* (A273)	Fleet tanker	
346	BW	HMS *Broadsword* (F88)	Type 22	
403	BX	HMS *Battleaxe* (F89)	Type 22	
330	BZ	HMS *Brazen* (F91)	Type 22	
335	CF	HMS *Cardiff* (D108)	Type 42	
—	CH	HMS *Challenger* (K07)	Seabed ops	
463	CP	HMS *Cleopatra* (F28)	Leander	
—	CU	RNAS Culdrose (HMS *Seahawk*)		
—	CW	HMS *Cornwall* (F99)	Type 22	
431	CY	HMS *Charybdis* (F75)	Leander	
—	DC	HMS *Dumbarton Castle* (P268)	Fishery protection	
—	DG	RFA *Diligence* (A132)	Maintenance	
423	DM	HMS *Diomede* (F16)	Leander	
464	DN	HMS *Danae* (F47)	Leander	
411	ED	HMS *Edinburgh* (D97)	Type 42	
434/5	ED	HMS *Endurance* (A171)	Ice Patrol	
—	EN	RFA *Engadine* (K08)	Helicopter support	
433	EU	HMS *Euryalus* (F15)	Leander	
420	EX	HMS *Exeter* (D89)	Type 42	
342	FA	RFA *Fort Austin* (A386)	Support ship	
404	FF	HMS *Fife* (D20)	County	
343	FG	RFA *Fort Grange* (A385)	Support ship	
—	FL	RNAY Fleetlands		
—	FS	HMS *Fearless* (L10)	Assault	
461	GA	HMS *Galatea* (F18)	Leander	
410	GC	HMS *Gloucester* (D96)	Type 42	
400	GL	HMS *Glamorgan* (D19)	County	
—	GN	RFA *Green Rover* (A268)	Fleet tanker	
—	GR	RFA *Sir Geraint* (L3027)	Landing ship	
—	GV	RFA *Gold Rover* (A271)	Fleet tanker	
344	GW	HMS *Glasgow* (D88)	Type 42	
—	GY	RFA *Grey Rover* (A269)	Fleet tanker	
—	H	HMS *Hermes* (R12)	Carrier	
415	HD	HMS *Hydra* (A144)	Hecla	
325	HE	HMS *Herald* (A138)	Hecla	
416	HL	HMS *Hecla* (A133)	Hecla	
475	HM	HMS *Hermione* (F58)	Leander	
414	HT	HMS *Hecate* (A137)	Hecla	
—	ID	HMS *Intrepid* (L11)	Assault	
465	JO	HMS *Juno* (F52)	Leander	
443	JP	HMS *Jupiter* (F60)	Leander	
—	L	HMS *Illustrious* (R06)	Carrier	

RN Code-Letters

Notes	Sqn code	Tail code	Name and Pennant Number	Type/task
	—	LC	HMS *Leeds Castle* (P258)	Fishery protection
	476	LE	HMS *Leander* (F109)	Leander
	—	LN	RFA *Sir Lancelot* (L3029)	Landing ship
	332	LP	HMS *Liverpool* (D92)	Type 42
	—	LS	RNAS Lee-on-Solent (HMS *Daedalus*)	
	360	MC	HMS *Manchester* (D95)	Type 42
	424	MV	HMS *Minerva* (F45)	Leander
	—	N	HMS *Invincible* (R05)	Carrier
	324	NA	HMS *Naiad* (F39)	Leander
	345	NC	HMS *Newcastle* (D87)	Type 42
	417	NM	HMS *Nottingham* (D91)	Type 42
	347	OD	RFA *Olmeda* (A124)	Fleet tanker
	347	ON	RFA *Olna* (A123)	Fleet tanker
	347	OW	RFA *Olwen* (A122)	Fleet tanker
	471	PB	HMS *Phoebe* (F42)	Leander
	445	PL	HMS *Plymouth* (F126)	Type 12
	454	PN	HMS *Penelope* (F127)	Leander
	—	PO	RNAS Portland (HMS *Osprey*)	
	—	PV	RFA *Sir Percival* (L3036)	Landing ship
	—	PW	Prestwick Airport (HMS *Gannet*)	
	—	R	HMS *Ark Royal* (R09)	Carrier
	436	RG	RFA *Regent* (A486)	Support ship
	462	RO	HMS *Rothesay* (F107)	Type 12
	437	RS	RFA *Resource* (A480)	Support ship
	—	RT	RFA *Reliant* (A131)	Helicopter support
	432	SC	HMS *Scylla* (F71)	Leander
	334	SN	HMS *Southampton* (D90)	Type 42
	450	SS	HMS *Sirius* (F40)	Leander
	—	TM	RFA *Sir Tristram* (L3505)	Landing ship
	347	TS	RFA *Tidespring* (A75)	Fleet tanker
	375	VB	HMS *Beaver* (F93)	Type 22
	—	VL	RNAS Yeovilton (HMS *Heron*)	
	—	WU	RNAY Wroughton	
	376	XB	HMS *Boxer* (F92)	Type 22
	407	YK	HMS *York* (D98)	Type 42
	456	YM	HMS *Yarmouth* (F101)	Type 12
			HMS *Brave* (F94)	Type 22
			HMS *London* (F95)	Type 22
			HMS *Sheffield* (F96)	Type 22
			HMS *Coventry* (F98)	Type 22

British Historic Aircraft in Overseas Markings

'Historic' aircraft carrying the markings of overseas air arms which can be seen in the UK, mainly preserved in museums and collections or taking part in air shows.

Serial	*Type (alternative identity)*	*Owner, operator and location*	*Notes*
Argentina			
A-517	FMA IA58 Pucara (G-BLRP)	Grampian Helicopters	
A-522	FMA IA58 Pucara (8768M)	FAA Museum, RNAS Yeovilton	
A-528	FMA IA58 Pucara (8769M)	Museum of Army Flying, Middle Wallop	
A-533	FMA IA58 Pucara (ZD486)	Museum of Army Flying, Middle Wallop	
A-549	FMA IA58 Pucara (ZD487)	Imperial War Museum, Duxford	
AE-409	Bell UH-1H	Museum of Army Flying, Middle Wallop	
AE-422	Bell UH-1H	FAA Museum, RNAS Yeovilton	
AE-520	Vertol CH-47C Chinook	RNAY Fleetlands	
656	Bell UH-1H (AE-409)	Museum of Army Flying, Middle Wallop	
0729	Beech T-34C Turbo Mentor [1-A-411]	FAA Museum, RNAS Yeovilton	
0767	Macchi MB339AA [4-A-116]	FAA Museum, RNAS Yeovilton	
PA-12	Sud SA330L Puma	Westlands, Weston-super-Mare	
Australia			
A2-4	Supermarine Seagull V (VH-ALB)	Battle of Britain Museum, Hendon	
A16-199	Lockheed Hudson IV (G-BEOX) [SF-R]	RAF Museum, Hendon	
Belgium			
FT-36	Lockheed T-33A	Dumfries & Galloway Aviation Museum, Tinwald Downs	
FT-37	Lockheed T-33A	RAF Alconbury	
FU-6	Republic F-84F Thunderstreak (52-7133)	RAF Museum/RAeS Medway Branch, Rochester	
HD-75	Hanriot HD1 (OO-APJ/G-AFDX/N75)	RAF Museum, Hendon	
Cambodia			
125	Morane MS733 Alcyon (G-SHOW/ F-BMQJ)	Booker Aircraft Museum	
Canada			
920	VS Stranraer (CF-BXO) [Q-N]	RAF Museum, Hendon	
5547	Hawker Hurricane II (G-HURI)	Privately owned, Coventry	
9059	Bristol Bolingbroke IVT	Privately owned, Portsmouth	
9893	Bristol Bolingbroke IVT	Privately owned, Duxford	
9940	Bristol Bolingbroke IVT	Royal Scottish Museum of Flight, East Fortune	
10038	Bristol Bolingbroke IVT (G-MKIV)	Privately owned, Duxford	
10201	Bristol Bolingbroke IVT	Strathallan Aircraft Collection	
18393	Avro Canada CF-100 (G-BCYK)	Imperial War Museum, Duxford	
20385	CCF AT-16 Harvard IV (G-BGPB)	Privately owned, Sandown	
Denmark			
E-402	Hawker Hunter F51	Lovaux, Hurn	
E-407	Hawker Hunter F51	Privately owned, Leicester	
E-408	Hawker Hunter F51 (8565M) [B]	RAF Brawdy, main gate	
E-412	Hawker Hunter F51	Tangmere Military Aviation Museum	
E-419	Hawker Hunter F51	North East Aircraft Museum, Usworth	
E-421	Hawker Hunter F51	Brooklands College of Technology, Surrey	
E-423	Hawker Hunter F51	Second World War Aircraft Preservation Society, Lasham	
E-424	Hawker Hunter F51	Lincolnshire Aviation Museum, East Kirkby	
E-425	Hawker Hunter F51	Midland Air Museum, Coventry	
E-427	Hawker Hunter F51 (G-9-447)	BAe Apprentice School, Brough	
E-430	Hawker Hunter F51	Privately owned, Faygate	
ET-271	Hawker Hunter T53	Booker Aircraft Museum	

Notes	Serial	Type (alternative identity)	Owner, operator and location
	ET-273	Hawker Hunter T7	Bomber County Aviation Museum, Cleethorpes
	L866	Consolidated Catalina (8466M)	RAF Cosford Aerospace Museum

Eire

	177	Percival Provost T1 (G-BLIW)	Privately owned, Shoreham
	178	Percival Provost T1 (G-BKOS)	Privately owned, Woodvale

Finland

	VI-3	Valtion Viima (G-BAAY)	Privately owned, White Waltham

France

	9	Dassault Mystere IVA	RAF Woodbridge
	19	Deperdussin Replica (BAPC136)	Leisure Sport, Thorpe Park
	25	Dassault Mystere IVA	RAF Woodbridge
	36	Dassault Mystere IVA [EABDR 8]	RAF Upper Heyford
	39	Nord 3400	Privately owned, Coventry
	45	SNCAN Stampe SV4C (G-BHFG)	Privately owned, Enstone
	46	Dassault Mystere IVA [EABDR 6]	RAF Upper Heyford
	50	Dassault Mystere IVA	RAF Woodbridge
	57	Dassault Mystere IVA [8-MT]	Imperial War Museum, Duxford
	59	Dassault Mystere IVA [314-TH]	Wales Aircraft Museum, Cardiff
	68	Nord 3400	Privately owned, Coventry
	70	Dassault Mystere IVA	Midland Air Museum, Coventry
	75	Dassault Mystere IVA	RAF Lakenheath
	79	Dassault Mystere IVA [8-NB]	Norfolk & Suffolk Aviation Museum, Flixton
	83	Dassault Mystere IVA [8-MS]	Newark Air Museum, Winthorpe
	84	Dassault Mystere IVA	Lashenden Air Warfare Museum, Headcorn
	85	Dassault Mystere IVA [8-MV]	Phoenix Aviation Museum, Bruntingthorpe
	92	MH Broussard (G-BJGW) [31-GW]	Privately owned, Duxford
	97	Dassault Mystere IVA	RAF Lakenheath
	99	Dassault Mystere IVA	RAF Lakenheath
	101	Dassault Mystere IVA [8-MN]	Bomber County Aviation Museum, Cleethorpes
	103	Nord Norecrin (G-BHXJ)	Privately owned, Popham
	104	Dassault Mystere IVA	RAF Bentwaters
	120	Stampe SV4C (G-AZGC)	Privately owned, Booker
	121	Dassault Mystere IVA [8-MY]	City of Norwich Aviation Museum
	124	Nord 3400	Privately owned, Coventry
	126	Dassault Mystere IVA	RAF Lakenheath
	127	Dassault Mystere IVA [EABDR 7]	RAF Upper Heyford
	133	Dassault Mystere IVA	RAF Woodbridge
	139	Dassault Mystere IVA [EABDR 9]	RAF Upper Heyford
	146	Dassualt Mystere IVA [8-MC]	North East Aircraft Museum, Usworth
	184	Dassault Mystere IVA	RAF Lakenheath, BDRT
	217	MH Broussard (G-BKPU)	Privately owned, Shawdene
	276	Dassault Mystere IVA	RAF Woodbridge
	309	Dassault Mystere IVA	RAF Lakenheath
	318	Dassault Mystere IVA	Dumfries & Galloway Aviation Museum, Tinwald Downs
	319	Dassault Mystere IVA [8-ND]	Rebel Air Museum, Andrewsfield
	1049	Morane MS230 (G-BJCL)	Privately owned, Duxford
	1076	Morane MS230 (G-AVEB)	Privately owned, Booker
	3398	Spad XII Replica (G-BFYO) [2]	Privately owned, St Just
	133722	Vought F4U-7 Corsair (NX1337A) [15F22]	Privately owned, Duxford/Sutton Bridge

Germany

	C19/18	Albatross replica (BAPC 118)	Privately owned, North Weald
	D5397/17	Albatross D.VA Replica (G-BFXL)	FAA Museum, RNAS Yeovilton
	5036	Bucker Jungmann (G-ATJX) [AT+JX]	Privately owned, Stapleford Tawney
	D2+600	CASA 352L (G-BFHG)	Aces High, Duxford
	1Z+EK	CASA 352L (N9012P)	Privately owned, Rochester
	N7+AA	CASA 352L	Privately owned, Coventry
	N8+AA	CASA 352L (G-BFHD)	Privately owned, Hurn
	N9+AA	CASA 352L (G-BECL)	Privately owned, Coventry
	475081	Fieseler Fi156C Storch (VP546/7362M)	RAF St Athan Historic Aircraft Collection
	CB+VD	Fieseler Fi156C Storch (D-EKMU)	Privately owned, Lympne
	28368	Flettner Fl282V Kolibri	Midland Air Museum, Coventry

Serial	Type (alternative identity)	Owner, operator and location	Notes
100143	Focke-Achgelis Fa330	Imperial War Museum, Duxford	
100502	Focke-Achgelis Fa330	Lincolnshire Aviation Museum, East Kirkby	
100509	Focke-Achgelis Fa330	Science Museum, South Kensington	
100545	Focke-Achgelis Fa330	Torbay Aircraft Museum, Paignton	
100549	Focke-Achgelis Fa330	Greater Manchester Museum of Science and Industry	
8	Focke Wulf FW190 Replica (G-WULF)	Privately owned, Elstree	
7334	Focke Wulf FW190 Replica (G-SYFW) [2+1]	Privately owned, Guernsey	
584219/38	Focke Wulf FW190F-8/UI (8470M)	RAF St Athan Historic Aircraft Collection	
733682	Focke Wulf FW190A-8/R6	Imperial War Museum, Lambeth	
4253/18	Fokker D.VII (G-BFPL)	Privately owned, Lower Upham	
5125/18	Fokker D.VII Replica (BAPC 110)	Leisure Sport, Thorpe Park	
8417/18	Fokker D.VII	RAF Museum Restoration Centre, Cardington	
150/17	Fokker Dr.1 Dreidekker Replica (BAPC 139)	Leisure Sport, Thorpe Park	
152/17	Fokker Dr.1 Dreidekker Replica (G-ATJM)	Privately owned, Sandown	
425/17	Fokker Dr.1 Dreidekker Replica (BAPC 133)	Torbay Aircraft Museum, Paignton	
425/17	Fokker Dr.1 Dreidekker Replica (G-BEFR)	Privately owned, St Athan	
102/18	Fokker Dr.1 Dreidekker Replica (BAPC 88)	FAA Museum, RNAS Yeovilton	
422/15	Fokker EIII replica (G-AVJO)	Privately owned, Booker	
22912	Hansa Brandenburg W.29 Replica (BAPC 138)	Leisure Sport, Thorpe Park	
701152	Heinkel He111H-23 (8471M) [NT+SL]	Battle of Britain Museum, Hendon	
120227	Heinkel He162 Salamander (8472M) [2]	RAF St Athan Historic Aircraft Collection	
120235	Heinkel He162 Salamander	Imperial War Museum, Lambeth	
14	Hispano HA1112 (C4K-235/ G-BJZZ)	Privately owned, Sandown	
1Z+NK	Junkers Ju52/3M (6316)	Imperial War Museum, Duxford	
494083	Junkers Ju87 D-3 (8474M) [RI+JK]	Battle of Britain Museum, Hendon	
360043	Junkers Ju88R-1 (PJ876/8475M) [D5+EV]	Battle of Britain Museum, Hendon	
7198/18	LVG C.VI (G-AANJ)	Shuttleworth Collection, Old Warden	
1190	Messerschmitt Bf109E-3	Privately owned, Hurn	
4101	Messerschmitt Bf109E-4 (DG200/ 8477M)	Battle of Britain Museum, Hendon	
10639	Messerschmitt Bf109G-2 (RN228/ 8478M)	RAF Benson, under restoration	
730301	Messerschmitt Bf110C-4 (AX772/ 8479M)	Battle of Britain Museum, Hendon	
191316	Messerschmitt Me163B Komet	Science Museum, South Kensington	
191614	Messerschmitt Me163B Komet (8481M)	RAF Cosford Aerospace Museum	
191659	Messerschmitt Me163B Komet	Royal Scottish Museum of Flight, East Fortune	
191660	Messerschmitt Me163B Komet	Imperial War Museum, Duxford	
191904	Messerschmitt Me163B Komet (8480M) [25]	RAF St Athan Historic Aircraft Collection	
112372	Messerschmitt Me262A-1 (VK893/ 8482M)	RAF St Athan Historic Aircraft Collection	
420430	Messerschmitt Me410A-1/U2 (8483M) [PD+VO]	RAF St Athan Historic Aircraft Collection	
ZA+WN	Morane 500 (G-AZMH)	Privately owned, Booker	
FI+S	Morane 505 (G-BIRW)	Royal Scottish Museum of Flight, East Fortune	
17	Nord 1002 (G-ATBG)	Privately owned, Sutton Bridge	
16+RF	Pilatus P-2 (U-110/G-PTWO)	Privately owned, Duxford	
1480	SNCAN Noralpha (G-BAYV)	Booker Aircraft Museum	

Greece

52-6541	Republic F-84F Thunderflash	North East Aircraft Museum, Usworth	
51-6151	Canadair F-86D Sabre	North East Aircraft Museum, Usworth	

Notes	Serial	Type (alternative identity)	Owner, operator and location
	Iraq		
	333	DH Vampire T55	Military Aircraft Preservation Group, Dukinfield, Greater Manchester
	Italy		
	MM19607	Canadair F-86E Sabre (XB733)	Privately owned, Much Hoole, Lancs
	MM5701	Fiat CR42 (BT474/8468M) [13-95]	Battle of Britain Museum, Hendon
	MM53211	Fiat G.46-4 (BAPC 79)	Privately owned, Lympne
	MM53432	NA T-6D (RM-11)	Privately owned, Staverton
	MM54137	NA T-6G Texan (G-CTKL)	Privately owned, Dorchester
	MM542540	Piper Super Cub	RAF Woodbridge, stored
	Netherlands		
	E-15	Fokker S-11 Instructor (G-BIYU)	Privately owned, Denham
	R-163	Piper Super Cub (G-BIRH)	Privately owned, Lee-on-Solent
	204/V	Lockheed SP-2H Neptune	RAF Cosford Aerospace Museum
	Norway		
	56321	Saab Safir (G-BKPY)	Newark Air Museum, Winthorpe
	Portugal		
	3460	Dornier 27 (G-BMFG)	Privately owned, Booker
	3497	Dornier 27 (G-BMFH)	Privately owned, Booker
	South Africa		
	6130	Lockheed Ventura II (AJ469)	RAF Museum Store, Henlow
	Spain		
	T2B-272	CASA C.352L	RAF Cosford Aerospace Museum
	HD5-1	Dornier Do24T-3 [58-1]	RAF Museum, Hendon
	C6-88	Hispano HA.1112	Privately owned, Stubbington
	T2-124	Bf-109K [FE-124]	Warbirds of GB, Bitteswell
	Sweden		
	35075	Saab J-35J Draken [40]	Duxford Aviation Society
	29640	Saab J-29F [08]	Midland Air Museum, Coventry
	Switzerland		
	J-108	Pilatus P-2 (G-BJAX)	Privately owned, Duxford
	U-125	Pilatus P-2 (G-BLKZ)	Privately owned, Goodwood
	U-142	Pilatus P-2 (G-BONE)	Privately owned, Southend
	J-1008	DH Vampire FB6	Mosquito Aircraft Museum, London Colney
	J-1172	DH Vampire FB6 (8487M)	Greater Manchester Museum of Science and Industry
	J-1523	DH Venom FB50 (G-VENI)	Privately owned, Cranfield
	J-1542	DH Venom FB50 (G-GONE)	Privately owned, Cranfield
	J-1601	DH Venom FB50 (G-VIDI)	Privately owned, Cranfield
	J-1605	DH Venom FB50 (G-BLID)	Aces High, Duxford
	J-1614	DH Venom FB50 (G-BLIE)	Privately owned, Glasgow
	J-1616	DH Venom FB50 (G-BLIF)	Aces High, Duxford
	J-1632	DH Venom FB50 (G-VNOM)	Privately owned, Cranfield
	J-1704	DH Venom FB54	RAF Cosford Aerospace Museum
	J-1758	DH Venom FB54 (G-BLSD)	Aces High, North Weald
	USA		
	0-17899	Convair VT-29B	Imperial War Museum, Duxford
	111989	Cessna L-19A Bird Dog (N33600)	Museum of Army Flying, Middle Wallop
	115042	NA T-6G Texan (G-BGHU) [TA-042]	Privately owned, Wellesbourne Mountford
	115302	Piper L-18C (G-BJTP)	Privately owned, Stoke Orchard, Glos
	121714	Grumman F8F-2B Bearcat (NX700H) [S/100]	Privately owned, Duxford
	12392	NA AT-6D Harvard III (FE905/LN-BNM)	RAF Museum Store, Cardington
	133854	NA Harvard III (G-SUES)	Privately owned, Biggin Hill
	14060	Lockheed T-33A [LN]	RAF Lakenheath
	14286	Lockheed T-33A [WK]	Imperial War Museum, Duxford
	14419	Lockheed T-33A [30-QC]	Midland Air Museum, Coventry
	146289	NA T-28 Trojan (N99153)	Norfolk & Suffolk Aviation Museum, Flixton
	150223	Westland Wessex	Sykes Helicopters, Hurn

Serial	*Type (alternative identity)*	*Owner, operator and location*	*Notes*
151632	NA TB-25N Mitchell (NL9494Z)	Privately owned, Coventry	
164	Beech 18 (G-BKGL)	British Aerial Museum, Duxford	
16718	Lockheed T-33A	RAF Sculthorpe	
16769	Lockheed T-33A	RAF Mildenhall	
17473	Lockheed T-33A	RAF Cosford Aerospace Museum	
181528	Piper J-3C-65 Cub	Privately owned, Southampton	
19252	Lockheed T-33A [314-UY]	Tangmere Military Aviation Museum	
231983	Boeing B-17G (F-BDRS) [IY-G]	Imperial War Museum, Duxford	
24535	Kaman HH-43F Huskie	Midland Air Museum, Coventry	
26	Boeing Stearman (G-BAVO)	Privately owned, Liverpool	
27767	Aeronca L-3A (G-BIHW)	Privately owned, Swansea	
2807	NA T-6G Texan (G-BHTH)	Privately owned, Liverpool	
29963	Lockheed T-33A	Wales Aircraft Museum, Cardiff	
315509	Douglas C-47D (G-BHUB)	Imperial War Museum, Duxford	
329417	Piper J-3C-65 Cub (G-BDHK)	Privately owned, Coleford	
329601	Piper J-3C-65 Cub (G-AXHR) [D-44]	Privately owned, Old Warden	
329934	Piper J-3C-65 Cub (G-BCPH) [72-B]	Privately owned, Booker	
34037	NA TB-25N Mitchell (429366/ N9115Z/151645/8838M)	Bomber Command Museum, Hendon	
413048	Piper J-3C-65 Cub (G-BCXJ) [39-E]	Privately owned, Compton Abbas	
41386	Thomas-Morse S4 Scout Replica (G-MJTD)	Privately owned, Hitchin	
42157	NA F-100D Super Sabre	North East Aviation Museum, Usworth	
42160	NA F-100D Super Sabre [FW-000]	Wales Aircraft Museum, Cardiff	
42163	NA F-100D Super Sabre [11-YG]	Dumfries & Galloway Aviation Museum Tinwald Downs	
42165	NA F-100D Super Sabre [11-ML]	Imperial War Museum, Duxford	
42174	NA F-100D Super Sabre	Midland Air Museum, Coventry	
42196	NA F-100D Super Sabre [LT]	Norfolk & Suffolk Aviation Museum, Flixton	
42204	NA F-100D Super Sabre [11-MQ]	RAF Alconbury	
42212	NA F-100D Super Sabre [LN]	RAF Sculthorpe	
42223	NA F-100D Super Sabre	Newark Air Museum, Winthorpe	
42239	NA F-100D Super Sabre [FW-239]	Phoenix Aviation Museum, Bruntingthorpe	
431171	NA B-25J Mitchell (N7614C)	Imperial War Museum, Duxford	
44	Piper L-18 Super Cub (G-BJLH) [K-33]	Privately owned, Liverpool	
454537	Piper L-4J Cub (G-BFDL) [04-J]	Privately owned, Prestwick	
461748	Boeing B-29A Superfortress (G-BHDK) [Y]	Imperial War Museum, Duxford	
463221	NA P-51D Mustang (N6340T) (really 473149) [G4-S]	Privately owned, Duxford	
472028	NA P-51D Mustang (41 IAF)	Privately owned, Teesside	
472216	NA P-51D Mustang (G-BIXL)	Privately owned, Duxford	
472258	NA P-51D Mustang (really 473979) [WZ-I]	Imperial War Museum, Duxford	
473543	NA P-51D Mustang (G-BLYW)	Privately owned, Woburn Green, Bucks	
479609	Piper J-3C-65 Cub (G-BHXY) [PR]	Privately owned, Barton	
479865	Piper J-3C-65 Cub (G-BHPK) [A-44]	Privately owned, Sywell	
480015	Piper J-3C-65 Cub (G-AKIB)	Privately owned, White Waltham	
480133	Piper J-3C-65 Cub (G-BDCD) [44-B]	Privately owned, Slinfold	
480594	Piper J-3C-65 Cub (G-BEDJ)	Privately owned, Ashford Hill	
483009	NA AT-6 Harvard (really 244540)	Epping Museum, North Weald	
483868	Boeing B-17G Fortress (N5237V)	Bomber Command Museum, Hendon	
485784	Boeing B-17G (G-BEDF) [K-G]	Privately owned, Duxford	
51-15227	NA T-6G Harvard (G-BKRA) [10]	Privately owned, Shoreham	
540	Piper L-4 Cub (G-BCNX)	Privately owned, Monewden	
54048	NA F-100D Super Sabre (really 42269) [LN]	RAF Lakenheath, at gate	
542265	NA F-100D Super Sabre [FW-2265]	RAF Wethersfield, at gate	
542447	Piper PA18-135 Super Cub (G-SCUB)	Privately owned, Anwick	
542457	Piper PA18-135 Super Cub (G-LION/R-167)	Privately owned, Orsett	
542474	Piper PA18-135 Super Cub (G-PCUB/R-164)	Privately owned, Redhill	
54433	Lockheed T-33A [WD]	Norfolk & Suffolk Aviation Museum, Flixton	
54439	Lockheed T-33A	North East Aviation Museum, Usworth	

Notes	*Serial*	*Type (alternative identity)*	*Owner, operator and location*
	5547	Lockheed T-33A (really 19036)	Newark Air Museum, Winthorpe
	60312	McDonnell F-101F Voodoo	RAF Alconbury, BDRT
	60689	Boeing B-52D Stratofortress	Imperial War Museum, Duxford
	62-494	Republic F-105G Thunderchief [LN] (really 24434)	RAF Lakenheath, BDRT
	63-428	Republic F-105G Thunderchief [JB] (really 24428)	RAF Upper Heyford
	63935	NA F-100F Super Sabre [11-MN]	RAF Alconbury
	63938	NA F-100F Super Sabre [11-MU]	Lashenden Air Warfare Museum, Headcorn
	70270	McDonnell F-101B Voodoo	RAF Woodbridge
	7797	Aeronca L-16A (G-BFAF)	Privately owned, Finmere
	80260	McDonnell F-101B Voodoo	RAF Bentwaters
	82062	DHC U-6A Beaver	Midland Air Museum, Coventry
	897	Aeronca Chief (G-BJEV)	Privately owned, Little Gransden
	P51D	NA P-51D Mustang (G-PSID) (really 4472258)	Warbirds of GB, Bitteswell

VI-3 Valtion Viima G-BAAY in Finnish AF markings. *PRM*

133722 F4U-7 Corsair NX1337A carries the markings of 15 Flotille, French Navy. *PRM*

Irish Army Air Corps Military Aircraft Markings

Serial	*Type (alternative identity)*	*Owner, operator and location*	*Notes*
34	Miles Magister	Irish Aviation Museum Store, Castlemoate House, Dublin	
141	Avro Anson	Irish Aviation Museum Store, Castlemoate House, Dublin	
164	DH Chipmunk	Engineering Wing, Baldonnel (stored)	
168	DH Chipmunk	Training Wing, Gormanston	
172	DH Chipmunk	Engineering Wing, Baldonnel	
173	DH Chipmunk	South East Aviation Enthusiasts, Waterford	
176	DH Dove	Civil Defence, Phoenix Park, Dublin	
181	Percival Provost T1	Fire Section, Baldonnel	
183	Percival Provost T1	Apprentice School, Baldonnel (stored)	
184	Percival Provost T1	Fire Section, Baldonnel	
187	DH Vampire T11	Aviation Society of Ireland, stored, Baldonnel	
191	DH Vampire T11	Irish Aviation Museum, Dublin	
192	DH Vampire T11	Institute of Technology, Bolton Street, in store, Baldonnel	
195	Sud Alouette III	No 1 Support Wing, Baldonnel	
196	Sud Alouette III	No 1 Support Wing, Baldonnel	
197	Sud Alouette III	No 1 Support Wing, Baldonnel	
198	DH Vampire T11 (XE977)	On display, Baldonnel	
199	DH Chipmunk	Training Wing, Gormanston	
202	Sud Alouette III	No 1 Support Wing, Baldonnel	
203	Cessna FR172H	No 2 Support Wing, Gormanston	
205	Cessna FR172H	No 2 Support Wing, Gormanston	
206	Cessna FR172H	No 2 Support Wing, Gormanston	
207	Cessna FR172H	No 2 Support Wing, Gormanston	
208	Cessna FR172H	No 2 Support Wing, Gormanston	
209	Cessna FR172H	No 2 Support Wing, Gormanston	
210	Cessna FR172H	No 2 Support Wing, Gormanston	
211	Sud Alouette III	No 1 Support Wing, Baldonnel	
212	Sud Alouette III	No 1 Support Wing, Baldonnel	
213	Sud Alouette III	No 1 Support Wing, Baldonnel	
214	Sud Alouette III	No 1 Support Wing, Baldonnel	
215	Fouga Super Magister	No 1 Support Wing, Baldonnel	
216	Fouga Super Magister	No 1 Support Wing, Baldonnel	
217	Fouga Super Magister	No 1 Support Wing, Baldonnel	
218	Fouga Super Magister	No 1 Support Wing, Baldonnel	
219	Fouga Super Magister	No 1 Support Wing, Baldonnel	
220	Fouga Super Magister	No 1 Support Wing, Baldonnel	
221	Fouga Super Magister [3-KE]	Engineering Wing, Baldonnel	
222	SIAI SF-260W Warrior	Training Wing, Baldonnel	
223	SIAI SF-260W Warrior	Training Wing, Baldonnel	
225	SIAI SF-260W Warrior	Training Wing, Baldonnel	
226	SIAI SF-260W Warrior	Training Wing, Baldonnel	
227	SIAI SF-260W Warrior	Training Wing, Baldonnel	
228	SIAI SF-260W Warrior	Training Wing, Baldonnel	
229	SIAI SF-260W Warrior	Training Wing, Baldonnel	
230	SIAI SF-260W Warrior	Training Wing, Baldonnel	
231	SIAI SF-260W Warrior	Training Wing, Baldonnel	
232	Beech King Air 200 (EI-BCY)	Maritime Squadron, Baldonnel	
233	SIAI SF-260MC	Engineering Wing, Baldonnel (stored)	
234	Beech King Air 200 (EI-BFJ)	Maritime Squadron, Baldonnel	
235	SIAI SF-260W Warrior	Training Wing, Baldonnel	
237	Aerospatiale Gazelle	Advanced Flying Training School, Baldonnel	
238	HS125/700B	Transport Squadron, Baldonnel	
240	Beech King Air 200	Transport Squadron, Baldonnel	
241	Aerospatiale Gazelle	Advanced Flying Training School Baldonnel	
243	Cessna FR172P	No 2 Support Wing, Gormanston	
245	SA365F Dauphin II	Naval Squadron, Baldonnel	

Overseas Military Aircraft Markings

Aircraft included in this section are a selection of those likely to be seen visiting UK civil and military airfields on transport flights, exchange visits, exercises and for air shows. It is not a comprehensive list of *all* aircraft operated by the air arms concerned.

Serial

AUSTRALIA
Royal Australian Air Force

Boeing 707-338C
A20-623
A20-624
A20-627
A20-629
Lockheed C-130H Hercules
A97-001
A97-002
A97-003
A97-004
A97-005
A97-006
A97-007
A97-008
A97-009
A97-010
A97-011
A97-012
Lockheed C130E Hercules
A97-159
A97-160
A97-167
A97-168
A97-171
A97-172
A97-177
A97-178
A97-180
A97-187
A97-189
A97-190
Lockheed P-3C Orion
Edinburgh, NSW
10 Sqn *
11 Sqn †
A9-656†
A9-657†
A9-658†
A9-659†
A9-660†
A9-661†
A9-662†
A9-663†
A9-664†
A9-665†
A9-751*
A9-752*
A9-753*
A9-754*
A9-755*

Serial

A9-756*
A9-757*
A9-758*
A9-759*
A9-760*

AUSTRIA
Oesterreichische Luftstreitkrafte

Saab 105ÖE (yellow)
1101/A
1102/B
1104/D
1105/E
1106/F
1107/G
1108/H
1109/I
1110/J
Saab 105ÖE (green)
1111/A
1112/B
1114/D
1116/F
1117/G
1119/I
1120/J
Saab 105ÖE (red)
1122/B
1123/C
1124/D
1125/E
1126/F
1127/G
1128/H
1129/I
1130/J
Saab 105ÖE (blue)
1131/A
1132/B
1133/C
1134/D
1135/E
1136/F
1137/G
1139/I
1140/J
Short SC7 Skyvan 3M
Tullin
5S-TA
5S-TB

Serial

BELGIUM
Force Aerienne Belge/ Belgische Luchtmacht

D-BD Alpha Jet
7/11 Smaldeel, Brustem
AT01
AT02
AT03
AT05
AT06
AT08
AT09
AT10
AT11
AT12
AT13
AT14
AT15
AT16
AT17
AT18
AT19
AT20
AT21
AT22
AT23
AT24
AT25
AT26
AT27
AT28
AT29
AT30
AT31
AT32
AT33
Dassault Mirage 5BA
1/8 Smaldeel, Bierset
2/42 Smaldeel, Florennes
BA01 2 Sm
BA02 2 Sm
BA03 8 Sm
BA04 2 Sm
BA05 1 Sm
BA08 2 Sm
BA10 1 Sm
BA11 2 Sm
BA13 2 Sm
BA15 1 Sm
BA16 1 Sm
BA17 2 Sm
BA18 8 Sm

Serial

BA20 8 Sm
BA21 1 Sm
BA22 1 Sm
BA23 8 Sm
BA26 1 Sm
BA27 8 Sm
BA29 8 Sm
BA30 2 Sm
BA31 1 Sm
BA33 1 Sm
BA37 1 Sm
BA39 1 Sm
BA42 8 Sm
BA43 1 Sm
BA44 1 Sm
BA45 8 Sm
BA46 1 Sm
BA48 1 Sm
BA50 2 Sm
BA51 8 Sm
BA52 8 Sm
BA53 2 Sm
BA54 2 Sm
BA56 2 Sm
BA57 1 Sm
BA59 2 Sm
BA60 8 Sm
BA62 2 Sm
BA63 8 Sm

Dassault Mirage 5BD

BD01 8 Sm
BD03 1 Sm
BD04 42 Sm
BD05 2 Sm
BD07 8 Sm
BD09 1 Sm
BD10 8 Sm
BD11 42 Sm
BD12 2 Sm
BD13 1 Sm
BD14 2 Sm
BD15 2 Sm

Dassault Mirage 5BR

BR03 42 Sm
BR04 42 Sm
BR08 42 Sm
BR09 42 Sm
BR10 42 Sm
BR12 42 Sm
BR13 42 Sm
BR14 42 Sm
BR15 42 Sm
BR17 42 Sm
BR19 42 Sm
BR20 42 Sm
BR21 42 Sm
BR22 42 Sm
BR23 42 Sm
BR24 42 Sm
BR25 42 Sm
BR26 42 Sm
BR27 42 Sm

Boeing 727-29C

21 Smaldeel, Melsbroek

CB01 21 Sm
CB02 21 Sm

Swearingen Merlin IIIA

21 Smaldeel, Melsbroek

CF01 21 Sm
CF02 21 Sm
CF04 21 Sm
CF05 21 Sm
CF06 21 Sm

Lockheed C-130H Hercules

20 Smaldeel, Melsbroek

CH01 20 Sm
CH02 20 Sm
CH03 20 Sm
CH04 20 Sm
CH05 20 Sm
CH06 20 Sm
CH07 20 Sm
CH08 20 Sm
CH09 20 Sm
CH10 20 Sm
CH11 20 Sm
CH12 20 Sm

Dassault Mystere 20

21 Smaldeel, Melsbroek

CM01 21 Sm
CM02 21 Sm

Hawker-Siddeley HS748 srs 2A

21 Smaldeel, Melsbroek

CS01 21 Sm
CS02 21 Sm
CS03 21 Sm

General Dynamics F-16A

349/350 Smaldeel, Bevekom (1 Wg)
23/31 Smaldeel, Kleine Brogel (10 Wg)

FA01 349 Sm
FA02 350 Sm
FA03 349 Sm
FA04 350 Sm
FA05 349 Sm
FA09 349 Sm
FA10 350 Sm
FA12 350 Sm
FA15 350 Sm
FA16 349 Sm
FA17 349 Sm
FA18 350 Sm
FA19 350 Sm
FA20 349 Sm
FA21 350 Sm
FA22 350 Sm
FA23 350 Sm
FA25 349 Sm
FA26 349 Sm
FA27 349 Sm
FA28 350 Sm
FA30 350 Sm
FA31 349 Sm
FA32 350 Sm
FA33 350 Sm
FA34 349 Sm
FA36 350 Sm
FA37 1 Wg
FA38 350 Sm
FA39
FA40 349 Sm
FA42 350 Sm
FA43 349 Sm
FA44 350 Sm
FA45 349 Sm
FA46 349 Sm
FA47 349 Sm
FA48 1 Wg
FA49 349 Sm
FA50
FA51 350 Sm
FA52 350 Sm
FA53 349 Sm
FA54 350 Sm
FA55 350 Sm
FA56
FA57 31 Sm
FA58 10 Wg
FA60 31 Sm
FA61 23 Sm
FA62 31 Sm
FA63 23 Sm
FA64
FA65 23 Sm
FA66 31 Sm
FA67 23 Sm
FA68 31 Sm
FA69 23 Sm
FA70 31 Sm
FA71 23 Sm
FA72 31 Sm
FA73 23 Sm
FA74 31 Sm
FA75 23 Sm
FA76 23 Sm
FA77 23 Sm
FA78 31 Sm
FA79 23 Sm
FA80 31 Sm
FA81 23 Sm
FA82 31 Sm
FA83 23 Sm
FA84 10 Wg
FA85 23 Sm
FA86 31 Sm
FA87 23 Sm
FA88 31 Sm
FA89 23 Sm
FA90 31 Sm
FA91 23 Sm
FA92 31 Sm
FA93 23 Sm
FA94 31 Sm
FA95 23 Sm
FA96 31 Sm

General Dynamics F-16B

1 Wing, Bevekom; 10 Wing, Kleine Brogel

FB01 10 Wg
FB02 1 Wg
FB03 1 Wg
FB04 1 Wg
FB05 1 Wg
FB06 1 Wg
FB07 10 Wg
FB08 1 Wg
FB09 1 Wg
FB10 10 Wg
FB11 1 Wg
FB12 1 Wg
FB13 10 Wg
FB14 10 Wg
FB15 10 Wg
FB17 10 Wg
FB18 10 Wg
FB19 10 Wg

Serial

FB20 10 Wg
Westland Sea King Mk48
40 Smaldeel, Koksijde
RS01
RS03
RS04
RS05
Siai Marchetti SF.260MB
Ecole de Pilotage Elementaire, Gossoncourt
ST03
ST04
ST07
ST09
ST11
ST12
ST14
ST15
ST16
ST17
ST18
ST19
ST20
ST21
ST22
ST23
ST24
ST25
ST26
ST27
ST29
ST30
ST31
ST32
ST33
ST34
ST35
ST36

Belgische Landmacht
Britten-Norman BN-2A Islander
15/16 Smaldeel, Brasschaat
B01/LA
B02/LB
B03/LC
B04/LD
B05/LE
B06/LF
B07/LG
B08/LH
B09/LI
B10/LJ
B11/LK
B12/LL

Belgische Zeemacht
Sud Alouette III
40 Smaldeel, Koksijde
M1 (OT-ZPA)
M2 (OT-ZPB)
M3 (OT-ZPC)

Serial

BRAZIL
Forca Aerea Brazileira
Lockheed C-130E Hercules
1 GT 1 Esq Afonsos
C-130 2451
C-130 2454
C-130 2455
C-130 2456
C-130 2457
C-130 2458
C-130 2459
C-130 2460
Lockheed KC-130H Hercules
1 GT 2 Esq Afonsos
C-130 2461
C-130 2462
Lockheed C-130H Hercules
1 GT 1 Esq Afonsos
C-130 2463
C-130 2464
C-130 2465

CANADA
Canadian Armed Forces
1st CAG, Sollingen West Germany
*409 Sqn, †421 Sqn, ‡439 Sqn
McDonnell Douglas CF-18A Hornet
188729*
188730*
188731*
188732*
188733*
188734*
188735*
188736*
188738*
188739*
188740*
188742*
188750*
McDonnell Douglas CF-18B Hornet
188918*
188919*
Lockheed C-130E Hercules
*429 Sqn, Winnipeg
†435 Sqn, Edmonton
‡436 Sqn, Trenton
130305
130306
130307
130308‡
130309
130310*
130311
130313†
130314‡
130315‡
130316
130317‡
130318
130319†
130320‡
130321‡
130322‡

Serial

130323‡
130324‡
130325
130326‡
130327‡
130328
Lockheed C-130H Hercules
130332
130333
130334
130335
DHC CC-132 Dash 7
No 412 Sqn
Lahr, West Germany
132001
132002
Canadair CT-133 Silver Star
1st CAG, Sollingen West Germany
133026
133052
133094
133315
133345
133405
133435
133490
133504
133542
133564
133571
133572
133581
133623
133648
Boeing CC-137 (B.707-374C)
437 Sqn, Ottawa
13701
13702
13703
13704
13705
Lockheed CP-140 Aurora
140101 407 Sqn
140102
140103 405 Sqn
140104 404 Sqn
140105
140106 404 Sqn
140107
140108
140109 407 Sqn
140110 415 Sqn
140111 415 Sqn
140112 415 Sqn
140113 415 Sqn
140114 415 Sqn
140115
140116 407 Sqn
140117 407 Sqn
140118 407 Sqn
Canadair CC-144 Challenger
No 412 Sqn, Lahr West Germany
144601
144602
144608
144609

Serial

CHILE
Fuerza Aérea de Chile
Lockheed C-130H Hercules
Grupo 10, Santiago
995
996

DENMARK
Kongelige Danske Flyvevaabnet
Saab A-35XD Draken
Eskadrille 725, Karup
A001
A002
A004
A005
A006
A007
A008
A009
A010
A011
A012
A014
A017
A018
A019
A020
Saab S-35XD Draken
Eskadrille 729, Karup
AR102
AR104
AR105
AR106
AR107
AR108
AR109
AR110
AR111
AR112
AR113
AR114
AR115
AR116
AR117
AR118
AR119
AR120
Saab Sk-35XD Draken
Karup
AT151 Esk 725
AT152 Esk 725
AT153 Esk 725
AT154 Esk 725
AT155 Esk 725
AT156 Esk 725
AT157 Esk 725
AT158 Esk 725
AT160 Esk 725
Lockheed C-130H Hercules
Eskadrille 721, Vaerlose
B678
B679
B680
Saab 17 Supporter
*Flyveskolan, Avno (FLSK), †Haerens Flyvetjaeneste (Danish Army), Vandel, ‡Eskadrille 721, Vaerlose
T401
T402
T403
T404
T405
T406
T407
T408‡
T409‡
T410†
T411†
T412†
T413†
T414†
T415†
T417†
T418†
T419‡
T420‡
T421*
T422*
T423*
T424*
T425*
T426*
T427*
T428*
T429*
T430*
T431*
T432*
Grumman Gulfstream III
Eskadrille 721, Vaerlose
F249
F313
F330
General Dynamics F-16A
*Eskadrille 723, Aalborg;
†Eskadrille 727, Skrydstrup;
‡Eskadrille 730, Skrydstrup
E174‡
E176*
E177‡
E178†
E180*
E181†
E182‡
E183*
E184*
E185‡
E187†
E188†
E189*
E190‡
E191‡
E192‡
E193‡
E194‡
E195*
E196*
E197‡
E198*
E199†
E200†
E201*
E202†
E203*
E596*
E597‡
E598†
E599*
E600‡
E601†
E602‡
E603‡
E604*
E605‡
E606†
E607*
E608*
E609†
E610†
E611†
General Dynamics F-16B
ET204*
ET205‡
ET206‡
ET207‡
ET208*
ET210‡
ET612‡
ET613†
ET614†
ET615†
Sikorsky S-61A
Eskadrille 722, Vaerlose
U240
U275
U276
U277
U278
U279
U280
U481

Sovaernets Flyvetjaeneste (Navy)
Westland Lynx HAS80
Eskadrille 722, Vaerlose
S134
S142
S170
S175
S181
S187
S191

Haerens Flyvetjaeneste (Army)
Hughes 500M
Vandel
H201
H202
H203
H205
H206
H207
H209
H210
H211
H212
H213

Serial

H244
H245
H246
H500

ECUADOR
Lockheed
C-130H Hercules
FAE-812
FAE-893

EGYPT
Al Quwwat al-Jawwiya
Ilmisriya

Lockheed
C-130H Hercules
1271/SU-BAB
1272/SU-BAC
1273/SU-BAD
1274/SU-BAE
1275/SU-BAF
1277/SU-BAI
1278/SU-BAJ
1279/SU-BAK
1280/SU-BAL
1281/SU-BAM
1282/SU-BAN
1283/SU-BAP
1284/SU-BAQ
1285/SU-BAR
1286/SU-BAS
1287/SU-BAT
1288/SU-BAU
1289/SU-BAV
1290/SU-BEW
1291/SU-BEX
1292/SU-BEY

FRANCE
Armee de l'Air

Aerospatiale TB-30
Epsilon
GE315, Cognac
01 VO
02 VJ
1 UA
2 118-UB
3
4 UC
5 UD
6 UE
7 UF
8 UG
9 UH
10 UI
11 UJ
12 UK
13 UL
14 UM
15 UN
16 UO
17 UP
18 UQ
19 UR
20 US
21 UT
22 UU
23 UV
24 UW
25 UX
26 UY
27 UZ
28 VA
29 VB

Serial

30 VC
31 VD
32 VE
33 VF
34 VG
35 VH
36 VI
37 VJ
38 VK
39 VL
40 VM
41 VN
42 VO
43 VP
44 VQ
45 VR
46 VS
47 VT
48 VU
49 VV
50 VW

Boeing KC-135F/
***KC-135FR**
ERV 93, Avord and
Mont de Marsan
38470/CA
38471/CB
38472/CC
38474/CE
38475/CF
312735/CG
312736/CH
312737/CI*
312738/CJ
312739/CK
312740/CL

CAARP CAP-20
GI 312, Salon de
Provence
1 VU
2 VV
3 VW
4 VX
5 VY
6 VZ

Cessna 310
045 AU
046 AV
185 AC
186 BI
187 BJ
188 BK
190 BL
192 BM
193 BG
194 BH
242 BW
244 AX
820 CL

Cessna 404
692 DX
815 DY

Cessna 411
185 AC
248 AB
F006 AD
F008 AE

D-BD Alpha Jet
*Patrouille de
France
ET 8, Cazaux;
GE 314, Tours;
CEAM (118), Mont de
Marsan

Serial

01
02 F-ZWRU
E1 8-NP
E3 118-BR
E4 314-LP
E5 118-BU
E6 8-NW
E7 314-LB
E8 314-LL
E9 314-LD
E10
E11 8-MP
E12 8-NC
E13 314-LH
E14
E15 314-LJ
E17 8-MR
E18 314-LM
E19 8-MK
E20 314-LO
E21 8-NY
E22 314-LQ
E23 8-MQ
E24 8-MA
E25 314-LT
E26 314-TK
E27 8-MU
E28 314-TL
E29 314-LV
E30 314-LW
E31 314-LX
E32 314-LY
E33 8-NL
E34 314-LZ
E35 314-TB
E36 314-TC
E37 314-TD
E38 314-TE
E39 314-TF
E40 8-MB
E41 8-MH
E42 314-TI
E43 314-TJ
E44 314-TN
E45 314-TM
E46 314-TO
E47 8-ND
E48 8-NZ
E49 314-TR
E50 314-TS
E51
E53
E55 F-TERE* (4)
E58 F-TERH* (7)
E59 F-TERI* (6)
E60
E61 F-TERJ* (8)
E63 F-TERL* (2)
E64 314-TT
E65 314-TU
E66 314-TV
E67 314-TW
E68 314-TX
E69 8-NH
E70 314-TY
E72 314-LF
E73 118-BT
E74 8-ND
E75 314-UD
E76 314-UE
E77 8-NH
E79 8-NS
E80
E81 8-NK

Serial	
E82	8-NX
E83	314-UJ
E84	314-UL
E85	314-UM
E86	314-LN
E87	314-LU
E88	8-MG
E89	314-UQ
E90	314-TH
E91	314-TG
E92	314-UT
E93	8-NT
E94	8-MO
E95	
E96	8-MJ
E97	314-LE
E98	314-LX
E99	8-MW
E100	
E101	8-NG
E102	8-ME
E103	314-TO
E104	314-LC
E105	314-VA
E106	314-VB
E107	F-TERK* (3)
E108	314-VC
E109	314-VD
E110	8-NB
E112	8-NQ
E113	8-NJ
E114	8-NN
E115	314-UF
E116	8-NV
E117	314-VG
E118	314-VH
E119	314-VI
E120	314-VJ
E121	314-VK
E122	314-VL
E123	314-VM
E124	
E125	314-TN
E126	314-VO
E127	8-MY
E128	8-NP
E129	314-VP
E130	8-MT
E131	314-VQ
E132	314-TL
E133	314-TY
E134	8-NE
E135	314-TZ
E136	314-VU
E137	8-MF
E138	8-NF
E139	8-MM
E140	314-UB
E141	314-LW
E142	8-ML
E143	314-VX
E144	314-VW
E146	314-VZ
E147	314-LA
E148	314-LC
E149	314-LD
E150	8-NO
E151	
E152	8-MC
E153	314-LL
E154	314-LN
E155	
E156	
E157	8-NI
E158	314-LR
E159	8-MD
E160	314-TM
E161	8-MN
E162	314-TA
E163	314-LS
E164	8-MS
E165	
E166	314-UC
E167	8-MV
E168	314-TJ
E169	314-LG
E170	F-TERM* (1)
E171	F-TERN* (5)
E172	F-TERO* (7)
E173	F-TERP*
E174	
E175	
E176	
E177	
E178	
E179	
E180	

Dassault Falcon 20C
EDT 60 and EDT 65, Villacoublay

1	CV
22	CS
49	OA EDT 60
79	CT
86	CG93 N EDT 60
104	CW
115	339-WL
124	CC
131	CD
138	CR
145	CV
167	L EDT 60
238	M EDT 60
260	A
268	K
291	P EDT 60
309	U EDT 60
422	L EDT 60
451	338-WN
463	339-WM
483	338-

Dassault Falcon 50

5	F-RAFI EDT 60
147	F-RAFJ EDT-60

Dassault Mirage F.1C
EC 5, Orange; EC 12, Cambrai; EC 30, Rheims; EC 118/24, Mont de Marsan

2	30-FG
3	118-AL
4	118-AM
5	
6	30-MA
8	5-OK
9	12-KB
10	30-SU
12	30-ST
13	30-FF
14	30-MS
15	30-FC
16	12-ZA
17	12-KC
18	12-KG
19	12-ZB
20	12-YD
21	30-MI
22	118-AN
23	30-FH
24	30-ME
25	12-ZC
26	12-ZI
27	30-SQ
29	12-YN
30	12-YC
31	30-MB
32	12-KD
33	30-FJ
35	
36	
37	30-FB
38	30-MT
39	12-KM
40	12-YA
41	30-SG
42	12-KI
43	12-YK
44	12-ZE
45	30-SR
47	30-SD
49	
50	30-SA
52	12-YG
54	30-MF
55	12-KH
60	30-MJ
62	
63	12-YJ
64	30-SP
67	30-SF
68	12-ZK
69	
70	30-SI
71	12-KJ
72	30-MO
74	12-ZJ
75	30-MI
76	30-MM
77	
78	12-ZL
79	30-SK
80	12-ZM
81	30-SH
82	30-SB
83	12-ZD
84	12-YO
85	30-FO
87	30-SJ
90	30-SO
100	30-FK
101	30-SC
102	12-ZG
103	30-MO
201	118-AK
202	5-OR
203	30-MD
204	
205	30-FI
206	5-OA
207	30-FE
208	5-OJ
210	30-SE
211	5-NN
213	12-ZR
214	5-OG
216	5-OL
217	30-MK
218	12-ZJ
219	12-KI
220	12-KL

Serial	
221	
223	5-NM
224	5-OI
225	118-AO
226	12-YO
227	12-KP
228	5-OH
229	5-ND
230	118-AP
231	12-YH
232	5-OT
233	30-MJ
234	30-SN
235	30-FP
236	5-OP
237	12-YI
238	5-NR
239	5-NJ
240	12-YB
241	5-AV
242	5-NA
243	5-NO
244	5-OQ
245	5-NI
246	5-NC
247	30-FR
248	12-YF
249	12-ZS
251	30-MH
252	5-ON
253	30-MC
254	12-ZM
255	5-NQ
256	30-FO
257	12-KO
258	12-YL
259	30-FA
260	5-OB
261	5-AV
262	30-MU
264	12-KN
265	5-NB
266	12-ZW
267	30-MP
268	5-OO
270	12-KE
271	30-FM
272	15-NG
273	12-ZN
274	5-OF
275	12-ZN
277	
278	5-OE
279	5-NK
280	5-NF
281	5-AU
282	5-AW
283	12-ZO

Dassault Mirage F.1CR
ER 33 Strasbourg

601	Istras
602	
603	33-NR
603	33-NB
606	33-ND
607	33-NE
608	33-NF
609	33-NG
610	33-NH
611	33-NI
612	33-NJ
613	33-NK
614	33-NL
615	33-NM
616	33-NN
617	33-NO
618	33-AA
619	33-AC
620	33-NA
621	33-NB
622	33-NC
623	33-ND
624	33-NE
625	33-NF
626	33-NG
627	33-NH
628	33-NI
629	33-NJ
630	33-NK
631	33-NL
632	33-NM
633	33-NN
634	33-NO
635	33-NP
636	33-NQ

Dassault Mirage 2000C
EC 2, Dijon; CEAM (118), Mont de Marsan

01	
03	
04	
1	2-EP
2	
3	118-AV
4	118-AW
5	118-AS
6	118-AY
8	2-EC
9	2-ED
10	2-EE
11	2-EF
12	2-EH
13	2-EI
14	2-EJ
15	2-EK
16	2-EL
17	2-EM
18	2-EN
19	2-LA
20	2-LE
21	2-LF
22	2-LG

Dassault Mirage 2000B
EC 2, Dijon

501	
502	118-AZ
503	118-AX
504	2-EG
505	2-ER
506	2-EQ
507	2-LC
508	2-LD

DHC6 Twin Otter
CEAM (118) Mont de Marsan; ET 63 Toulouse

292	OW
298	OY
300	OZ
603	82-PU
730	52-LF
742	52-LG
743	118-ID
745	118-IG
786	63-VV
790	63-VW

Douglas DC8F

45819	F-RAFC
45820	F-RAFA
46043	F-RAFD
46130	F-RAFF
46132	F-RAFB

Embraer Xingu
CEAM (118) Mont de Marsan; * GE 319 Avord; † ETT 43 Bordeaux; ‡ETT 44 Aix-en-Provence

054	118-IA
064	118-IB
072	YA*
073	YB*
075	YC*
076	YD*
078	YE*
080	YF*
082	YG*
084	YH*
086	YI*
089	YJ*
091	YK*
092	YL*
095	YM*
096	YN*
098	YO*
099	YP*
100	YR*
101	BW†
102	BX†
103	CT‡
105	CU‡
107	CV‡
108	CW‡
109	
110	
111	YQ*

Morane Saulnier Paris
ETT 41 Metz; ETT 43 Bordeaux; ETT 44 Aix-en-Provence; ET 65 Villacoublay; CEAM (118) Mont de Marsan

1	118-DB
14	070-MD
19	41-AR
20	
23	65-LA
24	65-LW
25	118-DI
26	65-LD
27	
29	43-BB
30	65-LI
34	65-LV
35	65-LN
36	
38	41-AT
44	65-LS
45	41-AR
51	
53	65-LO
54	
56	65-LP
57	
58	65-LB

Serial

59 65-LR
60 65-LQ
61 65-LY
62 118-DO
65 65-LZ
68 65-LF
70 65-LT
71 65-LC
73 41-AS
75 118-DC
77 118-DE
78 65-LU
79 65-LA
80 65-LM
81 65-LL
82 44-CM
91 65-LJ
93 65-LJ
94 65-LH
96
97 43-BA
100 NG
113 NI
114 NJ
115 OV
116 ON
117 AZ
118 NQ
119 NL

Nord 262 Fregate

Esc 70 Chateaudun;
*ET 65 Villacoublay

3 OH
58 MJ
64 AA*
66 AB*
67
68 AC*
76 AD*
77 AK*
78
80 AW*
81 AH*
83 AI*
86 70-MC
87 AN*
88 AL*
89 118-IR
91 AT*
92 AO*
93 AP*
94 AU
95 AR*
105 AE*
106 AY*
107 AX*
108 AG*
109 AM*
110 AS*

Nord Noratlas

ET 63 Toulouse;
CEAM (118) Mont de Marsan; CIFAS (328) Bordeaux

18 CR
25
28
41
66
84
94 YF
96 63-VH
100 328-EB
104 118-IF

Serial

113 63-VN
114 316-FQ
120 63-VA
122 63-WD
129 316-FA
146 63-WV
153 328-EH
155 328-EG
157 63-WK
162 328-EF
165 63-VK
169 63-VL
171 316-FR
172
180 63-VB
185 63-VG
188 316-FS
189 316-FN
191 63-WS
193 316-FU
194 316-FP
196 316-FO
199 63-WM
200 328-EK
201 63-VJ
202 63-VE

C-160 Transall

ET 61 Orleans (C160A/F); ET 64 Evreux (C160NG)

A02 61-MI
A04 61-BI
A06 61-ZB
F1 61-MA
F2 61-MB
F3 61-MC
F4 61-MD
F5 61-ME
F11 61-MF
F12 61-MG
F13 61-MH
F14 61-MI
F15 61-MJ
F16 61-MK
F17 61-ML
F18 61-MM
F42 61-MN
F43 61-MO
F44 61-MP
F45 61-MQ
F46 61-MR
F47 61-MS
F48 61-MT
F49 61-MU
F50 61-MV
F51 61-MW
F52 61-MX
F53 61-MY
F54 61-MZ
F55 61-ZC
F86 61-ZD
F87 61-ZE
F88 61-ZF
F89 61-ZG
F90 61-ZH
F91 61-ZI
F92 61-ZJ
F93 61-ZK
F94 61-ZL
F95 61-ZM
F96 61-ZN
F97 61-ZO
F98 61-ZP
F99 61-ZQ

Serial

F100 61-ZR
F153 61-ZS
F154 61-ZT
F155 61-ZU
F157 61-ZW
F158 61-ZX
F159 61-ZY
F160 61-ZZ
F201 64-GA
F202 64-GB
F203 64-GC
F204 64-GD
F205 64-GE
F206 64-GF
F207 64-GG
F208 64-GH
F210 64-GJ
F211 64-GK
F212 64-GL
F213 64-GM
F214 64-GN
F215 64-GO
F217 64-GQ
F218 64-GR
F219 64-GS
F220 ELINT
F221 ELINT
F222 64-GV
F223 64-GW
F224 64-GX
(Command Post Prototype)
F225 64-GY
F226 64-GZ
F227 64-GP

SEPECAT Jaguar A

EC 3 Nancy; EC 7 St Dizier; EC 11 Toul

A1 3-XJ
A2 3-XL
A5 7-PM
A6
A7 3-XK
A8 3-XL
A9 3-XD
A10 3-XH
A11 3-XA
A12 3-XI
A13 3-XM
A14
A15
A16 7-NG
A17 7-HC
A19 7-IG
A20 7-HE
A21 7-IA
A22 7-PC
A23 7-HO
A24 7-HH
A25 7-IB
A26 7-HJ
A27 11-MA
A28 11-MC
A29 7-HA
A31 7-NJ
A32 7-NL
A33 7-IH
A34 7-IL
A35 7-HG
A36 7-II
A37 7-PA
A38 7-IC
A39 7-IP

Serial	
A40	3-XC
A41	7-ND
A43	7-HD
A44	7-ID
A46	7-IM
A47	7-HP
A48	7-NH
A49	7-NO
A50	11-YM
A53	7-PG
A54	7-HM
A55	7-HN
A56	
A58	7-NM
A59	7-HB
A60	7-HF
A61	7-IF
A64	3-XB
A65	7-IO
A66	11-RT
A70	
A72	11-HJ
A73	7-PB
A74	
A75	11-RW
A76	7-HL
A79	
A80	7-IN
A82	11-YB
A83	118-AH
A84	
A85	11-YL
A86	11-MG
A87	11-RX
A88	11-RQ
A89	11-RG
A90	11-YI
A91	11-RJ
A92	11-MS
A93	11-MV
A94	11-ED
A95	11-EC
A96	11-
A97	11-YD
A98	11-EH
A99	
A100	11-R
A101	11-MF
A103	11-
A104	11-MP
A107	11-YC
A108	
A110	11-MD
A112	11-RM
A113	11-YA
A115	11-RH
A116	11-YD
A117	11-YE
A118	11-YF
A119	11-MV
A120	11-MM
A121	11-YN
A122	11-MO
A123	11-EL
A124	
A126	11-RB
A127	11-RK
A128	11-RI
A129	11-ER
A130	11-MB
A131	11-EE
A133	11-EF
A135	
A136	11-E
A137	11-ES
A138	7-NG
A139	11-EL
A140	11-YK
A141	11-RN
A142	7-NL
A143	11-MH
A144	11-RN
A145	
A146	118-AI
A148	11-YL
A149	11-EK
A150	118-AJ
A151	11-EB
A152	118-AG
A153	11-EX
A154	
A155	
A156	11-EH
A157	11-MQ
A158	11-EU
A159	11-EV
A160	

SEPECAT Jaguar E

Serial	
E1	
E2	3-XO
E3	7-NN
E4	7-PE
E5	118-AD
E6	11-ME
E7	
E8	7-PP
E9	7-PH
E10	3-XG
E11	3-XE
E12	7-PA
E13	7-PD
E15	11-YZ
E16	11-RF
E17	7-PI
E18	
E19	7-PK
E20	11-RV
E21	7-PO
E22	11-YY
E23	11-EI
E24	11-EM
E25	7-IK
E27	11-MA
E28	7-PJ
E29	7-IJ
E30	
E31	7-HI
E32	7-NE
E33	
E35	7-PF
E36	7-PL
E37	7-PQ
E38	7-NN
E39	11-YK
E40	7-PN

Aeronavale/Marine

Morane Saulnier Paris

ES 57, Landivisiau

32
33
40
41
42
46
47
48
85
87
88

Nord 262 Fregate

ES 2, Lann Bihoue; ES 3, Hyeres; ES 55, Aspretto; ES 56, Nimes-Garons; ES 11, Le Bourget

16
28
43
45
46
51 (565)
52
53
59 (25)
60 (565)
61
62
63
65
69
70
71 (25)
72
73
75
79
100
102
104 (115)

SA.321G Super Frelon

ES 20, St Raphael; 32 F, Lanveoc; 33 F, San Mandrier

101
102
105
106
118
120
122
134
137
141
144
148
149
159
160
162
163
164
165

Breguet 1050 Alizé

4F, Lann Bihoue; 6F, Nimes-Garons; ES 59, Hyeres

11
12
16
17
22
24
25
26
27
28
30
31

Serial

33
34
36
41
42
43
44
45
47
48
50
51
52
53
55
56
59
60
64
65
68
76
87

Breguet 1150 Atlantic

21F/22F, Nimes-Garons; 23F/24F, Lann Bihoue

3
5
7
9
15
17
21
23
25
27
31
35
38
44
45
47
48
49
51
52
54
66
67
68
ANG.01
ANG.02
ANG.03
ANG.04

Dassault Etendard IVM

16F, Landivisiau; ES 59, Hyeres

2
3
4
5
6
7
9
11
15
16
21
22
29
30

Serial

32
33
34
36
37
40
41
42
52
53
56
57
59
60
62
63
66

Dassault Etendard IVP

16F Landivisiau

101
103
107
108
109
114
115
117
118
120

Dassault Super Etendard

11F, Landivisiau; 14F, Landivisiau; 17F, Hyeres

1
2
3
4
5
6
7
8
9
10
11
12
13
14
15
16
17
18
19
20
21
23
24
25
26
27
28
29
30
31
32
33
34
35
37
38
39
40
41

Serial

42
43
44
45
46
47
48
49
50
51
52
53
54
55
57
58
59
60
61
62
63
64
66
70
71

Dassault Falcon 10(MER)

ES3, Hyeres; ES 57 Landivisiau

32
101
129
133
143
185

Dassault Falcon Guardian

48
65
72
77
80

Embraer Xingu

ES 11, Le Bourget; ES 52, Lann Bihoue

55
65
66
67
68
69
70
71
74
77
79
81
83
85
87
90

LTV F-8E (FN) Crusader

12F, Landivisiau

1
2
3
4
6
7
8
10
11
12

Serial

16
17
18
19
23
25
27
28
29
32
33
34
35
37
39
40
41

Piper Navajo
ES 2, Lann Bihoue;
ES 3, Hyeres
227
232
903
904
906
912
914
916
925
927
929
931

Westland Lynx HAS2 (FN)*; HAS4 (FN)†
31F, San Mandrier;
34F, Lanveoc; 35F,
Lanveoc; ES 20
St Raphael
03*
04*
260*
262*
263*
264*
265*
266*
267*
268*
270*
271*
272*
273*
274*
275*
276*
278*
621*
622*
623*
624*
625*
626*
627*
801†
802†
803†
804†
805†
806†
807†
808†
809†
810†
811†
812†
813†
814†

GREECE
Elliniki Aeroporia

Lockheed C-130H Hercules
356 Elefis
741
742
743
744
745
746
747
748
749
750
751
752

ISRAEL
Heyl ha'avir

Lockheed C-130H Hercules
4X-FBA/102
4X-FBB/106
4X-FBC/309

Lockheed C-130E Hercules
4X-FBE/304
4X-FBF/301
4X-FBG/310
4X-FBH/312
4X-FBI/314
4X-FBK/318
4X-FBL/313
4X-FBM/316
4X-FBN/307
4X-FBO/203
4X-FBP/208

Lockeed C-130H Hercules
4X-FBQ/420
4X-FBS/427
4X-FBT/435
4X-FBU/448
4X-FBW/436
4X-FBX/428

Lockheed KC-130H Hercules
4X-FBY/522
4X-FBZ/545

ITALY
Aeronautica Militare Italiano

Aeritalia G222
46 Aerobrigata, Pisa
MM62101
MM62102 46-20
MM62104 46-91
MM62105 46-82
MM62107
MM62108 46-30
MM62109 46-96
MM62110 46-81
MM62111 46-83
MM62112 46-85
MM62113 46-34
MM62114 46-80
MM62115 46-22
MM62116 46-35
MM62117 46-25
MM62118 46-24
MM62119 46-21
MM62120 46-90
MM62121 46-86
MM62122 46-23
MM62123 46-28
MM62124 46-88
MM62125 46-87
MM62126 46-26
MM62127 46-27
MM62128 46-89
MM62129 46-29
MM62130 46-31
MM62132 46-32
MM62133 46-93
MM62134 46-33

Aeritalia G222TCM
46 Aerobrigata, Pisa
MM62103 RS-35
MM62135 46-94
MM62136 46
MM62137 46-95
MM62138 46

Aeritalia G222RM
14° Stormo, Practica Di Mare
MM62139 14-20
MM62140 14-21
MM62141 14-22

Aermacchi MB339
*Frecce Tricolori
† Scula Volo Basico Iniziale Aviogetti, Lecce; ‡14° Stormo, Practica di Mare
MM54438
MM54439* 15
MM54440
MM54442
MM54445† 01
MM54446
MM54447† 02
MM54448† 03
MM54449† 04
MM54450‡ 14-30
MM54451‡ 14-31
MM54452‡ 14-32
MM54453† 05
MM54454† 06
MM54455† 07
MM54456† 10
MM54457† 11
MM54458† 12
MM54459† 13
MM54460† 14
MM54461† 15
MM54462
MM54463† 16
MM54464† 20
MM54465† 21
MM54467† 23
MM54468† 24
MM54469† 25
MM54470† 26
MM54471† 27
MM54472† 30
MM54473* 12
MM54474* 6
MM54475* 1
MM54476* 11

Serial

MM54477* 14
MM54478* 4
MM54479* 9
MM54480* 8
MM54481* 7
MM54482* 3
MM54483* 2
MM54485* 13
MM54486* 5
MM54487† 31
MM54488† 32
MM54489† 33
MM54490† 34
MM54491† 35
MM54492† 36
MM54493† 37
MM54494† 40
MM54495† 41
MM54496† 42
MM54497† 43
MM54498† 44
MM54499† 45
MM54500† 46
MM54501† 47
MM54503† 51
MM54504† 52
MM54505† 53
MM54506† 54
MM54507† 55
MM54508† 56
MM54509† 57
MM54510† 60
MM54511†
MM54512†
MM54513† 61
MM54514† 64
MM54515† 65
MM54516† 66
MM54517† 67
MM54518† 70

Grumman Gulfstream III

MM62022

Lockheed C-130H Hercules

46 Aerobrigata, Pisa
MM61988 46-02
MM61989 46-03
MM61990 46-04
MM61991 46-05
MM61992 46-06
MM61993 46-07
MM61994 46-08
MM61995 46-09
MM61997 46-11
MM61998 46-12
MM61999 46-13
MM62001 46-15

McDonnell Douglas DC9-32

31° Stormo, Rome
MM62012 31-12
MM62013 31-13

Panavia Tornado

*TTTE Cottesmore
6° Stormo, Ghedi
36° Stormo, Giola del Colle
MM586
MM587
MM7001 RS-01
MM7002* I-92
MM7003* I-93
MM7004* I-90
MM7005* I-91
MM7006 6-01
MM7007 6-02
MM7008
MM7009 6-04
MM7010 6-03
MM7011 6-10
MM7012 6-11
MM7013 6-05
MM7014 6-12
MM7015
MM7016 6-23
MM7017 6-14
MM7018 6-24
MM7019 6-22
MM7020 6-21
MM7021 6-30
MM7022 6-26
MM7023
MM7024 6-25
MM7025 6-31
MM7026 6-33
MM7027 6-32
MM7028 6-34
MM7029 6-35
MM7030 6-36
MM7031 6-37
MM7033 6-42
MM7034 6-41
MM7035 36-30
MM7036 36-31
MM7037
MM7038
MM7039
MM7040
MM7041
MM7042 36-50
MM7043 6-51
MM7044 36-42
MM7046 36-34
MM7047 36-37
MM7048
MM7049
MM7050 36-44
MM7051 36-43
MM7052 36-41
MM7053 36-45
MM7054
MM7055
MM7056 36-47
MM7057
MM7058
MM7059
MM7060
MM7061
MM7062 6-53
MM7063 36-51
MM7064
MM7065
MM7066
MM7067
MM7068
MM7069 6-61
MM7070
MM7071
MM7072
MM7073
MM7074
MM7075
MM7076
MM7077
MM7078
MM7079
MM7080
MM7081
MM7082
MM7083
MM7084
MM7085
MM7086
MM7087
MM7088
MM55000* I-42
MM55001* I-40
MM55002* I-41
MM55003* I-43
MM55004* I-44
MM55005 36-56
MM55006 6-15
MM55007 36-55
MM55008 6-20
MM55009 6-16
MM55010 6-50
MM55011 6-51

Piaggio-Douglas PD-808/ *PD-808-RM

14° Gruppo, Treviso-San Angelo;
31° Stormo, Roma-Ciampino
MM61948 31-48
MM61949 31-49
MM61950 31-50
MM61951 31-51
MM61952 31-52
MM61953 31-53
MM61954 31-54
MM61955 31-55
MM61956 31-56
MM61957 31-57
MM61958
MM61959
MM61960 31-60
MM61961 31-61
MM61962
MM61963 31-63
MM62014* 31-53
MM62015* 14-54
MM62016* 14-55
MM62017* 14-56

JORDAN

Al Quwwat Al-Jawwiya Alamalakiya Al-Urduniya

Lockheed C-130B Hercules

3 Sqn, Amman
340
341

Lockheed C-130H Hercules

3 Sqn, Amman
344
345
346
347

KUWAIT

Kuwait Air Force

McDonnell Douglas DC9-32

KAF 320
KAF 321

Lockheed L100-30 Hercules

KAF 322
KAF 323
KAF 324
KAF 325

Serial

LUXEMBOURG
NATO — Geilenkirchen
Boeing E-3A
LX-N90442
LX-N90443
LX-N90444
LX-N90445
LX-N90446
LX-N90447
LX-N90448
LX-N90449
LX-N90450
LX-N90451
LX-N90452
LX-N90453
LX-N90454
LX-N90455
LX-N90456
LX-N90457
LX-N90458
LX-N90459

NETHERLANDS
Koninklijke Luchmacht

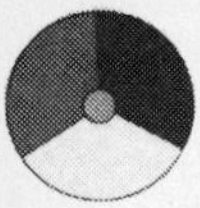

Fokker F-27-100 Friendship
334 Sqn, Soesterberg
C-1
C-2
C-3
Fokker F-27-300M Troopship
334 Sqn, Soesterberg
C-4
C-5
C-6
C-7
C-8
C-9
C-10
C-11
C-12
F-27-200MPA
M-1
M-2
General Dynamics F-16A/F16B*
306 Sqn, Volkel;
311 Sqn, Volkel;
312 Sqn, Volkel;
322 Sqn, Leeuwarden;
323 Sqn, Leeuwarden
Operational Conversion Unit (TCA), Leeuwarden
J192 311 Sqn
J193 312 Sqn
J194 311 Sqn
J195 311 Sqn
J196 311 Sqn
J197
J198
J199
J200
J201
J202
J203
J204
J205

Serial

J206
J207
J208* 306 Sqn
J209* 311 Sqn
J210*
J211*
J212 323 Sqn
J213 TCA
J214 323 Sqn
J215 TCA
J218 TCA
J219 TCA
J220 322 Sqn
J221 322 Sqn
J222 322 Sqn
J223 322 Sqn
J226 322 Sqn
J228 322 Sqn
J229 322 Sqn
J230 323 Sqn
J231 323 Sqn
J232 323 Sqn
J234 323 Sqn
J235 323 Sqn
J236 323 Sqn
J238 TCA
J239 TCA
J240 322 Sqn
J241 322 Sqn
J242 322 Sqn
J243 322 Sqn
J244 322 Sqn
J245 323 Sqn
J246 323 Sqn
J247 323 Sqn
J248 323 Sqn
J249 323 Sqn
J250 323 Sqn
J251 322 Sqn
J253 TCA
J254 323 Sqn
J255 323 Sqn
J256 323 Sqn
J257 322 Sqn
J258 311 Sqn
J259* TCA
J260* 322 Sqn
J261* 322 Sqn
J262* TCA
J263* 323 Sqn
J264* 322 Sqn
J265* TCA
J266* TCA
J267* TCA
J268* TCA
J269* TCA
J270* 322 Sqn
J616 311 Sqn
J617 311 Sqn
J618 311 Sqn
J619 311 Sqn
J620 311 Sqn
J622 311 Sqn
J623 311 Sqn
J624 311 Sqn
J625 311 Sqn
J626 311 Sqn
J627 311 Sqn
J628 306 Sqn
J629 311 Sqn
J630 306 Sqn
J631 306 Sqn
J632 306 Sqn
J633 306 Sqn

Serial

J635 306 Sqn
J636 306 Sqn
J637 306 Sqn
J638 306 Sqn
J639 311 Sqn
J640 306 Sqn
J641 306 Sqn
J642 311 Sqn
J643 306 Sqn
J644 306 Sqn
J645 306 Sqn
J646 306 Sqn TGP
J647
J648 306 Sqn
J649* 306 Sqn
J650* 312 Sqn
J651* 311 Sqn
J652* 311 Sqn
J653* 306 Sqn
J654* 311 Sqn
J655* 306 Sqn
J656* 312 Sqn
J657* 311 Sqn
J864 311 Sqn
J866 312 Sqn
J867 312 Sqn
J868 312 Sqn
J869 312 Sqn
J870 312 Sqn
J871 312 Sqn
J872 312 Sqn
J873 312 Sqn
J874 312 Sqn
J875 312 Sqn
J876 312 Sqn
J877 312 Sqn
J878 312 Sqn
J879 312 Sqn
J880 312 Sqn
J881 312 Sqn
J882* TCA
J883* TCA
J884* 312 Sqn
J885* TCA
Northrop NF-5A
313 Sqn, Twente;
314 Sqn, Eindhoven;
315 Sqn, Twente;
316 Sqn, Gilze-Rijen
K3001 313 Sqn
K3003 315 Sqn
K3004 313 Sqn
K3005 315 Sqn
K3007 315 Sqn
K3008 314 Sqn
K3011 315 Sqn
K3012 315 Sqn
K3013 314 Sqn
K3014 314 Sqn
K3015 314 Sqn
K3016 316 Sqn
K3017 316 Sqn
K3018 316 Sqn
K3019 315 Sqn
K3020 313 Sqn
K3021 314 Sqn
K3022 313 Sqn
K3023 316 Sqn
K3024 315 Sqn
K3025 315 Sqn
K3026 314 Sqn
K3027 316 Sqn
K3028 315 Sqn
K3030 313 Sqn

Serial

K3031 316 Sqn
K3032 315 Sqn
K3033 316 Sqn
K3035 313 Sqn
K3036 314 Sqn
K3039 313 Sqn
K3040 313 Sqn
K3041 313 Sqn
K3042 315 Sqn
K3043 316 Sqn
K3044 314 Sqn
K3045 315 Sqn
K3046 316 Sqn
K3047 316 Sqn
K3048 313 Sqn
K3049 314 Sqn
K3050 316 Sqn
K3051 315 Sqn
K3052 315 Sqn
K5054 316 Sqn
K3055 314 Sqn
K3056 315 Sqn
K3057 315 Sqn
K3058 313 Sqn
K3060 314 Sqn
K3061 314 Sqn
K3062 313 Sqn
K3063 316 Sqn
K3065 316 Sqn
K3066 316 Sqn
K3067 314 Sqn
K3068 314 Sqn
K3069 314 Sqn
K3070 314 Sqn
K3072 316 Sqn
K3073 316 Sqn

Northrop NF-5B
313 Sqn, Twente;
314 Sqn, Eindhoven;
315 Sqn, Twente;
316 Sqn, Gilze-Rijen
K4002 313 Sqn
K4003 315 Sqn
K4005 313 Sqn
K4006 313 Sqn
K4007 313 Sqn
K4008 316 Sqn
K4009 314 Sqn
K4010 313 Sqn
K4011 314 Sqn
K4012 313 Sqn
K4013 313 Sqn
K4014 313 Sqn
K4015 314 Sqn
K4016 313 Sqn
K4017 314 Sqn
K4018 313 Sqn
K4019 314 Sqn
K4020 314 Sqn
K4021 314 Sqn
K4023 316 Sqn
K4024 316 Sqn
K4025 313 Sqn
K4026 315 Sqn
K4027 315 Sqn
K4028 316 Sqn
K4029 313 Sqn
K4030 315 Sqn

Sud Alouette III
*Grasshoppers
298 Sqn,
Soesterberg;
300 Sqn, Deelan
A177

Serial

A208
A209
A217
A218
A226
A227
A235
A246
A247
A253
A254
A260
A261
A262
A267
A275
A281
A292
A293
A301
A302
A307
A319
A324
A336
A342
A343
A350*
A351*
A366
A374
A383
A390*
A391
A398*
A399
A407
A414
A451
A452
A453
A464
A465*
A470
A471
A482
A483
A488
A489
A494
A495
A499*
A500
A514
A515
A522
A528
A529
A535
A536
A542
A550

Marine Luchtvaartdienst

Lockheed P-3C Orion
320 Sqn, Valkenburg
300
301
302
303
304
305
306
307

Serial

308
309
310
311
312

Westland Lynx
7/860 Sqns, De Kooij
260 UH14A
261 UH14A
262 UH14A
264 UH14A
265 UH14A IS
266 SH14B PH
267 SH14B KB
268 SH14B PF
269 SH14B KB
270 SH14B BK
271 SH14B CB
272 SH14B
273 SH14B
274 SH14B PH
276 SH14C
277 SH14C
278 SH14C
279 SH14C
280 SH14C EV
281 SH14C
282 SH14C IS
283 SH14C

NEW ZEALAND

Royal New Zealand Air Force

Boeing 727-22C
40 Sqn, Whenuapai
NZ7271
NZ7272

Lockheed C-130H Hercules
40 Sqn, Whenuapai
NZ7001
NZ7002
NZ7003
NZ7004
NZ7005

Lockheed P-3B Orion
5 Sqn, Whenuapai
NZ4201
NZ4202
NZ4203
NZ4204
NZ4205
NZ4206

NIGERIA

Federal Nigerian Air Force

Lockheed C-130H Hercules
NAF-910
NAF-911
NAF-912
NAF-913
NAF-914
NAF-915
NAF-916
NAF-917
NAF-918

Serial

NORWAY
Kongelige Norske Luftforsvaret

Dassault Falcon 20 ECM
335 Skv, Gardermoen
041
053
0125

General Dynamics F-16A/*F-16B
331 Skv, Bosø; 332 Skv, Rygge; 334 Skv, Bosø

Serial	Unit
272	332 Skv
273	332 Skv
274	332 Skv
275	332 Skv
276	332 Skv
277	332 Skv
278	331 Skv
279	331 Skv
281	331 Skv
282	331 Skv
284	332 Skv
285	332 Skv
286	331 Skv
287	331 Skv
288	331 Skv
289	331 Skv
290	331 Skv
291	331 Skv
292	332 Skv
293	332 Skv
294	332 Skv
295	332 Skv
296	332 Skv
297	332 Skv
298	332 Skv
299	332 Skv
300	334 Skv
302*	332 Skv
303*	332 Skv
304*	332 Skv
305*	332 Skv
306*	332 Skv
307*	332 Skv
658	334 Skv
659	334 Skv
660	334 Skv
661	334 Skv
662	334 Skv
663	334 Skv
664	334 Skv
665	334 Skv
666	334 Skv
667	334 Skv
668	334 Skv
669	334 Skv
670	334 Skv
671	334 Skv
672	331 Skv
673	331 Skv
674	331 Skv
675	331 Skv
676	331 Skv
677	331 Skv
678	331 Skv
679	331 Skv
680	331 Skv
681	331 Skv
682	331 Skv
683	331 Skv
684	331 Skv
685	331 Skv
686	331 Skv
687	331 Skv
688	331 Skv
689*	334 Skv
690*	331 Skv
691*	331 Skv
692*	334 Skv
693*	334 Skv

Lockheed C-130H Hercules
335 Skv, Gardermoen
952
953
954
955
956
957

Lockheed P-3B Orion
333 Skv, Andøya
576
583
599
600
601
602
603

Northrop F-5A
336 Skv, Rygge; 338 Skv, Orland

Serial	Unit
125	336 Skv
128	338 Skv
129	338 Skv
130	336 Skv
131	338 Skv
132	338 Skv
133	336 Skv
134	338 Skv
164	338 Skv
207	336 Skv
208	336 Skv
209	338 Skv
210	338 Skv
214	338 Skv
215	338 Skv
220	338 Skv
222	338 Skv
225	338 Skv
227	338 Skv
228	338 Skv
369	336 Skv
370	338 Skv
371	338 Skv
372	338 Skv
373	338 Skv
374	336 Skv
375	338 Skv
376	338 Skv
563	338 Skv
565	336 Skv
566	338 Skv
568	338 Skv
571	338 Skv
573	338 Skv
574	338 Skv
575	336 Skv
577	338 Skv
895	338 Skv
896	338 Skv
897	336 Skv
898	338 Skv
901	338 Skv
902	338 Skv
904	338 Skv
905	338 Skv

Northrop RF-5A
336 Skv, Rygge
100
101
102
103
104
105
106
107
108
109
110
112
113
489
490

Northrop F-5B
336 Skv, Ryege; 338 Skv, Orland

Serial	Unit
135	338 Skv
136	336 Skv
241	338 Skv
242	338 Skv
243	338 Skv
244	336 Skv
387	336 Skv
594	338 Skv
595	338 Skv
906	336 Skv
907	338 Skv
908	338 Skv
909	338 Skv

Westland Sea King Mk43
330 Skv
060
062
066
068
069
070
071
072
073
074
189

Westland Lynx Mk86
337 Skv
207
216
228
232
235
237

OMAN
Al Quwwat al Jawwiya al Saltanat Oman

BAC 1-11 srs 485GD
45 Sqn, Seeb
551
552
553

Lockheed C-130H Hercules
45 Sqn, Seeb

Serial

501
502
503
Short Skyvan 3M
25 Sqn, Seeb
901
902
903
904
906
907
908
910
911
912
913
914
915
916

PORTUGAL
Forca Aerea Portuguesa
Cessna T-37C
*Asas de Portugal
102 Esq, Sintra
2401
2402
2403
2404*
2407*
2410
2411
2412
2415*
2417
2418
2419
2420
2421*
2422
2423*
2424
2425
2426*
2427
2428
2429*
2430
Lockheed
C-130H Hercules
501 Esq, Montijo
6801
6802
6803
6804
6805
Falcon 20
8101
8102

SAUDI ARABIA
Al Quwwat Al-Jawwiya as Sa' udiya
Lockheed
C-130 Hercules
451 C-130E
452 C-130E
455 C-130E
456 KC-130H
457 KC-130H
458 KC-130H
459 KC-130H
460 C-130H
461 C-130H

Serial

462 C-130H
463 C-130H
464 C-130H
465 C-130H
466 C-130H
467 C-130H
468 C-130H
469 C-130H
470 C-130H
1601 C-130H
1602 C-130H
1603 C-130H
1604 C-130H
1605 C-130H
1606 C-130E
1607 C-130E
1608 C-130E
1609 C-130E
1610 C-130E
1611 C-130E
1612 C-130H
1614 C-130H
1615 C-130H
1616 KC-130H
1617 KC-130H
1618 C-130H
1619 C-130H
1620 KC-130H
1621 KC-130H
Lockheed Jetstar
101
102

SINGAPORE
Republic of Singapore Air Force
Lockheed
C-130B Hercules
122 Sqn, Changi
720
721
Lockheed
C-130H Hercules
122 Sqn, Changi
724
725
730
731
732
733

SPAIN
Ejercito del Aire
Dassault Falcon 20
401 Esq, Madrid
TM.11-1/401-02
TM.11-2/401-03
TM.11-3/401-04
TM.11-4/401-05
Dassault Falcon 50
401 Esq, Madrid
T.16-1/401-09
Fokker F.27M Friendship 400MPA
802 Esq, Gando
D.2-01
D.2-02
D.2-03
Lockheed
C-130H Hercules
311 Esq/312 Esq, Zaragoza
T.10-2/311-02

Serial

T.10-3/311-03
T.10-4/311-04
T.10-8/311-05
T.10-9/311-06
T.10-10/312-04
Lockheed
KC-130H Hercules
312 Esq, Zaragosa
TK.10-5/312-01
TK.10-6/312-02
TK.10-7/312-03
TK.10-11/312-05
TK.10-12/312-06

SWEDEN
Kungl Svenska Flygvapnet
Lockheed
C-130E Hercules
F7, Satenäs
84001/841
84002/842
Lockheed
C-130H Hercules
F7, Satenäs
84003/843
84004/844
84005/845
84006/846
84007/847
84008/848
Cessna 404
87001/871
87002/872
87003/873
Metro III
88001/881

SWITZERLAND
Schweizerische Flugwaffe
Beech E-50
Twin Bonanza
A-711
A-712
A-713

THAILAND
Royal Thai Air Force
DC.8-62AF
60112 (HS-TGQ)

TURKEY
Turk Hava Kuvvetleri
Lockheed
C-130E Hercules
222 Sqn, Erkilet
ETI-00991
ETI-01468
ETI-12186
ETI-12947
ETI-13187
ETI-13188
ETI-13189
ETI-17949
Vickers V794
Viscount
8th VIP Unit, Yesilkoy
246
430
431

Serial

UNITED ARAB EMIRATES
United Arab Emirates Air Force

Abu Dhabi
Lockheed C-130H Hercules
1213
1214
Dubai
Lockheed C-130H Hercules
311
312

WEST GERMANY
Luftwaffe

Boeing 707-307C
FBS, Cologne/Bonn
10+01
10+02
10+03
10+04
Canadair CL601 Challenger
FBS, Cologne/Bonn
12+01
12+02
12+03
12+04
12+05
12+06
12+07
HFB 320 Hansa Jet
*FBS, Cologne/ Bonn;
†JBG32 Lechfeld;
‡Est 61, Ingolstadt
16+01*
16+02*
16+03*
16+04*
16+05*
16+06*
16+07‡
16+08‡
16+21†
16+22
16+23†
16+24†
16+25†
16+26†
16+27†
16+28†
VFW 614
FBS, Cologne/Bonn
17+01
17+02
17+03
Lockheed F-104G Starfighter
JBG 34, Memmingen
20+04†
20+05†
20+36
20+37†
20+38†
20+46†
20+49†
20+50†
20+56†
20+57†
20+64†
21+37

Serial

21+38†
21+42†
21+49
21+56†
21+63†
21+68†
21+69†
21+71†
21+91†
21+98†
21+99†
22+07†
22+32†
22+35†
22+38
22+39†
22+40†
22+41†
22+43†
22+44†
22+46†
22+48†
22+49†
22+55†
22+57†
22+58†
22+61†
22+65†
22+67†
22+90†
22+91†
22+92†
23+01†
23+24
23+30
23+32†
23+74†
23+92†
23+94†
23+97
24+11†
24+13
24+27†
24+38†
24+43†
24+46†
24+74†
25+14†
25+15†
25+17†
25+28†
25+35†
25+45†
25+50†
25+61†
25+74†
26+03†
26+04†
26+05†
26+13†
26+15†
26+20†
26+23†
26+24†
26+26†
26+28†
26+29†
26+30†
26+41†
26+42†
26+43†
26+45†
26+47
26+49†

Serial

McD RF-4E Phantom
AKG 51, Bremgarten;
AKG 52, Leck;
TSLW 1, Kaufbueren;
EST 61, Ingoldstadt
35+01 EST 61
35+02 AKG 52
35+03 AKG 51
35+04 AKG 51
35+05 AKG 52
35+06 AKG 51
35+08 AKG 52
35+09 AKG 52
35+10 AKG 52
35+11 AKG 52
35+12 AKG 51
35+13 AKG 52
35+14 AKG 52
35+17 AKG 52
35+18 AKG 52
35+19 AKG 51
35+20 AKG 52
35+21 AKG 52
35+22 AKG 51
35+24 AKG 52
35+25 AKG 51
35+26 AKG 52
35+27 AKG 51
35+28 AKG 51
35+29 AKG 51
35+31 AKG 52
35+32 AKG 52
35+33 AKG 51
35+34 AKG 51
35+35 AKG 51
35+36 AKG 52
35+37 AKG 52
35+38 AKG 51
35+39 AKG 52
35+40 AKG 51
35+41 AKG 52
35+42 AKG 52
35+43 AKG 52
35+44 AKG 51
35+46 AKG 51
35+48 AKG 51
35+49 AKG 51
35+50 AKG 51
35+51 AKG 51
35+52 AKG 52
35+53 AKG 52
35+54 AKG 52
35+56 AKG 51
35+57 AKG 51
35+58 AKG 51
35+59 AKG 51
35+60 AKG 52
35+61 AKG 51
35+62 TSLW 1
35+63 AKG 51
35+64 AKG 51
35+65 AKG 52
35+66 AKG 52
35+67 AKG 52
35+68 AKG 51
35+69 AKG 52
35+71 AKG 51
35+72 AKG 52
35+73 AKG 51
35+74 AKG 52
35+75 AKG 51
35+76 AKG 52
35+77 AKG 52

Serial	
35+78	AKG 51
35+79	AKG 52
35+80	AKG 52
35+81	AKG 51
35+82	AKG 51
35+83	EST 61
35+84	AKG 52
35+85	AKG 52
35+86	AKG 51
35+87	AKG 52
35+88	AKG 51

McD F-4F Phantom

JBG 35, Pferdsfeld;
JBG 36, Hopsten;
JG 71, Wittmundhafen;
JG 74, Neuberg;
TSLW 1, Kaufbueren;
EST 61, Ingoldstadt

Serial	
37+01	JBG 36
37+03	JG 71
37+04	TSLW 1
37+05	JG 74
37+06	JG 71
37+07	JBG 36
37+08	JG 71
37+09	JBG 35
37+10	JG 71
37+11	JG 74
37+12	JBG 36
37+13	JBG 35
37+14	TSLW 1
37+15	EST 61
37+16	EST 61
37+17	JBG 36
37+18	JBG 35
37+19	JG 71
37+20	JG 74
37+21	JBG 36
37+22	JBG 35
37+23	JG 71
37+24	JG 74
37+25	JBG 36
37+26	JBG 35
37+27	JG 71
37+28	JBG 35
37+29	JBG 36
37+30	JBG 35
37+31	JG 71
37+32	JG 74
37+33	JBG 36
37+34	JBG 35
37+35	JG 71
37+36	JG 74
37+37	JBG 36
37+38	JBG 35
37+39	JG 71
37+40	JG 74
37+41	JBG 36
37+42	JBG 35
37+43	JG 71
37+44	JG 74
37+45	JBG 36
37+46	JBG 35
37+47	JG 71
37+48	JG 74
37+49	JBG 36
37+50	JBG 35
37+51	JG 71
37+52	JG 74
37+53	JBG 36
37+54	JBG 35
37+55	JG 71
37+56	JG 74
37+57	JBG 36
37+58	JBG 35
37+60	JG 74
37+61	JBG 36
37+63	JG 71
37+64	JG 74
37+65	JBG 36
37+66	JBG 35
37+67	JG 71
37+69	JBG 36
37+70	JBG 35
37+71	JG 71
37+73	JBG 36
37+75	JG 71
37+76	JG 74
37+77	JBG 36
37+78	JBG 35
37+79	JG 71
37+80	JG 74
37+81	JBG 36
37+82	JBG 35
37+83	JG 71
37+84	JG 74
37+85	JBG 36
37+86	JG 71
37+88	JG 74
37+89	JBG 36
37+90	JBG 36
37+91	EST 61
37+92	JG 74
37+93	JBG 36
37+94	JBG 35
37+96	JG 74
37+97	JBG 36
37+98	JBG 35
37+99	
38+00	JG 74
38+01	JBG 36
38+02	JBG 35
38+03	JG 71
38+04	JG 74
38+05	JBG 36
38+06	JBG 35
38+07	JG 71
38+08	JG 74
38+09	JBG 36
38+10	JBG 35
38+11	JG 71
38+12	JG 74
38+13	JBG 36
38+14	JBG 35
38+15	JG 71
38+16	JG 74
38+17	JBG 36
38+18	JBG 35
38+20	JG 74
38+21	JBG 36
38+24	JG 74
38+25	JBG 36
38+26	JBG 35
38+27	JG 71
38+28	JG 74
38+29	JBG 36
38+30	JBG 35
38+31	JG 71
38+32	JG 74
38+33	JBG 36
38+34	JBG 35
38+36	JBG 74
38+37	JBG 36
38+38	JBG 35
38+39	JG 71
38+40	JG 74
38+42	JBG 35
38+43	JG 71
38+44	JG 74
38+45	JBG 36
38+46	JBG 35
38+47	JG 71
38+48	JG 74
38+49	JBG 36
38+50	JBG 35
38+51	JG 71
38+52	JG 74
38+53	JBG 36
38+54	JBG 35
38+55	JG 71
38+56	JG 74
38+57	JBG 36
38+58	JBG 35
38+59	JG 71
38+60	JG 74
38+61	JG 71
38+62	JBG 35
38+63	JG 71
38+64	JG 74
38+66	JG 71
38+67	JG 71
38+68	JG 74
38+69	JBG 36
38+70	JBG 35
38+72	JG 74
38+73	JBG 36
38+74	JBG 35
38+75	JBG 35

D-BD Alpha Jet

JBG 41, Husum;
JBG 43, Oldenburg;
JBG 49, Fürstenfeldbruk;
JBG 44, Beja (Portugal)

Serial	
40+01	EST 61
40+02	
40+03	JBG 49
40+04	JBG 43
40+05	JBG 49
40+06	JBG 49
40+07	JBG 49
40+08	JBG 44
40+09	JBG 41
40+10	JBG 41
40+11	JBG 43
40+12	JBG 44
40+13	JBG 43
40+14	JBG 43
40+15	JBG 41
40+16	JBG 41
40+17	JBG 49
40+18	JBG 49
40+20	JBG 43
40+21	JBG 41
40+22	JBG 41
40+23	JBG 49
40+24	JBG 43
40+25	JBG 49
40+26	JBG 41
40+27	JBG 43
40+28	JBG 41
40+29	JBG 49
40+30	JBG 49
40+31	JBG 43
40+32	JBG 43
40+33	JBG 41
40+34	JBG 41
40+35	JBG 49
40+36	JBG 43

Serial	
40+37	JBG 49
40+38	JBG 43
40+39	JBG 41
40+40	JBG 49
40+41	JBG 41
40+42	JBG 49
40+43	JBG 43
40+44	JBG 43
40+45	JBG 41
40+46	JBG 43
40+47	JBG 49
40+48	JBG 44
40+49	JBG 49
40+50	JBG 43
40+51	JBG 41
40+52	JBG 44
40+53	JBG 44
40+54	JBG 44
40+56	EST 61
40+57	JBG 43
40+58	JBG 43
40+59	JBG 49
40+60	JBG 41
40+61	JBG 43
40+62	JBG 41
40+63	JBG 41
40+64	JBG 49
40+65	JBG 49
40+66	JBG 44
40+67	JBG 49
40+68	JBG 41
40+69	JBG 43
40+70	JBG 41
40+71	JBG 44
40+72	JBG 44
40+73	JBG 49
40+74	JBG 41
40+75	JBG 43
40+77	JBG 49
40+78	JBG 43
40+79	JBG 43
40+80	JBG 43
40+81	JBG 41
40+82	JBG 49
40+83	JBG 41
40+84	JBG 49
40+85	JBG 49
40+86	JBG 43
40+87	JBG 43
40+88	JBG 41
40+89	JBG 41
40+90	JBG 49
40+91	JBG 49
40+92	JBG 43
40+93	JBG 44
40+94	JBG 44
40+95	JBG 43
40+96	JBG 49
40+97	JBG 49
40+98	JBG 41
40+99	JBG 41
41+00	JBG 43
41+01	JBG 43
41+02	JBG 41
41+03	JBG 41
41+04	JBG 49
41+05	JBG 43
41+06	JBG 44
41+07	JBG 49
41+08	JBG 49
41+09	JBG 49
41+10	
41+11	JBG 49
41+12	JBG 43

Serial	
41+13	LKO
41+14	JBG 41
41+15	JBG 41
41+16	JBG 44
41+17	JBG 44
41+18	JBG 43
41+19	JBG 43
41+20	JBG 41
41+21	JBG 41
41+22	JBG 44
41+23	JBG 44
41+24	JBG 41
41+25	JBG 49
41+26	JBG 49
41+27	JBG 43
41+28	JBG 43
41+29	JBG 44
41+30	JBG 44
41+31	JBG 41
41+32	JBG 41
41+33	JBG 41
41+34	JBG 43
41+35	JBG 49
41+36	JBG 49
41+37	JBG 49
41+38	JBG 49
41+39	JBG 43
41+40	JBG 43
41+41	JBG 41
41+42	JBG 43
41+43	JBG 43
41+44	JBG 49
41+45	JBG 49
41+46	JBG 43
41+47	JBG 41
41+48	JBG 41
41+49	JBG 49
41+50	JBG 49
41+51	JBG 43
41+52	JBG 43
41+53	JBG 41
41+54	JBG 41
41+55	JBG 49
41+56	JBG 49
41+57	JBG 43
41+58	JBG 43
41+59	JBG 41
41+60	JBG 41
41+61	JBG 49
41+62	JBG 49
41+63	JBG 43
41+64	JBG 43
41+65	JBG 41
41+66	JBG 41
41+67	JBG 49
41+68	JBG 49
41+70	JBG 43
41+71	JBG 41
41+72	JBG 41
41+73	JBG 41
41+74	JBG 41
41+75	JBG 41

Panavia Tornado
***Marinesflieger 1, Schleswig**
†TTTE Cottesmore;
JBG 31, Nörvenich;
JBG 32, Lechfeld;
JBG 33, Buchel;
JBG 38, Jever

Serial	
43+01/G-20†	
43+02/G-21†	
43+03/G-22†	
43+04/G-23†	
43+05/G-24†	
43+06/G-25†	
43+07/G-26†	
43+08/G-27†	
43+09/G-28†	
43+10/G-29†	
43+11/G-30†	
43+12/G-70†	
43+13/G-71†	
43+14/G-72†	
43+15/G-31†	
43+16/G-32†	
43+17/G-33†	
43+18/G-77†	
43+19/G-78†	
43+20/G-73†	
43+22	JBG 38
43+23/G-34†	
43+24/G-74†	
43+25/G-75†	
43+26/G-76†	
43+27	MFG 1
43+28	JBG 38
43+29/G-35†	
43+30	JBG 38
43+31/G-36†	
43+32	JBG 38
43+33	JBG 38
43+34	JBG 38
43+35/G-38†	
43+36	JBG 38
43+37/G-37†	
43+38	JBG 38
43+40	JBG 38
43+41	
43+42*	MFG 1
43+43*	JBG 38
43+44*	MFG 1
43+45*	MFG 1
43+46*	MFG 1
43+47*	MFG 1
43+48*	MFG 1
43+50*	MFG 1
43+51*	MFG 1
43+52*	MFG 1
43+53*	MFG 1
43+54*	MFG 1
43+55*	MFG 1
43+56*	MFG 1
43+57*	MFG 1
43+58*	MFG 1
43+59*	MFG 1
43+60*	MFG 1
43+61*	MFG 1
43+62*	MFG 1
43+63*	MFG 1
43+64*	MFG 1
43+65*	MFG 1
43+67*	MFG 1
43+68*	MFG 1
43+69*	MFG 1
43+70*	MFG 1
43+71*	MFG 1
43+72*	MFG 1
43+73*	MFG 1
43+74*	MFG 1
43+75*	MFG 1
43+76*	MFG 1
43+77*	MFG 1
43+78*	MFG 1
43+79	JBG 38
43+80*	MFG 1
43+81*	MFG 1
43+82*	MFG 1

Serial	
43+83*	MFG 1
43+84*	MFG 1
43+85*	MFG 1
43+86*	MFG 1
43+87*	MFG 1
43+88*	MFG 1
43+89*	MFG 1
43+90	JBG 38
43+91	JBG 38
43+92	JBG 31
43+94	JBG 31
43+95	JBG 32
43+96	JBG 31
43+97	JBG 31
43+98	JBG 31
43+99	JBG 31
44+00	JBG 31
44+01	JBG 38
44+02	JBG 31
44+03	JBG 31
44+04	JBG 31
44+05	JBG 38
44+06	JBG 31
44+07	JBG 31
44+08	JBG 38
44+09	JBG 31
44+10	JBG 38
44+11	JBG 38
44+12	JBG 31
44+13	JBG 38
44+14	JBG 31
44+15	JBG 38
44+16	JBG 31
44+17	JBG 38
44+18	JBG 31
44+19	JBG 31
44+20	JBG 38
44+21	JBG 31
44+22	JBG 31
44+23	JBG 31
44+24	JBG 38
44+25	JBG 38
44+26	JBG 31
44+27	JBG 31
44+28	JBG 31
44+29	JBG 31
44+30	JBG 31
44+31	JBG 31
44+32	JBG 31
44+33	JBG 31
44+34	JBG 31
44+35	JBG 31
44+36	JBG 32
44+37	JBG 32
44+38	JBG 32
44+39	JBG 32
44+40	JBG 31
44+41	JBG 31
44+42	JBG 32
44+43	JBG 32
44+44	JBG 31
44+46	JBG 32
44+47	JBG 31
44+48	JBG 31
44+49	JBG 31
44+50	JBG 32
44+51	JBG 32
44+52	JBG 31
44+53	JBG 32
44+54	JBG 32
44+55	JBG 32
44+56	JBG 32
44+57	
44+58	JBG 32

Serial	
44+59	JBG 32
44+60	JBG 32
44+61	JBG 32
44+62	JBG 32
44+63	JBG 32
44+64	JBG 32
44+65	TSLW
44+66	
44+67	JBG 32
44+68	JBG 32
44+69	JBG 32
44+70	JBG 32
44+71	JBG 32
44+72	JBG 33
44+73	JBG 33
44+74	JBG 33
44+75	JBG 33
44+76	JBG 32
44+77	JBG 32
44+78	JBG 32
44+79	JBG 32
44+80	JBG 32
44+81	JBG 32
44+82	JBG 32
44+83	JBG 32
44+84	JBG 32
44+85	JBG 32
44+86	JBG 33
44+87	JBG 33
44+88	JBG 33
44+89	JBG 33
44+90	
44+91	JBG 33
44+92	JBG 33
44+93	
44+94	
44+95	
44+96	
44+97	
44+98	
44+99	

Transall C-160
LTG 61, Landsberg;
LTG 62, Wunstorf;
LTG 63, Hohn

50+06	LTG 63
50+07	LTG 61
50+08	LTG 61
50+09	LTG 62
50+10	LTG 62
50+17	LTG 62
50+29	LTG 62
50+33	LTG 63
50+34	LTG 62
50+35	LTG 62
50+36	LTG 62
50+37	LTG 62
50+38	LTG 62
50+39	LTG 62
50+40	LTG 61
50+41	LTG 63
50+42	LTG 63
50+43	LTG 61
50+44	LTG 61
50+45	LTG 63
50+46	LTG 62
50+47	LTG 61
50+48	
50+49	LTG 61
50+50	LTG 63
50+51	LTG 61
50+52	LTG 62
50+53	LTG 62
50+54	LTG 63
50+55	LTG 62
50+56	LTG 63
50+57	LTG 61
50+58	LTG 63
50+59	LTG 63
50+60	LTG 62
50+61	LTG 63
50+62	LTG 61
50+64	LTG 61
50+65	LTG 62
50+66	LTG 61
50+67	LTG 63
50+68	LTG 61
50+69	LTG 63
50+70	EST 61
50+71	LTG 63
50+72	LTG 61
50+73	LTG 62
50+74	LTG 61
50+75	
50+76	LTG 63
50+77	LTG 63
50+78	LTG 62
50+79	LTG 63
50+80	LTG 61
50+81	LTG 62
50+82	LTG 63
50+83	LTG 62
50+84	LTG 63
50+85	LTG 61
50+86	LTG 61
50+87	LTG 63
50+88	LTG 61
50+89	LTG 62
50+90	LTG 63
50+91	LTG 62
50+92	LTG 61
50+93	LTG 61
50+94	LTG 62
50+95	LTG 63
50+96	LTG 61
50+97	LTG 62
50+98	LTG 61
50+99	LTG 61
51+00	LTG 63
51+01	LTG 62
51+02	LTG 63
51+03	LTG 62
51+04	LTG 61
51+05	LTG 62
51+06	LTG 63
51+07	LTG 62
51+08	LTG 63
51+09	LTG 63
51+10	LTG 61
51+11	LTG 62
51+12	LTG 63
51+13	LTG 61
51+14	LTG 63
51+15	LTG 61

Dornier Do.28D-2 Skyservant
***Marinesflieger, Kiel**

58+05	
58+06	
58+08	LTG 62
58+09	LTG 62
58+10	
58+11	
58+13	
58+14	LTG 62
58+15	JBG 31

Overseas Serials

Serial

58+16
58+17
58+18 LTG 63
58+20 JGB 31
58+21
58+23 LTG 61
58+24
58+26 LTG 62
58+27
58+28 JBG 35
58+29 LTG 61
58+30 LTG 63
58+31
58+32 JG 74
58+33
58+34 LTG 62
58+36 LTG 62
58+37
58+38 LTG 62
58+39 LTG 62
58+40
58+41
58+42
58+43
58+44
58+46 LTG 62
58+47
58+49 JBG 49
58+50 JBG 33
58+51
58+52 LTG 62
58+53 JBG 32
58+54 AKG 51
58+55 JBG 32
58+57
58+58 JBG 33
58+59 JBG 34
58+60 LTG 62
58+61 JBG 34
58+62 JBG 36
58+64
58+65 JG 71
58+66 JBG 38
58+67 JBG 38
58+68 LTG 62
58+69 LTG 62
58+70 LTG 62
58+71 LTG 61
58+72 AKG 51
58+73 JBG 31
58+74 JBG 41
58+75
58+76 JBG 41
58+77 JBG 49
58+78 JBG 31
58+79 LTG 62
58+80 JBG 33

Serial

58+81 LTG 62
58+82 JBG 43
58+83
58+84 JBG 43
58+85 JBG 33
58+86 JBG 49
58+87 JBG 49
58+89 JBG 49
58+90
58+91
58+92 JBG 36
58+93
58+94 JBG 35
58+95
58+96
58+97
58+98 AKG 52
58+99 JG 71
59+00 FBS
59+01 FBS
59+02 FBS
59+03 FBS
59+04 FBS
59+05 FBS
59+06*
59+07*
59+08*
59+09*
59+10*
59+11*
59+12*
59+13*
59+14*
59+15*
59+16*
59+17*
59+18*
59+19*
59+20*
59+21*
59+22*
59+23*
59+24*
59+25*

Breguet
1151 Atlantic
***Marinesflieger 3**
Nordholz

61+01*
61+02*
61+03*
61+04*
61+05*
61+06*
61+07*
61+08*
61+09*

Serial

61+10*
61+11*
61+12*
61+13*
61+14*
61+15*
61+16*
61+17*
61+19*
61+20*

Westland
Lynx Mk88
***Marinesflieger 3**,
Nordholz

83+01*
83+02*
83+03*
83+04*
83+05*
83+06*
83+07*
83+08*
83+09*
83+10*
83+11*
83+12*

Westland Sea
King HAS.41
***Marinesflieger 5**,
Kiel

89+50*
89+51*
89+53*
89+54*
89+55*
89+56*
89+57*
89+58*
89+59*
89+60*
89+61*
89+62*
89+63*
89+65*
89+66*
89+67*
89+68*
89+69*
89+70*
89+71*

English Electric
Canberra B2
EST 61, Manching

99+34
99+35

BD09 Dassault Mirage 5BD from No 1 Squadron Belgian AF. *PRM*

AT08 D-BD Alphajet of the Belgian AF. *DJM*

LX-N90456 a NATO operated Boeing E-3A Sentry. *PRM*

133 Northrop F-5A of No 336 Skv Royal Norwegian AF. *PRM*

50+96 Transall C-160 of LTG61 German Air Force. *APM*

01078 Lockheed TR-1A is based at RAF Alconbury. *PRM*

80-565 GD F-16A is operated by 496TS/50TFW at Hahn. *PRM*

40465 Shorts C-23A Shepa of 322MAW/10MAS. *APM*

18898 GrummanOV-1D Mohawk of the US Army. *DJM*

90006 Lockheed C-5A Galaxy, USAF 436 MAW. *PRM*

60186 Lockheed C-141B Starlifter, USAF 443 MAW. *PRM*

159316 Lockheed P-3C Orion, USN VP-45 Squadron. *DJM*

US Military Aircraft Markings

All USAF aircraft have been allocated a fiscal year (FY) number since 1921. Individual aircraft are given a serial according to the fiscal year in which they are ordered. The numbers commence at 0001 and are prefixed with the year of allocation. For example F-111E 68-0001 was the first aircraft ordered in 1968. The fiscal year (FY) serial is carried on the technical bloc which is usually stencilled on the left-hand side of the aircraft just below the cockpit. The number displayed on the fin is a corruption of the FY serial. Most tactical aircraft carry the fiscal year in small figures followed by the last three digits of the serial in large figures. For example F-111F 70-2362 carries 70362 on its tail. An exception to this practice is the F-5E which carries the five digits of the production serial without the fiscal year. For example the FY serial of the F-5E which displays 01532 is 74-01532. Large transport and tanker aircraft such as C-130s and KC-135s usually display a five-figure number commencing with the last digit of the appropriate fiscal year and four figures of the production number. An example of this is EC-135H 61-0282 which displays 10282 on its fin. Aircraft of more than 10 years vintage which might duplicate a five-figure number of a more modern type in service, are prefixed 0-.

USN serials follow a straightforward numerical sequence which commenced, for the present series, with the allocation of 00001 to an SB2C Helldiver by the Bureau of Aeronautics in 1940. Numbers in the 160000 series are presently being issued. They are usually carried in full on the rear fuselage of the aircraft and displayed either as a four- or five-figure sequence or in full on the fin.

UK based USAF Aircraft

The following aircraft are normally based in the UK. They are listed in alphabetical order of type with individual aircraft in serial number order, as depicted on the aircraft. The number in brackets is either the alternative presentation of the five-figure number commencing with the last digit of the fiscal year, or the fiscal year where a five-figure serial is presented on the aircraft. Where it is possible to identify the allocation of aircraft to individual squadrons by means of colours carried on fin or cockpit edge, this is also provided.

Serial	*Notes*
Lockheed TR-1A	
(95RS/17RW, RAF Alconbury)	
01068 (FY80)	
01070 (FY80)	
01072 (FY80)	
01077 (FY80)	
01078 (FY80)	
01079 (FY80)	
01081 (FY80)	
McDonnell-Douglas RF-4C Phantom	
(AR: 1TRS/10TRW, RAF Alconbury)	
68-554 (80554)	
68-555 (80555)	
68-557 (80557)	
68-561 (80561)	
68-563 (80563)	
68-565 (80565)	
68-567 (80567)	
68-568 (80568)	
68-580 (80580)	
68-583 (80583)	
68-589 (80589)	
69-369 (90369)	
69-370 (90370)	
69-378 (90378)	
69-380 (90380)	
69-381 (90381)	
69-382 (90382)	
69-384 (90384)	
71-259 (10259)	
72-146 (20146)	

Notes	Serial	Notes	Serial
	Northrop F-5E Tiger II		80-215 (00215) pr
	(527AS/10TRW, RAF Alconbury)		80-216 (00216) pr
	FY74		80-217 (00217) y
	01532		80-218 (00218) gy
	01534		80-219 (00219) gy
	01534 Replica at Alconbury gate		80-220 (00220) bl
	01535		80-227 (00227) gy
	01542		80-228 (00228) pr
	01543		80-229 (00229) bk
	01544		80-230 (00230) bk
	01545		80-231 (00231) gy
	01547		80-232 (00232) bl
	01549		80-233 (00233) r
	01551		80-234 (00234) bl
	01553		80-235 (00235) r
	01554		80-236 (00236) r
	01556		80-237 (00237) bk
	01559		80-270 (00270) r
	01560		80-271 (00271) bl
	01563		80-272 (00272) y
	01566		80-273 (00273) gy
	01568		80-274 (00274) pr
	01569		80-275 (00275) bk
			80-276 (00276) y
	Fairchild A-10A Thunderbolt II		80-277 (00277) bk
	WR: 81TFW:		80-278 (00278) r
	78TFS red (r) Woodbridge		80-279 (00279) pr
	91TFS blue (bl) Woodbridge		80-280 (00280) bl
	92TFS yellow (y) Bentwaters		80-281 (00281) y
	509TFS grey (gy) Bentwaters		81-939 (10939) gy
	510TFS purple (pr) Bentwaters		81-940 (10940) bk
	511TFS black (bk) Bentwaters		81-941 (10941) r
	79-217 (90217)		81-942 (10942) bl
	79-218 (90218) y		81-943 (10943) y
	79-219 (90219) bk		81-944 (10944) pr
	79-220 (90220) gy		81-947 (10947) gy
	79-221 (90221) pr		81-948 (10948) gy
	79-224 (90224) gy		81-949 (10949) bk
	79-225 (90225) bl		81-950 (10950) bl
	80-143 (00143) r		81-951 (10951) bl
	80-144 (00144) gy		81-952 (10952) pr
	80-145 (00145) y		81-953 (10953) gy
	80-146 (00146) bk		81-954 (10954) y
	80-147 (00147) pr		81-955 (10955) bk
	80-155 (00155) pr		81-956 (10956) bl
	80-156 (00156) bk		81-957 (10957) y
	80-157 (00157) bk		81-960 (10960) r
	80-158 (00158) bl		81-961 (10961) r
	80-159 (00159) y		81-962 (10962) bl
	80-160 (00160) pr		81-963 (10963) y
	80-167 (00167) r		81-964 (10964) gy
	80-168 (00168) y		81-965 (10965) pr
	80-169 (00169) pr		81-966 (10966) pr
	80-170 (00170) gy		81-967 (10967) bk
	80-171 (00171) bl		81-976 (10976) bl
	80-172 (00172) bk		81-977 (10977) y
	80-179 (00179) r		81-978 (10978) r
	80-180 (00180) bl		81-979 (10979) gy
	80-181 (00181) y		81-980 (10980) pr
	80-183 (00183) pr		81-981 (10981) bk
	80-184 (00184) bk		81-982 (10982) r
	80-185 (00185)		81-983 (10983) bl
	80-192 (00192) y		81-984 (10984) r
	80-194 (00194) gy		81-985 (10985) y
	80-195 (00195) pr		81-986 (10986) bk
	80-196 (00196) bk		81-987 (10987) gy
	80-203 (00203) r		81-988 (10988) pr
	80-204 (00204) bl		81-990 (10990) gy
	80-205 (00205) bl		81-991 (10991) bl
	80-206 (00206) y		81-992 (10992) y
	80-207 (00207) y		82-646 (20646) pr
	80-208 (00208) gy		82-647 (20647) bk
			82-649 (20649) bl
			82-650 (20650) pr

Serial	Notes
82-654 (20654) r	
82-655 (20655) bl	
82-656 (20656) y	
82-657 (20657) gy	
82-658 (20658) r	
82-659 (20659) bk	

Sikorsky HH-53C
(67 ARRS, RAF Woodbridge)

Serial	Notes
5784 (FY69)	
5785 (FY69)	
5796 (FY69)	
5797 (FY69)	
8284 (FY68)	

General Dynamics EF-111A Raven
(UH: RAF Upper Heyford)
66ECIO/42ECS grey

Serial	Notes
66-030 (60030)	
66-033 (60033)	
66-037 (60037)	
66-039 (60039)	
66-041 (60041)	
66-055 (60055)	
66-056 (60056)	
66-057 (60057)	
67-032 (70032)	
67-034 (70034)	
67-035 (70035)	
67-041 (70041)	
67-052 (70052)	
67-053 (70053)	

General Dynamics F-111E
(UH: 20TFW, RAF Upper Heyford)
55TFS blue/white (bl)
77TFS red (r)
79TFS yellow/black (y)

Serial	Notes
67-119 (70119) bl	
67-120 (70120) r	
67-121 (70121) bl	
67-122 (70122) y	
67-123 (70123) y	
68-001 (80001) r	
68-002 (80002) y	
68-004 (80004) bl	
68-005 (80005) bl	
68-006 (80006) bl	
68-007 (80007) r	
68-009 (80009) r	
68-010 (80010) y	
68-011 (80011) r	
68-013 (80013) y	
68-014 (80014) bl	
68-015 (80015) bl	
68-016 (80016) bl	
68-017 (80017) r	
680-20 (80020) multi	
68-021 (80021) r	
68-022 (80022) y	
68-023 (80023) y	
68-025 (80025) bl	
68-026 (80026) bl	
68-027 (80027) r	
68-028 (80028) r	
68-029 (80029) r	
68-030 (80030) y	
68-031 (80031) r	
68-032 (80032) y	
68-033 (80033) y	
68-034 (80034) bl	
68-035 (80035) bl	
68-036 (80036) bl	
68-037 (80037) r	
68-038 (80038) r	
68-039 (80039) r	
68-040 (80040) y	
68-041 (80041) r	
68-043 (80043) y	
68-044 (80044) bl	
68-046 (80046) bl	
68-047 (80047) r	
68-048 (80048) r	
68-049 (80049) r	
68-050 (80050) y	
68-051 (80051) r	
68-052 (80052) y	
68-053 (80053) y	
68-054 (80054) bl	
680-55 (80055) bl	
68-056 (80056) bl	
68-059 (80059) r	
68-061 (80061) r	
68-062 (80062) y	
68-063 (80063) y	
68-064 (80064) bl	
68-065 (80065) bl	
68-066 (80066) bl	
68-067 (80067) r	
68-068 (80068) r	
68-069 (80069) r	
68-071 (80071) r	
68-072 (80072) y	
68-073 (80073) y	
68-074 (80074) bl	
68-075 (80075) bl	
68-076 (80076) bl	
68-077 (80077) r	
68-078 (80078) r	
68-079 (80079) y	
68-080 (80080) y	
68-082 (80082) y	
68-083 (80083) y	
68-084 (80084) bl	

General Dynamics F-111F
(LN: 48TFW, RAF Lakenheath)
492 TFS blue (bl)
493 TFS yellow (y)
494 TFS red (r)
495 TFS green (gn)

Serial	Notes
70-362 (02362) bl	
70-363 (02363) y	
70-364 (02364) bl	
70-365 (02365) bl	
70-368 (02368) bl	
70-369 (02369) bl	
70-370 (02370) bl	
70-371 (02371) gn	
70-372 (02372) r	
70-373 (02373) bl	
70-374 (02374) y	
70-375 (02375) bl	
70-376 (02376) y	
70-378 (02378) r	
70-379 (02379) r	
70-381 (02381) y	
70-382 (02382) y	
70-383 (02383) y	
70-384 (02384) r	
70-385 (02385) gn	
70-386 (02386) y	
70-387 (02387) gn	
70-389 (02389) r	
70-390 (02390) multi	

Notes	Serial
	70-391 (02391) gn
	70-392 (02392) gn
	70-394 (02394) bl
	70-396 (02396) bl
	70-397 (02397) y
	70-398 (02398) gn
	70-399 (02399) bl
	70-401 (02401) r
	70-402 (02402) y
	70-403 (02403) bl
	70-404 (02404) y
	70-405 (02405) r
	70-406 (02406) bl
	70-408 (02408) r
	70-409 (02409) r
	70-411 (02411) bl
	70-412 (02412) gn
	70-413 (02413) r
	70-414 (02414) gn
	70-415 (02415) y
	70-417 (02417) r
	70-418 (02418) bl
	70-419 (02419) gn
	71-883 (10883) y
	71-884 (10884) gn
	71-885 (10885) gn
	71-886 (10886) bl
	71-887 (10887) y
	71-888 (10888) bl
	71-889 (10889) y
	71-890 (10890) y
	71-891 (10891) y
	71-892 (10892) y
	71-893 (10893) bl
	71-894 (10894) gn
	72-442 (21442) r
	72-443 (21443) r
	72-444 (21444) r
	72-445 (21445) gn
	72-446 (21446) gn

Notes	Serial
	72-448 (21448) multi
	72-449 (21449) y
	72-450 (21450) y
	72-451 (21451) y
	72-452 (21452) y
	73-707 (30707) r
	73-708 (30708) r
	73-710 (30710) r
	73-711 (30711) gn
	73-712 (30712) gn
	73-713 (30713) gn
	73-715 (30715) r
	74-177 (40177) bl
	74-178 (40178) gn
	74-180 (40180) bl
	74-181 (40181) bl
	74-182 (40182) y
	74-183 (40183) gn
	74-184 (40184) y
	74-185 (40185) r

Lockheed C-130 Hercules
(67ARRS/39 ARRW, RAF Woodbridge)

50962 (FY65) HC-130H
60220 (FY66) HC-130P
95820 (FY69) HC-130N
95823 (FY69) HC-130N
95826 (FY69) HC-130N
95827 (FY69) HC-130N

Boeing EC-135H
(513TAW/10 ACCS, Mildenhall)
FY61

10282 EC-135H
10285 EC-135H
10286 EC-135H
10291 EC-135H

UK based US Navy Aircraft

Beech UC-12B
(8G: Naval Air Facility, RAF Mildenhall)
1322/8D (161322)
1503/8G (161503)

European based USAF Aircraft

These aircraft are normally based in Western Europe with the USAFE. They are shown in numerical order of type designation, with individual aircraft in serial number order as carried on the aircraft. An alternative five-figure presentation of the serial is shown in brackets where appropriate. Fiscal year (FY) details are also provided if necessary. The unit allocation and operating bases are given for most aircraft.

Serial

Bell UH-1N
67ARRS
Det 2 Ramstein*
Det 9 Zaragoza†
FY69
96603†
96606*
96607*
96608*
96609*
96611†
96630†

McDonnell Douglas RF-4C Phantom
(ZR: 26TRW/38TRS Zweibrucken)
64-001 (41001)
67-451 (70451)
67-469 (70469)
68-577 (80577)
68-590 (80590)
69-360 (90360)
69-361 (90361)
69-364 (90364)
69-365 (90365)
69-366 (90366)
69-367 (90367)
69-368 (90368)
69-371 (90371)
69-372 (90372)
69-374 (90374)
71-249 (10249)
71-251 (10251)
71-254 (10254)
72-152 (20152)
72-153 (20153)

McDonnell Douglas F-4E Phantom
(RS: 86TFW Ramstein
SP: 52TFW Spangdahlem)
23 TFS blue-white (bl)
81 TFS yellow/black (y)
480 TFS red/white (r)
67-343 (70343) RS
68-372 (80372) RS
68-375 (80375) RS
68-377 (80377) RS
68-378 (80378) RS
68-381 (80381) RS
68-384 (80384) RS
68-386 (80386) RS
68-388 (80388) RS
68-393 (80393) RS
68-394 (80394) RS
68-401 (80401) RS
68-403 (80403) RS
68-404 (80404) RS

Serial

68-408 (80408) RS
68-411 (80411) RS
68-413 (80413) RS
68-438 (80438) RS
68-440 (80440) RS
68-441 (80441) RS
68-442 (80442) RS
68-444 (80444) RS
68-445 (80445) RS
68-459 (80459) RS
68-460 (80460) RS
68-465 (80465) RS
68-467 (80467) RS
68-476 (80476) RS
68-480 (80480) RS
68-481 (80481) RS
68-496 (80496) RS
68-506 (80506) RS
68-507 (80507) RS
68-508 (80508) RS
68-509 (80509) RS
68-516 (80516) RS
68-517 (80517) RS
68-527 (80527) RS
68-528 (80528) RS
68-529 (80529) RS
68-531 (80531) RS
68-533 (80533) RS
68-534 (80534) RS
68-538 (80538) RS
69-244 (90244) RS
69-249 (90249) RS
69-260 (90260) RS
69-264 (90264) RS
69-278 (90278) RS
7-1247 (10247) SP y
71-079 (11079) SP r
72-139 (20139) SP bl
72-159 (20159) SP y
72-160 (20160) bl
72-165 (20165) SP r
72-166 (20166) SP y
72-167 (20167) SP r
72-407 (21407) SP r
72-477 (21477) SP r
72-482 (21482) SP bl
72-483 (21483) SP r
72-485 (21485) SP r
74-038 (41038) y
74-044 (41044) SP bl
74-045 (41045) SP y
74-048 (41048) SP r
74-049 (41049) SP r
74-050 (41050) SP r
740-52 (41052) SP r
74-053 (41053) SP y
74-056 (41056) SP y
74-057 (41057) SP r
74-059 (41059) SP bl
74-060 (41060) SP y

Serial

74-622 (41622) SP bl
74-628 (41628) SP r
74-630 (41630) SP y
74-633 (41633) SP bl
74-634 (41634) SP y
74-635 (41635) SP r
74-636 (41636) SP y
74-638 (41638) SP y
74-639 (41639) SP bl
74-640 (41640)
74-641 (41641) SP bl
74-642 (41642) SP y
74-644 (41644) SP r
74-645 (41645) SP y
74-647 (41647) SP y
74-648 (41648) SP y
74-650 (40650) SP bl
74-650 (41650) SP y
74-651 (41651) SP bl
74-652 (40652) SP r
74-652 (41652) SP bl
74-653 (40653) SP r
74-653 (41653) SP bl
74-654 (40654) SP bl
74-656 (40656) SP r
74-657 (40657) SP y
74-659 (40659) SP r
74-662 (40662) SP bl
74-663 (40663) SP y
74-664 (40664) SP bl

McDonnell Douglas F-4G Phantom
(SP 52TFW Spangdahlem)
23 TFS blue-white (bl)
81 TFS yellow/black (y)
480 TFS red/white (r)
69-202 (97202) y
69-212 (97212) bl
69-228 (97228) bl
69-234 (97234) r
69-236 (97236) r
69-241 (90241) bl
69-247 (90247) y
69-248 (90248) r
69-250 (90250) r
69-253 (90253) r
69-255 (90255) bl
69-262 (97262) bl
69-268 (97268) bl
69-269 (90269) r
69-270 (97270) r
69-285 (90285) y
69-286 (90286) —
69-293 (97293) y
69-295 (97295) y
69-546 (97546) bl
69-556 (97556) y
69-558 (97558) r

Serial

69-566 (97566) bl
69-579 (97579) r
69-582 (97582) y
69-587 (97587) y

McDonnell Douglas C-9A Nightingale
(435TAW/55AAS Rhein Main)
FY71
10876
10879
10880
10881
10882

Beech C-12
(*58 MAS Ramstein
†7005ABS Stuttgart
‡JUSMG Madrid
**MAAG Athens
§ MAAG, Ankara
‡‡JUSMG Turkey)
22549 (FY76)† C-12A
22550 (FY76)† C-12A
22932 (FY77)† C-12A
22933 (FY77)† C-12A
30498 (FY83)* C-12A
31212 (FY83)‡ C-12A
31218 (FY73)** C-12A
40161 (FY84)* C-12F
40162 (FY84)* C-12F
40163 (FY84)* C-12F
40164 (FY84)* C-12F
40165 (FY84)* C-12F
40166 (FY84)* C-12F
60173 (FY70)§ C-12A

McDonnell Douglas F-15C/‡F-15D Eagle
CR: Soesterberg 32TFS orange
BT: 36TFW Bitburg
22TFS red (r)
53TFS yellow (y)
525TFS blue (b)
79-004 (90004)‡ CR
79-005 (90005)‡ CR
79-006 (90006)‡ BT bl
79-007 (90007)‡ BT y
79-008 (90008)‡ BT bl
79-009 (90009)‡ BT y
79-010 (90010)‡ BT y
79-011 (90011)‡ BT r
79-012 (90012)‡ BT r
79-015 (90015) CR
79-016 (90016) CR
79-017 (90017) CR
79-018 (90018) CR
79-019 (90019) CR
79-020 (90020) CR
79-021 (90021) CR
79-022 (90022) BT r
79-023 (90023) CR
79-024 (90024) CR
79-025 (90025) BT bl
79-026 (90026) CR
79-027 (90027) CR
79-028 (90028) CR
79-029 (90029) CR
79-030 (90030) CR
79-031 (90031) CR
79-032 (90032) CR
79-033 (90033) CR

Serial

79-034 (90034) CR
79-035 (90035) BT bl
790-36 (90036) BT multi
79-037 (90037) BT bl
79-038 (90038) BT bl
79-039 (90039) BT bl
79-041 (90041) BT bl
79-042 (90042) BT bl
79-043 (90043) BT bl
79-045 (90045) BT bl
79-046 (90046) BT bl
79-047 (90047) BT bl
79-048 (90048) BT y
79-049 (90049) BT r
79-050 (90050) BT bl
79-051 (90051) BT r
79-052 (90052) BT r
790-53 (90053) BT y
79-054 (90054) BT r
79-055 (90055) BT bl
79-056 (90056) BT r
79-057 (90057) BT r
79-058 (90058) BT bl
79-059 (90059) BT r
79-060 (90060) BT r
79-061 (90061) BT bl
79-062 (90062) BT bl
79-063 (90063) BT r
79-064 (90064) BT r
79-065 (90065) BT r
79-066 (90066) BT bl
79-067 (90067) BT bl
79-068 (90068) BT bl
79-069 (90069) BT y
79-070 (90070) BT y
79-072 (90072) BT y
79-073 (90073) BT y
79-074 (90074) BT y
79-075 (90075) BT y
79-076 (90076) BT y
79-077 (90077) BT y
79-078 (90078) BT y
79-079 (90079) BT r
79-080 (90080) BT y
79-081 (90081) BT y
80-002 (00002) BT bl
80-003 (00003) BT y
80-004 (00004) BT r
80-005 (00005) BT multi
80-006 (00006) BT r
80-009 (00009) BT r
80-010 (00010) BT r
80-011 (00011) BT y
80-012 (00012) BT y
80-013 (00013) BT y
80-014 (00014) BT y
80-015 (00015) BT y
80-016 (00016) BT r
80-017 (00017) BT bl
80-018 (00018) BT bl
80-019 (00019) BT bl
80-020 (00020) BT bl
80-021 (00021) BT r
80-022 (00022) BT r
80-023 (00023) BT r
80-024 (00024) BT bl
80-026 (00026) BT r
80-028 (00028) BT y
80-029 (00029) BT bl
80-031 (00031) BT r
80-032 (00032) BT bl
81-045 (10045) CR
81-046 (10046) CR
81-047 (10047) CR

Serial

81-048 (10048) CR
81-049 (10049) CR
81-065 (10065)‡ CR
81-066 (10066)‡ CR

General Dynamics F-16A/‡F-16B
(HR: 50TFW Hahn)
10TFS blue (bl)
313TFS white (w)
496TFS red (r)
(TJ: 401TFW Torrejon)
612TFS blue (bl)
613TFS yellow/black (y)
614TFS red (r)
80-543 (00543) HR w
80-544 (00544) HR w
80-545 (00545) HR w
80-546 (00546) HR w
80-555 (00555) HR w
80-556 (00556) HR bl
80-558 (00558) HR bl
80-559 (00559) HR bl
80-560 (00560) HR r
80-561 (00561) HR r
80-562 (00562) HR r
80-563 (00563) HR r
80-565 (00565) HR r
80-572 (00572) HR multi
80-574 (00574) HR w
80-575 (00575) HR w
80-576 (00576) HR w
80-577 (00577) HR bl
80-585 (00585) HR w
80-586 (00586) HR bl
80-587 (00587) HR bl
80-588 (00588) HR bl
80-589 (00589) HR bl
80-590 (00590) HR bl
80-591 (00591) HR bl
80-592 (00592) HR r
80-601 (00601) HR r
80-602 (00602) HR bl
80-603 (00603) HR r
80-604 (00604) HR r
80-605 (00605) HR r
80-606 (00606) HR r
80-607 (00607) HR r
80-608 (00608) HR r
80-610 (00610) HR bl
80-612 (00612) HR multi
80-613 (00613) HR bl
80-614 (00614) HR bl
80-615 (00615) HR bl
80-616 (00616) HR bl
80-618 (00618) HR w
80-619 (00619) HR w
80-620 (00620) HR bl
80-622 (00622) HR w
80-636 (00636)‡ HR w
80-637 (00637)‡ HR bl
81-665 (10665) HR w
81-666 (10666) HR r
81-669 (10669) HR bl
81-671 (10671) HR w
81-672 (10672) HR bl
81-673 (10673) HR bl
81-674 (10674) HR r
81-675 (10675) HR bl
81-680 (10680) HR r
81-681 (10681) HR w
81-682 (10682) HR w
81-694 (10694) HR r
81-695 (10695) HR w

Serial

81-696 (10696) HR w
81-697 (10697) HR r
81-698 (10698) HR r
81-699 (10699) HR bl
81-700 (10700) HR bl
81-707 (10707) HR r
81-709 (10709) HR r
81-710 (10710) HR bl
81-711 (10711) HR bl
81-712 (10712) HR w
81-713 (10713) HR w
81-721 (10721) HR w
81-722 (10722) HR multi
81-723 (10723) HR r
81-731 (10731) HR w
81-732 (10732) HR w
81-737 (10737) HR multi
81-738 (10738) HR multi
81-757 (10757) HR bl
81-758 (10758) HR bl
81-759 (10759) HR r
81-788 (10788) TJ bl
81-790 (10790) TJ bl
81-792 (10792) TJ bl
81-794 (10794) TJ bl
81-796 (10796) TJ bl
81-798 (10798) TJ bl
81-800 (10800) TJ r
81-802 (10802) TJ r
81-804 (10804) TJ r
81-806 (10806) TJ r
81-807 (10807) TJ r
81-810 (10810) TJ r
81-818 (10818)‡ HR bl
81-819 (10819)‡ HR w
81-820 (10820)‡ HR r
81-821 (10821)‡ TJ r
81-822 (10822)‡ TJ r
82-002 (21002) TJ multi
82-004 (21004) TJ r
82-007 (21007) TJ r
82-009 (21009) TJ r
82-011 (21011) TJ r
82-013 (21013) TJ bl
82-015 (21015) TJ bl
82-018 (21018) TJ y
82-020 (21020) TJ y
82-022 (21022) TJ y
82-024 (21024) TJ bl
82-025 (21025) TJ bl
82-031 (21031)‡ HR r
82-035 (21035)‡ HR bl
82-047 (21047)‡ TJ r
82-900 (20900) TJ r
82-902 (20902) TJ r
82-904 (20904) TJ r
82-906 (20906) TJ r
82-908 (20908) TJ r
82-911 (20911) TJ r
82-914 (20914) TJ multi
82-918 (20918) TJ r
82-920 (20920) TJ r
82-922 (20922) TJ multi
82-924 (20924) TJ r
82-927 (20927) TJ r
82-928 (20928) TJ bl
82-931 (20931) TJ bl
82-933 (20933) TJ r
82-936 (20936) TJ y
82-938 (20938) TJ y
82-941 (20941) TJ y
82-943 (20943) TJ y
82-944 (20944) TJ y
82-946 (20946) TJ y

Serial

82-948 (20948) TJ y
82-949 (20949) TJ y
82-952 (20952) TJ y
82-954 (20954) TJ r
82-955 (20955) TJ y
82-957 (20957) TJ y
82-959 (20959) TJ y
82-962 (20962) TJ y
82-964 (20964) TJ y
82-965 (20965) TJ y
82-968 (20968) TJ y
82-970 (20970) TJ y
82-975 (20975) TJ y
82-977 (20977) TJ y
82-980 (20980) TJ y
82-981 (20981) TJ y
82-982 (20982) TJ bl
82-986 (20986) TJ bl
82-988 (20988) TJ bl
82-991 (20991) TJ bl
82-993 (20993) TJ bl
82-996 (20996) TJ bl
82-998 (20998) TJ bl
82-999 (20999) TJ r
83-066 (31066) TJ bl
83-067 (31067) TJ bl
83-068 (31068) TJ bl
83-069 (31069) TJ bl
83-071 (31071) TJ y
83-074 (31074) TJ y
83-079 (31079) TJ y
83-166 (31166)‡ TJ y
83-167 (31167)‡ TJ y
83-168 (31168)‡ TJ bl
83-169 (31169)‡ TJ bl

General Dynamics F-16C/F-16D‡
(RS: 86TFW Ramstein)
84-238 (41238) RS
84-239 (41239) RS
84-240 (41240) RS
84-266 (41266) RS
84-267 (41267) RS
84-323 (41323)‡ RS
84-324 (41324)‡ RS

Gates C-21A Learjet
(*58MAS Ramstein
†7005ABS Stuttgart)
FY84
40081†
40082†
40083†
40084*
40085*
40086*

Shorts C-23A Sherpa
(322MAW/10MAS Zweibrucken)
FY83
30512 *Zweibrucken*
30513 *Ramstein*
FY84
40458 *Sembach*
40459 *Spangdahlem*
40460 *Hahn*
40461 *Rhein Main*
40462
Mildenhall/ Lakenheath

Serial

40463 *Bitburg*
40464 *Zaragosa*
40465 *Alconbury*
40466 *Bentwaters/ Woodbridge*
40467 *Upper Heyford*
40468 *Greenham Common*
40469 *Soesterberg*
40470 *Torrejon*
40471 *Wiesbaden*
40472 *Aviano*
40473

North American T-39A/CT-39A
(†1868FCS Rhein Main
‡7005ABS Stuttgart)
10684 (FY61)‡
24453 (FY62)†

Cessna T-41 Mescalero
FY65
55186 (N5186F) Spangdahlem
55187 (N5187F) Torrejon
55188 (N5188F) Ramstein

Sikorsky CH-53C
(601TCW Sembach)
01625 (FY70)
01626 (FY70)
01629 (FY70)
01630 (FY70)
10924 (FY68)
10928 (FY68)
10930 (FY68)
10932 (FY68)

Lockheed C-130E Hercules
(435TAW Rhein Main: 37TAS; *7405 OS)
01260 (FY70)
01264 (FY70)
01271 (FY70)
01274 (FY70)
10935 (FY68)
10938 (FY68)
10943 (FY68)
10946 (FY68)
10947 (FY68)
17681 (FY64)
18240 (FY64)
21819 (FY62)*
21822 (FY62)*
21828 (FY62)*
37885 (FY63)
40502 (FY64)
40527 (FY64)
40550 (FY64)
96566 (FY69)
96582 (FY69)
96583 (FY69)

Serial

Lockheed MC-130E Hercules
(7SOS Rhein Main)
40523 (FY64)
40551 (FY64)
40555 (FY64)
40561 (FY64)
40566 (FY64)

Serial

Lockheed VC-140B Jetstar
(58MAS Ramstein)
12489 (FY61)
12491 (FY61)
24198 (FY62)
24200 (FY62)
24201 (FY62)

Serial

European based US Army Aircraft

Bell AH-1S (FM) Cobra
2nd Armoured Cavalry Regiment: Feucht
11th Armoured Cavalry Regiment: Fulda
3rd Aviation Battalion (Combat), 'B' Co: Giebelstadt
3rd Aviation Battalion (Combat), 'C' Co: Schweinfurt
8th Aviation Battalion (Combat), 'B' Co: Mainz-Finthen
8th Aviation Battalion (Combat), 'C' Co: Mainz-Finthen
501st Aviation Battalion (Combat), 'B' Co: Ansbach
501st Aviation Battalion (Combat), 'C' Co: Illesheim
503rd Aviation Battalion (Combat), 'B' Co: Hanau
503rd Aviation Battalion (Combat), 'C' Co: Hanau

FY68
15007 8 B Co
15015 3 C Co
15036 503 C Co
15038 501 B Co
15046 501 B Co
15057 501 C Co
15069 501 B Co
15084 503 B Co
15085 2 ACR
15092 503 B Co
15093 8 B Co
15104 503 C Co
15105 2 ACR
15106 3 B Co
15110 503 B Co
15112 501 C Co
15113 503 C Co
15116 2 ACR
15131 8 C Co
15134 501 B Co
15142 11 ACR
15152 501 B Co
15167 501 B Co
15173 501 B Co
15180 503 B Co
15208 503 C Co

FY66
15249 503 B Co
15250 2 ACR
15252 11 ACR
15254 2 ACR
15261 2 ACR
15263 8 B Co
15264 3 B Co
15266 2 ACR
15273 11 ACR
15275 503 C Co
15286 2 ACR
15289 8 B Co
15290 2 ACR
15292 8 C Co
15293 501 C Co
15295 2 ACR
15315 503 B Co
15316 3 C Co
15321 8 C Co
15322 501 B Co
15324 501 C Co
15328 503 B Co
15335 11 ACR
15348 3 C Co
15350 3 C Co
15356 11 ACR

FY67
15450 2 ACR
15452 8 C Co
15455 2 ACR
15456 501 C Co
15457 503 C Co
15459 2 ACR
15460 8 B Co
15470 11 ACR
15473 11 ACR
15475 11 ACR
15477 3 C Co
15479 3 B Co
15480 503 B Co
15489 8 B Co
15490 503 B Co
15491 8 C Co
15497 2 ACR
15506 3 B Co
15508 501 C Co
15512 3 B Co
15520 501 C Co
15522 3 B Co
15528 3 B Co
15530 3 B Co
15535 3 C Co
15540 8 C Co
15548 3 B Co
15551 501 C Co
15565 3 C Co
15571 8 B Co
15572 11 ACR
15587 501 C Co
15593 11 ACR
15610 2 ACR
15613 8 C Co
15614 8 B Co
15617 503 B Co
15621 2 ACR
15624 501 B Co
15633 501 C Co
15642 8 C Co
15643 2 ACR
15650 503 B Co
15652 503 B Co
15658 11 ACR
15659 2 ACR
15662 11 ACR
15664 3 C Co
15665 8 C Co
15666 11 ACR
15675 11 ACR
15679 8 C Co
15682 8 B Co
15683 501 B Co
15701 2 ACR
15710 503 B Co
15716 503 C Co
15717 3 B Co
15721 3 C Co
15736 3 C Co
15741 503 C Co
15745 8 B Co
15757 503 C Co
15762 501 B Co
15764 3 B Co
15769 8 C Co
15771 503 B Co
15772 8 B Co
15775 503 C Co
15776 503 C Co
15784 8 B Co
15789 501 C Co
15790 3 C Co
15805 501 B Co
15815 501 B Co
15822 2 ACR
15829 501 C Co
15833 8 C Co

Serial
15842 501 B Co
15852 503 C Co
15860 8 C Co
15863 3 C Co

FY70
15947 501 C Co
15950 501 C Co
15951 503 C Co
15952 11 ACR
15958 11 ACR
15959 8 C Co
15961 8 C Co
15970 3 B Co
15971 3 C Co
15995 2 ACR
16012 3 C Co
16016 3 C Co
16048 3 C Co
16054 501 B Co
16091 501 B Co

FY69
16411 3 C Co
16422 501 B Co
16426 501 B Co
16429 3 B Co
16431 3 B Co
16432 503 B Co
16433 8 B Co
16434 503 B Co
16436 503 C Co
16445 8 B Co

FY68
17023 503 C Co
17028 503 B Co
17047 11 ACR
17049 8 B Co
17062 503 C Co
17063 503 B Co
17066 501 C Co
17067 501 C Co
17070 501 C Co
17074 503 C Co
17076 501 B Co
17078 8 B Co
17079 503 B Co
17082 503 C Co
17085 503 C Co
17087 501 C Co
17088 11 ACR
17092 503 B Co
17095 8 C Co
17100 501 B Co
17101 503 C Co
17104 501 B Co
17105 501 C Co
17108 501 C Co
17111 8 C Co
17112 503 B Co

FY71
20998 11 ACR
21014 503 C Co
21028 503 C Co
21035 2 ACR

FY78
23118 3 B Co

FY79
23189 3 B Co
23190 3 B Co

Serial
23194 3 B Co
23199 3 C Co
23200 3 C Co
23235 3 C Co

FY81
23526 11 ACR
23527 11 ACR
23528 8 C Co
23529 8 C Co
23530 8 C Co
23531 8 B Co
23532 8 C Co
23533 8 B Co
23534 8 B Co
23535 8 B Co
23536 8 B Co
23537 3 B Co
23538 3 B Co
23539 3 C Co
23540 3 B Co

Grumman V-1 Mohawk
(*OV-1B; ‡OV-1C, †OV-1D, §RV-1D)
73CIC, Stuttgart
14239 (FY64)*
14244 (FY64)*
14246 (FY64)*
14247 (FY64)*
14248 (FY64)*
14256 (FY64)*
14258 (FY64)*
14261 (FY64)*
14268 (FY64)*
14269 (FY64)*
14270 (FY64)*
15930 (FY68)†
15938 (FY68)†
15940 (FY68)†
15951 (FY68)†
16996 (FY68)†
17004 (FY69)†
17007 (FY69)†
17008 (FY69)†
18898 (FY67)‡
18899 (FY67)‡
18905 (FY67)‡
18909 (FY67)‡
18919 (FY67)‡
18921 (FY67)‡
25886 (FY62)*
25891 (FY62)§
25897 (FY62)§

Beech C-12A Super King Air
($=C-12C, @=RC-12D)
(* 25AvCo, Stuttgart;
† HQ/USEUCOM;
‡ 56AvCo, Vicenza
§ 207AvCo
**1MIB, Wiesbaden
††2MIB/330 ASACo, Stuttgart)
22253 (FY73)*
22254 (FY73)§
22255 (FY73)†
22260 (FY73)‡
22261 (FY73)†
22262 (FY73)§
22556 (FY76)‡
22557 (FY76)§

Serial
22558 (FY76)†
22564 (FY76)‡
22931 (FY77)†
22944 (FY77)‡
22950 (FY77)§
23126$ (FY78)§
23127$ (FY78)§
23128$ (FY78)§
23132$ (FY78)
23141@ (FY78)**
23142@ (FY78)**
23143@ (FY78)**
23144@ (FY78)††
23371@ (FY80)††
23373@ (FY80)††
23374@ (FY80)††
23375@ (FY80)**
23376@ (FY80)††
23377@ (FY80)**
23378@ (FY80)††
23542@ (FY81)**

Beech U-21A King Air
(* EU-21A; 7th Signals Bgde)
18000 (FY66)*
18010 (FY66) Berlin Bgd
18013 (FY66)*
18014 (FY66) 56th AvCo
18019 (FY66) 56th AvCo
18025 (FY66) 56th AvCo
18027 (FY66)*
18037 (FY66)
18040 (FY66)
18048 (FY67)
18049 (FY67) 14th AvCo
18050 (FY67)
18058 (FY67) 5th Corps
18078 (FY67) 7th Corps
18080 (FY67) 56th AvCo
18116 (FY67) 56th AvCo

Boeing-Vertol CH-47C Chinook
(* 180AvCo, Schwabisch Hall;
† 205AvCo, Mainz-Finthen;
‡ 295AvCo, Coleman Barracks)
15002 (FY70)*
15005 (FY70)†
15007 (FY70)†
15012 (FY70)‡
15020 (FY70)*
15028 (FY70)†
15029 (FY70)†
15030 (FY70)†
15032 (FY70)†
15829 (FY68)‡
15831 (FY68)‡
15838 (FY68)†
15846 (FY68)*
15847 (FY68)†
15849 (FY68)‡
15851 (FY68)†
15856 (FY68)*
15865 (FY68)*
15867 (FY68)*
15868 (FY68)*
15990 (FY68)‡
15995 (FY68)*
15997 (FY68)*
16005 (FY68)†

Serial

16006 (FY68)*
16008 (FY68)‡
16009 (FY68)†
17106 (FY69)†
17114 (FY69)‡
17116 (FY69)*
17117 (FY69)‡
17118 (FY69)*
17126 (FY69)†
18516 (FY67)‡
18531 (FY67)†
18533 (FY67)‡
18540 (FY67)*
18548 (FY67)*
20946 (FY71)†
20950 (FY71)†
20951 (FY71)†
20952 (FY71)†
20953 (FY71)†
20954 (FY71)‡
22277 (FY74)†
22281 (FY74)*
22283 (FY74)‡
22284 (FY74)‡
22285 (FY74)†
22286 (FY74)†
22291 (FY74)‡
22293 (FY74)‡
22676 (FY76)†
22677 (FY76)‡
22678 (FY76)‡
22679 (FY76)‡
22681 (FY76)*
22683 (FY76)*
22684 (FY76)*
23394 (FY79)*
23395 (FY79)†
23396 (FY79)*
23398 (FY79)‡
24734 (FY85)
24735 (FY85)
24736 (FY85)
24737 (FY85)
24739 (FY85)
24740 (FY85)
24742 (FY85)

Sikorsky UH-60A Blackhawk

3rd Aviation Battalion (Combat), 'D' Co and 'E' Co: Giebelstadt
8th Aviation Battalion (Combat), 'D' Co: Mainz-Finthen
8th Aviation Battalion (Combat), 'E' Co: Wiesbaden
48th Aviation Co: Wiesbaden
203rd Aviation Co: Wertheim
205th AVIM Battalion: Hanau
207th Aviation Co: Heidelburg
394th AVIM Battalion: Nellingen
421st Medical Co, 1st Platoon: Wiesbaden
421st Medical Co, 2nd Platoon: Schweinfurt
421st Medical Co, 3rd Platoon: Wiesbaden
421st Medical Co, 4th Platoon: Darmstadt
501st Aviation Battalion (Combat), 'D' Co and 'E' Co: Ansbach
503rd Aviation Battalion (Combat), 'D' Co and 'E' Co: Hanau

Serial

FY80
23425 3 E Co
23427 3 E Co
23428 3 E Co
23431 3 E Co
23432 3 E Co
23433 3 E Co
23436 3 E Co
23438 3 E Co
23439 3 E Co
23440 3 E Co
23441 3 E Co
23442 3 E Co
23443 3 E Co
23489 394
23490 394

FY81
23568 205
23571 3 E Co
23572 205
23573 205
23575 48
23578 48
23579 48
23580 48
23581 503 E Co
23582 48
23583 503 E Co
23584 503 E Co
23585 503 E Co
23586 503 E Co
23587 48
23588 48
23589 48
23590 48
23591 48
23592 48
23593 48
23594 501 E Co
23595 501 E Co
23596 48
23597 48
23598 48
23599 48
23602 503 E Co
23603 503 E Co
23604 503 E Co
23605 503 E Co
23606 503 E Co
23607 8 E Co
23608 501 E Co
23609 503 E Co
23610 503 E Co
23613 501 E Co
23614 503 E Co
23615 503 E Co
23616 8 E Co
23617 503 D Co
23618 503 E Co
23622 8 E Co
23623 8 D Co
23624 8 E Co
23625 8 E Co
23626 8 E Co

Serial

FY82
23660 501 E Co
23661 501 E Co
23662 501 E Co
23663 501 E Co
23664 501 E Co
23665 8 E Co
23666 8 E Co
23667 8 E Co
23668 8 E Co
23669 8 E Co
23672 203
23673 203
23674 203
23675 421 4 Pl
23676 421 2 Pl
23682 8 E Co
23683 8 E Co
23684 8 E Co
23685 8 E Co
23686 8 E Co
23690 501 E Co
23691 501 E Co
23692 501 E Co
23693 501 E Co
23694 501 E Co
23695 203
23696 203
23697 203
23698 203
23699 203
23700 —
23701 207
23702 207
23703 203
23704 203
23705 203
23706 203
23707 203
23721 203
23722 203
23723 421 4 Pl
23726 421 4
23727 421 4
23729 421 2 Pl
23730 421 2 Pl
23731 —
23733 421 4 Pl
23735 421
23736 —
23737 421 4 Pl
23738 421 2 Pl
23739 421 4 Pl
23740 —
23741 421 2 Pl
23743 421 2 Pl
23744 501 D Co
23745 394
23746 421 2 Pl
23749 421
23750 421
23751 421
23752 421
23753 421
23754 421
23755 421
23756 421

European based US Navy Aircraft

Serial

Grumman C-1A Trader
(VR-24 Sigonella)
136756 [JM46]
136757 [JM45]
146025 [JM41]
146028 [JM42]
146034 [JM43]
146049 [JM44]
146051 [JM51]

Grumman C-2A Greyhound
(VR-24 Sigonella)
148148 [JM20)
155123 [JM25]
155124 [JM24]
162142 [JM22]
162143 [JM23]
162144 [JM24]
162145 [JM25]

Serial

Douglas EA-3B Skywarrior
(VQ-2 Rota)
144850 [JQ12]
144852 [JQ18]
146448 [JQ14]
146453 [JQ15]
146454 [JQ16]
146455 [JQ17]

Beech UC-12B Super King Air
(8C) NAF Sigonella;
(8D) NAF Rota
1197 [8D] (161197)
1323 [8C] (161323)
1517 [8D] (161517)

Serial

NA CT-39G Sabreliner
(VR-24 Sigonella)
159361 [JM30]
159362 [JM31]
159363 [JM32]

Sikorsky RH-53D Sea Stallion
(VR-24 Sigonella)
158690 [JM50]
158691 [JM51]

Lockheed C-130F Hercules
(VR-22: Rota)
149790 [JL790]
149794 [JL794]
149797 [JL797]
149801 [JL801]

US based USAF Aircraft

The following aircraft are normally based in the USA but are likely to be seen visiting the UK from time to time. They are listed in numerical progression by the serial actually carried on the aircraft externally. Fiscal year information is provided, together with details of mark variations and in some cases operating units. The types are also in numerical order, commencing with the E-**3**B and concluding with the C-**141**B.

Serial/Wing

Boeing E-3B/C Sentry
(552AW&CW)
(bk: 963AW&CS)
00137 (FY80) C
00138 (FY80) C
00139 (FY80) C
10004 (FY81) C
10005 (FY81) C
11407 (FY71) B bk
11408 (FY71) B
20006 (FY82) C
20007 (FY82) C
30008 (FY83) C
30009 (FY83) C
31674 (FY73) C
(Boeing)
31675 (FY73) B
50556 (FY75) B r
50557 (FY75) B
50558 (FY75) B
50559 (FY75) B
50560 (FY75) B bk
61604 (FY76) B
61605 (FY76) B r
61606 (FY76) B
61607 (FY76) B
70351 (FY77) B bk
70352 (FY77) B
70353 (FY77) B
70354 (FY77) B
70355 (FY77) B
70356 (FY77) B
80576 (FY78) B
80577 (FY78) B r
80578 (FY78) B bk
90001 (FY79) B
90002 (FY79) B
90003 (FY79) B r

Boeing E-4B
(1ACCS)
31676 (FY73)
31677 (FY73)
40787 (FY74)
50125 (FY75)

Boeing B-52G Stratofortress

FY57

Serial	Wing
76468	2 BW
76469	93 BW
76470	2 BW
76471	2 BW
76472	93 BW
76473	93 BW
76474	379 BW
76475	92 BW
76476	32 BW
76477	32 BW
76478	32 BW
76479	93 BW
76480	93 BW
76483	93 BW
76484	93 BW
76485	93 BW
76486	93 BW
76487	93 BW
76488	42 BW
76489	32 BW
76490	93 BW
76491	2 BW
76492	93 BW
76494	
76495	93 BW
76497	379 BW
76498	416 BW
76499	92 BW
76500	92 BW
76501	416 BW
76502	93 BW
76503	93 BW
76504	93 BW
76505	42 BW
76506	42 BW
76508	416 BW
76509	97 BW
76510	32 BW
76511	97 BW
76512	93 BW
76513	97 BW
76514	42 BW
76515	93 BW
76516	416 BW
76517	93 BW
76518	93 BW
76519	2 BW
76520	2 BW

FY58

Serial	Wing
80158	93 BW
80159	32 BW
80160	93 BW
80162	42 BW
80163	93 BW
80164	93 BW
80165	379 BW
80166	93 BW
80167	32 BW
80168	92 BW
80170	32 BW
80171	93 BW
80172	97 BW
80173	379 BW
80175	92 BW
80176	32 BW
80177	32 BW
80178	32 BW
80179	379 BW
80181	92 BW
80182	379 BW
80183	93 BW
80184	92 BW
80185	93 BW
80186	97 BW
80189	32 BW
80190	32 BW
80191	93 BW
80192	2 BW
80193	93 BW
80194	92 BW
80195	93 BW
80197	416 BW
80199	97 BW
80200	97 BW
80202	32 BW
80203	93 BW
80204	6512 TS
80205	2 BW
80206	93 BW
80207	42 BW
80210	93 BW
80211	97 BW
80212	42 BW
80213	32 BW
80214	93 BW
80216	2 BW
80217	379 BW
80218	416 BW
80219	2 BW
80220	93 BW
80221	2 BW
80222	93 BW
80223	93 BW
80224	97 BW
80225	2 BW
80226	379 BW
80227	92 BW
80229	92 BW
80230	93 BW
80231	416 BW
80232	92 BW
80233	93 BW
80234	379 BW
80235	42 BW
80236	379 BW
80237	379 BW

Serial/Wing

80238	416 BW
80239	32 BW
80240	416 BW
80241	93 BW
80242	2 BW
80243	93 BW
80244	379 BW
80245	6512 TS
80247	93 BW
80248	93 BW
80249	32 BW
80250	2 BW
80251	379 BW
80252	97 BW
80253	2 BW
80254	93 BW
80255	32 BW
80257	32 BW
80258	2 BW

FY59

92564	93 BW
92565	2 BW
92566	416 BW
92567	416 BW
92568	416 BW
92569	93 BW
92570	93 BW
92571	93 BW
92572	416 BW
92573	32 BW
92575	93 BW
92577	2 BW
92578	97 BW
92579	2 BW
92580	97 BW
92581	93 BW
92582	2 BW
92583	93 BW
92584	92 BW
92585	379 BW
92586	416 BW
92587	93 BW
92588	2 BW
92589	379 BW
92590	97 BW
92591	93 BW
92592	32 BW
92593	92 BW
92594	2 BW
92595	2 BW
92596	2 BW
92597	416 BW
92598	2 BW
92599	2 BW
92601	416 BW
92602	97 BW

Boeing B-52H Stratofortress

FY60

00001	5 BW
00002	7 BW
00003	5 BW
00004	7 BW
00005	7 BW
00007	7 BW
00008	5 BW
00009	410 BW
00010	96 BW
00011	5 BW
00012	28 BW
00013	7 BW
00014	7 BW
00015	7 BW
00016	410 BW
00017	7 BW
00018	96 BW
00019	7 BW
00020	319 BW
00021	28 BW
00022	96 BW
00023	410 BW
00024	7 BW
00025	7 BW
00026	28 BW
00028	96 BW
00029	96 BW
00030	28 BW
00031	410 BW
00032	5 BW
00033	7 BW
00034	28 BW
00035	319 BW
00036	5 BW
00037	410 BW
00038	28 BW
00040	5 BW
00041	410 BW
00042	28 BW
00043	319 BW
00044	410 BW
00045	7 BW
00046	7 BW
00047	319 BW
00048	28 BW
00049	96 BW
00050	28 BW
00051	7 BW
00052	7 BW
00053	319 BW
00054	28 BW
00055	96 BW
00056	5 BW
00057	7 BW
00058	7 BW
00059	319 BW
00060	5 BW
00061	7 BW
00062	96 BW

FY61

10001	410 BW
10002	410 BW
10003	7 BW
10004	28 BW
10005	96 BW
10006	410 BW
10007	410 BW
10008	410 BW
10009	96 BW
10010	319 BW
10011	5 BW
10012	7 BW
10013	5 BW
10014	7 BW
10015	7 BW
10016	7 BW
10017	96 BW
10018	7 BW
10019	319 BW
10020	96 BW
10021	28 BW
10022	96 BW
10023	7 BW
10024	7 BW
10025	7 BW
10026	5 BW
10027	96 BW
10028	410 BW
10029	5 BW
10030	
10031	96 BW
10032	96 BW
10034	7 BW
10035	7 BW
10036	410 BW
10037	
10038	96 BW
10039	96 BW
10040	410 BW

Lockheed C-5A Galaxy

(60 MAW: Travis AFB, California
433 MAW/68 TAS AFRES, Kelly AFB, Texas
436 MAW: Dover AFB, Delaware
443 MAW: Altus AFB, Oklahoma)

FY70

00445	436 MAW
00446	60 MAW
00447	436 MAW
00448	436 MAW
00449	60 MAW
00450	60 MAW
00451	60 MAW
00452	436 MAW
00453	60 MAW
00454	436 MAW
00455	436 MAW
00456	436 MAW
00457	60 MAW
00458	60 MAW
00459	60 MAW
00460	436 MAW
00461	60 MAW
00462	443 MAW
00463	436 MAW
00464	436 MAW
00465	436 MAW
00466	443 MAW
00467	443 MAW

FY66

68304	436 MAW
68305	60 MAW
68306	60 MAW
68307	436 MAW

FY67

70167	60 MAW
70168	436 MAW
70169	60 MAW

Serial/Wing

70170 105 MAG
70171 60 MAW
70173 436 MAW
70174 60 MAW

FY68
80211 60 MAW
80212 436 MAW
80213 60 MAW
80214 436 MAW
80215 436 MAW
80216 60 MAW
80217 436 MAW
80219 60 MAW
80220 436 MAW
80221 60 MAW
80222 436 MAW
80223 60 MAW
80224 436 MAW
80225 436 MAW
80226 60 MAW
80228 60 MAW

FY69
90001 60 MAW
90002† 433 MAW
90003 436 MAW
90004 436 MAW
90005 60 MAW
90006 436 MAW
90007 436 MAW
90008 60 MAW
90009 60 MAW
90010 60 MAW
90011 60 MAW
90012 60 MAW
90013 60 MAW
90014 443 MAW
90015* 137 MAS
90016† 433 MAW/ 68 TAS
90017 436 MAW
90018 60 MAW
90019 436 MAW
90020 60 MAW
90021 436 MAW
90022 60 MAW
90023 60 MAW
90024 60 MAW
90025 60 MAW
90026 436 MAW
90027 436 MAW

Lockheed C-5B Galaxy
31285 (FY85)
4 (FY84)

Lockheed SR-71A
(9SRW/99SRS)
(No 4 Detachment: RAF Mildenhall)

FY64
17950
17952
17953
17956
17957
17958
17959
17960
17961
17962
17963
17964
17967
17968
17969
17970
17971
17972
17974
17975
17976
17979
17980
17981

Boeing EC-18B
(Air Force Systems Command)

FY81
10891
10892
10893
10894
10895
10896
10897
10898

Grumman C-20A Gulfstream III
(89 MAW)

FY83
30500
30501
30502

McDonnell-Douglas KC-10A Extender
(2 BW* 22 ARW† 68 ARG‡)
20190 (FY82)*
20191 (FY82)†
20192 (FY82)*
20193 (FY82)†
30075 (FY83)*
30076 (FY83)†
30077 (FY83)*
30078 (FY83)†
30079 (FY83)*
30080 (FY83)†
30081 (FY83)*
30082 (FY83)†
40185 (FY84)†
40186 (FY84)*
40187 (FY84)†
40188 (FY84)
40189 (FY84)†
40190 (FY84)*
40191 (FY84)†
40192 (FY84)
50027 (FY85)†
50028 (FY85)*
50029 (FY85)
50030 (FY85)
50031 (FY85)
50032 (FY85)
50033 (FY85)
50034 (FY85)
50035 (FY85)
50036 (FY85)
50037 (FY85)
90433 (FY79)*
90434 (FY79)*
91710 (FY79)*
91711 (FY79)*
91712 (FY79)*
91713 (FY79)*
91946 (FY79)†
91947 (FY79)*
91948 (FY79)†
91949 (FY79)†
91950 (FY79)†
91951 (FY79)†

Lockheed C-130E/ DC-130E@/ EC-130E$/ WC-130E‡/ MC-130E§ Hercules
(*ANG, Air National Guard;
†AFRES, Air Force Reserve)

FY70
01259 317 TAW
01260 435 TAW
01261 317 TAW
01262 317 TAW
01263 317 TAW
01264 435 TAW
01265 317 TAW
01266 317 TAW
01267 317 TAW
01268 317 TAW
01269 317 TAW
01270 317 TAW
01271 435 TAW
01272 317 TAW
01273 317 TAW
01274 435 TAW
01275 317 TAW
01276 317 TAW

FY68
10934 317 TAW
10935 435 TAW
10937 317 TAW
10938 435 TAW
10939 317 TAW
10940 317 TAW
10941 317 TAW
10942 317 TAW
10943 435 TAW
10945 317 TAW
10946 435 TAW
10947 435 TAW
10948 314 TAW
10949 314 TAW
10950 314 TAW

FY61
12358* 115 TAS
12359* 115 TAS

Serial/Wing	
12360‡	54 WRS
12361	314 TAW
12362	314 TAW
12363	314 TAW
12364@	314 TAW
12365‡	53 WRS
12366‡	54 WRS
12367*	115 TAS
12368	314 TAW
12369	314 TAW
12370*	115 TAS
12371	314 TAW
12372*	115 TAS
12373*	115 TAS
FY64	
17680	314 TAW
17681	435 TAW
18240	435 TAW
FY72	
21288	374 TAW
21289	374 TAW
21290	374 TAW
21291	314 TAW
21292	314 TAW
21293	314 TAW
21294	314 TAW
21295	314 TAW
21296	314 TAW
21298	314 TAW
21299	374 TAW
FY62	
21784*	130 TAS
21786*	109 TAS
21787*	130 TAS
21788*	130 TAS
21789†	337 TAS
21790*	130 TAS
21792*	115 TAS
21793*	115 TAS
21794†	337 TAS
21795*	130 TAS
21798*	130 TAS
21799*	115 TAS
21801*	115 TAS
21803†	337 TAS
21804*	130 TAS
21806†	756 TAS
21807†	337 TAS
21808†	337 TAS
21810†	337 TAS
21811*	115 TAS
21812*	109 TAS
21816†	337 TAS
21817*	109 TAS
21820†	337 TAS
21821	314 TAW
21822	7405 OS
21823†	337 TAS
21824*	130 TAS
21826*	115 TAS
21827	314 TAW
21829*	109 TAS
21830†	337 TAS
21833*	115 TAS
21834†	756 TAS
21835†	756 TAS
21837*	109 TAS
21838†	337 TAS

Serial/Wing	
21839†	756 TAS
21842*	115 TAS
21844†	756 TAS
21846*	109 TAS
21847†	756 TAS
21848†	756 TAS
21849†	337 TAS
21850†	337 TAS
21851*	115 TAS
21852†	756 TAS
21855	314 TAW
21856*	109 TAS
21858†	337 TAS
21859	374 TAW
21860†	337 TAS
21862*	115 TAS
21864*	109 TAS
21866†	337 TAS
FY63	
37764†	357 TAS
37765	314 TAW
37767	314 TAW
37768	314 TAW
37769	314 TAW
37770†	357 TAS
37771	314 TAW
37773$	193 ECS [PA]
37776	317 TAW
37777	374 TAW
37778	314 TAW
37779	17 TAS
37781	314 TAW
37782	62 MAW
37783$	193 ECS [PA]
37784	62 MAW
37786	314 TAW
37788	62 MAW
37790	314 TAW
37791	314 TAW
37792	62 MAW
37793	314 TAW
37794	314 TAW
37795	314 TAW
37796	314 TAW
37799	314 TAW
37800	374 TAW
37803	374 TAW
37804	17 TAS
37805†	357 TAS
37806	314 TAW
37807	435 TAW
37808	314 TAW
37809	317 TAW
37811	374 TAW
37812	374 TAW
37813	317 TAW
37814	62 MAW
37815$	193 ECS [PA]
37816$	193 ECS [PA]
37817†	357 TAS
37818	17 TAS
37819	374 TAW
37820	314 TAW
37821	317 TAW
37822†	357 TAS
37823	317 TAS
37824	374 TAW
37825	374 TAW
37826†	327 TAS
37828$	193 ECS [PA]

Serial/Wing	
37829	17 TAS
37830	17 TAS
37831	17 TAS
37832†	327 TAS
37833†	327 TAS
37834†	327 TAS
37835	314 TAW
37836	314 TAW
37837	17 TAS
37838	314 TAW
37839	314 TAW
37840	374 TAW
37841	314 TAW
37842	62 MAW
37845	317 TAW
37846	17 TAS
37847	317 TAW
37848†	327 TAS
37849	317 TAW
37850	314 TAS
37851	17 TAS
37852†	357 TAS
37853†	327 TAS
37854	62 MAW
37856†	357 TAS
37857	314 TAW
37858	36 TAS
37859	374 TAW
37860	314 TAW
37861	314 TAW
37863†	357 TAS
37864	314 TAW
37865	374 TAW
37866	314 TAW
37867†	327 TAS
37868	374 TAW
37869$	193 ECS [PA]
37871	317 TAW
37872	17 TAS
37874	62 MAW
37876	314 TAW
37877	374 TAW
37879	374 TAW
37880	62 MAW
37881	374 TAW
37882	314 TAW
37883†	327 TAS
37884	317 TAW
37885	435 TAW
37887	314 TAW
37888	314 TAW
37889	314 TAW
37890	317 TAW
37891	62 MAW
37892†	327 TAS
37893	62 MAW
37894	314 TAW
37895	374 TAW
37896	314 TAW
37897	374 TAW
37898	314 TAW
37899	317 TAW
39810	317 TAW
39811	314 TAW
39812	314 TAW
39813	314 TAW
39814	314 TAW
39815	314 TAW
39816$	193 ECS [PA]
39817$	193 ECS [PA]

Serial/Wing

FY64
40495 317 TAW
40496 317 TAW
40497 374 TAW
40498 317 TAW
40499 317 TAW
40500 17 TAS
40501 317 TAW
40502 435 TAW
40503 374 TAW
40504 317 TAW
40510 62 MAW
40512 62 MAW
40513 314 TAW
40514 374 TAW
40515 374 TAW
40517 317 TAW
40518 374 TAW
40519 62 MAW
40520 374 TAW
40521 62 MAW
40523§ 7 SOS
40524 62 MAW
40525 317 TAW
40526 317 TAW
40527 435 TAW
40529 317 TAW
40530 314 TAW
40531 317 TAW
40533 314 TAW
40534 374 TAW
40535 314 TAW
40537 317 TAW
40538 314 TAW
40540 317 TAW
40541 317 TAW
40542 317 TAW
40544 374 TAW
40549 314 TAW
40550 435 TAW
40551§ 7 SOS
40552† 54 WRS
40553† 54 WRS
40554† 54 WRS
40555§ 7 SOS
40556 374 TAW
40557 314 TAW
40560 314 TAW
40561§ 7 SOS
40566§ 7 SOS
40569 314 TAW
40570 317 TAW

FY69
96566 435 TAW
96579 314 TAW
96580 317 TAW
96582 435 TAW
96583 435 TAW

Lockheed C-130H$/WC-130H‡/MC-130H§ Hercules
(*ANG, Air National Guard
†AFRES, Air Force Reserve)

FY80
00320* 158 TAS
00321* 158 TAS
00322* 158 TAS
00323* 158 TAS
00324* 158 TAS
00325* 158 TAS
00326* 158 TAS
00332* 158 TAS

FY81
10626† 700 TAS
10627† 700 TAS
10628† 700 TAS
10629† 700 TAS
10630† 700 TAS
10631† 700 TAS

FY64
14861‡ 54 WRS
14866‡ 920 WRG

FY82
20054* 144 TAS
20055* 144 TAS
20056* 144 TAS
20057* 144 TAS
20058* 144 TAS
20059* 144 TAS
20060* 144 TAS
20061* 144 TAS

FY83
30483* 139 TAS
30486* 139 TAS
30487* 139 TAS
30488* 139 TAS
30489* 139 TAS
30490* 139 TAS
30491* 139 TAS
30492* 139 TAS
30493* 139 TAS
31212§

FY73
31580 314 TAW
31581$ 41 ECS [DM]
31582 374 TAW
31583$ 41 ECS [DM]
31584$ 41 ECS [DM]
31585$ 41 ECS [DM]
31586$ 41 ECS [DM]
31587$ 41 ECS [DM]
31588$ 41 ECS [DM]
31590 314 TAW
31592 41 ECS [DM]
31594$ 41 ECS [DM]
31595$ 41 ECS [DM]
31597 374 TAW
31598 374 TAW

FY84
40204
40205
40206
40207
40208
40209
40210
40211
40212
40213
40275
40276

FY74
41658 463 TAW
41659 463 TAW
41660 463 TAW
41661 463 TAW
41662 463 TAW
41663 463 TAW
41664 463 TAW
41665 463 TAW
41666 463 TAW
41667 463 TAW
41668 463 TAW
41669 463 TAW
41670 463 TAW
41671 463 TAW
41673 463 TAW
41674 463 TAW
41675 463 TAW
41676 463 TAW
41677 463 TAW
41679 463 TAW
41680 463 TAW
41681 463 TAW
41682 463 TAW
41684 463 TAW
41685 463 TAW
41687 463 TAW
41688 463 TAW
41689 463 TAW
41690 463 TAW
41691 463 TAW
41692 463 TAW
42061 463 TAW
42062 463 TAW
42063 463 TAW
42065 463 TAW
42066 463 TAW
42067 463 TAW
42069 463 TAW
42070 463 TAW
42071 463 TAW
42072 463 TAW
42130 463 TAW
42131 463 TAW
42132 463 TAW
42133 463 TAW
42134 463 TAW

FY85
50011
50012

FY65
50963‡ 54 WRS
50964‡† 920 WRG
50966‡ 54 WRS
50967‡† 920 WRG
50968‡ 54 WRS
50969‡† 920 WRG
50972‡† 920 WRG
50976‡ 54 WRS
50977‡† 920 WRG
50980‡† 920 WRG
50984‡ 54 WRS
50985‡ 54 WRS

FY78
80806* 185 TAS
80807* 185 TAS
80808* 185 TAS
80809* 185 TAS

Serial/Type/Wing		
80810*	185 TAS	
80811*	185 TAS	
80812*	185 TAS	
80813*	185 TAS	

FY79

90473*	183 TAS	
90474*	183 TAS	
90475*	183 TAS	
90476*	183 TAS	
90477*	183 TAS	
90478*	183 TAS	
90479*	183 TAS	
90480*	183 TAS	

Boeing C-135 Stratotanker
(*ANG, Air National Guard;
†AFRES, Air Force Reserve)

FY60

00313	KC-135A	410 BW
00314	KC-135A	410 BW
00315	KC-135A	320 BW
00316	KC-135A	93 BW
00317	KC-135A	93 BW
00318	KC-135A	416 BW
00319	KC-135A	320 BW
00320	KC-135A	7 BW
00321	KC-135A	379 BW
00322	KC-135A	410 BW
00323	KC-135A	28 BW
00324	KC-135A	7 BW
00325	KC-135A	379 BW
00326	KC-135A	379 BW
00327	KC-135A	376 SW
00328	KC-135A	7 BW
00329	KC-135A	93 BW
00330	KC-135A	19 ARW
00331	KC-135A	93 BW
00332	KC-135A	320 BW
00333	KC-135A	319 BW
00334	KC-135A	96 BW
00335	KC-135Q	380 BW
00336	KC-135Q	380 BW
00337	KC-135Q	380 BW
00339	KC-135Q	376 SW
00341	KC-135A	380 BW
00342	KC-135Q	9 SRW
00343	KC-135Q	380 BW
00344	KC-135Q	376 SW
00345	KC-135Q	9 SRW
00346	KC-135Q	380 BW
00347	KC-135A	340 ARG
00348	KC-135A	93 BW
00349	KC-135A	410 BW
00350	KC-135A	19 ARW
00351	KC-135A	340 ARG
00353	KC-135A	384 ARW
00355	KC-135A	416 BW
00356	KC-135A	305 ARW
00357	KC-135A	305 ARW
00358	KC-135A	410 BW
00359	KC-135A	376 SW
00360	KC-135A	410 BW
00361	KC-135A	340 ARG
00362	KC-135A	305 ARW
00363	KC-135A	92 BW
00364	KC-135A	410 BW
00365	KC-135A	410 BW

Serial/Type/Wing		
00366	KC-135A	410 BW
00367	KC-135A	93 BW
00372	C-135E	4950 TW
00374	EC-135E	4950 TW
00375	C-135E	4950 TW
00376	C-135E	55 SRW
00377	C-135A	4950 TW
00378	C-135A	55 SRW

FY61

10261	EC-135L	305 ARW
10262	EC-135A	28 BW
10263	EC-135L	305 ARW
10264	KC-135A	42 BW
10266	KC-135A	97 BW
10267	KC-135A	97 BW
10268	KC-135A	384 ARW
10269	EC-135L	305 ARW
10270	KC-135A	319 BW
10271	KC-135A	5 BW
10272	KC-135A	97 BW
10274	EC-135H	6 ACCS
10275	KC-135A	97 BW
10276	KC-135A	97 BW
10277	KC-135A	97 BW
10278	EC-135A	28 BW
10279	EC-135L	305 ARW
10280	KC-135A	340 ARG
10281	KC-135A	28 BW
10282	EC-135H	10 ACCS
10283	EC-135L	305 ARW
10284	KC-135A	7 BW
10285	EC-135H	10 ACCS
10286	EC-135H	10 ACCS
10287	EC-135A	28 BW
10288	KC-135A	28 BW
10289	EC-135A	28 BW
10290	KC-135A	97 BW
10291	EC-135H	10 ACCS
10292	KC-135A	97 BW
10293	KC-135R	384 ARW
10294	KC-135A	416 BW
10295	KC-135A	97 BW
10297	EC-135A	28 BW
10298	KC-135A	384 ARW
10299	KC-135A	410 BW
10300	KC-135A	22 ARW
10302	KC-135A	93 BW
10303	KC-135A	97 BW
10304	KC-135A	93 BW
10305	KC-135A	305 ARW
10306	KC-135A	93 BW
10307	KC-135A	93 BW
10308	KC-135A	376 SW
10309	KC-135A	93 BW
10310	KC-135A	93 BW
10311	KC-135A	5 BW
10312	KC-135A	384 ARW
10313	KC-135A	320 BW
10314	KC-135A	7 BW
10315	KC-135A	305 ARW
10317	KC-135A	410 BW
10318	KC-135A	410 BW
10320	KC-135A	42 BW
10321	KC-135A	19 ARW
10323	KC-135A	22 ARW
10324	KC-135A	93 BW
10325	KC-135A	42 BW
10326	EC-135N	4950 TW
10327	EC-135N	4950 TW
10329	EC-135E	4950 TW

Serial/Type/Wing		
10330	EC-135E	4950 TW
12662	RC-135S	6 SW
12663	RC-135S	6 SW
12665	WC-135B	55 WRS
12666	WC-135B	55 WRS
12667	WC-135B	552 AW/CW
12668	C-135C	15 ABW
12669	C-135C	4950 TW
12670	WC-135B	55 WRS
12671	C-135C	89 MAW
12672	WC-135B	55 WRS
12673	WC-135B	55 WRS
12674	WC-135B	55 WRS

FY64

14828	KC-135A	509 BW
14829	KC-135A	22 ARW
14830	KC-135A	5 BW
14831	KC-135A	5 BW
14832	KC-135A	96 BW
14833	KC-135A	97 BW
14834	KC-135A	340 ARG
14835	KC-135A	5 BW
14836	KC-135A	320 BW
14837	KC-135A	319 BW
14838	KC-135A	93 BW
14839	KC-135A	19 ARW
14840	KC-135A	376 SW
14841	RC-135V	55 SRW
14842	RC-135V	55 SRW
14843	RC-135V	55 SRW
14844	RC-135V	55 SRW
14845	RC-135V	55 SRW
14846	RC-135V	55 SRW
14847	RC-135U	55 SRW
14848	RC-135V	55 SRW
14849	RC-135U	55 SRW

FY62

23497	KC-135A	93 BW
23498	KC-135A	92 BW
23499	KC-135A	93 BW
23500	KC-135A	380 BW
23501	KC-135A	42 BW
23502	KC-135A	509 BW
23503	KC-135A	42 BW
23504	KC-135A	319 BW
23505	KC-135A	509 BW
23506	KC-135A	416 BW
23507	KC-135A	96 BW
23508	KC-135A	416 BW
23509	KC-135A	93 BW
23510	KC-135A	376 SW
23511	KC-135A	416 BW
23512	KC-135A	93 BW
23513	KC-135A	416 BW
23514	KC-135A	416 BW
23515	KC-135A	410 BW
23516	KC-135A	416 BW
23517	KC-135A	7 BW
23518	KC-135A	96 BW
23519	KC-135A	416 BW
23520	KC-135A	340 ARG
23521	KC-135A	93 BW
23523	KC-135A	509 BW
23524	KC-135A	380 BW
23525	KC-135A	340 ARG
23526	KC-135A	416 BW
23527	KC-135A	93 BW
23528	KC-135A	96 BW
23529	KC-135A	509 BW

USAF (US based)

Serial	Type	Wing
23530	KC-135A	509 BW
23531	KC-135A	509 BW
23532	KC-135A	509 BW
23533	KC-135A	379 BW
23534	KC-135A	340 ARG
23537	KC-135A	509 BW
23538	KC-135A	509 BW
23539	KC-135A	93 BW
23540	KC-135A	509 BW
23541	KC-135A	340 ARG
23542	KC-135A	42 BW
23543	KC-135A	93 BW
23544	KC-135A	2 BW
23545	KC-135A	380 BW
23546	KC-135A	42 BW
23547	KC-135A	42 BW
23548	KC-135A	93 BW
23549	KC-135A	416 BW
23550	KC-135A	384 ARW
23551	KC-135A	19 ARW
23552	KC-135A	96 BW
23553	KC-135A	42 BW
23554	KC-135A	319 BW
23555	KC-135A	93 BW
23556	KC-135A	93 BW
23557	KC-135A	93 BW
23558	KC-135A	96 BW
23559	KC-135A	93 BW
23560	KC-135A	509 BW
23561	KC-135A	96 BW
23562	KC-135A	384 ARW
23563	KC-135A	93 BW
23564	KC-135A	97 BW
23565	KC-135A	305 ARW
23566	KC-135A	22 ARW
23567	KC-135A	340 ARG
23568	KC-135A	509 BW
23569	KC-135A	384 ARW
23570	EC-135G	28 BW
23571	KC-135A	93 BW
23572	KC-135A	340 ARG
23573	KC-135A	42 BW
23574	KC-135A	305 ARG
23575	KC-135A	42 BW
23576	KC-135A	93 BW
23577	KC-135A	305 ARW
23578	KC-135A	42 BW
23579	EC-135G	28 BW
23580	KC-135A	42 BW
23581	EC-135C	55 SRW
23582	EC-135C	55 SRW
23583	EC-135C	28 BW
23584	EC-135J	9 ACCS
23585	EC-135C	55 SRW
24125	C-135B	58 MAS
24126	C-135B	89 MAW
24127	C-135B	89 MAW
24128	RC-135X	6 SW
24129	C-135B	89 MAW
24130	C-135B	89 MAW
24131	RC-135W	55 SRW
24132	RC-135W	55 SRW
24133	EC-135B	55 SRW
24134	RC-135W	55 SRW
24135	RC-135W	55 SRW
24138	RC-135W	55 SRW
24139	RC-135W	55 SRW
26000	VC-137C	89 MAW
FY72		
27000	C137C	89 MAW

Serial	Type	Wing
FY63		
37976	KC-135A	93 BW
37977	KC-135A	42 BW
37978	KC-135A	305 ARW
37979	KC-135A	42 BW
37980	KC-135A	305 ARW
37981	KC-135A	384 ARW
37982	KC-135A	384 ARW
37983	KC-135A	305 ARW
37984	KC-135A	93 BW
37985	KC-135A	42 BW
37986	KC-135A	320 BW
37987	KC-135A	410 BW
37988	KC-135A	93 BW
37990	KC-135A	305 ARW
37991	KC-135A	5 BW
37992	KC-135A	93 BW
37993	KC-135A	2 BW
37994	EC-135G	305 ARW
37995	KC-135A	509 BW
37996	KC-135A	305 ARW
37997	KC-135A	319 BW
37998	KC-135A	380 BW
37999	KC-135A	5 BW
38000	KC-135A	22 ARW
38001	EC-135G	28 BW
38002	KC-135A	28 BW
38003	KC-135A	93 BW
38004	KC-135A	28 BW
38005	KC-135A	2 BW
38006	KC-135A	379 BW
38007	KC-135A	379 BW
38008	KC-135A	319 BW
38009	KC-135A	305 ARW
38010	KC-135A	22 ARW
38011	KC-135A	96 BW
38012	KC-135A	97 BW
38013	KC-135A	28 BW
38014	KC-135A	22 ARW
38015	KC-135A	93 BW
38016	KC-135A	93 BW
38017	KC-135A	22 ARW
38018	KC-135A	93 BW
38019	KC-135A	22 ARW
38020	KC-135A	376 SW
38021	KC-135A	28 BW
38022	KC-135A	93 BW
38023	KC-135A	93 BW
38024	KC-135A	22 ARW
38025	KC-135A	305 ARW
38026	KC-135A	22 ARW
38027	KC-135A	42 BW
38028	KC-135A	305 ARW
38029	KC-135A	380 BW
38030	KC-135A	305 ARW
38031	KC-135A	305 ARW
38032	KC-135A	28 BW
38033	KC-135A	305 ARW
38034	KC-135A	28 BW
38035	KC-135A	2 BW
38036	KC-135A	93 BW
38037	KC-135A	2 BW
38038	KC-135A	93 BW
38039	KC-135A	379 BW
38040	KC-135A	305 ARW
38041	KC-135A	2 BW
38043	KC-135A	42 BW
38044	KC-135A	2 BW
38045	KC-135A	92 BW
38046	EC-135C	55 SRW
38047	EC-135C	55 SRW

Serial	Type	Wing
38048	EC-135C	6 ACCS
38049	EC-135C	55 SRW
38050	EC-135C	55 SRW
38051	EC-135C	55 SRW
38052	EC-135C	55 SRW
38053	EC-135C	55 SRW
38054	EC-135C	55 SRW
38055	EC-135J	9 ACCS
38056	EC-135J	9 ACCS
38057	EC-135J	9 ACCS
38058	KC-135D	305 ARW
38059	KC-135D	305 ARW
38060	KC-135D	305 ARW
38061	KC-135D	305 ARW
38871	KC-135A	305 ARW
38872	KC-135A	19 ARW
38873	KC-135A	320 BW
38874	KC-135A	319 BW
38875	KC-135A	340 ARG
38876	KC-135A	93 BW
38877	KC-135A	384 ARW
38878	KC-135A	93 BW
38879	KC-135A	320 BW
38880	KC-135A	384 ARW
38881	KC-135A	380 BW
38883	KC-135A	305 ARW
38884	KC-135A	410 BW
38885	KC-135A	320 BW
38886	KC-135A	96 BW
38887	KC-135A	19 ARW
38888	KC-135A	28 BW
39792	RC-135V	55 SRW
FY55		
53118	EC-135K	8 TDCS
53125	EC-135Y	CinC CC
53130	KC-135A	7 BW
53136	KC-135A	22 ARW
53137	KC-135A	2 BW
53139	KC-135A	92 BW
53141*	KC-135E	154 ARS
53142	KC-135A	340 ARG
53143*	KC-135E	197 ARS
53145†	KC-135A	314 ARS
53146*	KC-135A	154 ARS
FY56		
63591	KC-135A	380 BW
63592	KC-135A	380 BW
63593*	KC-135A	154 ARS
63594	KC-135A	5 BW
63595	KC-135A	22 ARW
63600	KC-135A	2 BW
63601	KC-135A	93 BW
63603	KC-135A	384 ARW
63604*	KC-135A	117 ARS
63606*	KC-135A	132 ARS
63607*	KC-135E	151 ARS
63608	KC-135A	340 ARG
63609*	KC-135E	151 ARS
63610	KC-135A	92 BW
63611*	KC-135A	145 ARS
63612*	KC-135E	126 ARS
63614	KC-135A	19 ARW
63615	KC-135A	19 ARW
63616	KC-135A	93 BW
63617	KC-135A	340 ARG
63619	KC-135A	2 BW
63620	KC-135A	384 ARW
63621	KC-135A	7 BW
63622*	KC-135A	132 ARS

Serial/Type/Wing		
63623†	KC-135A	336 ARS
63624	KC-135A	384 ARW
63625	KC-135A	96 BW
63626*	KC-135E	147 ARS
63627	KC-135A	2 BW
63630*	KC-135A	154 ARS
63631*	KC-135E	117 ARS
63632	KC-135A	92 BW
63633	KC-135A	380 BW
63634	KC-135A	19 ARW
63635	KC-135A	96 BW
63636	KC-135A	19 ARW
63637	KC-135A	42 BW
63638*	KC-135E	197 ARS
63639	KC-135A	96 BW
63640*	KC-135A	132 ARS
63641*	KC-135A	117 ARS
63642	KC-135A	92 BW
63643*	KC-135E	151 ARS
63644	KC-135A	92 BW
63645	KC-135A	93 BW
63646	KC-135A	92 BW
63647	KC-135A	305 ARW
63648*	KC-135E	145 ARS
63649	KC-135A	2 BW
63650*	KC-135A	133 ARS
63651	KC-135A	92 BW
63652	KC-135A	92 BW
63653	KC-135A	92 BW
63654*	KC-135A	132 ARS
63656	KC-135A	7 BW
63658	KC-135A	42 BW
FY57		
71418	KC-135A	42 BW
71419	KC-135A	92 BW
71420	KC-135A	7 BW
71421	KC-135A	92 BW
71422†	KC-135A	72 ARS
71423*	KC-135A	116 ARS
71425*	KC-135E	154 ARS
71426*	KC-135A	154 ARS
71427	KC-135A	384 ARW
71428*	KC-135A	116 ARS
71429*	KC-135A	117 ARS
71430	KC-135A	92 BW
71431*	KC-135E	116 ARS
71432	KC-135A	93 BW
71433*	KC-135E	197 ARS
71434*	KC-135A	116 ARS
71435	KC-135A	93 BW
71436	KC-135A	7 BW
71437	KC-135A	92 BW
71438†	KC-135E	72 ARS
71439	KC-135A	92 BW
71440	KC-135A	93 BW
71441	KC-135A	92 BW
71443*	KC-135A	132 ARS
71445*	KC-135A	145 ARS
71447	KC-135A	92 BW
71448*	KC-135A	154 ARS
71450*	KC-135A	132 ARS
71451	KC-135A	2 BW
71452*	KC-135E	197 ARS
71453	KC-135A	7 BW
71454*	KC-135A	197 ARS
71455*	KC-135E	151 ARS
71456	KC-135A	340 ARG
71458*	KC-135E	108 ARS
71459	KC-135A	93 BW
71460*	KC-135A	117 ARS

Serial/Type/Wing		
71461	KC-135A	2 BW
71462	KC-135A	340 ARG
71463*	KC-135A	117 ARS
71464*	KC-135E	145 ARS
71465*	KC-135E	154 ARS
71467	KC-135A	93 BW
71468†	KC-135A	336 ARS
71469	KC-135A	93 BW
71470	KC-135A	7 BW
71471	KC-135A	19 ARW
71472	KC-135A	22 ARW
71473	KC-135A	93 BW
71474	KC-135A	19 ARW
71475*	KC-135E	197 ARS
71476	KC-135A	305 ARW
71477	KC-135A	340 ARG
71478*	KC-135E	151 ARS
71479†	KC-135A	336 ARS
71480*	KC-135E	108 ARS
71481*	KC-135A	154 ARS
71482*	KC-135A	117 ARS
71483	KC-135A	340 ARG
71484*	KC-135E	197 ARS
71485*	KC-135E	151 ARS
71486	KC-135A	19 ARW
71487	KC-135A	93 BW
71488	KC-135A	2 BW
71490	KC-135A	93 BW
71491*	KC-135A	132 ARS
71492	KC-135A	2 BW
71493	KC-135A	7 BW
71494*	KC-135A	154 ARS
71495*	KC-135E	197 ARS
71496*	KC-135E	197 ARS
71497	KC-135A	92 BW
71499	KC-135A	384 ARW
71501*	KC-135A	116 ARS
71502	KC-135A	384 ARW
71503*	KC-135E	151 ARS
71504†	KC-135A	72 ARS
71505*	KC-135A	132 ARS
71506	KC-135A	93 BW
71507*	KC-135A	145 ARS
71508	KC-135A	384 ARW
71509*	KC-135E	147 ARS
71510*	KC-135E	191 ARS
71511†	KC-135A	314 ARS
71512†	KC-135A	336 ARS
71514	KC-135A	340 ARG
72589	KC-135E	CinC SAC
72590	KC-135A	68 ARG
72591	KC-135A	68 ARG
72592	KC-135A	93 BW
72593	KC-135A	68 ARG
72594*	KC-135E	108 ARS
72595*	KC-135E	147 ARS
72596	KC-135A	5 BW
72597	KC-135A	93 BW
72598†	KC-135A	336 ARS
72599	KC-135A	319 BW
72600*	KC-135E	116 ARS
72601	KC-135A	97 BW
72602	KC-135A	7 BW
72603†	KC-135A	336 ARS
72604*	KC-135E	126 ARS
72605	KC-135A	19 ARW
72606*	KC-135E	150 ARS
72607*	KC-135E	147 ARS
72608*	KC-135E	147 ARS
72609	KC-135A	19 ARW

Serial/Type/Wing		
FY58		
80001	KC-135A	320 BW
80003*	KC-135E	108 ARS
80004	KC-135A	93 BW
80005	KC-135A	7 BW
80006*	KC-135E	191 ARS
80008*	KC-135E	145 ARS
80009	KC-135A	5 BW
80010	KC-135A	93 BW
80011	KC-135A	305 ARW
80012*	KC-135E	191 ARS
80013†	KC-135A	72 ARS
80014	KC-135A	379 BW
80015	KC-135A	320 BW
80016	KC-135A	92 BW
80017*	KC-135A	145 ARS
80018†	KC-135A	314 ARS
80019	EC-135P	6 ACCS
80020*	KC-135A	116 ARS
80021	KC-135A	68 ARG
80022	EC-135P	6 ACCS
80023	KC-135A	68 ARG
80024*	KC-135E	126 ARS
80025	KC-135A	68 ARG
80027	KC-135A	19 ARW
80028	KC-135A	68 ARG
80029	KC-135A	68 ARG
80030	KC-135A	42 BW
80032*	KC-135E	116 ARS
80033	KC-135A	305 ARW
80034	KC-135A	68 ARG
80035	KC-135A	379 BW
80036	KC-135A	19 ARW
80037	KC-135A	93 BW
80038	KC-135A	319 BW
80040*	KC-135E	150 ARS
80041†	KC-135A	72 ARS
80042	KC-135A	380 BW
80043*	KC-135E	191 ARS
80044	KC-135A	19 ARW
80045	KC-135Q	380 BW
80046	KC-135Q	380 BW
80047	KC-135Q	380 BW
80049	KC-135Q	380 BW
80050	KC-135Q	376 SW
80051	KC-135A	320 BW
80052†	KC-135A	336 ARS
80053†	KC-135A	314 ARS
80054	KC-135Q	9 SRW
80055	KC-135Q	380 BW
80056	KC-135A	92 BW
80057*	KC-135E	108 ARS
80058†	KC-135A	314 ARS
80059	KC-135A	5 BW
80060	KC-135Q	380 BW
80061	KC-135Q	380 BW
80062	KC-135Q	9 SRW
80063	KC-135A	320 BW
80064†	KC-135A	314 ARS
80065	KC-135Q	380 BW
80066	KC-135A	19 ARW
80067*	KC-135E	108 ARS
80068*	KC-135E	108 ARS
80069	KC-135Q	376 SW
80070	KC-135A	410 BW
80071	KC-135Q	9 SRW
80072	KC-135Q	380 BW
80073	KC-135A	96 BW
80074	KC-135Q	9 SRW
80075	KC-135A	320 BW
80076	KC-135A	19 ARW

Serial	Type	Wing
80077	KC-135Q	9 SRW
80078*	KC-135E	150 ARS
80079	KC-135A	7 BW
80080*	KC-135E	191 ARS
80081	KC-135A	42 BW
80082*	KC-135A	116 ARS
80083	KC-135A	320 BW
80084	KC-135Q	9 SRW
80085†	KC-135A	336 ARS
80086	KC-135Q	9 SRW
80087*	KC-135E	150 ARS
80088	KC-135Q	9 SRW
80089	KC-135Q	9 SRW
80090†	KC-135A	314 ARS
80091	KC-135A	5 BW
80092	KC-135A	28 BW
80093	KC-135A	93 BW
80094	KC-135Q	9 SRW
80095	KC-135Q	9 SRW
80096†	KC-135A	314 ARS
80097	KC-135A	7 BW
80098	KC-135A	5 BW
80099	KC-135Q	9 SRW
80100	KC-135A	7 BW
80102	KC-135A	96 BW
80103	KC-135Q	9 SRW
80104	KC-135A	92 BW
80105	KC-135A	92 BW
80106	KC-135A	93 BW
80107*	KC-135E	191 ARS
80108†	KC-135A	314 ARS
80109	KC-135A	96 BW
80110	KC-135A	319 BW
80111*	KC-135E	126 ARS
80112	KC-135Q	9 SRW
80113	KC-135A	96 BW
80114	KC-135A	96 BW
80115*	KC-135E	150 ARS
80116	KC-135A	96 BW
80117	KC-135Q	9 SRW
80118	KC-135A	19 ARW
80119	KC-135A	5 BW
80120	KC-135A	5 BW
80121	KC-135A	68 ARG
80122	KC-135A	92 BW
80123	KC-135A	379 BW
80124	KC-135A	305 ARW
80125	KC-135Q	9 SRW
80126	KC-135A	305 ARW
80128	KC-135A	5 BW
80129	KC-135Q	9 SRW
80130	KC-135A	7 BW
86970	EC-137B	89 MAW
86971	EC-137B	89 MAW
86972	EC-137B	89 MAW

FY59

Serial	Type	Wing
91443	KC-135A	92 BW
91444	KC-135A	92 BW
91445*	KC-135A	116 ARS
91446	KC-135A	5 BW
91447	KC-135A	305 ARW
91448*	KC-135A	133 ARS
91449	KC-135A	19 ARW
91450*	KC-135A	133 ARS
91451†	KC-135A	72 ARS
91452*	KC-135A	116 ARS
91453	KC-135R	28 BW
91454	KC-135A	19 ARW
91455	KC-135R	28 BW
91456*	KC-135E	126 ARS
91457*	KC-135E	147 ARS
91458	KC-135A	19 ARW
91459	KC-135A	19 ARW
91460	KC-135Q	9 SRW
91461	KC-135A	19 ARW
91462	KC-135Q	380 BW
91463	KC-135A	93 BW
91464	KC-135Q	9 SRW
91466	KC-135A	19 ARW
91467	KC-135Q	380 BW
91468	KC-135Q	9 SRW
91469	KC-135A	380 BW
91470	KC-135Q	9 SRW
91471	KC-135Q	380 BW
91472	KC-135A	97 BW
91473*	KC-135E	191 ARS
91474	KC-135Q	9 SRW
91475	KC-135A	319 BW
91476*	KC-135A	126 ARS
91477†	KC-135A	72 ARS
91478	KC-135A	93 BW
91479*	KC-135E	126 ARS
91480	KC-135Q	9 SRW
91482	KC-135A	384 ARW
91483	KC-135A	93 BW
91484*	KC-135E	147 ARS
91485*	KC-135E	150 ARS
91486	KC-135A	5 BW
91487*	KC-135E	108 ARS
91488	KC-135A	319 BW
91489*	KC-135E	191 ARS
91490	KC-135Q	9 SRW
91492	KC-135A	319 BW
91493	KC-135A	319 BW
91494*	KC-135A	133 ARS
91495	KC-135E	319 BW
91496	KC-135E	7 BW
91497*	KC-135E	150 ARS
91498	KC-135A	92 BW
91499*	KC-135A	133 ARS
91500	KC-135A	319 BW
91501*	KC-135A	116 ARS
91502	KC-135A	384 ARW
91503	KC-135A	42 BW
91504	KC-135Q	9 SRW
91505*	KC-135A	133 ARS
91506*	KC-135E	147 ARS
91507	KC-135A	42 BW
91508	KC-135A	19 ARW
91509*	KC-135A	133 ARS
91510	KC-135Q	380 BW
91511	KC-135A	42 BW
91512	KC-135Q	9 SRW
91513	KC-135Q	9 SRW
91514	KC-135A	55 SRW
91515	KC-135A	379 BW
91516	KC-135A	379 BW
91517	KC-135A	379 BW
91518	EC-135K	8 TDCS
91519*	KC-135E	126 ARS
91520	KC-135Q	9 SRW
91521	KC-135A	68 ARG
91522	KC-135A	410 BW
91523	KC-135Q	9 SRW

Lockheed C-141B Starlifter
(60 MAW: Travis AFB, California
62 MAW: McChord AFB, Washington
63 MAW: Norton AFB, California
437 MAW: Charleston AFB, S Carolina
438 MAW: McGuire AFB, New Jersey
443 MAW: Altus AFB, Oklahoma)

FY61

Serial	Wing
12778	438MAW

FY63

Serial	Wing
38075	60 MAW
38076	438 MAW
38078	437 MAW
38079	437 MAW
38080	438 MAW
38081	62 MAW
38082	62 MAW
38083	438 MAW
38084	63 MAW
38085	63 MAW
38086	62 MAW
38087	63 MAW
38088	60 MAW
38089	438 MAW
38090	438 MAW

FY64

Serial	Wing
40609	62 MAW
40610	437 MAW
40611	437 MAW
40612	437 MAW
40613	437 MAW
40614	63 MAW
40615	437 MAW
40616	438 MAW
40617	63 MAW
40618	437 MAW
40619	443 MAW
40620	438 MAW
40621	438 MAW
40622	438 MAW
40623	438 MAW
40625	438 MAW
40626	438 MAW
40627	438 MAW
40628	438 MAW
40629	437 MAW
40630	437 MAW
40631	437 MAW
40632	60 MAW
40633	438 MAW
40634	63 MAW
40635	62 MAW
40636	63 MAW
40637	60 MAW
40638	438 MAW
40639	438 MAW
40640	60 MAW
40642	60 MAW
40643	60 MAW
40644	437 MAW
40645	60 MAW
40646	437 MAW
40648	60 MAW
40649	437 MAW
40650	438 MAW
40651	438 MAW
40653	63 MAW

FY65

Serial	Wing
50216	63 MAW

Serial	Wing
50217	437 MAW
50218	437 MAW
50219	60 MAW
50220	437 MAW
50221	438 MAW
50222	437 MAW
50223	438 MAW
50224	438 MAW
50225	63 MAW
50226	443 MAW
50227	62 MAW
50228	62 MAW
50229	62 MAW
50230	60 MAW
50231	60 MAW
50232	62 MAW
50233	60 MAW
50234	60 MAW
50235	62 MAW
50236	438 MAW
50237	62 MAW
50238	60 MAW
50239	60 MAW
50240	62 MAW
50241	62 MAW
50242	60 MAW
50243	62 MAW
50244	62 MAW
50245	60 MAW
50246	60 MAW
50247	60 MAW
50248	62 MAW
50249	60 MAW
50250	60 MAW
50251	60 MAW
50252	60 MAW
50253	62 MAW
50254	60 MAW
50255	62 MAW
50256	60 MAW
50257	62 MAW
50258	62 MAW
50259	60 MAW
50260	60 MAW
50261	438 MAW
50262	443 MAW
50263	62 MAW
50264	62 MAW
50265	438 MAW
50266	437 MAW
50267	437 MAW
50268	60 MAW
50269	437 MAW
50270	437 MAW
50271	438 MAW
50272	437 MAW
50273	437 MAW
50275	437 MAW
50276	437 MAW
50277	62 MAW
50278	60 MAW
50279	437 MAW
50280	62 MAW
59397	63 MAW
59398	60 MAW
59399	62 MAW
59400	63 MAW
59401	437 MAW
59402	63 MAW
59403	60 MAW
59404	63 MAW
59405	60 MAW
59406	63 MAW
59408	437 MAW
59409	438 MAW
59410	62 MAW
59411	438 MAW
59412	438 MAW
59413	438 MAW
59414	63 MAW
FY66	
60126	438 MAW
60128	63 MAW
60129	62 MAW
60130	63 MAW
60131	437 MAW
60132	438 MAW
60133	438 MAW
60134	437 MAW
60135	437 MAW
60136	63 MAW
60137	63 MAW
60138	63 MAW
60139	63 MAW
60140	438 MAW
60141	62 MAW
60142	62 MAW
60143	63 MAW
60144	437 MAW
60145	62 MAW
60146	438 MAW
60147	60 MAW
60148	63 MAW
60149	438 MAW
60150	63 MAW
60151	60 MAW
60152	437 MAW
60153	63 MAW
60154	438 MAW
60155	438 MAW
60156	63 MAW
60157	438 MAW
60158	62 MAW
60159	62 MAW
60160	63 MAW
60161	62 MAW
60162	438 MAW
60163	437 MAW
60164	63 MAW
60165	62 MAW
60166	438 MAW
60167	437 MAW
60168	437 MAW
60169	438 MAW
60170	438 MAW
60171	63 MAW
60172	63 MAW
60173	438 MAW
60174	438 MAW
60175	63 MAW
60176	62 MAW
60177	63 MAW
60178	437 MAW
60179	63 MAW
60180	63 MAW
60181	63 MAW
60182	63 MAW
60183	438 MAW
60184	63 MAW
60185	60 MAW
60186	443 MAW
60187	437 MAW
60188	443 MAW
60189	60 MAW
60190	63 MAW
60191	60 MAW
60192	62 MAW
60193	63 MAW
60194	437 MAW
60195	437 MAW
60196	437 MAW
60197	62 MAW
60198	63 MAW
60199	443 MAW
60200	63 MAW
60201	63 MAW
60202	437 MAW
60203	437 MAW
60204	438 MAW
60205	63 MAW
60206	62 MAW
60207	438 MAW
60208	63 MAW
60209	437 MAW
67944	60 MAW
67945	437 MAW
67946	63 MAW
67947	437 MAW
67948	438 MAW
67949	63 MAW
67950	438 MAW
67951	62 MAW
67952	63 MAW
67953	438 MAW
67954	438 MAW
67955	437 MAW
67956	437 MAW
67957	63 MAW
67958	63 MAW
67959	63 MAW
FY67	
70001	63 MAW
70002	437 MAW
70003	443 MAW
70004	437 MAW
70005	63 MAW
70007	438 MAW
70009	63 MAW
70010	437 MAW
70011	437 MAW
70012	437 MAW
70013	438 MAW
70014	437 MAW
70015	63 MAW
70016	437 MAW
70018	62 MAW
70019	438 MAW
70020	438 MAW
70021	438 MAW
70022	443 MAW
70023	63 MAW
70024	438 MAW
70025	60 MAW
70026	437 MAW
70027	438 MAW
70028	63 MAW
70029	63 MAW
70031	60 MAW
70164	62 MAW
70165	438 MAW
70166	443 MAW

US based US Navy Aircraft

Serial/Wing

Although only a small number of the following Lockheed P-3 Orions are based in Europe, more than half of the aircraft listed have visited or detached to the UK during recent years.

Lockheed P-3 Orion

Barbers Point NAS
VC-1; VP-1
Brunswick NAS
VP-8; VP-10; VP-11; VP-23; VP-26; VP-44
Jacksonville NAS
CNO; CinC LANT; VP-5; VP-16; VP-24; VP-30; VP-45; VP-49; VP-56
Moffett Field NAS
VP-91
New Orleans NAS
VP-94
Patuxent River NAS
NRL; VX-1; VXN-8
Rota NAS (Spain)
VQ-2; VR-22
Selfridge ANGB
VP-93
South Weymouth NAS
VP-92
Warminster NAF
NADC
Willow Grove NAS
VP-64; VP-66

P-3A
(‡EP-3A; †EP-3E; **UP-3A; *RP-3A; §VP-3A)

148883**	NADC
148888 [JQ-23]†	VQ-2
148889**	NADC
149667*	VXN-8
149668 [JQ-21]†	VQ-2
149670*	NRL
149673 [JA-6]‡	VX-1
149674‡	NRL
149676§	CNO
149677 [JQ-20]**	VQ-2
150494 [JQ-25]†	VQ-2
150495**	Keflavik
150496§	CinC LANT
150500*	VXN-8
150502 [JQ-22]†	VQ-2
150503 [JQ-26]†	VQ-2
150505 [JQ-24]†	VQ-2
150511§	CinC AFSE
150515§	HQ USMC
150517 [LL-17]	VP-30
150527 [JB]**	VXN-8
150528 [JB-528]**	VXN-8
150604 [LV-00]	VP-66
150605	VC-1
150607**	NRL
151351 [LZ-3]	VP-94
151354 [LW-15]	VP-68
151359 [LZ-2]	VP-94
151360 [LW-12]	VP-68
151361 [LW-1]	VP-68
151364 [LZ-7]	VP-94
151370 [LZ-6]	VP-94
151371 [LZ-00]	VP-94
151376 [LZ-10]	VP-94
151382 [LZ-11]	VP-94
151384 [LW-4]	VP-68
151390 [LW-3]	VP-68
151392 [LW-2]	VP-68
151395 [LH-10]	VP-93
152140 [LV-12]	VP-66
152143 [LU-2]	VP-64
152146 [LV-4]	VP-66
152147 [LU-5]	VP-64
152148 [LV-11]	VP-66
152152 [LU-10]	VP-64
152154 [LU-7]	VP-64
152156 [LV-10]	VP-66
152157 [LU-1]	VP-64
152158 [LU-4]	VP-64
152160 [LV-3]	VP-66
152162 [LV-7]	VP-66
152163 [LV-5]	VP-66
152165 [LU-11]	VP-64
152166 [LY-1]	VP-92
152168 [LY-6]	VP-92
152169 [LY-3]	VP-92
152170 [LY-10]	VP-92
152174 [LU-3]	VP-64
152180 [LV-6]	VP-66
152181 [LU-6]	VP-64
152183 [LV-1]	VP-66
152184 [LU-12]	VP-64
152185 [LV-2]	VP-66
152186 [LY-5]	VP-92

P-3B
(†EP-3B; *RP-3D)

152718 [LT-1]	VP-62
152723 [LH-5]	VP-93
152725 [LZ-12]	VP-94
152726 [PM-4]	VP-91
152727 [LZ-3]	VP-94
152728 [LT-3]	VP-62
152730 [LT-4]	VP-62
152735 [LW-7]	VP-68
152737 [PM-2]	VP-91
152738 [LZ-1]	VP-94
152740 [PM-1]	VP-91
152741 [LY-10]	VP-92
152743 [LT-6]	VP-62
152744 [PM-3]	VP-91
152746 [PM-6]	VP-91
152747 [PM-10]	VP-91
152748 [LW-3]	VP-68
152750 [LT-7]	VP-62
152752 [PM-5]	VP-91
152755 [LY-]	VP-92
152756 [PM-11]	VP-91
152760 [LH-3]	VP-93
152762 [LT-10]	VP-62
152763 [PM-7]	VP-91
152764 [LZ-4]	VP-94
153414 [LT-5]	VP-68
153416 [LW-10]	VP-68
153417 [LY-1]	VP-92
153418 [LW-1]	VP-68
153421 [LY-1]	VP-92
153422 [LW-00]	VP-68
153425 [LW-4]	VP-68
153426 [LT-11]	VP-62
153427 [LY-3]	VP-92
153429 [LW-6]	VP-68
153430 [LT-2]	VP-62
153431 [LW-5]	VP-68
153433 [LY-12]	VP-92
153434 [LL-24]	VP-30
153435 [LY-4]	VP-92
153436 [LY-5]	VP-92
153442†	NRL
153443 [O1]*	VXN-8
153446 [LW-10]	VP-68
153452 [LW-1]	VP-68
154577 [LL-25]	VP-30
154581 [LZ-10]	VP-94

P-3C
(*RP-3D)

156507 [LL-39]	VP-30
156510 [LN-40]	VP-45
156511 [LL-37]	VP-30
156516 [LR-4]	VP-24
156517 [YB-35]	VP-1
156518 [LQ-2]	VP-56
156520 [YB-3]	VP-1
156522 [LQ-3]	VP-56
156523 [LQ-9]	VP-56
156524 [LL-33]	VP-30
156525 [LL-32]	VP-30
156526 [LL-31]	VP-30
156527 [LP-2]	VP-49
156528 [LL-31]	VP-30
156529 [LL-32]	VP-30
156530 [LQ-5]	VP-56
157310 [LR-1]	VP-24
157311 [LR-2]	VP-24
157312 [LR-3]	VP-24
157313 [LP-4]	VP-49
157314 [LP-3]	VP-49
157315 [LP-5]	VP-49
157316 [LL-36]	VP-30
157318 [LL-38]	VP-30
157319 [LP-1]	VP-49
157321 [LQ-6]	VP-56
157322 [LQ-4]	VP-56
157323 [LQ-8]	VP-56
157324 [LQ-1]	VP-56
157326 [JA-5]	VX-1
158204	NADC
158206 [JA-3]	VX-1
158223 [QE-3]	VP-40
158226 [QE-5]	VP-40
158227*	VXN-8
158563 [JA-4]	VX-1
158564 [LR-5]	VP-24

Serial/Wing		Serial/Wing		Serial/Wing	
158565 [LA-1]	VP-5	160761 [LM-1]	VP-44	161132 [LL-60]	VP-30
158566 [LA-4]	VP-5	160762 [LM-2]	VP-44	161329 [LE-9]	VP-11
158567 [LA-6]	VP-5	160763 [LM-3]	VP-44	161330 [LE-8]	VP-11
158568 [LP-9]	VP-49	160764 [LM-4]	VP-44	161331 [LE-1]	VP-11
158569 [LN-45]	VP-45	160765 [LM-5]	VP-44	161332 [LE-2]	VP-11
158570 [LN-42]	VP-45	160766 [LM-6]	VP-44	161333 [LE-3]	VP-11
158571 [LA-8]	VP-5	160767 [LJ-7]	VP-23	161334 [LE-4]	VP-11
158572 [LN-43]	VP-45	160768 [LJ-8]	VP-23	161335 [LE-5]	VP-11
158573 [LN-44]	VP-45	160769 [LJ-9]	VP-23	161336 [LE-6]	VP-11
158913 [QE-12]	VP-40	160770 [LJ-5]	VP-23	161337 [LE-7]	VP-11
158919 [LQ-1]	VP-56	160999 [LJ-6]	VP-23	161338 [LC-81]	VP-8
158920 [LP-7]	VP-49	161000 [LJ-1]	VP-23	161339 [LC-82]	VP-8
158922 [LA-7]	VP-5	161001 [LL-52]	VP-30	161340 [LC-83]	VP-8
158923 [LA-9]	VP-5	161002 [LJ-2]	VP-23	161404 [LC-84]	VP-8
158924 [LA-5]	VP-5	161003 [LJ-3]	VP-23	161405 [LC-85]	VP-8
158926 [LN-41]	VP-45	161004 [LJ-4]	VP-23	161406 [LC-86]	VP-8
158927 [LP-8]	VP-49	161005 [LK-5]	VP-26	161407 [LC-87]	VP-8
158929 [LP-6]	VP-49	161006 [LK-6]	VP-26	161408 [LC-88]	VP-8
158931 [LA-3]	VP-5	161007 [LK-7]	VP-26	161409 [LC-89]	VP-8
158932 [LA-2]	VP-5	161008 [LK-8]	VP-26	161411 [LL-30]	VP-30
158933 [LN-46]	VP-45	161009 [LK-9]	VP-26	161412 [LL-61]	VP-30
158934 [LR-6]	VP-24	161010 [LK-4]	VP-26	161413 [LL-62]	VP-30
158935 [LR-7]	VP-24	161011 [LK-1]	VP-26	161414 [LL-63]	VP-30
159318 [LN-47]	VP-45	161012 [LK-2]	VP-26	161415 [LL-64]	VP-30
159319 [LN-48]	VP-45	161013 [LK-3]	VP-26	161585 [JA-1]	VX-1
159320 [LR-8]	VP-24	161014 [LL-53]	VP-30	161586 [LF-6]	VP-16
159321 [QE-1]	VP-40	161121 [LL-54]	VP-30	161587 [LF-7]	VP-16
159322 [LR-9]	VP-24	161122 [LL-55]	VP-30	161588 [LF-8]	VP-16
159326 [QE-6]	VP-40	161123 [LD-3]	VP-10	161589 [LF-9]	VP-16
159327 [QE-7]	VP-40	161124 [LD-4]	VP-10	161590 [LL-65]	VP-30
159889	NADC	161125 [LD-5]	VP-10	161591 [LF-1]	VP-16
160291	NADC	161126 [LD-6]	VP-10	161592 [LF-2]	VP-16
160292 [LL-50]	VP-30	161127 [LD-7]	VP-10	161593 [LF-3]	VP-16
160293 [LL-51]	VP-30	161128 [LD-8]	VP-10	161594 [LF-4]	VP-16
160610 [LM-9]	VP-44	161129 [LD-9]	VP-10	161595 [LF-5]	VP-16
160611 [LM-8]	VP-44	161130 [LD-2]	VP-10	161596 [LL-66]	VP-30
160612 [LM-7]	VP-44	161131 [LD-1]	VP-10		

Civil Registered Aircraft in Military Service

Grumman Gulfstream III
(Government of Saudi Arabia)

107 HZ109
HZ108

Lockheed C-130H Hercules
(Government of Saudi Arabia)

HZ114 HZ116
HZ115 HZ117

Lockheed P-3 Orion
(NOAA)
N42RF (159773) WP-3D
N43RF (159875) WP-3D

North American Sabre 75A
(Federal Aviation Administration)

N51 N55 N59 N63
N52 N56 N60 N64
N53 N57 N61 N65
N54 N58 N62

North American F-100F Super Sabre
(Flight Refuelling Ltd, Hurn/Flight Systems, Decimomannu)

N414FS N417FS
N415FS N418FS
N416FS N419FS

Dassault Falcon 20DC
(Flight Refuelling Ltd/FRADU, RNAS Yeovilton)

N900FR (N22FE)
N901FR (N37FE)
N902FR (N2FE/N23FR)
N903FR (N5FE/N25FR)
N904FR (N3FE/N24FR)
N905FR (N32FE)
N906FR (N33FE)
N907FR (N23FE)
N908FR (N27FE)
N909FR (N28FE)